ZHU RONGJI
ON THE RECORD

ZHU RONGJI
ON THE RECORD

The Road to Reform
1998–2003

Zhu Rongji
Translated by June Y. Mei

Forewords by
Henry A. Kissinger
Helmut Schmidt

BROOKINGS INSTITUTION PRESS
Washington, D.C.

Copyright © 2015
FOREIGN LANGUAGES PRESS
Beijing, China

The Library of Congress cataloged the first volume as follows:

Zhu, Rongji, 1928–
    [Works. Selections. English]
    Zhu Rongji on the record : the road to reform, 1991–1997 / Zhu Rongji ; translated by June Y. Mei ; forewords by Henry A. Kissinger, Helmut Schmidt.
        pages   cm
    Includes bibliographical references and index.
    ISBN 978-0-8157-2519-0 (hardcover : alk. paper) –
    ISBN 978-0-8157-2518-3 (pbk. : alk. paper)
    1. China—Politics and government—1976–2002. 2. China—Economic conditions—1976–2000. 3. China—Economic policy—1976–2000. 4. Speeches, addresses, etc., Chinese. I. Title.
    DS779.29.Z478.A513 2013
    951.05'9—dc23   2013023421

ISBN 978-0-8157-2627-2 (hardcover : alk. paper)
ISBN 978-0-8157-2628-9 (pbk : alk. paper)

9 8 7 6 5 4 3 2 1

Printed on acid-free paper

Typeset in Minion

Composition by Cynthia Stock
Silver Spring, Maryland

CONTENTS

1999

2000

2001

PUBLICATION NOTE

The four-volume Chinese version of *Zhu Rongji on the Record* (*Zhu Rongji Jianghua Shilu*) was published in China in 2011. It included 348 important speeches, articles, letters and directives, as well as 272 photos and 30 photocopies of his directives, letters and inscriptions from his term as Vice Premier (April 1991–March 1998) and his term as Premier (March 1998–March 2003).

The two-volume English edition features 111 of these speeches, articles, letters, and directives, 54 of which are included in the first volume and 57 in the second. The materials are arranged chronologically, with the first volume covering the period from September 1991 to December 1997. This second volume covers the period from March 1998 to February 2003. The author personally selected and approved all materials included in this book.

These materials were edited from audio-visual materials, transcripts and manuscripts, and most of them are being published for the first time in English. Some brief annotations have been added by the editors and translator, and most captions and subheadings were added by the editors. Due to the unavailability of transcripts in the original languages, remarks by foreign guests in conversations with the author have been translated from the Chinese edition.

Li Bingjun, Lian Yong, Zhang Changyi, Xie Minggan, Lin Zhaomu, Lu Jing and Hou Chun participated in the editorial work, and Ma Dongsheng and Li Lijun helped compile and collate relevant materials.

FOREWORD
HENRY A. KISSINGER

It is commonplace to refer to China's enormous strides of the past decades as an "economic miracle." Yet in essence a miracle is an event beyond human performance or comprehension. China's reform and development was a policy course adopted by top officials and carried out through the efforts and vitality of the Chinese people. Even if the feats this course involved could not easily be duplicated, they can be studied and mined for practical lessons within China and beyond.

With *Zhu Rongji on the Record*, China's former Premier Zhu Rongji has made a valuable contribution to this process. He has collected dozens of speeches, dialogues, and internal memoranda reflecting his engagement with the major economic, political, and social issues of his era. They cover a period when China, under the leadership of President Jiang Zemin and with Zhu as Vice Premier and subsequently Premier, overhauled its financial system, tamed escalating inflation, concluded arduous negotiations on its entry into the World Trade Organization, lifted tens of millions out of poverty, launched an ambitious development program for its western regions, joined the ranks of the world's largest economies, and made a successful bid for the 2008 Olympics.

By any standard, it was a period of momentous change. It was particularly noteworthy for witnessing the construction of a new set of links between China and the international system—in trade, financial markets, science and education, diplomacy, and many other fields. In its depth and breadth, this integration of China into international architecture had no precedent in previous eras of Chinese history. What Jiang, Zhu, and their colleagues oversaw reflected their considered judgment about China's interests and necessities. The implications were global. The elaboration of the links they fostered will form an essential, perhaps decisive, component of 21st-century world order.

Given this record of extraordinary achievement, one might expect to find in these pages a record of triumphs and exultation. What Zhu provides is something more complex, more sober, and ultimately bolder. He has been as direct in his editorial selections as he was in his leadership style in office and has not shied away from difficult or sensitive issues. The challenges of balancing growth with environmental preservation; the pitfalls of domestic and international financial instability; the daunting endeavor of reforming China's stock exchanges, labor regulations, infrastructure programs, and grain and natural-resources markets; the urgent task of uprooting malfeasance and preventing financial abuses; the complexities of encouraging growth while ensuring quality and consistency— readers will find forthright discussions of all of these issues in Zhu's book. The picture that emerges is one of the immensity of the task of governing China and addressing its contemporary challenges—and of the boldness and creativity of the generation charged with turning Deng Xiaoping's reform-and-opening-up concept into a reality.

For scholars outside of China, the publication of this book stands as a significant contribution to the historical record. On major debates over China's reform path, which English-speaking readers once knew of only in general terms, Zhu sheds considerable historical light. He publishes here his written instructions to colleagues and transcripts of his internal remarks on policy issues. These include Zhu's watershed March 1992 analysis of Deng Xiaoping's "Southern Tour" talks, in which Zhu stressed—at a crucial period in China's internal debate—the imperative of bold but sustainable growth. This candid discussion earned a crucial endorsement from Jiang Zemin, who ordered it distributed to cadres nationwide, and it became the basis for many of Zhu's subsequent efforts. Scholars will have a chance to study too the conclusions Zhu drew from the 1997 Asian financial crisis, and the lessons he distilled for China's policy course.

Zhu Rongji on the Record also functions as a case study in practical statecraft. Because China's reform program was so sweeping, and the projects being implemented were of such scale and complexity, Zhu had occasion to reflect on almost every aspect of modern economic management and social development. The problems addressed in this book range across industries—railways, coal, finance, automobile manufacturing, real estate—and their relevance reaches well beyond China. Economists, business strategists, and policymakers will all find in these pages thought-provoking examples of how a penetrating mind grappled with one of the most significant reform programs in modern history. They will appreciate the creativity of his proposals, the scope and ambition of his vision, his resoluteness in crisis, and his strategic acuity—marked by a determination, as Zhu puts it, to "unify our thinking, and see the entire country as one single chessboard."

For many years now I have been fortunate to count Premier Zhu as a friend, and to learn from his insights. It brings great satisfaction to know that with this edition of *Zhu Rongji on the Record,* a broader audience of English-speaking readers will be able to appreciate his vigorous personality and acute analyses.

FOREWORD
HELMUT SCHMIDT

During the late 1960s I had an inkling that China was regaining its status as a world power. However, since Germany and China had no diplomatic ties, I traveled to East Asia hoping to look at China from the perspective of the Japanese, the South Koreans, the Thai people, and the Australians. In 1972, as one outcome of these travels, Germany and China established diplomatic relations. Three years later, I visited China for the first time at the invitation of Zhou Enlai, but owing to Zhou's illness, I was received by Mao Zedong and by Deng Xiaoping. In the following decades I visited China some 12 or 15 times and witnessed firsthand China's phenomenal economic, educational, and social upswing since the late 1970s.

Throughout the four millenniums of its existence, Chinese civilization has shown a fascinating vitality. Considering China's relative decay during the 19th century and its riven internal and external conditions during the first decades of the 20th century, China's rather explosive renaissance in the past three decades seems almost unbelievable.

After 1978 Deng set up a stunning evolutionary process of step-by-step economic reforms. He anticipated that if structural and economic reforms were introduced simultaneously, it might lead to chaos. Later developments in the former Soviet Union appeared to justify this view. After 1989 the risk of a rollback in China appeared a possibility. However, with his five-week trip to southern provinces and cities in early 1992, Deng successfully affirmed that the movement toward a market-oriented economy would continue. Without the paramount leadership of Deng Xiaoping, China's new rise would certainly never have occurred. Yet it has been Zhu Rongji's outstanding achievements as Vice-Premier, central bank Governor, and as Premier that consolidated Deng's legacy to present-day China.

The first years of China's economic transformation resembled an ecstatic rush. Severe signs of a dangerous overheating were soon noticeable. Inflation became a serious problem, especially in the early 1990s when China suffered double-digit inflation rates of more than 20 percent. Obviously, a framework that allowed for a steady and sustainable growth had to be established, and it became the main driving force of Zhu's work. In a speech in March 1992, he outlined the need for broad structural reforms and technological progress alongside the process of further economic opening. To turn the spirit of Deng's southern talks into reality, a sound macroeconomic environment, a modern financial system, and an efficient industrial sector were essential.

I first met Zhu Rongji in 1993, when he was still Vice Premier and had become fully responsible for economic affairs. Although Zhu was educated as a technical engineer, his economic insight was remarkable, surpassing that of most other political leaders in the world I have met.

In 1993 Zhu launched widespread reforms to restructure China's financial sector. As one result, the People's Bank of China became a genuine central bank that was now able to conduct a nationally unified monetary policy. At the same time, Zhu addressed the need to shift fiscal power to the central government as its share of tax revenues had fallen sharply during the 1980s. A federal-style tax-streaming system with centralized tax administration replaced a rather complicated system in which all taxes were collected at the local level. This put the central government's financial resources on a much healthier foundation than before and meant they could be redistributed to provinces with less dynamic economies.

In the wake of improved macroeconomic controls, inflationary pressures decreased, and between 1995 and 1997 China's high-flying economy managed to make a "soft landing." When Asia was hit by a severe financial crisis in 1997 and 1998, China was affected only slightly, mainly because of its capital controls but also with the help of massive infrastructure projects. Guided by Zhu's economic expertise, China's leadership kept the renminbi from being devalued and refrained from taking part in a damaging "race to the bottom." After the Asian crisis, Zhu emphasized the need for effective financial market regulation and oversight in order to prevent harmful speculation. The global financial meltdown after the collapse of Lehman Brothers almost 10 years later demonstrated that Western political leaders had regrettably failed to draw similar lessons.

When he was appointed Premier in 1998, Zhu accelerated the pace of reforming China's huge sector of state-owned enterprises (SOEs). By the mid-1990s many of China's SOEs were showing low profitability and severe losses. Nonperforming loans against them had become a major problem for China's financial sector. By "grasping the large, releasing the small," privatizing was successfully pushed further, while keeping pillar industries fully under state control. Market forces were enhanced, allowing for bankruptcies and layoffs. When Zhu finished his term as Premier in 2003, the SOEs' estimated contribution to GDP had been reduced to 35%. As the related speeches and papers in this volume impressively reveal, he addressed frankly the problems caused by this far-reaching corporate restructuring rather than avoiding them.

Throughout his political career, Zhu has always been a man of action, eager to implement the next feasible steps of reforms, yet always doing so with far-sightedness. I remember a conversation with Zhu in the late 1990s about China's possible membership in the World Trade Organization (WTO). In contrast to Zhu, I did not think that such a binding external commitment would be a forceful impetus for China's further reform. Zhu's perception certainly proved to be right. The formal entry into WTO in December 2001 was a crucial milestone in China's successful transformation into a market-oriented economy.

Today, China is already number two in the world economy, and it will become its biggest player within the next 15 or 20 years. Between 1989 and 2012 China's economic growth averaged 9% a year. The overall standard of living improved considerably, even though its population increased dramatically to 1.3 billion. Of course, huge problems still remain to be tackled: growing disparities within society as well as between coastal, central, and western provinces; the need for a comprehensive social security system; the rural exodus into ever-expanding megacities; and severe air pollution. These provide only a rough idea of the challenges ahead.

Western perceptions of China's new economic strength are often marked by uneasiness. However, those believing in the mechanism of competition should consider the emergence of a new competitor an inspiring force rather than a threat. The ascent of the Japanese economy after the Second World War did not prove harmful to the Western world, nor has the rise of the inescapable economic and technological competition with China, which instead has revitalized the West's own strengths. At the same time, the West must accept that China will choose its own way to evolve.

This highly informative collection of speeches, minutes, and letters by Zhu Rongji deserves widespread attention. It is a unique historical document of China's unprecedented economic evolution over the past few decades. And it gives a fascinating insight into the political work of Zhu Rongji—an exceptionally gifted statesman and a dear friend.

Being congratulated by Jiang Zemin on being named Premier by the first session of the Ninth National People's Congress on March 17, 1998. (Photograph by Wang Jianmin, Xinhua News Agency)

Chairing and speaking at the first plenary meeting of the State Council in Zhongnanhai, Beijing, on March 24, 1998. At right is Li Lanqing, Politburo member and Vice Premier. (Photograph by Liu Jianguo, Xinhua News Agency)

Responding to questions from Chinese and foreign reporters at a press conference during the first session of the Ninth National People's Congress on March 19, 1998. (Photograph by Zhao Yingxin, Xinhua News Agency)

Delivering the "Report on the Work of the Government" at the second session of the Ninth National People's Congress on March 5, 1999. (Photograph by Ju Peng, Xinhua News Agency)

In conversation with Jiang Zemin at the opening of the third session of the Ninth National People's Congress in the Great Hall of the People on March 5, 2000. (Photograph by Wang Xinqing, Xinhua News Agency)

In conversation with Hu Jintao at the opening of the 15th Congress of the Chinese Communist Party in the Great Hall of the People on September 12, 1997. (Photograph by Lan Hongguang, Xinhua News Agency)

Group photo of the State Council leadership on January 27, 2003. From left to right: Ismail Amat, Luo Gan, Wen Jiabao, Qian Qizhen, Zhu Rongji, Li Lanqing, Wu Bangguo, Chi Haotian, Wu Yi, and Wang Zhongyu.

On an inspection tour of Jishou University, Jishou, Hunan Province, on April 7, 2001.

Note from The Brookings Institution

JOHN L. THORNTON
Chair, Board of Trustees

I met Zhu Rongji in the mid-1990s when as Vice Premier he was responsible, in addition to many other matters, for the first overseas listings of China's state-owned enterprises (SOEs). I was Chairman of Goldman Sachs Asia at the time and had relatively close contact with Vice Premier Zhu and Wang Qishan, then Governor of China Construction Bank, as we worked on the Hong Kong listing of China Mobile. This was completed in October 1997, three months after the resumption of Chinese sovereignty in Hong Kong, and it inaugurated an era in which China's largest SOEs would become publicly listed companies. Today, China Mobile stands as the world's largest mobile phone company with over 790 million subscribers.

After Zhu became Premier in 1998, he continued his total commitment to the reforms that propelled China's rapidly expanding economy. Our association has continued to the present day: Zhu was the founding Dean of the Tsinghua University School of Economics and Management (SEM) and has been the Honorary Chairman of its Advisory Board since its inception in 2000. As a member of the Board from the beginning and as its chair between 2010 and 2013, I have had the pleasure of working with the former Premier as SEM has continued to strive to become a world-leading business school.

The Zhu Rongji I have known for two decades is very much the man who emerges in the pages that follow. Courageous, decisive, inquisitive, grounded, and very funny, he mastered both the macro and micro of whatever issue he faced. His searing intellect and force of personality were famous and could be intimidating. ("If you argue with me, I might turn red in the face on the spot. . . . Although I'm not very forbearing, I never target others and never bear a grudge.") One contribution of this volume is to show the other defining qualities of Zhu as a leader: his quest for ideas from both inside and outside China, an openness to persuasive argument, and the ability to adjust the details of policy even as his determination to execute the overall vision never wavered.

The volume overflows with Zhu's insights, singular personality, and leadership style. The selections, made by Zhu himself, also chart the history of some of the most challenging economic issues faced by China during this pivotal period in its development. They will be valuable to scholars and serious students who seek to better understand the country.

The opening selection of volume 2 is exemplary. It is Zhu's speech to the first plenary session of the State Council that he chaired after becoming Premier in the spring of 1998. Confiding that he had "barely slept" the night before thinking about what he should say, Zhu puts his prepared remarks aside and tells the roomful of senior officials that they had been given a "historic opportunity as [China] moves between two centuries." Zhu acknowledges the formidable obstacles to achieving this goal—official corruption and arrogance being the most dangerous—but he exhorts his colleagues to take the plunge:

> Comrades, from this day on, we are a single entity bound together by fate. You must be determined to jump into the abyss with me! Actually, not to jump in, but to find clever ways to overcome the various obstacles before us, to avoid all the dangers and pitfalls, till we triumphantly reach the other side of the course. Let us bind our fates together and with a strong sense of responsibility complete our tasks as quickly as possible, so that we may be accountable to the people.

A fascinating aspect of Zhu's speech is how in 1998 he foreshadows the priorities President Xi Jinping would adopt 15 years later. Pointing to corruption, high-handedness, and a bureaucratic work style as the sources of the people's discontent with the Party, Zhu orders his ministers to set a simpler, more modest example. When visiting the provinces, leaders should "travel light," reducing the size of entourages and dispensing with formal greeting ceremonies, banquets, and sendoffs. They should also avoid "fancy hotels and famous scenic spots." In daily work, the number of meetings should be reduced and the ones that are necessary shortened and simplified. Meaningless activities should be eliminated entirely: "We must stop cutting ribbons—what are leading members of the State Council doing at such activities?" The image of the good official Zhu has in mind are closely echoed in the Eight Regulations to Improve Working Style announced by Xi shortly after taking the Party helm in 2013.

Through occasional but startling vignettes, volume 2 also deepens our understanding of Zhu the man. In a speech to college students in 2001, for instance, he relates a painful anecdote with a candidness rarely seen from a senior leader in any country:

> I remember very clearly how my son, when he was a little over 10 years old [at the height of the Cultural Revolution], wanted to grow vegetables on our balcony. One day he found a tattered piece of linoleum that he put on the balcony, preparing to put soil on it in order to grow vegetables. As soon as I saw this, I told him that no matter how poor we were, we could

not take things from others. Then I casually slapped him on the ear. It was the first time I had ever struck him, and it was also the last.

He told me that he had taken nothing from anyone, that he had retrieved this broken piece of linoleum from the trash. At the time I very much regretted hitting him, but perhaps because as a father I couldn't get off my high horse, I said, "All right then, I shouldn't have hit you. But we must bring this piece of linoleum back regardless of whether it belongs to someone or if it came from the trash." Then I accompanied him in throwing this piece of linoleum back into the trash heap. I feel very bad whenever I think of this.

Zhu ranks among a handful of truly extraordinary statesmen whom I have encountered. In an essay collected in volume 1, Zhu remembered one of his university professors who had a deep influence on him. In 1950, Zhang Mingtao, the Dean of Tsinghua's Electrical Engineering Department, told an assembly of patriotic students who wanted to know how they should serve their country that they must first strive to become individuals who were upright, incorruptible, and "rigorously painstaking" in pursuit of the truth. The professor called on them to become "Chinese with backbone." Hearing it that day, it was a phrase Zhu would never forget. And none may be more apt in describing Zhu Rongji himself—a Chinese with backbone.

1

SPEECH AT THE FIRST PLENARY SESSION OF THE STATE COUNCIL[1]

March 24, 1998

Last night I barely slept, thinking about today's speech. Because this is a plenary meeting of the State Council, I had earlier asked the State Council Research Office to draft a speech, which since then has been revised several times and commented on by all the Vice Premiers and State Councilors. It is a very comprehensive draft, but I'm not going to read it today. It will be printed and distributed to all of you. Instead, this is an impromptu speech for which I take full responsibility. Consider it for your reference only.

I'd like to focus on three topics: (1) the most urgent issues to be resolved this year; (2) reforms of government agencies—if this is not handled well now, the stability of our entire society and the normal operations of government will be at risk; and (3) the need for a major change in the style and mode of work in this administration—without such a change, we won't be able to accomplish our mission. However, I'm going to discuss these issues in reverse order, starting with the State Council's style and mode of work.

Transforming the Government's Style and Mode of Work

Colleagues, the first session of the Ninth National People's Congress clearly has great expectations of our administration, and the media both at home and abroad all place great hope in it. We must therefore ask how we can achieve the weighty task that the people have entrusted us with. I expressed my true feelings in this regard at the press conference at the conclusion of that first session.[2] Subsequently, many comrades asked me, how come you didn't leave any wiggle

---

1. On March 24, 1998, Zhu Rongji chaired the First Plenary Session of the State Council at Zhongnanhai. Participants included the members of the State Council Plenum and leading members of its various agencies, administrative departments, and directly controlled operating units. The official version of Zhu's speech distributed to participants was published under the title "Govern Effectively, Cleanly and Efficiently, and Perform Well the Tasks of This Trans-Century Administration" in *Selected Important Essays since the 15th Party Congress*, vol. 1 (Beijing: People's Publishing House, 2000). This chapter is based on a recording of Zhu's impromptu speech at the conference.

2. See *Zhu Rongji Meets the Press* (Oxford University Press, 2011), chap. 19.

room at all in your remarks? They raised the question out of concern for me, in that they felt these things could not be accomplished, not even in five years, let alone three. So why did I say that? Because I feel deeply that this administration is being given a historic opportunity as it moves between two centuries, a chance not only to carry on what has come before but also to open up the way forward. If we were to pass up this opportunity, it would be hard for China to achieve things in the next century.

So far, the reforms and opening up initiated by Deng Xiaoping have achieved unprecedented success, the two administrations led by Li Peng have created good macroeconomic conditions, and our nation's economy has become quite strong. All this has laid a good foundation for our future work. But many latent crises are brewing in our country, which may erupt at any time. I don't mean a crisis of government—the collective leadership of the Party Central Committee with Jiang Zemin at its core is strong and united and can steer us through even the most complex situation. Those of you engaged in economic work all know that the problems in this sphere are very serious right now, that people are dissatisfied with us in many respects.

In particular, our officials are corrupt, there is disparity between the rich and the poor, some grassroots officials lord it over others, some senior officials are too bureaucratic and have little regard for the interests of the people—all this has left the people very dissatisfied! The one thing they are still satisfied with, however, is the economy: it continues to grow, prices are falling and not rising, and there's no problem with maintaining basic living standards. If this administration doesn't enact basic reforms aimed at existing shortcomings and lay down a good foundation, it will indeed be hard to achieve much in China into the next century.

I'm the oldest person here, and of those present today, even the "young" ones are no longer young. Having worked for several decades, we have a profound understanding of how hard it is to transition from a planned economy to a socialist market economy. We know, too, the shortcomings of a planned economy. Therefore we have to come up with a relatively good way to gradually resolve [these] and transition to a genuine socialist market economy. We need those of you here who are familiar with both the old and new systems to assume positions of leadership. However, we can't simply promote the good talkers, who can reel off a lot of theory but fail to understand conditions in China or the way its economy has been operating for the past few decades—that would be very dangerous. Instead we need young and capable officials, and once we identify them we should let them rise to the top, perhaps even promote them to a second-in-command position to train them and prepare them for promotion. But this cannot be done in a single step—you need to use a bit of authority to resolve these problems.

Chairman Mao was the core of the first generation of leaders, and Deng Xiaoping was the core of the second generation. Now we have established the third generation of collective leadership with Jiang Zemin at its core. It is leading us as we navigate the domestic economic waters without the slightest volatility. It was a great blessing for the Chinese people that there was not even a hint of it when Deng Xiaoping passed away. One might say that this administration brings together some of today's best leading cadres. I'm not saying this team is perfect, but the consensus both in China and abroad is that this team is quite dependable, capable, experienced, and able to cope with complex situations. We should all feel satisfaction and pride at being part of this transcentury leadership team.

When I said that a "minefield" and an "abyss" lie before this administration, I was not the least bit mistaken, though of course we will avoid such pitfalls. But it's going to be very tough to do so! Colleagues, from this day on, we are "a single entity bound together by fate." You must be determined to "jump" into the abyss with me! Actually, not to jump in, but to find clever ways to overcome the various obstacles before us, to avoid all the dangers and pitfalls, till we triumphantly reach the other side of the course. Let us bind our fates together and with a strong sense of responsibility complete our tasks as quickly as possible, so that we may be accountable to the people.

We must strive hard and govern well and make this a clean, efficient, and "cheap government," in the sense ascribed by Marx. In *The Civil War in France*, he took the phrase to mean a lean, low-cost government that does not waste the sweat and blood of its people. We must lead by example and become this sort of government; otherwise we won't accomplish this task. It won't work to go on as we have been doing. Each and every one of us, starting with myself, and you, comrades—who have hundreds of thousands or millions following you—must lead by example and be a role model. If the leadership team of the State Council, including all of us here, can do this, we will be able to reverse the current bad trends in society.

I'd like to mention a motto that may be of some help here—one that I put my faith in as soon as I took up my post in Shanghai: "The people respect me not because of my ability, but because of my fairness." That is to say, people respect my authority not because I have such great abilities, for even if I were more capable I wouldn't necessarily be better than others. They accept my authority because I am fair in my dealings. "Officials do not fear my sternness, they fear my probity." Officials below me aren't afraid of me because of my sternness, they're afraid because I'm not corrupt, because there's no shit on my ass. If I can walk tall and sit straight, I can dare to expose your bad behavior. "From fairness comes light, and from incorruptibility comes authority." You can only understand things clearly if you are fair, and you can only have authority if you aren't corrupt.

I always adhered to this principle when I was working in Shanghai. I constantly reminded myself to be fair, even if I wasn't always able to achieve this. I also strove to be clean—even in minor matters, I made sure to consider whether it was consistent with Party regulations and never risked being careless about it. I made the same demands of those working beside me and of my family members. Also, as my secretary frequently reminded me, it is essential to monitor each other. Provided we all work at it, I think we can change the unhealthy trends in society today.

Let me lay out five expectations in the hope that we will encourage one another to live up to them.

1. We Must Never Forget That We Are Servants of the People. We must serve our people with heart and soul and must not seek special privileges. When the Disciplinary Commission of the Central Committee recently investigated several regions and departments, its inspection teams found a lot of problems. What I hadn't expected was that many of those involved were old friends of mine. Is such disregard of rules and regulations even the least bit appropriate for public servants? Do they think that having climbed to their positions, they can do as they please and enjoy whatever they want? How can we let this go on?!

2. We Must Discharge Our Duties Faithfully and Dare to Speak the Truth. If everyone in this administration were "Mr. Nice Guy," we'd be letting the people down. We have to be the "bad guys." Don't think that "our society has now become a society of mediocrities in which no one wants to offend anybody. It's enough that I don't sink to their level." This sort of thinking won't do. First of all, you can go ahead and offend me. I may not have a lot of forbearance and lose my temper easily. If you argue with me, I might turn red in the face on the spot. But I bear this proverb in mind: "Be tolerant and you will be great; forgo desires and you will be strong." If you don't crave anything, you will be strong and fear nothing. This is my motto. Although I'm not very forbearing, I never target others and never bear a grudge. The facts prove this. On the contrary, if someone dares to speak up, dares to contradict me to my face, puts me in an awkward position, I'll give such a person important responsibilities. Of course I can't do this with just anyone, especially if he doesn't have the ability. However, I absolutely will not bear a grudge.

To give you an example, Liu Jibin[3] of this administration and I once got into a raging argument over the issuance of Treasury bonds. At the time I was very upset with him, and even today I still think that he was wrong. His way of issuing

---

3. Liu Jibin was then Chairman of the State Commission for Science, Technology, and Industry for National Defense. From June 1988 to March 1998 he was Vice Minister of Finance.

Treasury bonds will not work—didn't last year prove that my method was the correct one? We can't have a market auction—that would force interest rates so high that the nation couldn't afford it. China has a special circumstance—the interest on Treasury bonds is higher than that of bank deposits. What other country in the world has a situation like this? If you have a market auction for Treasury bonds, you'll only be paying high interest to those speculators. But Jibin is a very upright and capable person, and I think it very appropriate to appoint him chairman of the State Commission for Science, Technology, and Industry for National Defense. Therefore, comrades, please set your minds at ease about me. At times, I may lose my temper with you, I may argue with you, I may even say some unpleasant things to you, because "it is easier to change the course of a river than to change a person's character." It's not that I'm unwilling to change—it's just that I haven't been able to change. But in my lifetime I've only been targeted; I've never targeted others.

We should all dare to offend not only leaders like ourselves, but also those below us. Otherwise, our nation's laws and rules will be ineffective. I place a great deal of trust in you. I'm not afraid that you might seek revenge, but I am afraid that you'll be reluctant to offend others. You must first dare to offend us, then dare to offend those in your charge: you must keep watch over them.

In some departments, section heads are the bosses. When governors and mayors come to call, they won't even bother to look at them—that's not good. This type of behavior can be found at the State Planning Commission, and the locals react very negatively to it. When officials from local governments arrive to submit a report, they'll find a young woman sitting there who won't offer them a chair, let alone look at them. This has become a "dictatorship of the section chiefs"—how can we allow this? I'm not saying that all section heads are like this, just that if there are any, they should be replaced immediately. Such people are not fit to be section heads; they're not true public servants. They should be sent off to learn how to change their attitudes.

3. We Must Govern with a Strict Hand and Not Be Afraid to Offend Anyone. Governing strictly means being more rigorous, and not casually letting things go. This isn't a question of letting a person slip off the hook—it's an institutional question. Otherwise, the fate of our country might "slip away." As I've just said, many of us are afraid that speaking the truth will give offense, and we're afraid others might be displeased—although it won't be so easy to fool me. We must get into the habit of daring to speak the truth.

4. We Must Be Clean and Honest and See That Corruption Is Punished. Before we can punish corruption, we must be clean and honest ourselves. Otherwise it won't be possible to punish corruption.

5. We Must Study Diligently and Work Hard. We have a great deal to learn about a lot of new things. In the past, we never encountered anything like the Asian financial crisis, so the only thing to do was to learn lessons from it. Our embassies abroad all wired us reports, and I read their analyses of the Asian financial crisis one by one. Although their information was much the same and was copied from newspapers, it helped broaden my knowledge. I read more than 100 telegrams, all the sections of foreign newspapers that dealt with the Asian financial crisis, and at least 3 Hong Kong papers every day—especially the economics pages. If I had not done this, how would I know the state of the stock markets and the price of a barrel of oil? If you don't study, how can you cope with an unpredictable situation such as this? If you don't read reports, don't watch TV, don't read the papers, don't watch *Topics in Focus,* if you don't know about people's woes and try to understand them, how can you do your work? The most letters I may have signed off on were from the public.

Colleagues, you must care about the woes of our people. You won't know until you've read about them. Many things are utterly outrageous—they make your hair stand on end, and your blood pressure will go up after learning about them. I've been working at the State Council for eight years now, and I deeply feel that it's very easy to come up with an idea. You can come up with many ideas—they can cover heaven and earth, past and present—and you can cite all the classics. It's also not so hard to set a policy—provided you humbly listen to the views of all the departments concerned and draw on the collective wisdom, you can come up with a good policy. But it's very hard to implement it. It's not as if you just write a lot of directives and the people below will faithfully execute them—it's nothing of the sort. The hardest thing is to implement.

One insight I've gained in the past eight years is that to get something done, you won't be able to implement it without convening eight or ten meetings. If you issued a document, it would be considered a success if 20% of its contents were implemented. Without double-checking, implementation just won't happen. Whenever any ministry or commission makes a decision or sets a policy, its people must go down [to lower levels] to check and to implement. You have to talk about it again and again, and think about it again and again.

For a good example, you only have to look at Xinjiang cotton, which received a sizable contribution from our national Treasury. We simply couldn't sell it, and millions of bales were stockpiled in national warehouses. But we couldn't stop buying it, because if we did so the farmers would stop planting cotton. Another problem: because the price of Xinjiang cotton is higher than foreign cotton, everyone wanted to use imported cotton. We had plenty of our own, yet people were going all out to import cotton, and smuggling was rampant. I used economic and administrative measures to deal with this and have lost count of how many meetings we held. Did we implement? Yes, [but] so far, we've only sold several hundred thousand bales of Xinjiang cotton. It's difficult!

Did you see the TV program about the "March 15 campaign?" This was a special report on illegal pyramid sales. What are pyramid sales? It's where one person brings in 10 people, and 10 people bring in 100. They sold fake and shoddy goods and ruined the lives of participants and their families. They sold so-called medical equipment to sick people, causing them to spend every last penny on this. Patients who were still able to stand beforehand wound up bedridden after using this equipment. Meanwhile, some of the people in the sales networks were making several thousand renminbi in only a few days and as much as RMB 10,000 in a month. I felt heartsick after watching this program, and yet Li Lanqing told me that he had issued a directive last year to put a halt to pyramid sales. I was shown the document and agreed with it. Now over a year has passed, but it seems that there's a lot of resistance to dealing with this matter. Wang Zhongfu,[4] I'm not criticizing you—a lot of the agencies under the Bureau of Industry and Commerce may not listen to you because they belong to local governments, some of which are very corrupt! But you still have a minor shortcoming. After Lanqing issued this important directive, you still printed up [a document] on the management of pyramid sales—isn't that admitting it's all right not to ban them?

Pyramid sales often touch on local interests, which means that officials as well as unsavory elements of society are all involved in them. Furthermore, if people in the pyramid sales networks try to pull out, they'll be badly beaten. What kind of market economy is this? It's the downright worst sort of feudal behavior. That's why it absolutely must be halted—how can we let it continue to harm people?

When I first started working at the State Council, I was rudely welcomed by the "stock disaster" at the Shenzhen Stock Exchange—the whole country was trading stocks then. In Chengdu alone there were over 100,000 traders. I still have photos taken from rooftops showing mobs of people everywhere—over 100,000 of them speculating in stocks as if they were at a donkey market. Sichuan's leaders asked me, "What shall we do?" My answer: you must decisively put an end to this; that is, it must not be allowed.

And how can you end it without firm resolve? Colleagues, you must implement, implement, and implement again. After sending down documents, if you don't follow up on their implementation by checking in person, very few people will pay any attention to you. Right now, the heads of some of our companies and officials in some localities who are in charge of economic work are both

---

4. Wang Zhongfu was then Director of the State Administration of Industry and Commerce.

Chairing and speaking at the first plenary meeting of the State Council on March 24, 1998. Attendees included Politburo Standing Committee member and Vice Premier Li Lanqing (second from right), Politburo members and Vice Premiers Qian Qizhen (fourth from right), Wu Bangguo (first from right), and Wen Jiabao (fifth from right), and Politburo member, State Councilor, and Secretary of the Central Political and Legal Affairs Committee of the Party Central Committee Luo Gan (sixth from right). (Photograph by Liu Jianguo, Xinhua News Agency)

ignorant and bold. They know nothing about economics, yet blindly give directions as boldly as can be.

With these companies, you won't know what's going on until you check, but once you do you'll be shocked. The ones reported to me are all billions of renminbi in the red. The China Rural Development Investment Trust Company, for example, has lost RMB 6.8 billion, and the Everbright International Investment Trust Company RMB 5 billion. Recently, the head office of the China Nonferrous Metals Industries Corporation was speculating in international futures. It was speculating wildly on the London Futures Exchange, to the shock of foreigners. Later realizing that the corporation housed a pack of bunglers, they targeted it, and in the end it lost $770 million—that's RMB 6 billion. Isn't that a crime against the people? And the banks were accessories to the crime.

The China Nonferrous Metals Industries Corporation borrowed money from abroad for its speculating and faced no limits, which is entirely against the rules. Who provided the guarantees? The Hunan branch of the Bank of China. That branch's president must not only be fired, he must never be allowed to work in banking again. As I see it, he should be put in jail. Even the head office of the Bank of China can't give guarantees like that, let alone a provincial branch. The leadership team is extremely important. It's these half-baked people we should be afraid of. If you say he doesn't understand the subject, he can still go on and on talking about it and even say a few sentences in a foreign language, making your head spin. In fact, he knows nothing whatsoever yet is bold as can be on the surface. That sort of person must be replaced! Don't be afraid to offend people.

We are a "single entity bound together by fate." If we encourage each other, support and help each other, we can become a role model for the entire nation's government system. Hence we must jointly agree to "Three Ground Rules."

The first ground rule is that when we make inspection tours around the country, we should travel light. That is to say, we should reduce the size of our entourages, do away with formal greeting ceremonies and not have company for meals, greetings, or sendoffs. We should take the lead. When the State Council's premier, vice premiers, and state councilors go on inspection tours, they should bring along only one person ranked higher than vice minister, and at most one department or division head from the other related agencies. Many problems basically can't be solved at lower levels, so there's no need to bring so many people. Otherwise, we wouldn't have enough vice ministers to go around. The State Council has [only] so many vice premiers—how can they accompany everyone? Don't send big gangs of people down and let them wine and dine—that will be a bad influence on the ethos there. All the provinces and municipalities are doing this right now, and people are grumbling about it. There's too much wining and dining, so I'm adding one more thing: don't have company for meals, and don't greet and send off. Regarding company for meals, the rule was very strict when I first arrived at the State Council—we were asked not to have company. In the end I had no way out, so I agreed to do it only once. When I first arrived at a locality, the provincial Party secretary and governor would have one meal with me. Then they started dining with me once upon arrival and again when I was about to go back. Now I feel we can no longer keep compromising—we should all eat on our own. What's the point of getting together? It's gotten so that if you have something to discuss, you won't be able to discuss it, and the whole thing becomes very crass. Lanqing says let's publish this rule in the papers, because then we can all say that this is a State Council rule and we don't want to violate it. Actually, it's enough just for a single provincial leader to accompany us. When we go down we're representing the government, so the provincial Party secretary needn't keep us company.

The second ground rule is that we must simplify meetings. We need to shorten the time they take, reduce the number of participants, and avoid fancy hotels and famous scenic spots. We can have our meetings in poorer places. Then everyone can visit the poor, so we can demonstrate that the State Council cares about the people.

The third ground rule is that we have to cut down on the "whirlwind of meetings." Other than the activities centrally organized by the Party Central Committee and the State Council, leading members of the State Council generally should not attend meetings convened by various departments, local governments, or units. We have to cut down on this trend of having meetings about everything, speaking a lot of empty words, and in the end still getting nothing done. For ministry meetings organized by the State Council where the minister is to make a speech, you can report to the vice premier or state councilor in charge ahead of time, get their opinions in person, and then just attend the meeting. In the past, a lot of our time was soaked up by these meetings, and it was impossible to think about the issues.

We have to make one more rule about certain activities. Leading members of the State Council must not participate in activities like receiving guests, posing for pictures with people, giving out prizes, cutting ribbons, or attending publication ceremonies or film premieres. We must stop cutting ribbons—what are leading members of the State Council doing at such activities? In other countries, serving officials don't do these kinds of things. Apart from activities centrally organized by the State Council, in general we shouldn't get involved. We also mustn't send congratulatory letters or telegrams to all sorts of working meetings at the various agencies, and we mustn't write inscriptions or sign autographs, except for [security signatures on] envelopes. This rule only applies to all of you here. We should focus our energies on studying and handling major issues, particularly on investigating at the grassroots level and determining the actual state of affairs.

At the moment, it's very hard for us to see what is really going on when we visit. The locals arrange everything in advance, but if we suddenly change their arrangements, we can spot problems right away. Henceforth we must think of some way not to warn them of an impending inspection and decide what we want to see once we're there. That way the locals won't have time to deceive us. Otherwise we won't be seeing the true situation, and the policies we set won't accord with reality. We must encourage each other to live up to these "five expectations" and "three ground rules."

On the Reform of Government Agencies

The time has come to devote a considerable amount of energy to this subject. The head of each ministry must personally take charge. Otherwise the agencies won't be able to carry out their normal work, and there'll be big problems: rockets won't be launched and planes won't be able to fly. We must keep work attitudes of departmental staff stable, must elevate their thinking, and give them a sense of security—this is a very important matter. However, you absolutely must not fail to seriously implement the reform out of these considerations, nor should you reform half-heartedly—that is impermissible. After this conference, all departments will have to start drawing up plans immediately to determine three things: functions, job descriptions, and numbers.

If functions aren't defined, departments will keep passing the buck to each other. If job descriptions aren't determined, we can't determine personnel numbers. This matter must be given priority. The vice premiers and state councilors in charge of the various departments will be responsible for this work, and they must deal with it personally. The task will be particularly difficult for several agencies having overlapping functions, notably the State Planning Commission, the State Economic and Trade Commission, the Ministry of Foreign Trade, and the State Commission for Science, Technology, and Industry for National Defense. In principle, each function should be handled by only one agency and not by several. To the greatest extent possible, the State Planning Commission should help the State Council come up with ideas on major issues such as macroeconomic controls, paying timely attention to the balance of the total national economy and overall trends. It should be less involved in concrete work.

The next focus of attention should be staffing positions and staff numbers. We have already resolved to cut the total staff of the State Council by half. The State Council must take the lead in this. The number of vice premiers has been reduced from six in the previous administration to four; state councilors from eight to five, and two of them even have double portfolios. The number of deputy secretaries-general at the State Council has been cut by half, from ten to five, and the [State Council's] staff by half. Without a 50% reduction of the State Council's staff, the ministries will refuse to follow suit. We need a highly efficient State Council. Unless we downsize, we can't be efficient; we'll just keep getting involved in things we shouldn't be involved in and keep passing the buck.

After streamlining the agencies, it will be somewhat easier to build a clean government. Right now it takes money to get anything done. Even Ministry of Finance officials who are in charge of fee collections want money, and recently some people have even requested money for annual enterprise inspections. The fiscal and tax agencies are very unpopular at present, particularly the tax bureaus directly responsible to the central government—you need to go down there and inspect the situation. The greatest public outcry is directed at law enforcement agencies that break the law and most likely harbor corruption in their units.

To put it bluntly, public security and judicial agencies are too much to take, as one can see from an episode of *Topics in Focus* reporting on how fees are collected on a certain stretch of road in Shanxi Province. The traffic police wear military overcoats, and as soon as a vehicle approaches, they order the driver to stop and give him a ticket for RMB 60. If the driver shows the slightest sign of objecting, they immediately increase it to RMB 120, and if he still objects, it's RMB 240. Isn't that gouging the people? What kind of law enforcement agency is that? Jia Chunwang,[5] I'm now about to give you a "tough job"—hand over all your toll-collecting to the Ministry of Transportation, and have the Ministry of Public Security get out of this business. Although you'll lose a very considerable sum of extra income, the state can consider giving you more subsidies in the future. We can discuss this further, but the work of collecting tolls must be given to the Ministry of Transportation. We must enact a policy of "separate channels for collections and expenditures" in all our work, so that those who collect the money are not in charge of using it.

As soon as possible, the State Council's various departments must each define their functions, and once the rules are in place, nobody should be allowed to break them. We must try our best to start operating normally by the end of the year—some ministries might be able to do it sooner.

What will happen to the half of the staff who will be moved out? These people are also precious assets, and we must make proper arrangements for them. Those who cannot be assigned jobs immediately should first be assigned to targeted learning and continue to receive their wages and subsidies as usual. Of the 30,000 or more working in central government agencies, 54% are under the age of 40, so they can still learn. I am asking Song Defu[6] and Chen Zhili[7] to talk this over and come up with a master plan for training and study. We must work meticulously on their morale and let them play the greatest possible role.

As I understand it, officials in our government agencies aren't too uneasy right now and are mentally prepared to move elsewhere—their income might even be higher afterward. Everyone, please get a firm grip on the reform of government agencies—we must win the first battle, and under no circumstances can anything go wrong. Also, we mustn't create misunderstandings. Some people have told me that they heard that publicly supported institutions are also going to trim half their staff, and that enterprises directly controlled by ministries will be doing the same. How is that possible? If that were the case, where would our outplaced staff go? If enterprises laid workers off or placed them elsewhere, it would be because productivity is poor and cannot be improved without cutting staff. We're talking about the placement of government agency staff.

We only have one expectation of publicly supported institutions—that their subsidies be gradually reduced. Although the educational system can't survive without "imperial rations,"[8] it has to get rid of excess personnel. Some research units will also have to cut some support staff; otherwise they'll have a hard time

---

5. Jia Chunwang was then Minister of Public Security.

6. Song Defu was then Minister of Human Resources.

7. Chen Zhili was then Minister of Education.

8. Translator's note: that is, it must be paid for by the government and supported by budgetary expenditures.

raising the pay of the researchers. Reforms and adjustments are indeed needed at enterprises and publicly supported institutions under the various ministries, but we didn't ask them to trim their staff by half. We have to make this very clear, or else it will lead to unnecessary panic. I expect that some problems will arise in the course of reforming government agencies—please report these in a timely way.

Regarding This Year's Work

Presiding over yesterday's meeting of the Party Central Committee's leading group on economics and finance, Jiang Zemin made an important speech in which he agreed in principle with our report on urgent current tasks and instructed us to focus on implementing it. Our report was basically concerned with the "One Assurance, Three Implementations and Five Reforms" that I had described during the press conference at the end of the first session of the Ninth National People's Congress.

1. Ensure That This Year's Economic Growth Rate Reaches 8%. Why must we ensure 8%? Because right now we're riding a tiger and can't dismount. The Ninth Five-Year Plan has set the rate at 8%, and if we fail to reach that, the public will lose confidence. Our tentative assessment is that it shouldn't be too hard to realize 8% growth this year—if we work at it, it can still be achieved. But there are two things we absolutely must not do:

—First, the banks must not loosen the money supply and we mustn't produce goods that are simply stockpiled—that would be tantamount to "suicide."

—Second, we mustn't try to "do it big and do it fast," and start up redundant construction projects.

Right now we do need to do some infrastructure construction projects, but we can take that in a broader sense to include agriculture, forestry, waterworks, railways, highways, new technologies, and upgrading existing enterprise technologies, as well as large-scale housing development. We have the wherewithal for increasing investments in these areas because in the past few years our monetary policy was fairly tight and we controlled the issuance of money. Now we can have a bit more bank credit lending, particularly because our foreign exchange reserves this year won't grow as quickly as they did last year. As of the end of February, our foreign exchange reserves didn't grow and even shrank a bit, which correspondingly reduced the amount of renminbi locked in by the forex. Last year [the forex reserves] grew by $100 million a day, but this year they've ceased to grow and have even shrunk a bit.

2. Lower Bank Interest Rates. Tonight we will announce that the bank interest rate will drop by 0.6%. This will lighten the burden on state-owned enterprises

(SOEs) by almost RMB 30 billion a year, which will help SOEs improve their production. At the same time, it might lead to a reduction in bank deposits, but the long-term interest rate hasn't dropped, only the short-term rate, so the impact shouldn't be too great.

3. Encourage Reemployment. The key to reforming SOEs is reemployment. The publicity departments haven't done enough in this area and need to do more to change people's views on choosing jobs. Financial arrangements have long since been made for the funding of the "three-thirds" system,[9] and the finance departments of both the central and local governments have reserved a portion of their money to ensure the basic living standards of laid-off workers in the period before reemployment.

This afternoon, Wu Bangguo and I will be going to the Northeast as Jiang Zemin has entrusted us with convening a meeting of the Party secretaries, provincial governors, and the autonomous region chairmen of three provinces and one autonomous region. That is a preparatory meeting for the national conference on reemployment work, and we'll be listening to the participants' feedback on our plan. In addition, this May we'll convene a national conference on reemployment work. I think that if we clearly explain the issue of reemployment and make proper arrangements, we'll definitely be able to encourage our SOEs to strengthen themselves while putting the minds of the laid-off workers at ease, which will lay the groundwork for our reforms this year.

4. Reform the Circulation System for Edible Grain. This reform is crucial, and we must solve the problem before the summer harvest. The purchase funds of the Agricultural Development Bank must operate in a closed system, and we're preparing to have a conference on the subject this April.

5. Reform the Housing and Health Care Systems. Pilot programs are now under way in all localities. Since each locality has its own ways of doing things, our job is to standardize these, solve some key issues of principle, and push the housing and health care reforms a step further forward. Housing reforms in particular, if matched by [supporting] policies, will be very helpful in reaching 8% growth this year.

Colleagues, we will be working together for five years, and must be earnest and united. The members of the State Council's standing committee are united. We

---

9. The "three-thirds system" refers to a State Council regulation regarding laid-off workers who were receiving reemployment services. Their enterprises, society at large, and government finance departments were each to be responsible for one-third of their basic living costs, including those for health care and old-age insurance costs.

trust you and support you, and you must also believe that we are putting our entire heart and soul into the tasks here. I see no [fundamental] contradictions between us, but there will be differences of opinion, and we cannot guarantee that we will have unanimous views on every question. We have been educated by the Party for many years and will put the big picture foremost, act democratically, and make the State Council's leadership work accord with realities. Will there be contradictions and disunity between the leading members of the State Council? Don't worry—there won't be any! We are entirely unanimous on the big questions, and you needn't have any worries. We are all candid people who speak our minds freely, and the State Council will definitely act democratically and listen humbly to your views.

Under a system now being introduced, we will no longer publish the State Council General Office's "*Yesterday's Developments*" and will replace this with the daily directives of the leading members of the State Council. We will try to publish these directives within two days—this way, the leading members of the State Council will be able to communicate about developments at any time. I'm still not fully familiar with the work of the other vice premiers yet, I'm more familiar with fiscal and financial work, and even these I don't have great familiarity with. In the future we'll have to solve this [communications] problem, and the leading members of the State Council must learn about each other's work on a daily basis.

We must also maintain consistent positions externally in order to avoid making it hard for those below to do their work. Please go about your work boldly—you have been elevated to leadership positions by the Party after careful consideration, and we both trust and support you. At the same time, I urge you to monitor us without any reservations. Something I can definitely do is self-consciously accept the monitoring of my colleagues.

2

On the Proper Reassignment, Resettlement, and Reemployment of Laid-off Workers[1]

March 25 and 26, 1998

The Party Central Committee and the State Council have decided to help large and medium state-owned enterprises out of their difficulties over a period of roughly three years through reforms, restructuring, transformation, and the strengthening of enterprise management. We will also do our best to start establishing a modern enterprise system at the majority of large and medium pillar SOEs by the end of the century. The conditions for achieving this goal are definitely present, and the key is to do a good job of reassigning, resettling, and reemploying laid-off workers.

March 25, 1998

Although laying off, reassigning, resettling, and reemploying surplus staff at SOEs will create temporary difficulties for some workers, this move is fundamentally conducive to healthy economic growth and to all-round social development. Furthermore, it is in the long-term interest of the working class. Handling this job well is an essential requirement of socialism and a responsibility that should be borne by the Party and the government. It has great bearing not only on the success or failure of SOE reform but also on social stability and the consolidation of political power. It is one of our most pressing current tasks. We must take all necessary measures to handle this matter well. I'd like to highlight four issues regarding the reassignment, resettlement, and reemployment of laid-off workers.

---

1. On May 14–16, 1998, the Party Central Committee and the State Council convened a conference in Beijing on ensuring the basic livelihoods of laid-off workers and their reemployment. To arrive at a clear understanding of the actual situation and prepare for the conference, Zhu Rongji went on an inspection and study tour of Jilin Province on March 24–26, 1998. He also chaired discussions in Changchun with the principal Party and government leaders in charge of this work in Liaoning, Jilin, Heilongjiang, and Inner Mongolia, and listened to their reports and recommendations for reassigning, resettling, and reemploying laid-off workers. These are his main remarks during the two meetings.

1. The Key to Resolving Difficulties of Large and Medium SOEs within Three Years Is Reducing Staff. As facts indicate, there are three main reasons for SOE difficulties: redundant construction, blind construction, and a bloated workforce.

Redundant construction is a persistent problem because these projects are all under way and can't be halted. If they're not completed, several tens of billions of renminbi will be wasted. If they are to be completed, several additional tens of billions will have to be invested, while other SOEs that have been producing the same types of goods will face ruin.

Blind construction is perpetuated by a desire to show some so-called political accomplishments, and it takes place even if there's no money for it. With basically no capital, such projects rely entirely on bank loans. They are also another form of redundant construction, so they have no way to repay the loans and can only produce losses. I've often issued grave warnings against these two problems: don't launch any more ordinary industrial projects. Not even one type of industrial product is in short supply.

Yet redundant and blind construction projects are far from coming to a halt. Beginning right now, we must make a determined effort to put an end to construction of this nature. The Ministry of Finance will absolutely not provide so much as a penny to capitalize any ordinary industrial project. We cannot casually put the Ministry's money into such projects and expose it to risks. Its funds should be used mainly to resolve issues that are in the public interest, such as infrastructure and public welfare. Implementing reemployment projects is in the public interest—the Ministry's money should be used for this type of work, not for doing projects haphazardly.

At present, a prominent problem and heavy burden at SOEs is that of overstaffing. Not only are there more people than work, but they're also constantly squabbling, which has an impact on the zeal of workers and productivity of the enterprise. Trimming staff is an important measure to achieve the goal of getting large and medium SOEs out of their difficulties within three years, in addition to halting redundant and blind construction. As the socialist market economy develops and grows more open to the outside, market competition will intensify by the day. The continued use of administrative means to protect loss-making enterprises won't work. We must follow a path of encouraging mergers, standardizing bankruptcies, streaming layoffs, reducing staff, and implementing reemployment projects. Only by reducing personnel numbers can the problem of loss-making at SOEs be addressed reasonably well.

2. The Laying Off and Reassignment of Surplus Staff Is the Way to Go. This is a major policy and a fundamental measure for invigorating SOEs. We absolutely mustn't [think that] SOEs should hire more people simply because China has a large population in need of jobs—that won't work. Enterprises will lose their

Chairing a meeting of leaders from Liaoning, Jilin, and Heilongjiang provinces and the Inner Mongolia Autonomous Region on March 25, 1998, held in Changchun, Jilin Province. In the first row are Politburo member and Vice Premier Wu Bangguo (first from right), Chairman of the State Economic and Trade Commission Sheng Huaren (third from right), and Governor of the People's Bank of China Dai Xianglong (fourth from right). At this meeting, Zhu Rongji stressed that every means possible should be used to properly resettle laid-off workers and to implement reemployment projects.

competitiveness if they have too many people, and those that cannot compete won't be able to survive.

Our country has a population of 1.2 billion, which will reach 1.3 billion by the end of the century. Employment is a major issue. Nevertheless, we can't just keep stuffing people into SOEs. We must turn SOEs into modern enterprises. If something can be done by three people, they mustn't use five. SOEs must be competitive, they must be able to engage in competition—only then can they survive. Only when SOEs become truly productive will they have the wherewithal to place surplus staff and to continually refine social insurance institutions.

We can't let people in enterprises muddle along, with "one person working, one person watching, and one person making trouble." Work can't be done well that way. The last two people must be asked to leave—don't let one keep watching, and even more so, don't let the other keep making trouble. Just keep one person working there. Reducing staff is the direction SOE reforms and development must take—enterprises must reduce. Therefore it is essential to implement projects for suitably placing those who are laid off and for gradually facilitating their reemployment. And precisely because our country's current social insurance institutions are still incomplete and fall far short of meeting needs, SOEs must take on the responsibility of placing and facilitating reemployment for the people they lay off. This is an important aspect of a social security system with Chinese characteristics.

3. We Must Guarantee the Basic Livelihoods of Those Laid Off in Accordance with Policy. Under a "three-thirds" principle, the State Council is proposing that enterprises, society, and fiscal departments each cover one-third of the basic costs of living (including health insurance and pension premiums) of workers who go into reemployment centers. Given the present capacities of these three entities, this is entirely doable.

For enterprises, this is not a large share of the burden. In Shanghai, the basic cost of living of a laid-off worker, including health insurance and pension payments, is RMB 4,000 a year, whereas a worker's average annual wage is about RMB 10,000, so RMB 4,000 isn't even half the annual citywide wage. An enterprise that pays one-third [of basic living costs] is in fact only paying one-sixth of the original wage, so most enterprises are entirely able to cope with this.

Some enterprises in exceptionally difficult circumstances will have to be propped up by fiscal departments. The one-third from these departments will not be very difficult to cover either. Just now you said that about 2 million workers in your four provinces have been laid off. Of these, only 1.1 million are from SOEs. Their problems must be resolved first. In fact, the average income of your workers here is lower than in Shanghai. Their basic living costs will only require RMB 4 billion at most. The fiscal departments should cover one-third, which is about 1.3 billion, but of this, the Ministry of Finance will subsidize about 30%, so not that much remains to be made up by the fiscal departments of the four provinces, and you should be able to come up with that. Fiscal subsidies from the central government will take the form of transfer payments of special funds to the old industrial bases in central, western, and northeast China.

At present, there are many channels for [raising] aid funds in society, so society should also be able to come up with its one-third. This funding is assured particularly because we've now increased the withholding for unemployment insurance. With less redundant and blind construction and less extravagance and waste, this problem can be solved.

4. We Must Use Every Conceivable Means to Implement Reemployment Projects. This is the ultimate way to reassign and resettle laid-off workers. The key to implementing reemployment projects is to change these workers' thinking about choosing jobs. Having been to Tianjin and Shanghai on inspection tours, I feel that right now it isn't that there are no job openings; it's that many laid-off workers aren't willing to take the jobs at hand. Some enterprises are head over heels in debt and owe money to the banks, yet they hire migrant workers from outside to do the landscaping and cleaning inside the factories because their laid-off workers won't do these things—how can that be? In Tianjin, Zhang

Hearing about the resolution of difficulties and reemployment of workers at the Tianjin Knitwear Factory on February 12, 1998. (Photograph by Chen Guoxing, Tianjin Daily)

Lichang[2] told me that some laid-off workers regard work like newspaper delivery to be relatively "noble" and acceptable. Why, I then asked, can't they deliver takeout food? When you want to buy a pizza in the United States, for example, you make a phone call and it will be delivered. He said the laid-off workers aren't willing to do that, let alone landscaping and cleaning.

At a future national conference, we should invite some responsible person from the All-China Federation of Trade Unions to talk about this subject. There's a lot of potential in the service industries, such as housekeeping and hourly work. We mustn't think that this kind of work lowers your social status; rather, we should regard this as equally noble work. Besides, many families have urgent need of such services, and with such help will be able to do their own jobs better. This is entirely honorable work.

Yesterday, Zhang Dejiang[3] told me that some villages in Jilin Province have people bring live pigs to sell in large cities like Beijing. Although agricultural production in Jilin last year declined by 10 billion jin,[4] farmer incomes not only did

2. Zhang Lichang was then Party Secretary of Tianjin.
3. Zhang Dejiang was then Party Secretary of Jilin.
4. One jin is equal to 0.5 kilogram.

not go down, they even increased slightly, mainly because people have developed a variety of operations such as processing animal feed, raising livestock, and animal husbandry. The special groups of villagers selling pigs in Shanghai and Beijing aren't organized by the government, and they're not consuming "imperial rations."[5] This operation has invigorated the rural economy, increased farmers' incomes, and provided conveniences to urban residents. However, we can't allow pyramid sales—pyramid sales can result in disaster for entire families. The State Council is about to issue a notice putting a firm halt to such activities.

Provided that the leadership at all levels takes it very seriously and adopts practical and effective measures, we will certainly be able to solve the reemployment problem.

March 26, 1998

This has been a very good meeting—it has been fully democratic and has achieved our goal of letting everyone speak freely, exchange information, pose questions, and further promote consensus. You've raised many excellent points, and these have given us many insights. Now I'd like to say a few words about the scope and standards of the basic livelihood of laid-off workers and about reemployment projects for retirees.

1. The Question of Scope. Why are the Party Central Committee and the State Council attaching so much importance to reassigning, resettling, and reemploying laid-off workers? Why has our new administration come here to discuss this issue as soon as we came into office? The main consideration here is to ensure social stability by guaranteeing the basic livelihood of laid-off workers and facilitating their reemployment. Without social stability, social development cannot take place. And if laid-off workers have no guarantee of a basic living, if they cannot be reemployed, society cannot be stable. Therefore one of the most important tasks of Party committees and governments at all levels now and in the future will be to ensure a basic livelihood for those laid off and to use every means conceivable to implement reemployment projects—this affects the entire big picture of reform, development, and stability. Our leading officials and all departments must devote great energy to this problem.

In Tianjin I visited a reemployment center, in Shanghai I discussed this issue with the parties concerned, and yesterday I visited the Changchun reemployment center. The reemployment centers in these places are using modern technologies to share information between job-seekers and would-be employers.

---

5. Translator's note: that is, they are not paid by the government and not supported by budgetary expenditures.

They are doing a good job of organizing and managing the labor force and helping laid-off workers find ways to make a living. These efforts are extremely significant but have just gotten started and must be strengthened.

In ensuring the basic livelihood of laid-off workers, we must consider where the focus should be. If we were to come up with a policy covering all laid-off workers, then some who left their factories years ago would show up asking for "policy implementation." This would create unnecessary headaches for enterprises experiencing difficulty or losses and for some local governments.

As Wu Bangguo[6] pointed out yesterday, enterprise layoffs are not a result of reforms. Yet some people mistakenly think that 10 million or more workers have been laid off because of the Party Central Committee and State Council's policy of "encouraging mergers and acquisitions, standardizing bankruptcies, laying off and reassigning [or otherwise] trimming staff and thus raising productivity, and implementing reemployment projects." This view is entirely wrong. The central authorities suggested this policy in January of last year, then formally issued a document in March[7] consisting of measures aimed at solving problems. But in some instances, such as arbitrary bankruptcies and mergers, they were seen as workers being laid off with no one taking care of them. In fact, there have long been layoffs everywhere; it's just that nobody called them that. In Jilin, they were called "vacations," while in other places they were called "the halting or half-halting of production" or "closures." In reality, the workers had been laid off long ago.

Many enterprises have been unable to pay wages since 1994—isn't that laying people off? It's even worse than layoffs. When workers are laid off, although technically they are still associated with the factory, they are told to go home, and the factory basically does not take care of them. At the time that the central authorities still didn't have a policy, enterprises and locals had no means of doing so.

Yesterday, I chatted a bit with several job-seekers at the Changchun reemployment center who were all "on vacation" and not being taken care of by the enterprises. Only one worker from the Changchun No. 1 Food Factory received RMB 130 in the first month of his "vacation," and he hasn't gotten so much as a penny ever since. So how can one say that layoffs are caused by policies of the central authorities? Besides, it's inevitable in the course of events that staff will be laid off.

Of the three reasons why SOEs are in difficulties, isn't overstaffing a very important one? If an enterprise is able to support only one person but has three people there, can it run well without laying off those two [extra] people? If we

---

6. Wu Bangguo was then a Politburo member and Vice Premier.

7. This refers to the "Supplementary Notice of the State Council on Questions Related to Pilot Programs on SOE Mergers and Bankruptcies and Employee Reemployment in Certain Cities."

go on like this, our enterprises won't be able to compete at all and just won't be well run. Why are workers being laid off? Because enterprises are losing money and can't compete. Without reducing staff, they won't be able to improve productivity—it's as simple as that.

The fact that more than 10 million people are laid off right now also reflects the inevitability of this course of events. That's why we must be clear about this relationship. These [problems] were created in the past, some owing to the economic overheating of 1993 and some to [events] several decades ago. They're all a result of history, so don't hold it against anyone now. The key issue is how to solve this problem.

In its documents, the State Council must make it clear that in ensuring the basic livelihood of laid-off workers, the scope and emphasis should be on those who have not yet dissolved their employment relationship with their factories and who have also entered reemployment centers. To this day, a good many enterprises still haven't established reemployment centers—this must be resolved as local conditions permit. Workers who left their factories quite a few years ago won't all be able to come back even if their employment relationship hasn't been dissolved. Some checking will have to be done [to determine their status]. For example, workers who have already found jobs won't be able to go back to their original enterprise to claim payments for basic living.

Government, enterprises, and society should be responsible for relief and subsidy payments to workers who left their enterprises many years ago but never dissolved their employment relationship with their enterprises and are now "homeless." This is complex and concrete work. We must come up with specific measures and let each locale deal with them in accordance with local circumstances.

The key still lies in reemployment. If we can achieve reemployment, nobody will run to the enterprises seeking "policy implementation." I suggest that after the national working conference on reemployment concludes, the Northeast region should hold a meeting at an appropriate time to share their experiences in and methods of reemployment.

In setting up reemployment centers, the most important thing is to assign highly competent officials and to make good use of modern technologies. We must establish an application system for future layoffs. It absolutely won't do to forcibly lay people off without establishing reemployment centers and without being able to ensure the basic livelihood of laid-off workers—the government and trade unions would have to intervene.

From now on, all laid-off workers must join reemployment centers—this must become an established system. We're not forbidding worker layoffs; rather, laid-off workers must join reemployment centers so that their basic livelihoods can be ensured. Enterprises will be required to file applications because the

Hearing about the living conditions of the family of a laid-off worker from the Jilin Brake Factory on March 25, 1998. (Photograph by Lan Hongguang, Xinhua News Agency)

government has to subsidize the basic living costs of laid-off workers. If enterprises don't file applications, how can subsidies be provided? Moreover, profitable enterprises are absolutely prohibited from receiving government subsidies for the workers they lay off. If they're not incurring losses, they may not apply to the government for the basic living costs of their laid-off workers. Only those enterprises in great difficulty and unable to even come up with one-sixth of the wages of their laid-off workers may apply for subsidies—this principle must be made clear.

As for the scope of ensuring the basic livelihood of laid-off workers, I have already given this some thought in Beijing and fear that after the national conference on reemployment and after we hear the views of all parties, we'll still have to make revisions in the methods to be used. The Ministry of Labor and Social Security and the State Economic and Trade Commission should organize studies on how the reemployment centers in the various provinces are run and exactly how broad the reach of the reemployment centers established by enterprises is.

2. The Question of Standards. I want to emphasize two points: first, "three-thirds" is a principle, but it isn't absolute. I'm not saying that all enterprises should get one-third of their subsidies from fiscal departments—the fraction will depend on actual circumstances. If an enterprise is truly in great difficulties and can't come up with even one-third, then government fiscal departments will have to prop it up with some extra subsidies. If an enterprise is in less difficulty and doesn't need a one-third subsidy, then don't give it so much. The standard subsidy per laid-off worker should be determined by all locales as circumstances warrant in each case.

3. Wages in Arrears and Retiree Pensions. Although this issue isn't directly concerned with reassigning, resettling, and reemploying laid-off workers, it seems to be the foremost problem in many places. With its many contradictions, it can easily elicit social sympathy and affect social stability.

Some point out that while laid-off workers are more numerous than retirees, there still aren't many cases of them petitioning collectively the way retirees do. This is because they're still young and can find a bit of work now and then or perhaps can still rely on their parents. Retirees have no one to rely on, so if they don't get their pensions, they'll become "homeless." That's why they deserve some explanation or satisfaction. The main cause of this problem is that pension funds don't earn enough to accumulate the necessary funds to cover their outlays. This issue merits a lot of attention, and we'll have to study it carefully once we return to Beijing.

Retiree pensions and wages in arrears are indeed a major problem that has wide impact and affects social stability. We must therefore take measures to properly address it.

First, we have to expand the coverage of pension insurance. That is, urban and township enterprises under all types of ownership, including foreign-invested and cooperative structures, must participate in the social pool and pay pension premiums. Since newly established enterprises don't need to make immediate use of their pension funds, their payments can be channeled into the social pool. We can't go on relying on SOE pensions alone.

Nowadays some places have two employees supporting one retiree, or even one employee supporting one retiree. With one generation supporting two or three, SOEs simply don't have enough pension funds and there's a great danger of spending money that has yet to be collected. Therefore we must expand pension coverage. The young people at newly formed enterprises must make contributions. Foreign-invested enterprises in particular should be subject to strict oversight and required to pay pension premiums. This isn't related to the investment environment. Premiums have to be paid in every country, and pension standards in developed countries are even much higher than in ours.

Second, the collection rate of pension premiums needs to be raised. It won't do for enterprises that have the money to refuse to pay. Their books must be checked—the Ministry of Labor and Social Security must strengthen its work in this area.

Third, pension funds need stronger management. As of last year, RMB 9.4 billion of pension funds had been misused and misappropriated—this must not be allowed to continue. The central authorities have now ruled that these funds may not be used for speculating in stocks or real estate. People think these ventures provide high returns, whereas in fact the risks are very great and all the money could be lost in one instant.

We are making it a hard and fast rule that pension funds may only be used to buy Treasury bonds or be deposited in banks and nothing else. To use them for other purposes will constitute a violation of the law and the people concerned will lose their jobs. To prevent misappropriation and embezzlement, these funds must be managed like "a chariot with three drivers": labor and social security departments will be in charge of collecting the money and depositing it into special bank accounts; and when these departments want to allocate money to enterprises, they will have to fill out a requisition that must be reviewed and approved by the fiscal departments before the funds can be withdrawn from the special bank accounts. Unless they see the reviews of the fiscal departments, banks will be unable to release the money. We must make this very clear.

This administration is going to change its work style and not focus its energy and attention on doing projects. It's absolutely wrong to see this as political accomplishment. What it can result in instead is "a moment of fame and a lifetime of castigation." While you have a project under way, it is called a "political accomplishment" and makes you feel glorious at the ribbon-cutting. Then once the project goes into production, it might lose money and be shut down. After a few years, you've moved elsewhere and received a promotion, but people will curse you for a lifetime! This administration will absolutely not do this sort of thing.

Starting with myself, we will not designate projects to be done. Our energies will be focused on the welfare of the people. Production can develop only after people are highly motivated. We must rely closely on the people and serve them with heart and soul. We have no choice but to focus on social insurance. The unemployment rate in other countries is very high—in Europe, it's over 10%, which is much higher than our rate. But others have well-rounded social security systems, so even if people lose their jobs, they can get by.

Under our current conditions, with social security systems still incomplete, it is very difficult to reform SOEs. They can't force people out, and it's very hard for them to go bankrupt. We now have criteria for enterprise bankruptcies so they can't arbitrarily go bankrupt on their own. The former way of going bankrupt won't work. Why? After a self-initiated bankruptcy, assets are used first to repay debts and to pay taxes, so the enterprises just don't have any money to resettle people. Besides, their assets aren't worth much anyway—there's not even enough to cover their debts—so how can they go bankrupt? If enterprises are to go bankrupt, there will have to be strict review procedures.

At the moment, pension funds are heavily indebted. I'd like to ask the Ministry of Finance, the Ministry of Labor and Social Security, and the State Council Office of Restructuring of the Economic System to study this matter jointly. An instrument used in the West to cover shortages in pension funds consists of a type of Treasury bond that only pays interest and doesn't repay the principal. In the past, the United States issued 100-year Treasury bonds. At that time, the American social security system was still incomplete, and these bonds only paid interest, not principal. There was an element of social charity in this, and many wealthy people were still willing to buy [these bonds] because they were guaranteed.

Another method is to levy a social security tax at some point in the future. During a recent study trip to the United States, Xiang Huaicheng[8] noted that $800 billion of its annual fiscal revenues of $1.6 trillion comes from income and sales taxes. Of the remaining $800 billion, $400 billion derives from a social security tax collected from individuals. By contrast, individual income taxes don't bring in much, only $200 billion. In the future, we'll have to refine our tax system and consider levying a social security tax. Otherwise, we won't be able to establish a social security fund.

In sum, we must strengthen management in all areas, increase income while limiting outlays, and gradually build up our country's social security system. Of course if we can solve the problems of redundant construction and money owed to banks for grain-related losses, our country would be able to free up several tens of billions of renminbi for this purpose and provide an extra allocation in the budget for social security. But enterprises will still have to deal with the temporary difficulties at present, and they can't refuse to pay the retirement stipends and pensions of retirees. It won't do for them to make excuses and say they can't afford to pay pension premiums—we must increase the collection rates. Not having paid pension premiums for a year or two, some enterprises that have yet to shut down are truly in difficulty, as they must still make pension payments to their retirees. Unemployment insurance must also be strengthened. It should be increased by two percentage points, one percentage point coming from individuals and the other from enterprises. These amounts will mainly be used for the reemployment of laid-off workers from SOEs, and unemployment relief will have to depend on the original one percentage point.

8. Xiang Huaicheng was then Minister of Finance.

3

Reforms of Government Agencies
Require Strong Determination,
Steady Steps, and Solid Work[1]

April 10, 1998

This special seminar for provincial-level officials on reforming government agencies is very timely, and I am fully supportive of it. I'd like to bring two points to your attention now.

1. The Reforms Must Go Forward, and
Government Must Be Separated from Enterprises

I'm going to open with a story first reported by the *Topics in Focus* program on CCTV, about a factory in a certain city that produced "Sanmei" wine, a well-known brand. When the enterprise was acquired by the Sanjiu Group, the trademark should also have been transferred. Instead the municipal Party secretary told the municipal finance department to buy the trademark, and it became the property of the government. Although the enterprise had already been acquired by the Sanjiu Group, municipal authorities just wouldn't turn over the brand name—the Party secretary even talked as if they had every reason not to. This is really lax management! If our provincial Party secretaries, governors, and mayors all intervene in the economy like that, how can China's economy take a turn for the better? How can we build a socialist market economy? If enterprises were all directed by the whims of senior officials, what competition would there be to speak of? That would still just amount to "eating from the same big pot"!

A second thing that merits our serious attention arises out of the recent "milk war" in Shanghai, where enterprises were selling milk at prices below their production costs. This is indicative of a systemic problem: factories that lose money don't have to assume responsibility; they can just go on owing

---

1. On March 31–April 11, 1998, the National School of Administration, in conjunction with the Organization Department of the Party Central Committee, the Ministry of Human Resources, and the Office for Public Sector Reform, organized a special seminar for provincial-level officials on promoting reforms of government agencies. This is the main part of Zhu Rongji's remarks at a discussion with seminar participants.

money to the banks, letting the banks pay up. This is also the result of administrative intervention. If you do some research, you'll find that wherever an enterprise is losing money in spades yet continues to produce, you'll find that it's backed either by the municipal Party secretary or by the mayor. The loser is the country, as the debts all lie with the banks. Should there be a financial crisis, the consequences would be unthinkable. Therefore we can't continue combining government with enterprises, and we can't allow administrative interference to continue.

Well, Then, What Should the Government Be in Charge Of? First and foremost, the government should regulate markets—it must firmly regulate the markets and must do that well. But at the moment the government isn't regulating markets. It's operating them. With a direct link between government and economic interests, however, competition cannot be fair.

Second, the government should regulate quality. The Bureau of Quality and Technical Supervision should be moved out of the State Economic and Trade Commission and put under the direct leadership of the State Council to elevate its position. Although this department doesn't have a higher rank, the State Council is determined to strengthen it and is preparing to assign several vice ministers to enhance its leadership. To reiterate, the government should be regulating markets and quality. It should not be directing production and operations of enterprises, and not ordering banks to lend to enterprises. More than anything else, this is a systemic problem, but it also demonstrates that government agencies are overstaffed. If they had fewer people, they wouldn't have so much time and energy for administrative interventions.

The key to transforming government functions is the separation of government from enterprises. That is why we are abolishing the industrial ministries with these reforms and turning them into national bureaus under the State Economic and Trade Commission. As facts have shown, you can't do a good job by letting industrial ministries run enterprises. In the past, there were eight ministries of machine building, for example, yet they couldn't run the machine-building industry well. Now things are much more complex and even harder to manage well. Systemically speaking, industrial ministries think in terms of the interests of their own sectors. It's very hard for them to supervise their enterprises in a serious manner as they are more inclined to [just] ask the central government for funding and for [favorable] policies.

This administration has decided that industrial departments should not be responsible for managing enterprises. As just mentioned, they are being converted to national bureaus and put under the leadership of the State Economic and Trade Commission. What should these industrial bureaus be doing? They should be planning, drawing up sector policies, arranging project assignments, preventing redundant construction, and so on. In short, there will be no direct ties between industrial bureaus and enterprises.

How Will the Government Oversee Enterprises in the Future? We will establish a system of special inspectors in state-owned enterprises. In fact, these will be supervisory committees dispatched by the State Council, but to avoid confusing them with the supervisory committees required by the Corporation Law, we will call them special inspectors. They will be delegated by the State Council, and each special inspector will be assigned four assistants, who will mainly be people familiar with accounting, auditing, finance, and supervision. This will constitute a fundamental change in the enterprise management system.

The main task of the special inspectors will be to check the books, and they will not intervene in state-owned enterprise (SOE) management or operations. Inspectors will examine the books twice a year, analyze and assess the financial status of SOEs, and determine whether they are making or losing money; at the same time, they will be assessing the performance of the SOEs' key leaders. After the inspectors' reports are reviewed by agencies like the State Economic and Trade Commission, they will be submitted to the State Council; then, through the personnel departments, the State Council will determine rewards or punishments and will hire or fire key SOE leaders, as circumstances warrant. Why do we have to do it this way? Let me give some examples.

At one point, the head office of a certain corporation borrowed $1.1 billion in forex without permission from the State Planning Commission or the State Administration of Foreign Exchange and used it for business purposes and futures trading. Last year, we discovered that it had lost $150 million and quickly took measures to change its leadership team. As we have since learned, the total losses amounted to $770 million—they had some nerve!

Another company that was originally doing very well and had never shown signs of any problems over the course of many years was exposed last year. We sent someone to investigate and found it had lost RMB 6.8 billion. We immediately abolished this unit and put it under the receivership of the China Construction Bank. In the end, these losses were all borne by the state.

Colleagues, if our SOEs hadn't acted without prior approval, failed to report after the fact, and lost tons of money, would our country be in such difficulties today? The State Council's decision to send special inspectors to large SOEs and enterprise groups was based on full and careful consideration [of these matters]. It is essential if we are to separate government from enterprises and is a major change in the way China manages SOEs, and it is consistent with international practice. If we don't do this, the goal of getting most large and medium SOEs out of their difficulties within three years will just be empty talk.

When our special inspectors check the books of SOEs, they will initially have to work with the fiscal accounting systems already in use and then gradually establish a modern system that accords with international practices of enterprise accounting. This work should start at enterprises already visited by the special inspectors and then be integrated with the auditing practices of industrial and commercial departments, making full use of the inspection results of these departments. If necessary, qualified accounting firms may be asked to assist in this endeavor. The SOEs examined by special inspectors need no longer conduct thorough unscheduled fiscal inspections, and they can also dispense with ordinary audits. Provided the special inspectors dare speak the truth and aren't afraid to offend people, they'll be able to unearth problems.

Why Should Personnel Departments Be in Charge of This Work? The key to whether SOEs can be well run lies with their leadership teams and with those first in command. And we must put constraints on people who utterly disregard laws and regulations. We'll send someone to keep an eye on them and on their books. If they don't work out, they'll be removed and replaced by others who are up to the task. The practice of sending special inspectors is a new one and it's best to proceed carefully at the beginning.

The first step is to choose good people. The current special inspectors and their professional assistants were all rigorously selected. There may not be many of them at the outset, but they must be fair and incorruptible—you must be straight yourself before you can set others straight. People with criminal records will not be allowed to do this work, nor will people who love to wine and dine— we cannot ruin the reputation [of the inspectors] right from the start.

The second step is to provide good training. Personnel departments should call on domestic and foreign experts and scholars to compile teaching materials in the shortest possible time, so we can begin the training this month.

The third step is to have rewards, punishments, and oversight. We must strengthen the education of special inspectors, and they must be highly disciplined. Those who don't work hard or who neglect their duties should be punished. In short, we must win the opening battle.

How Should We Manage Local SOEs? We must aim for a method that combines local industrial departments and bureaus and doesn't let them run enterprises anymore. Choose some outstanding officials to oversee enterprises and to supervise factory directors. We have proposed a 16-character guideline for streaming off government agency staff that includes "reassigning them with [the same] job titles, providing them with targeted training, strengthening enterprises, and optimizing structures."

Why did we add "strengthening enterprises?" At first, many people suggested "strengthening the front lines" or "strengthening the grass roots," but in the end we still stayed with "strengthening enterprises," because enterprises are the foundation. If they aren't run well, everything is meaningless.

To strengthen enterprises, we must send them the most outstanding officials. In the past, if an entrepreneur ran an enterprise well, he would be transferred and become a vice minister or a bureau chief, so all the [capable] people were siphoned off. Now we have to reverse this practice and send the best people to the enterprises. The government mustn't interfere with their management or operations and must give them a free hand to do their work. At the same time, we must have special inspectors keeping an eye on them—even capable people cannot be without restraints. We have to solve this problem through the socialist market economy and the enterprise system. Reform of government agencies is both an inevitable demand and a pressing need of the evolving situation. Such action is critical for the resolution of deep-level contradictions and for the success of various other reforms and developments.

If agency reforms are done well, if all levels of government can truly become streamlined and efficient, if officials become highly motivated and take charge of the things government should be in charge of, if weak links can be strengthened, if the command system is responsive, if work is done more efficiently, and if the guidelines and policies of the Party are properly implemented—everything else will be easy to deal with. You must all fully recognize this and become more self-aware. Even if you meet with difficulties, resistance, and risks, you must tackle these head-on and work hard to do a good job.

Government Reform Requires Great Determination, a Steady Pace, and Solid Work

Our proposal to trim 50% of agency staffs was not groundless. The government will no longer directly run enterprises. Its management systems and work methods must be fundamentally transformed so staffing can be reduced. In the past, there were more people than work, talent was underutilized, and things that shouldn't have been done were done—this can't go on any longer. We must transform government functions, improve work methods and work styles, and truly achieve streamlining and high efficiency.

To Do All This, We Must First Have Great Determination. After returning from my trip abroad, the first thing I did was to go over documents—I hadn't signed off on any documents for 10 days. I discovered that one of these documents, submitted to the State Council on January 7, was a request from the All-China Federation of the Disabled for the Ministry of Finance to cover the interest on their poverty-relief loans. The State Council General Office sent this request to the various departments for their opinions, and it wasn't until April 8 that there were any results for me to sign off on. It took three months to come up with a solution, which set me thinking.

This was not an isolated incident—there are many such cases. This administration absolutely cannot go on like this. First, if you want a loan, the unit submitting the request should take the initiative to make the contacts, to ask the bank for a loan, and see what the bank thinks; then it should go to the Ministry of Finance to ask it to cover the interest, and see what the ministry thinks. You must do the legwork and give good reasons to persuade the bank and the ministry. After they agree, then submit your request to the State Council for approval. If they don't agree, include their dissenting views in your submission. Otherwise, the State Council will send this document back to you, indicating that the submitting unit did not fulfill all its obligations. If you have reported all the dissenting views and coordinated everything you can coordinate, then you have discharged your obligations.

The State Council will then go over the opinions of all the units involved, and the vice premier in charge will judge whether something should be done— he will be able to make decisions. Major policy decisions must ultimately be submitted to the premier for approval. In the past, if something came up, the bureau chief and section chief of the State Council Secretariat would convene a meeting of all the parties concerned to coordinate matters. If there were differences of opinion, a deputy secretary-general of the State Council would have to contact the ministers concerned to obtain a consensus. We can't do things this way anymore. The State Council Secretariat has neither the responsibility nor the power to coordinate. This work is now the responsibility of the various ministries of the State Council.

You should seek out the ministries in charge yourself, going door-to-door to coordinate. If no consensus can be reached and the State Council must coordinate, you should first factually report the results of your own efforts to the State Council. Then the leading members of the State Council will be able to make a decision, and if necessary, a deputy secretary-general can coordinate at the request of the vice premier in charge.

Unless we are determined to change our work style, we won't be able to improve our efficiency or alter the practice of having more people than work. Therefore I am asking the General Office of the State Council to take the lead and be a role model in this streamlining of government agencies.

What will happen to staff who are reassigned? The staff of the State Council are of high caliber and should be sent where they can be more useful, where they can make full use of their talents. At present the leadership of many departments is weak and needs boosting and strengthening. Take commercial banks, for instance—send capable vice ministers to act as their vice presidents. Likewise, the State Administration of Taxation, the State Bureau of Industry and Commerce, and the State Bureau of Quality and Technical Supervision all need to be strengthened, and the units directly under them especially need strengthening. Although the status of agencies needn't be raised, high-ranking officials can be assigned to them. A minister can become vice minister at another ministry, while a vice minister can take a second-ranking job at another vice-ministerial agency. Departments and bureaus can do likewise.

We are also preparing to assign a group of department and bureau chiefs who are in their prime and have completed training to institutions of higher learning to flesh out the leadership structures there. In addition, some younger staff with the [appropriate] educational background can pursue studies leading to higher degrees or credentials that will make them assets in positions where they are needed. That's why in trimming agency staff we are at the same time strengthening the entire structures of government agencies, enterprises, and related units.

It's time to be determined to do this. The overall atmosphere is ripe, as even government agency staff themselves understand that the current situation is unworkable, that it is inefficient, and that we cannot bear this financial burden. People in enterprises act differently from those in [government] agencies. They're not relying on "imperial rations"[2]—they'll have to find their own means of making a living, and they'll have to think of ways to make the enterprises run well.

Second, the Pace Must Be Steady. Some at this study seminar are in favor of initiating reforms at the provincial level of government this year. With only 30,000-odd people in its ranks, the State Council system will be somewhat less difficult to reform. By contrast, local agencies altogether employ 8 million Party and government workers. This includes 5.3 million civil servants alone. Cutting them by half affects 2.6 million people—the difficulties of streaming so many people are considerable. I suggest that you don't make a move this year and let the national agencies take the first step while you learn from their experience. You must "think things through and then move."

This year, you should first do the planning and figure out where the streamed people will go—draw up the plan for agency reform and then start next year. Finalize the program for the "three determinations"[3] before the end of next year and determine which people are to be trimmed. We can't call this completing the job—it will take three years to complete the job; that is, it will take until 2001 to make arrangements for all the people. In other words, by the end of this year

2. Translator's note: that is, they are not paid by the government and not supported by budgetary expenditures.

3. Translator's note: determining the functions, structure, and staffing of each agency.

for national government agencies and the end of next year for local government agencies, the people who are to be trimmed should leave their places of work. They will continue to receive their wages as before, and after targeted training, within roughly three years' time, they will gradually be reassigned to places they are more needed.

How should you reassign local government staff? Apart from strengthening SOEs, it is very important to have them strengthen the grass roots. The current caliber of some grassroots officials is really too poor: some of them exhibit downright disregard for the law and lord it over the people. Of course the vast majority of grassroots officials are still good people and problems arise only among a minority. That's why we should strengthen the grass roots and send qualified people to take the place of unqualified ones.

Quite a few people have said that in the course of streaming off people, we should take measures to optimize the ranks of our civil servants. How do we optimize? This absolutely does not mean keeping all those who are qualified, asking only the unqualified ones to leave. I feel that we must send those outstanding ones to SOEs and to the grass roots, send them where they are more needed. Those who stay at the agencies should be combinations of strong and weak people. It won't necessarily work well to put several strong people together. Our main goal is really to strengthen the SOEs and grass roots.

Third, the Work Must Be Substantive. The reform of government agencies is going to affect the personal interests of most officials, so there's bound to be some volatility in their sentiments. We again stress that those who are reassigned should not be discriminated against, that their state-mandated wages and benefits must absolutely not be reduced. They should get the same wages as before— this is an important measure for keeping the ranks of the officials stable. At the same time, we must extend our ideological work in a down-to-earth way to every person so that all feel they are being treated fairly by the organization.

For this round of adjustments to national agencies, we conducted repeated studies of how to deal with ministerial-level officials. As for [projected changes at] the vice ministerial level, I've studied them twice with people at the Organization Department of the Central Committee, but we haven't completely settled on them yet. I've had talks with many ministers and vice ministers. I hope that all levels of local government will also act in this spirit and make proper arrangements for their staff, sending them to the most appropriate places. This not only shows trust in them but is also required by our work.

To carry out ideological work, you must have discussions with people. You must figure out what they're thinking and investigate comprehensively. Do meticulous and solid work—that is the only way to demonstrate a responsible attitude toward the personnel of government agencies.

Although this round of government agency reforms is a medium-sized pro-gram, it still involves fairly big steps. When I was traveling abroad, all the foreign leaders who met with me commented, "It can't be easy for you to make such big decisions!" Although big, these steps haven't caused any major instability in Beijing [so far]; everything appears basically stable. Provided we have great determination, our steps are steady, and our work is solid, I feel there won't be any major trouble.

Overall, the great majority of our officials are indeed good people who will abide by organizational decisions, as illustrated in the case of Song Ruixiang, who used to be Minister of Geology and Mineral Resources. After we established the new Ministry of Land and Resources, we gave a great deal of thought to what arrangements to make for this ministerial official. We ultimately decided to assign him to the post of Deputy Party Secretary and Executive Vice Director of the State Environmental Administration, where the work is related to his own and he retains his ministerial rank. Although it wasn't easy for him to accept this decision, he recently wrote me a letter indicating that he completely accepts the organization's assignments. I feel we should learn from his spirit of looking at the big picture! That's why I think that as long as our work touches their hearts, people will be understanding and amenable to reason. If we deal with them bureaucratically, handle things sloppily, and neglect ideological work altogether, substituting it with mere proclamations, then there's bound to be trouble.

4

KEY ASPECTS OF REFORM OF THE GRAIN CIRCULATION SYSTEM[1]

June 3, 1998

After late April's national conference on reform of the grain circulation system, the State Council dispatched five investigative teams to more than 10 provinces to promote and check on implementation of the spirit of the conference. We could see from the situation in these places that the leaders at all levels are taking this task very seriously and focusing on it very hard. However, the work is progressing unevenly; particularly at the county and township levels, it hasn't been addressed forcefully enough, and the spirit of the conference hasn't been fully implemented.

During an inspection tour of Anhui Province, I met the director of a county-level grain bureau who spoke ever so glibly about "the four separations and one refinement" (the separation of government from enterprises, of storage from operation, of central responsibilities from local responsibilities, and of old fiscal grain accounts from new grain accounts, and the refinement of a new grain pricing system), but who couldn't get to the point when explaining what the focus of current work should be. As this shows, we still have a lot of work to do if we are to gain a deep understanding of the spirit of the "State Council Decision on Further Reform of the Grain-Circulation System" as well as its various programs and policies, and if we are to know how to implement them.

Through these investigations, we sensed that the details of some policies still needed to be refined. Therefore after returning to Beijing, we conducted further studies on policies that needed more clarification and issued a supplementary notice. Yesterday, the Executive Committee of the State Council reviewed and

1. On June 3, 1998, the State Council held a national video teleconference on grain purchases and sales. Responsible members of the Party Central Committee and the State Council departments concerned attended at the main venue in Beijing. Participants at other venues included leading government officials from the provinces, autonomous regions, centrally administered municipalities, cities (prefectures), and counties; officials responsible for grain, fiscal work, and financial work; and officials responsible for local development and planning (or economic) commissions, finance bureaus, agricultural bureaus, industrial and commercial bureaus, pricing bureaus, grain bureaus, the Agricultural Development Bank, and the Agricultural Bank. Teleconferencing venues were set up all the way down to the county level. These are Zhu Rongji's main remarks at the conference.

passed the "Regulations on Grain Purchases," and these will be issued very soon. In the future we will still have to draw up regulations on grain sales and other appropriate regulations so that all the programs and policies on grain will have a basis in law. At present, the central programs and policies regarding reform of the grain circulation system and proper handling of grain purchases and sales are already quite complete and very explicit. Our meeting today includes all levels down to the county so that we can brief all of you about these central programs and policies and the results of our studies. We will also be making arrangements for further reforms of the grain-circulation system and grain purchases and sales.

The Prerequisite for Grain Reforms

All parts of the country must first and foremost earnestly study the documents from the central government and come to a deep and genuine understanding of their essence—this is the prerequisite for doing a good job of grain reforms. I recently read an internal Xinhua news report on a speech made by the director of the provincial grain department of a certain major grain-producing province. Much of this speech does not accord with reality. He was very aggravated, felt very put upon, exaggerated the difficulties, and only emphasized the responsibilities of others without critically examining his own work. How can a leader like this handle grain reforms well? This isn't a problem of a single individual. Rather, it reflects the feelings of a group of people within the grain system. If we don't change some people, if we don't replace some people, if we don't arrest some people, it will be very hard for these reforms of the grain circulation system to succeed. Those who aren't up to the job must be replaced, those with serious problems must be removed, and those who have broken criminal laws must be arrested. Otherwise, reforms of the grain circulation system cannot be conducted successfully.

Within the grain system nationwide, grain purchase funds in the amount of RMB 200 billion or more have been lost, in arrears, or misused. If we continue losing tens of billions of renminbi a year, neither the national and local governments nor the banks will be able to cope with such a heavy burden. Handling reforms of the grain circulation system well will have a major impact on the entire big picture. We must unify our thinking and our actions, implement all the central programs and policies on this reform without cutting any corners, and strive for depth in this work.

Our most important job right now is to implement and bring to fruition the three policies of purchasing farmers' surplus grain without limits at the protected prices, having state-owned grain purchase-and-storage enterprises sell at profitable prices, and having a closed system of operations for the Agricultural

Development Bank's grain purchase funds. This will accelerate the pace of self-reform within grain enterprises. Now I'd like to reemphasize a few points.

Farmers' Surplus Grain Must Be Purchased without Caps[2] at the Protected Prices

This policy is the foundation of all our current work on grain. Only by buying surplus grain without caps at protected prices will we be able to protect farmers' interests, ensure that they remain highly motivated, and be sure of a steady increase in grain production. Only then can the sourcing of grain be firmly in the hands of state-owned grain purchase-and-storage enterprises, and only then can they direct the market price of grain and be able to sell it at profitable prices.

These state-owned grain purchase-and-storage enterprises owe money to the banks largely because during bumper harvests they failed to properly implement uncapped purchases of surplus grain at protected prices, thereby causing farmers to sell their grain cheaply to private dealers. Private dealers have low operating costs, so they are able to sell their grain at lower prices, which then push the market price of grain down. By contrast, state-owned grain purchase-and-storage enterprises have many employees, large expenditures, and high operating costs, so their grain is priced higher than that from private dealers and doesn't sell well. The poorer their sales, the less willing they are to purchase grain without caps, and the greater its availability to private dealers. Meanwhile, in order to pay wages and bonuses, the state-owned grain stations and granaries operate "in reverse," selling grain at low prices and at a loss, creating a vicious cycle. If the state-owned grain purchase-and-storage enterprises can buy up all of the farmers' surplus grain at protected prices, they will control the supply of grain and be in a position to direct the market price of grain, so they will be able to sell profitably. Therefore the most basic step enabling them to sell at a profit and stop losing money is to buy at protected prices without limits.

During the summer harvest last year, we stressed that surplus grain should be purchased from farmers without limits and at protected prices. This [directive] was resolutely and successfully implemented everywhere and was very popular with the farmers. But we didn't persevere. By the time of the autumn harvest, our purchases weren't entirely open-ended, causing a great deal of grain to wind up in the hands of private dealers. Right now, the market price of grain is lower than the protected price, so why won't farmers sell to the state-owned grain stations and granaries at the protected price and instead sell to private dealers at the market price?

2. Translator's note: "unlimited," "open-ended," or "uncapped" grain purchases refer to the government purchasing, at protected prices, as much grain as farmers wish to sell.

The problem lies with the state-owned grain purchase-and-storage enterprises themselves—they failed to make the process convenient for the farmers and failed to make uncapped purchases. Some state-owned grain stations and granaries only purchased limited quantities during limited hours and lowered both the grading and the pricing of the grain. Some workers had a poor service attitude: when presented with grain that was a bit high in water content or natural impurities, instead of buying it after deducting for the water and impurities, they would tell farmers to take it home. Faced with such inconveniences, farmers would rather sell their grain to private dealers for a few fen less per jin.[3]

Furthermore, labor service companies and staff affiliated with some state-owned grain stations and granaries buy grain from farmers at low prices and then sell it at protected prices to the stations and granaries, making a profit by doing so. Some state-owned grain stations and granaries carry out proxy collections of fees planned by the township and retained by the village, in which case farmers receive no cash for their grain and so are unwilling to sell to the stations and granaries. Some locales issue guaranteed-purchase cards or impose other types of grain purchase quotas, so they don't purchase directly without limits, and such actions also give rise to reselling [of the quotas]. These problems have impeded the implementation of the policy of purchasing surplus grain without limits at protected prices, harmed the interests of the farmers, and must be thoroughly resolved.

Purchases of this year's summer harvest are about to begin, and grain departments everywhere must resolutely make uncapped purchases of surplus grain from farmers at protected prices. State-owned grain purchase-and-storage enterprises must improve their service attitudes and execute this policy in earnest. They should make it convenient for farmers to sell grain and not have them stand in long lines. Grain must be purchased year-round from farmers, and it is forbidden to limit, halt, or forgo purchases. Grading and pricing must not be lowered. And farmers shouldn't be told to take poorer-quality grain home—the price of such grain can be determined by deducting for water content, impurities, and other quality issues, and it can be dried by heating or airing after it is purchased.

We must also ensure that farmers who sell grain can receive cash in a timely manner. When purchasing grain, apart from collecting agricultural tax in accordance with national regulations, state-owned grain stations and granaries are not allowed to do any proxy collections or collect any proxy payments of fees "planned by the township and retained by the village" or any other taxes. Likewise, township officials and village heads are not allowed to collect township-planned and village-retained fees at grain stations and granaries. Any officials and staff of state-owned grain stations and granaries who break the country's laws or

---

3. One jin is equal to 0.5 kilogram.

violate [Party] discipline must be resolutely investigated and punished. In short, it is forbidden to buy grain at low prices from farmers under any pretext. The Agricultural Development Bank must ensure the supply of funds for grain purchases.

The grain purchase market must be managed well. Only state-owned grain purchase-and-storage enterprises are permitted to buy grain from farmers. All private dealers, grain merchants, and other companies are prohibited from buying grain directly from villages. The bureaus of industry and commerce everywhere must step up inspections, and each infringement must be strictly punished when it is discovered, going so far as to cancel operating licenses [of violators]. Grain-processing enterprises and other entities that use grain can make purchases at grain markets at the county level or above. Grain sales must be freed up and invigorated. We must permit enterprises and individuals from other areas to buy grain at markets at the county level or above and allow sales to take place through multiple channels.

We Must Be Determined to Sell Grain Profitably

This is an important measure to prevent continuing losses at state-owned grain purchase-and-storage enterprises and to enable them to gradually absorb the losses and debts they have incurred. If they can't sell grain at a profit, they won't be able to recoup their costs and make enough money to survive and grow.

Grain prices have been relatively low for the past two years. One problem here is not only that some locales have failed to make uncapped purchases of surplus grain at protected prices, thereby losing grain supplies, but also that state-owned grain purchase-and storage enterprises are selling grain at low, money-losing prices. Our studies indicate that this problem is much more serious than we had thought. In order to pay wages and bonuses and to put up buildings, some state-owned grain purchase-and-storage enterprises were even willing to sell grain at low prices to private dealers. On the one hand they were selling grain at low prices, and on the other they were running up bank debts. This gave private dealers and private grain-processing enterprises a source of low-cost grain, while also greatly increasing the losses and bank debts of the state enterprises. Once private grain-processing enterprises gained control of low-cost grain, they could manipulate retail prices in the entire grain market, making it very hard for state-owned grain purchase-and-storage enterprises to sell their supplies at profitable prices. Now private grain-processing enterprises can be found all over the map, and they aren't small in scale either. Many private rice factories obtain their grain from state-owned grain purchase-and-storage enterprises that sell to them at a loss.

During my study trip to Anhui, I had my secretary and a colleague from the State Planning Commission pretend to be "private dealers" and buy grain from three private grain-processing factories. These three factories all boasted, "We can give you as much grain as you want, and we can sell it to you right away." Would they dare brag like this if they weren't colluding with some state-owned grain departments? Another private factory was processing 150 tons of rice daily, several tens of thousands of tons annually. It couldn't possibly operate on such a large scale if it depended on individual farm families for its supply of grain. In fact, grain from state-owned grain purchase-and-storage enterprises was being shipped to it by the truckload—how can we let this happen?!

These enterprises sell the rice they bought at protected prices to private dealers at a loss-making lower price, so dealers can make a profit by selling the processed rice for a mere RMB 0.8–0.9 per jin, whereas our state-owned grain storage-and-purchase enterprises will lose money unless they can sell their processed rice for RMB 1–1.2 per jin. Of course their rice won't sell! And if it doesn't sell, they have no choice but to follow the market and sell at lower loss-making prices, letting the private dealers lead them around by the nose. First the private dealers sell at low prices, then the state-owned grain enterprises follow them in lowering prices, and they might go so far as to sell to the private dealers at still lower prices. This way, the state's tens of billions of renminbi in annual grain subsidies doesn't really subsidize the farmers: the money winds up in the pockets of the private dealers, with some corrupt elements profiting from all this. It's really heartbreaking!

The reason why state-owned grain enterprises aren't able to sell profitably is that they themselves are selling grain at loss-making low prices. This is mainly because the system doesn't make sense—we cannot go on without reforming it! To reform the grain system, we must be clear about what created this situation. We must analyze the causes clearly. It isn't enough to merely feel aggravated and put upon and not recognize the problems in ourselves.

We believe that once the state-owned grain enterprises manage to get all the grain in their hands by selling it without limits at protected prices, they will be able to sell it upon adding their costs and necessary profits. Then they will gradually make a profit and stop losing money. After all, there isn't anyone who can compete with the state-owned grain enterprises. Who can offer the protected prices? Only the state has this capability. If its grain enterprises don't make open-ended purchases of surplus grain at protected prices and also sell it at a loss, they won't be able to sell profitably, and losses will inevitably mount.

Through this round of investigations, we discovered an area of grain policy that still lacks clarity: it concerns the stage at which the price is supposed to return a profit. Originally this wasn't stated very clearly. We now stress that this should be the stage of purchase and storage. That is, we are asking grain purchase-and-storage enterprises such as state-owned grain stations and granaries (including their affiliated grain-processing factories that don't yet have separate budgets) to sell grain at a price composed of a base purchase price to which is added a reasonable processing cost and the smallest possible profit—they should not lose money. Those state-owned grain-processing factories, wholesale and retail enterprises that have separate budgets, should abide by this principle: they should be able to afford to buy and be able to afford to sell. Starting with their purchase price, they should determine the sales price for themselves, and they should be responsible for their own profits and losses.

At the moment, however, the lower limits for retail prices of grain are also regulated in quite a few places, as a result of a biased understanding of the policy of selling grain at a profit. State-owned grain retail stores are independently budgeted and responsible for their own profits and losses. They have different channels for sourcing and different purchase prices so they should also have different sales prices, and you can't regulate their lowest sales price. If it was regulated and they were unable to sell their grain, how would they be able to pay wages? Who would be responsible? State-owned grain retail stores are responsible for their own profits and losses, and the state cannot subsidize them.

At present, many state-owned grain retail stores can obtain supplies from private dealers. This helps absorb the grain dispersed across society as quickly as possible, and it creates conditions for state-owned grain purchase-and-storage enterprises to sell at a profit. Once the private dealers sell off all their grain, state-owned grain purchase-and-storage enterprises will be able to control the market and guide prices, and they will be able to truly operate profitably. From now on, the lowest sales prices of state-owned grain retail stores must not be regulated, and those that have been regulated must be corrected.

Grain Purchase Funds Must Be Used in a Closed System

A closed system enables us to supervise the way state-owned grain purchase-and-storage enterprises are implementing state grain purchase policies. It prevents misuse and misappropriation, while ensuring that the supply of funds for purchasing grain is both adequate and timely.

The state is establishing the Agricultural Development Bank for the purpose of enabling grain purchase funds to be used in a closed system. This bank must strictly enforce "linking loans to inventory" and "having the money follow the grain." It must insist on "full settlements in both money and grain, and full repayments of loans." After state-owned grain purchase-and-storage enterprises sell their grain, they must repay both principal and interest in full to the Agricultural Development Bank. For each jin of grain they buy, they will get one jin's worth of money; if they bought at the fixed price, they get the fixed price; and if they bought at the protected price, they get the protected price. For each jin of grain they sell, these enterprises must repay both principal and interest to the

Agricultural Development Bank; otherwise, the bank will not lend to them the next time they purchase grain. Here the Agricultural Development Bank will play a decisive role in overseeing and ensuring the proper use of funds. This is a huge responsibility, one that may have bearing on the very success or failure of this reform of the grain circulation system.

To ensure that the policy of "linking inventory to loans" is truly implemented, the Agricultural Development Bank must thoroughly check the grain reserves of state-owned grain purchase-and-storage enterprises. It must check to see how much money they have borrowed, how much grain they have bought, and whether or not they're misusing grain purchase funds. Banks absolutely have the right to check accounts—this is international practice. State-owned grain purchase-and-storage enterprises must provide relevant information unconditionally. If they don't honestly tell the Agricultural Development Bank how much grain they've bought and sold and how much grain they've stored, the bank will not lend to them. Only by doing so can we strengthen oversight and prevent new monetary losses, more debts to banks, and misappropriation.

The Agricultural Bank must go deep into the grass roots and improve services. If state-owned grain stations and granaries are selling grain at low, money-losing prices, for example, the Bank can't simply cut off loans to them. On the one hand, it must be responsible to the country and strengthen its oversight of state-owned grain purchase-and-storage enterprises; and when it discovers problems, it must report these in a timely way to the government departments in charge so that they can deal with these issues firmly. On the other hand, it must improve its service attitude and ensure that grain purchase funds are delivered in a timely way and do not cause delays in grain purchases. The Agricultural Development Bank must act as the nation's gatekeeper, and it must do its work well. All levels of government, particularly the county level, must support the Bank's work and join with it in defending the nation's interests. All commercial banks must also actively support the closed-system operations of grain purchase funds.

Loans for businesses affiliated with grain purchase-and-storage enterprises have already been hived off from the Agricultural Development Bank, and it will now specialize in lending to grain purchase-and-storage enterprises. These state-owned enterprises may open accounts only at the Agricultural Development Bank, not at any other banks. If any commercial banks allow these enterprises to open accounts, they must be dealt with firmly.

State-Owned Enterprises Must Do a Good Job of Reforming Themselves

This is the basic way for state-owned grain purchase-and-storage enterprises to solve their problems. Right now, the grain system is greatly overstaffed. It costs several tens of billions of renminbi a year to feed its 4 million or more current and retired employees, and all of this is factored into the cost of grain. If the cost of grain is extremely high, how can they make money selling at those prices? Therefore we must be resolved to trim staffing by half.

Of the 3.1 million people currently employed in the grain system, only about 1.5 million are really engaged in purchasing and storing grain. The other 1.6 million were streamed off long ago; it's just that they haven't been completely detached from the system. So trimming staff by half won't in fact be as hard as you might imagine, and most of the problems can be resolved once the 1.6 million who have already left are completely detached from the state-owned grain purchase-and-storage enterprises. At some of the state-owned grain retail stores I saw in Anhui, grain sales accounted for only 20% of total sales, and they are entirely capable of being responsible for their own profits and losses.

Crude management and serious waste are quite pervasive at state-owned grain purchase-and-storage enterprises, which is another major reason why their operating costs are high and they find it hard to make money. Henceforth all these enterprises must be independently budgeted and must be responsible for their own profits and losses. Apart from purchasing, which will be monopolized by state-owned grain purchase-and-storage enterprises, all other work—including processing, wholesaling, and retailing—must be open to market competition. In other words, improve operational management and lower costs through competition.

We must establish a complete system of rules and regulations as quickly as possible, strengthen internal management, cut unnecessary expenses, block loopholes, and prevent waste. Only by cutting expenses will state-owned grain purchase-and-storage enterprises become competitive in the market. Only then will conditions be favorable for making a profit from sales, and only then will there be economic benefits.

Through this conference today, we want everyone to clearly understand that the key to deepening reforms of the grain circulation system and handling grain purchases well is to focus on the four main points of the "three policies and one reform."[4] Of these, buying surplus grain from farmers without caps at protected prices lays the foundation for encouraging farmers to remain enthusiastic about growing grain and for implementing the sale of grain at profitable prices. Selling grain at a profit is the key to halting losses and gradually absorbing past debts. Operating grain purchase funds in a closed system is the way to ensure

4. The "three policies" are to make uncapped purchases of surplus grain from farmers at the protected prices, have grain purchase-and-storage enterprises sell grain at profitable prices, and operate grain purchase funds in a closed system. The "one reform" is to accelerate self-reform at grain enterprises.

that losses or misappropriations do not continue and that funds are supplied in full and in a timely way. And the self-reform of grain enterprises provides the conditions for them to successfully implement the "three policies." I believe that we will undoubtedly do a good job of reforming the grain circulation system provided we are unified in our thinking and in our actions, and provided that we work together as one to do so.

5

A Conversation with U.S. Treasury Secretary Robert E. Rubin[1]

June 26, 1998

ZRJ: You certainly work quickly. Just yesterday I saw you on TV in the United States, and today you're in Beijing. Moreover, you've already paid lightning visits to the People's Bank of China and the Ministry of Finance.

RER: Yes, although I only talked with them for a short time, it was very productive. I'm not a diplomat and can dispense with the formalities. We only discussed substantive issues.

ZRJ: Although you're not a diplomat, your words are more valuable than those of a diplomat.

RER: That's why I have to be careful when I speak, especially when I'm commenting on the markets.

ZRJ: We welcome you to China. Recently, the United States intervened in the yen exchange rate and was very successful. We congratulate you on this. But your task is still a very difficult one. Today's yen exchange rate has fallen again, to JPY 142.35 = US$1.

RER: You're quite right—this is a very difficult task. We came up with $2 billion in a single day. That's a very large sum, but the basic way to solve the devaluation of the yen is for Japan to take action.

ZRJ: Judging from the news coming out of Tokyo, Japan hasn't taken any measures. It seems that the yen will remain in a state of neither collapsing nor improving. The Southeast Asian countries are very worried about this.

---

1. This conversation took place at the Hall of Purple Light in Zhongnanhai, Beijing, where Zhu Rongji met with Secretary Rubin.

Meeting with U.S. Treasury Secretary Robert Rubin at the Hall of Purple Light, Zhongnanhai, Beijing, on June 26, 1998. (Photograph by Li Shengnan, Xinhua News Agency)

RER: I think you might discuss this with President Bill Clinton when you meet with him tomorrow. I've discussed it with him many times, and he feels that ultimately it will be up to Japan to improve the yen situation.

ZRJ: I'm very worried about the current state of the yen. Some people estimate that by the end of this year, the yen exchange rate might drop to JPY 180 = US$1. Do you think this is possible?

RER: This is very hard to predict right now. Some economists think that the yen exchange rate might eventually fall to 160–180 yen to the dollar. That would be very bad news for Asia. We have to think of some way to avoid such a situation and persuade Asian countries to pressure Japan.

ZRJ: There's one view that the yen exchange rate this year will be 180, and next year it will be 230. This might be somewhat overstated, but most people think that the yen will break through 150 this year. The continued devaluation of the yen is indeed bad news for Southeast Asia, and it will further worsen the financial crisis in the region. But no matter what, China won't break its promise not to devalue the renminbi. If we were to also follow [Japan] in devaluing, that would be a catastrophe for Asian nations.

RER: It would also be catastrophic for the entire global economy.

ZRJ: No matter what benefits devaluation might bring us, we cannot do that. It would do too much harm to others, and in the end we would also harm ourselves. As to how long we can hold out, I can't say, and even if I said something people wouldn't believe me.

RER: We can say that China is one of the most creditworthy countries in the world today. China has the fullest respect from the international community, whether it be in economics or in handling other issues. That's why the United States and China should join hands and jointly resolve the current crisis.

ZRJ: I said just now that the renminbi won't be devalued—that much we can do. Exports account for only 20% of China's domestic production. Even though there was negative growth in our foreign trade in May, we can use our domestic markets to make up for foreign markets. The problem now is that we, too, are facing some difficulties: there were many redundant projects in the past, market supply is greater than demand, state-owned enterprises are not producing enough, and workers are unemployed. In increasing domestic demand, putting money into the industrial sector won't yield any results, so we can only invest in infrastructure construction. But the repayment period of infrastructure projects is quite long. It won't do to rely entirely on bank loans; we still need investment from the financial departments.

Fortunately, for the past few years our fiscal policy has been tight, so we're now capable of doing this. In comparison with last year, fixed asset investments grew by 10% during the first quarter of this year, by 15% during the second quarter, and are expected to grow by 20% in the third quarter. These investments will drive the production of the materials of production and promote operations at industrial enterprises. In the first quarter of this year, our GDP growth rate was 7.2%; it might be only 6.8% in the second quarter, and we estimate it will reach 8% in the third quarter and 9–10% in the fourth quarter. This way, even if we don't meet our target of 8% growth for the whole year, we won't be too far off. Right now, 8% has become a psychological number. Even if we reached 7.9%, our Hong Kong compatriots would be dissatisfied.

RER: This is very interesting. I'm not familiar with the situation in China! But I think what foreigners are concerned about isn't a particular percentage; rather it's whether or not these statistics are accurate and whether or not they accord with international standards. China's creditworthiness is very good right now, and even if your growth rate reached only 5–6%, it wouldn't have a great impact on you. The key is what measures you're taking and how you handle the relation between immediate benefits and long-term benefits. What the international community is most concerned about is whether or not you can continue to stay the course on reforms.

ZRJ: If there hadn't been an Asian financial crisis, our economic growth rate might have exceeded 8%. Now the Asian financial crisis has had a major impact on our growth, and under these circumstances, it's no simple matter for our growth rate to reach 7%, or even a bit more than 6%. But we also realize that 8% is a psychological number—it's much more significant to people in the East than to Westerners. If this year's growth rate were to reach 7.9%, the very next day the Hong Kong media would say, "The renminbi is about to be devalued." You said just now that you don't understand China. I think this kind of modesty is to be cherished.

However, I feel that if we really can't reach 8%, there's no need to force the issue. Actually, it would be very easy to reach 8%. For example, we could loosen the money supply and make large investments regardless of whether or not they're for redundant projects, but we won't do such a stupid thing. As for your question just now about whether or not our statistics are accurate, I also don't know, but I can assure you that the figures for this year won't be less accurate than those for last year.

Our reforms are proceeding according to plan, and may perhaps be stepped up; otherwise, we won't be able to ensure our economic growth. The reforms of our banking system in particular are progressing noticeably more quickly. We've learned a lot from the Asian financial crisis, and if we don't speed up the reforms, we won't be able to stabilize our finances. Recently we shut down several banks. We feel that no matter what their backgrounds may be, if they have problems, then those that should be shut down should be resolutely shut down.

The problems that recently emerged in Japan gave us a bit more confidence. In the past, some people felt that the Chinese banking system was the worst in the world. Now it gives me some slight consolation—maybe we're not the worst in the world—at most we're second worst. The worst is the Japanese system.

RER: You could be right. The Chinese and Japanese situations are different—China dares to look straight at its own problems and do something to solve them, whereas Japan seems to lack confidence and doesn't have specific measures for solving its problems. That's the difference between the two countries.

Mr. Premier, I know there are four major banks in China. Internationally, some people are estimating that the bad loans at these banks are as high as 25–30%—of course these aren't your official figures. But regardless of what the figure actually is, I think China may be somewhat lacking in skills in this area. What plans do you have in this regard?

ZRJ: There's some accuracy in the 25% figure you cite, but this 25% isn't bad loans; we might call them nonperforming loans. Nonperforming loans aren't the same as irrecoverable loans. Of course 25% nonperforming loans is still a rather large number, but the percentage of bad loans and doubtful loans isn't very large. A very important point is that most of these nonperforming loans were created in 1992 and 1993 when real estate was overheated, and to this day they haven't been fully resolved. During the course of financial reforms in the next few years, very few new nonperforming loans will be created, and the existing ones will be reduced in number year by year. Our goal is to reduce them by two percentage points or more. At present, our banking operations are moving in the direction of prudent management and rigorously controlling nonperforming loans.

In your country, you're often questioned by your Congress. It's the same for me—I'm often criticized in our country. Some say I'm a "loan miser," that I'm too stingy about lending money. Some economists have told me, "Now's the time to loosen the money supply, print more money, and stimulate the economy, but your banks are unwilling to make loans."

RER: Your discussions in China about these issues are very interesting. How about this: we switch places, you answer to the U.S. Congress and I'll answer to the Chinese people. How about it?

ZRJ: I can't do your job.

RER: May I ask yet another question? In light of the crises that have occurred in Southeast Asia and Japan, what should the United States do that might be helpful?

ZRJ: I feel that right now, the United States is the only country that can influence Japan. No other country can do that. If the United States continues to exert its influence on Japan, Japan still has the power to stabilize the yen. If the United States wavers on this issue, the yen will continue to fall. This would be bad for the Southeast Asian countries and would also be a major blow to Hong Kong. On the other side, it would also impact the United States. Some people are already wondering if the U.S. economy is doing too well just now, if stock prices are too high, so everyone is waiting for them to come down. Given these circumstances, we don't want to see the entire world economy being affected. As for China, we can only make sure the renminbi doesn't devalue, but we don't have the ability to influence Japan.

RER: All of us, including President Clinton, have been closely following the yen devaluation all along, but so far we haven't found an effective way to persuade the Japanese to take decisive measures and turn things around. We can continue to pressure the Japanese, but if the Japanese government doesn't act, then it's still useless. You're very right: the U.S. economy can be just as easily hurt and we're also trying to avoid that. Also, we're very concerned about the issue of Hong Kong. May I ask how you see Hong Kong's exchange rate?

ZRJ: The current link between the Hong Kong dollar and the U.S. dollar is a tiger that we are riding and can't dismount from. There's no other way; we can only stay the course. The Hong Kong dollar will continue to be affected by international impacts, but I think Hong Kong will be able to withstand them, and the central government will also support Hong Kong at all costs.

RER: I'd like to ask another question. Our chief representative has made a new proposal in the negotiations over China's joining the WTO [World Trade Organization]. The U.S. trade deficit with China will reach $60 billion this year. As you know, trade issues in the United States are affected by politics, and this is a very difficult problem that might lead to a wave of trade protectionism. We feel that the new American proposal is in the interest of both sides and hope that the Chinese side will give serious consideration to our proposal.

ZRJ: Don't believe those figures of $50 billion or $60 billion. You should do what President Clinton said and fire all the people who came up with those numbers. If we had a $50 billion trade surplus, China's forex reserves would be as much as US$300 billion, highest in the world.

RER: That's exactly the direction you're moving in.

ZRJ: This is purely a question of how you calculate it.

RER: Even if it's calculated using the Chinese method, that's still quite a sizable figure.

ZRJ: Of the products we export, 54% are processing trade exports. That is to say, raw materials are imported from the United States, Japan, and elsewhere, then processed in China and reexported. China doesn't benefit much from this; it only gains a few jobs. If we really had a $50 billion surplus, then China wouldn't be the way it is now—we wouldn't have so many problems, and my job as Premier would be much easier.

RER: I agree with you and we could discuss methods of calculation, but you should also agree with me that China has had a trade surplus with the United States for many years, and it's continuing to increase.

ZRJ: All along we've been trying to find a way to resolve this problem. During this China trip of President Clinton's, we've signed $3 billion of contracts to purchase equipment from you, which is more than the $2 billion of aid you gave Japan. We had originally hoped to also reach an agreement whereby the United States would promise to give China permanent most favored nation status and agree to China's joining the WTO at the end of next year, while at the same time China would propose a timetable for further opening up its telecommunications and financial sectors, but this didn't win the appreciation of the American side, and instead you made even more stringent demands. We feel this was very regrettable. Of course, we're still negotiating about this.

RER: There may be some new progress now.

ZRJ: If the talks succeed, the United States would be helping us, and at the same time we would be more able to help resolve the financial crisis in Southeast Asia.

RER: I certainly hope so.

ZRJ: I hear you'll also be visiting several Southeast Asian nations?

RER: Yes, I still have to visit Malaysia, Thailand, and the Republic of Korea. The main purpose is to demonstrate our support for the countries that are carrying out reforms. I think that even if Japan were to take some measures, and if in addition there are joint efforts by countries like Korea and Thailand, it would still take quite a while to really solve the current problems.

ZRJ: The Japanese originally could have done a lot, but they didn't do it. So far, we've spent $4 billion to help Thailand, South Korea, and Indonesia. I told the Japanese that in lending money to these countries, we are in fact helping them repay their debts to you.

RER: Thank you for meeting with me.

6

CRACK DOWN HARD ON SMUGGLING[1]

July 15, 1998

This national conference on cracking down on smuggling is yet another very important meeting convened by the Party Central Committee and the State Council this year. At its opening, Jiang Zemin met with all the participants and delivered a major speech reflecting deep thought and emotion. His words were powerful, occupied the moral high ground, and were infused with concern for the nation. They offer us vital guidance as we rapidly launch a major project nationwide in a special joint action to crack down hard on smuggling, and as we intensify the fight against corruption and endeavor to run the Party and government with a stricter hand. In keeping with Jiang Zemin's important speech and with the demands of this conference, all locales, departments, and sectors must align their thinking, strengthen their leadership, and make meticulous arrangements to swiftly and surely crack down on smuggling all across the country. Now I'd like to draw on the discussions at this conference to underline a few points.

The Urgency of Launching and Intensifying a Major Struggle against Smuggling

Brazen smuggling is currently a prominent problem in the social and economic life of our nation. The decision to launch a fierce and intense nationwide campaign against smuggling is an important move of the Party Central Committee and the State Council in response to this situation. It will have a wide

---

1. The Party Central Committee and the State Council convened a national antismuggling working conference on July 13–15, 1998. Participants included representatives responsible for this work from the provinces, autonomous regions, centrally administered municipalities, the Xinjiang Construction Corps, the departments concerned of the Party Central Committee and the State Council, the four general departments of the People's Liberation Army, and the headquarters of the navy, air force, and People's Armed Police. Zhu Rongji's speech at this conference was a call for the initiation and deployment of a rapidly unfolding major antismuggling joint action under a nationwide special project. Originally titled "Unify Our Thinking, Strengthen Leadership, Rapidly and Fiercely Crack Down on Smuggling," this speech was previously published in *Selected Important Essays since the 15th Party Congress*, vol. 1 (Beijing: People's Publishing House, 2000). This is the main part of the speech.

impact: on whether we reach our target for economic growth this year; whether our reforms, opening up, and modernization proceed smoothly; and whether an incorruptible work style can be further strengthened within our Party. We should be highly determined, act decisively and resolutely, and produce significant results.

Over the past few years, all locales and departments have engaged in a great deal of antismuggling work, with clear results. This success must be recognized. At the same time, we must fully acknowledge that the current fight against smuggling is still facing a very grim situation. The scope of smuggling activities, the variety of goods smuggled, and the sums involved are all unprecedented. Criminal activities are growing worse by the day—in the use of fake approval documents, fake papers, and fake seals; in deceptions springing from nonreporting and concealment; and in the disguised use of processing trade zones and tax-bonded zones.

Smuggling is most severe in the case of the "two oils" (industrial and edible), the "two motorized vehicles" (automobiles and motorcycles), the "two raw materials" (for textiles and petrochemicals), cigarettes, and pirated CDs. Added to these are large quantities of over a hundred types of goods, including plywood, cameras, light-sensitive materials, cathode-ray tubes, compressors, mobile phones, computers, rubber, pharmaceuticals, Western liquors, and detergents. The departments concerned estimate that as much as a hundred billion renminbi worth of goods are smuggled in every year.

This increasingly brazen smuggling is already posing a serious economic, social, and political threat to our nation. It is creating huge losses to our economy and our tax revenues, [adversely] impacting our domestic markets and national industries, and disrupting our market order. Because of its large scale, smuggling is compounding the difficulties in the reform and development of our state-owned enterprises. Some enterprises are to some extent unable to operate at full capacity, face operational difficulties, and must increase layoffs because smuggled goods have taken over part of our domestic markets. We should also recognize that large-scale smuggling is impeding the implementation of Party and government programs and policies, is leading some locales and units to ignore administrative orders, and is promoting departmentalism, localism, and a tendency to have no one in charge.

In effect, smuggling is corrupting our officials, undermining social mores, and tempting people to commit many crimes—all in all, it is fostering social corruption and political decadence. If we allow it to go on unchecked, it will not only seriously affect the smooth progress of our reforms, opening up, and modernization, but it will also wreck our economy, wreck our political authority, and wreck our Party. Therefore this crackdown on smuggling is not only a major economic struggle but also a challenging political endeavor.

Inspecting confiscated smuggled goods in the Huangpu Customs warehouse, Guangdong Province, on October 24, 1998.

One noteworthy development over the past few years has been the proliferation of smuggling by legal persons. The involvement of legal persons with special status is particularly serious as it has brought domestic and outside parties into collusion, helped smuggling to become widespread, and given it protection. Particularly troubling to the general public is the involvement of Party, government, and military agencies in some locales, as well as of judiciary agencies and their affiliated units and staff. This is the crux of the current brazenness and growing intensity of smuggling, and it adds to the complexity and arduousness of the fight against it. Until we can fundamentally solve the problem of smuggling by legal persons, particularly by legal persons with special status, we won't be able to thoroughly smash the bravado of the evil forces of smuggling.

Why Is Smuggling So Brazen in Spite of Our Repeated Crackdowns?

One of the main reasons for this brazenness is that the leading officials of some locales and departments don't sufficiently understand the harm smuggling causes and have various types of misguided attitudes toward it. Some say, "You can get rich by smuggling," "Smuggling can invigorate the economy," "You can crack down on smuggling, but mustn't kill it," or "Cracking down on smuggling will [negatively] affect reform and opening up." These are entirely bizarre theories—they are utterly far-fetched!

Smuggling is a crime that can only lead to quick riches for the very few while inevitably harming the interests of the vast majority. Smuggling will not only ruin reform and opening up, it will also disrupt the economy and absolutely not invigorate it. To say that "you can crack down on smuggling, but mustn't kill it" is, in itself, condoning and tolerating smuggling, giving it a boost. The leaders of some locales and units pay lip service to cracking down on smuggling, while in fact keeping one eye open and the other eye shut, even going so far as to tolerate and support smuggling. For the sake of the interests of a small sector, a small group, or some individuals, they do not mind undermining the interests of the country.

Second, there is a close connection between smuggling and corruption, which is related to crass behavior within the Party among those who have no regard for politics and principles. Wherever smuggling becomes prevalent, corruption intensifies; corruption protects smuggling while smuggling damages the economy and harms the nation. Many facts prove that wherever smuggling is serious, corruption is also very serious. Crass behavior within the Party makes it impossible to effectively halt smuggling and corruption. When cases of smuggling are investigated, the perpetrators will seek favors from all sides, create layer upon layer of obstacles, and make it impossible for the case to be thoroughly investigated and handled according to the law.

Moreover, the present antismuggling institutions and systems are inadequate, oversight is weak, enforcement is lax, and crackdowns are not forceful enough—these are also major reasons why smuggling is so brazen. The Customs Law of the People's Republic of China promulgated back in 1987 stated clearly that smuggled goods must be confiscated, that fines as high as the value of these goods may be levied, and that criminal liability should be pursued for actions that constitute smuggling. This law has not been enforced in a long time. The law enforcement and judicial agencies in some places substitute fines for confiscation, they substitute fines for customs duties, and they substitute fines for criminal penalties. This is tantamount to condoning smuggling and promotes its spread.

Since the reforms and opening up began, our Party has consistently attached great importance to cracking down on economic crimes, which include smuggling. As early as 1982, Deng Xiaoping urged: "We must employ dual tactics. That is, we must unswervingly pursue the policy of opening to the outside world and stimulating the economy and, at the same time, wage a resolute struggle against economic crime. There is no question that without such a struggle the overall policy will fail."[2]

Ever since then, we have waged an unceasing campaign against smuggling. Over the past few years, Jiang Zemin has issued a series of important directives

---

2. See "Combat Economic Crime," in *Selected Works of Deng Xiaoping*, 2nd ed., vol. 2 (Beijing: Foreign Languages Press, 1995), p. 396.

in this regard, noting that whether we happen to be at the central or local level, we're all in the same boat. We all must be good shipmates, face the winds and waves together, and move ahead unswervingly down the path of socialism with Chinese characteristics. If we do not have a common goal and all do as we please, particularly if we tolerate the growth of smuggling and the spread of corruption, once the boat capsizes, we'll all go overboard. These words are anchored in deep emotion and deep thought, and are worth our reflecting on.

The day before yesterday, upon greeting participants at this conference, Jiang Zemin again stressed that in order to stem the current momentum of brazen smuggling, we must have great determination, act swiftly, use tough measures, and punish severely. We have to strike out hard at this sort of serious criminal activity and absolutely not let up. All locales, departments, and sectors must thoroughly understand the essence of the speeches of Deng Xiaoping and Jiang Zemin. From this high ground—of reform, opening up, and modernization; of upholding our nation's economic security and realizing the sustained, rapid, and healthy development of our national economy; and of fighting corruption and ensuring the long-term good governance of our country—we must fully recognize the importance and urgency of cracking down on smuggling and more consciously launch the fight against smuggling with high resolve and more effective measures, so that we may firmly halt the momentum of brazen smuggling.

Several Issues in Launching the Fight against Smuggling

Jiang Zemin's important speech the day before yesterday and State Councilor Wu Yi's work report clearly lay out the overall goals and general work plans for launching the fight against smuggling. We should all understand these thoroughly and implement them well. I'd like to emphasize three points here.

1. Stress the Key Areas and Be Clear about the Mission. In order to strike a swift and severe blow against smuggling, the special program I mentioned earlier—a joint nationwide action of the Party Central Committee and State Council— will focus with concentrated energy on the period from July until the end of the year. All locales, departments, and sectors must take immediate action, launch a powerful offensive against smuggling, and deal it an annihilating blow.

To conduct this joint action and special program successfully, we must carefully integrate the general with the specific and stress the key areas, which in commodity smuggling consist of industrial oil, automobiles, cigarettes, and pirated CDs. We also have to crack down firmly on the smuggling of edible oil, motorcycles, raw materials for petrochemicals and textiles, mobile phones, and computers. Geographically, the key smuggling areas are the coastal regions of Guangdong and Guangxi, especially maritime (or riverine) smuggling in the Pearl River

Delta, as well as along the Beilun River on the Sino-Vietnamese border. Smuggling in these areas involves large quantities, covers vast territories, and has an extremely adverse impact. Smuggling in the coastal regions of Fujian and Zhejiang as well as along their inland borders must also be addressed more forcefully.

As for the methods and channels of smuggling, it is essential to crack down on the use of fake approval documents, invoices, and seals for imports and exports, in addition to nonreporting, concealment, and the use of processing trade zones and tax-bonded zones (or warehouses). We must turn to special measures to crack down more forcefully on these key commodities, geographic areas, and channels. I would emphasize cracking down on two activities here: smuggling through the use of the processing trade, and smuggling by legal persons, particularly by legal persons with special status.

Since reforms and opening up began, the processing trade has played an important and positive role in the development of our country's economy—this must be fully affirmed. But the processing trade has also created many problems. Especially in the past few years, there have been more and more instances of smuggling in this area of trade. It operates on an even greater scale than maritime smuggling and also causes considerable harm.

In the first half of this year, the processing trade accounted for 54% of our country's exports and during the first five months alone was responsible for 157 major cases of smuggling nationwide valued at RMB 1.1 billion, which was 45% of the total value of all smuggling cases. Among these cases, a fairly large proportion involved foreign-invested enterprises. If we cannot put a halt to this type of smuggling, we won't be able to turn serious smuggling around. Therefore we should be confident that we are justified in cracking down on smuggling through the processing trade. We must strengthen oversight of the processing trade in accordance with the law, and we must resolutely uncover, also in accordance with the law, instances in which processing trade enterprises and foreign-invested enterprises are selling usage rights to their registration books, selling raw materials or finished goods domestically without permission, or avoiding taxes. We must strictly control the approvals for new processing trade projects, and the departments involved must focus hard on studying and drawing up concrete ways to do this.

Smuggling by legal persons—including [commercial] enterprises and publicly funded enterprises, as well as Party, government, and military agencies in some locales—and by companies run by law enforcement and judicial agencies as well as their affiliated companies involves huge sums, is very serious, employs despicable methods, and creates great harm. It is time to come down especially hard on legal persons engaged in smuggling, especially those with special status. We have to have strict punishment for those who organize, plan, and participate in smuggling as well as those who support them behind the scenes, and we should trace the responsibilities of the principal leaders of the main agencies and units in charge. The Party, government, and military agencies and judicial departments of all locales must seriously investigate smuggling or its protectors, including the companies operated by and affiliated with the subordinate units of all these entities. The effect of this joint action and special program against smuggling will depend in large part on the progress and results achieved by cracking down on smuggling by legal persons.

This joint action and special program against smuggling should include the following three measures:

—Quickly block the evil wind of smuggling and prevent new cases from happening. To do this, we must continue to implement the program of "capturing at sea, blocking along coasts, checking at ports, managing markets and punishing severely," so as to integrate cracking down with prevention.

—Thoroughly investigate the smuggling cases that have already occurred and strike out fiercely at the smugglers. A few should be executed in accordance with the law, killing one to warn the many; we should intimidate the forces of smuggling and educate the officials and the public.

—Deal with the matter comprehensively, treating both the symptoms and the disease, so as to fundamentally address the problem of laxity in combating smuggling. In short, we have to create new conditions for attacking and preventing smuggling.

2. Focus Our Energies on Major Cases and Deal a Firm Blow to Smuggler Bravado. Our prior experience in combating smuggling indicates that we can only intimidate smugglers by thoroughly investigating major cases and striking the perpetrators hard. Only then will we be able to better educate officials and public alike.

When smuggling in Haifeng County in Guangdong Province grew increasingly brazen in the early 1980s, the situation was quickly turned around only after the county Party secretary at that time, who condoned and supported smuggling, was firmly and severely punished as required by law. Likewise, the brazen smuggling in Rushan City in Shandong Province in 1993 was addressed by executing the chief smugglers in keeping with the law and giving a suspended death sentence to the municipal Party secretary at that time, actions that immediately warned the many by killing one. Therefore in order to intensify the fight against smuggling and achieve notable results, we must concentrate our energies on making breakthroughs in a batch of representative cases that involve huge sums and serious offenses, and we must quickly and severely punish smugglers in accordance with the law.

Our investigation of major smuggling cases must be more forceful. In regions and units where smuggling is rampant and major cases have remained unresolved for a long time, the central government and provincial (or autonomous region or centrally administered municipality) governments should organize special forces to handle investigations directly. We should strengthen the guidance we give to those working on these cases. The main leaders should personally oversee major cases; for those that involve many departments or locales, the ones concerned should handle the cases jointly and increase their efficiency by doing so.

These investigations have to be carried out in earnest, have to tackle the tough issues, and must resolutely sweep aside all obstacles and interference. No matter what units or persons may be involved, all have to be thoroughly investigated. Punishments must then be meted out swiftly and severely in accordance with the law, and there must be absolutely no holding back. Smugglers of the worst sort who commit the most serious offenses must receive the most severe penalties allowed by the law. We must be forceful in halting the practice of asking for special treatment. If anyone asks for special treatment, we should urge the [Party] disciplinary committees and supervisory departments to investigate them. We can even have CCTV's *Topics in Focus* program interview them, so that smugglers and those who protect them or request special treatment for them have no place to hide. We have to establish an antismuggling reporting system to promote forcefulness in the investigations conducted by all locales and departments. We must focus on resolving major cases that have yet to be resolved and handle them in accordance with the law. We must strengthen oversight by the public and by the media and publicize the outcomes of investigations into major cases in a timely way, so as to strengthen our ability to intimidate the forces behind smuggling.

3. Intensify Reforms and Establish a New Antismuggling System. To meet the needs of the new situation in combating smuggling, the Party Central Committee and the State Council have decided to undertake major reforms of the antismuggling system.

First, we will establish a national antismuggling police force. It will consist of a professional anticrime force that specializes in combating smuggling, with authority to investigate, detain, arrest, and make preliminary inquiries in accordance with the law. It will be managed under the dual vertical leadership of Customs and Public Security, with Customs taking the lead. It will deploy its police and carry out antismuggling missions under the unified direction of Customs. This police force will have no responsibilities for maintaining social order or combating other types of crimes, and it will have no hierarchical relationship with local public security authorities.

Because smuggling's unique features distinguish it from other economic and criminal offenses—it is a crime that transcends borders and boundaries and leaves behind fleeting clues—decisive measures must be taken on the spot. Therefore a national antismuggling police force will facilitate a rapid and forceful crackdown on smuggling. This reform measure is rooted in our country's realities but draws on standard international practices.

Second, antismuggling actions will be undertaken jointly and handled by one authority. In order to correct the shortcomings of many departments that employ nonstandard actions against smuggling, as well as repair the policies being made by many agencies and reduce confusion and disorder, public security and industrial and commercial law enforcement departments will, under Customs leadership, establish a system of taking joint action to pursue smugglers. Meanwhile cases of smuggling, once discovered, will be handled solely by Customs. Cases that do not constitute smuggling will all be turned over to Customs for administrative penalties. Whenever smuggling is suspected, the information will all be sent to the antismuggling police force for investigation. Customs will turn over all smuggled contraband and funds found to the national treasury in a timely manner, and no unit will be allowed to retain any of these for its own purposes.

Third, we will reform the current system for managing fines and money confiscated in the course of combating smuggling and insist on a "dual-track collection and payment system." All such fines and funds are to be turned over in their entirety to the central fiscal authorities. The central fiscal authorities will retain 30% for making up [evaded] taxes. Of the remaining portion, 50% will be used to improve the equipment and case handling of antismuggling departments and to reward those units and individuals that earned merits in their work. The other 50% will be rebated to provincial fiscal authorities for unified deployment by the various provinces, autonomous regions, and centrally administered municipalities, to be used primarily for antismuggling work. A portion of the fines and confiscated money from smuggling should also be used to support and reward antidrug forces. The central fiscal authorities should simplify procedures for rebates and improve the efficiency of their work.

The above reform measures will enable us to strengthen our antismuggling forces and also ensure that we can systemically and institutionally crack down on smuggling in a forceful and timely way. This is in line with the fact that we must govern according to law and administer according to law and is absolutely necessary. All parties concerned must implement these measures seriously.

Even as we continually intensify the struggle against smuggling, we must do a good job of integrating the crackdown with the strengthening of legal institutions, the strengthening of order, the strengthening of oversight, and the punishment of corruption. The Party, government, and military agencies in all locales as well as judicial departments must resolutely close down all the companies they run and affiliated companies, and must cut themselves off entirely from these companies and affiliates in terms of staffing, finances, and materials within a specified time.

We've talked about doing this for several years but so far we haven't executed well. Party and government agencies as well as the military and armed police all rely on "imperial rations"[3] and absolutely must not run commercial companies. We now have to be determined to focus hard on resolving this problem. The issues are complex, and we must first delink, then rectify. We have to comprehensively clean up and resolutely abolish the markets in which smuggled goods are traded and strike hard at the selling of smuggled goods.

At present, our legal system is still imperfect, and some existing laws and regulations lack force. In view of the developing situation and the needs of the fight against smuggling, we have to focus urgently on revising and drafting the relevant laws and regulations, refining and perfecting the various management systems, and enforcing the laws strictly, so that the fight against smuggling is put on the path of the rule of law.

Strengthen Leadership and Focus on Implementation

The task of launching and intensifying the crackdown on smuggling is a very important and arduous one in both the short and long term. All levels of Party committees and government must give it high priority and firmly strengthen their leadership over it. In addition, all locales, departments, and sectors must think in terms of politics, the big picture, and discipline, and truly align their thinking and their actions with the plans and demands of the Party Central Committee and the State Council. They must gradually set up a system of anti-smuggling leadership responsibilities. Particularly where smuggling is rampant, Party and government leaders must tackle this job personally and truly assume these responsibilities. In cases where leadership is weak, where the crackdown lacks force, where people may even seem to be obeying but are actually resisting, and where a locale or unit has failed to turn rampant smuggling around within a designated time, we must strictly trace the responsibilities of the principal Party and government leaders concerned.

Public security, industrial-commercial, and supervisory departments as well as courts and procuratorates at all levels must treat combating smuggling as a major task. All departments concerned should work together closely both in handling and managing issues, should coordinate their actions and address issues comprehensively, and should share the duties and tasks of combating smuggling. We must broadly mobilize the people and fully rely on them so as to create a social environment in which smuggling evokes the same response as "a

---

3. Translator's note: that is, they are paid by the government and supported by budgetary expenditures.

rat crossing the street: everyone will want it to be hit." We must construct a wall of iron to prevent and combat smuggling.

To judge the effectiveness of this joint antismuggling program, we'll have to see whether smuggling in key commodities, in key areas, and via key channels is indeed checked. We'll have to see if major smuggling cases and smugglers can be thoroughly investigated and dealt with. And we'll have to see if the people are truly satisfied with the results of the crackdown. The State Council will be organizing a comprehensive study of the progress in the fight against smuggling.

Furthermore, we must continue to rectify and strengthen the ranks of Customs to meet the demands of both the arduous struggle against smuggling and implementation of the new system to combat it. The key is to build a Customs team of high caliber and great fighting strength. The Party Central Committee and the State Council are placing very high hopes and trust in Customs. Overall, our Customs team is a good one, one that has achieved a great deal. However, the problems that have been exposed in it are also quite serious.

Some Customs staff take bribes to overlook smuggling or even participate in it. Records show that from 1993 to 1997 we uncovered 211 such cases, and that 303 people were involved. These are just the cases that have been exposed—perhaps some have yet to come to light.

Customs is the main agency and force for combating smuggling. To set others straight, you must be straight yourself. If you are crooked, how can you set others straight? Customs must be clean and self-disciplined, it must deal severely with corruption, and must be firm in eliminating the bad apples in its ranks. In particular, it must rectify and strengthen its leadership team, resolutely transferring away those who are weak and inept, of poor caliber, or unsuited to serve as leaders. In their place, it must bring in a group of truly impartial people who are not afraid to offend, who embody the spirit of [self-] sacrifice, and who have the professional expertise to reinforce the leadership team.

Customs must also cultivate an antismuggling force that has professional integrity, is efficient and incorruptible, and practices strict discipline. It must constantly strengthen education in anticorruption activities and professional ethics among its ranks and improve the caliber of its staff in all areas. Each and every Customs staff member should be filled with a sense of moral authority; have the courage to stick to principles; dare to offend others; truly carry out the sacred duties entrusted to him by the Party and by the people; be loyal to the Party, to the people, and to the country; and be a strong warrior in the fight against smuggling.

The antismuggling divisions of the public security and industrial and commercial departments must also properly clean up their ranks, must strengthen their leadership teams at all levels in particular, and must take the initiative in seriously and responsibly carrying out the fight against smuggling. We must augment and improve the equipment used to combat smuggling and be determined to install container-scanning systems at all ports. We must also increase equipment such as antismuggling speedboats and helicopters and strengthen our ability to combat smuggling.

Launching this large-scale, nationwide joint action and special program against smuggling is a major move by the Party Central Committee and the State Council to ensure that we can successfully meet our economic targets this year and that our economy grows in a healthy way. It is also an important measure for intensifying the struggle against corruption and strengthening the development of a clean Party and government. It affects the entire big picture and has enormous significance. Let us uphold Deng Xiaoping Theory, be firmly united around the Party center with Jiang Zemin at its core, bolster our spirits, act together as one, and win new victories in the war against smuggling.

7

Rebuilding after the Floods with the Same Spirit Displayed in Combating Them[1]

August 31–September 10, 1998

O ur country has been ravaged by exceptionally serious floods this year. Flooding in the Yangtze River basin was the worst in history—worse than in 1931 and also worse than the unusually heavy floods of 1954. And the floods in Northeast China were of a magnitude seen only once every 300 years. Although a terrible thing, these floods have drawn all our people together. Had they not been so united, and had it not been for the decisive power of the People's Liberation Army (PLA) in particular, the consequences of these floods would have been unthinkable.

August 31, 1998, in Heilongjiang Province

We have just heard the reports of the Heilongjiang provincial Party committee and provincial government as well as leading members from various State Council departments. I agree with their views in principle and want to again emphasize two points.

1. Our Victory in the Face of Disastrous Flooding. We have again won a decisive victory in the face of flooding that is seldom encountered. It was made possible by the pulling together of the country's entire Party, entire army, and entire population.

The flooding this year along the Nen and Songhua rivers was historic, something you encounter once in 300 or maybe even 500 years. Because soldiers and civilians were united in their efforts and particularly because of the PLA's efforts, we were spared even greater catastrophe and losses and survived this challenging moment. We witnessed many truly heroic deeds during this event. In the absence of wars, we haven't seen this sort of spirit and such moving deeds in a long time. Officers and soldiers did not hesitate to sacrifice their own lives to

---

1. On August 28–September 1 and September 7–12, 1998, Zhu Rongji visited Inner Mongolia, Heilongjiang, Jilin, Hubei, Jiangxi, Hunan, Chongqing, and Sichuan to inspect flood relief work and post-flood rebuilding efforts. These are the main remarks he made during those visits.

save those of the people—again and again they offered to risk their own chances of survival for the sake of ordinary people, which was incredibly touching.

Every evening, when I see these reports on TV, I am moved to tears. I feel that this was a live battle drill for the armed forces, a major test for them. Our PLA is an army we can truly count on, an army that can overcome any foe. In fighting the deluge, our Chinese people also demonstrated that they are a great people, with a strong ability to pull together. The unity between soldiers and civilians, between officials and the public, and between the Party and the people was greatly strengthened. Unlike the past, when officials were widely criticized by the public for corruption and bureaucratism, this time everyone acknowledged that most of our officials were in the front lines, and only a very few fled elsewhere. At a critical moment, the Chinese Communist Party was up to the test and served the people with its entire heart and soul. That's why, although this flooding was a catastrophe resulting in losses of over RMB 160 billion nationwide, in return it taught us a lesson, acting like a gigantic force pulling all our people together, so a bad thing can still turn into a good thing. We cannot overstate the extent to which our victory over the flooding has bolstered our spirits.

For the country as a whole, it has been a decisive victory. And though we still can't be careless or lax about the Jing River and Lake Hong, the most dangerous period for the country has passed. We must study these experiences in earnest and commend those who acted with outstanding courage to fight the flooding. We should shower praise and recognition especially on those from the PLA who directed operations.

2. Rebuilding in the Aftermath of the Flooding. Now that we have achieved a decisive victory over the flooding, we should quickly shift the emphasis of our work to post-flood rebuilding. This rebuilding includes resuming production, making arrangements for the winter, and rebuilding homes. In resuming production, we must restore and rebuild various projects that were destroyed by the floods.

The key task, however, is to solve the question of how the flood victims will get through this winter, and we must take special care to prevent a major epidemic after a disaster of this proportion. As Zhang Wenkang[2] just noted, during the Yangtze flooding of 1931, 145,000 people drowned and over 3 million died of disease; in the major flooding of 1954, 33,000 people died, mostly from disease. This time the massive flooding took far fewer lives—more than 1,300 altogether. In Heilongjiang, for instance, no one died—in view of the enormity of the floods, this was truly remarkable.

Now we have to focus on disease prevention and getting through the winter. In organizing the resumption of production, making living arrangements, and

2. Zhang Wenkang was then Minister of Health.

In conversation with national model worker Ma Yongshun in Harbin, Heilongjiang Province, on August 31, 1998.

in rebuilding homes, we must learn from the lessons of the past. We mustn't simply restore everything to the way it used to be; rather, we have to rebuild in a way that makes more sense. The State Council had earlier suggested an approach that I will repeat here, and I urge you all to take note.

First, *"close off the mountains and plant trees, and revert farmland back to forests."* I discussed this issue today with Ma Yongshun.[3] These past few years we've really cut down far too many trees, which has resulted in a great deal of erosion. Chairman Mao and Premier Zhou [Enlai] were both very serious about protecting our water resources and the environment, and they issued many ecological directives. But in carrying these out, we created many problems that repeatedly devastated our forests. In the past few years we've also emphasized the protection of forests and of ecological resources, yet deforestation has remained very severe. Although this year's flooding is undoubtedly related to climate change, it also has something to do with environmental degradation.

3. Ma Yongshun was a forestry worker in the Tieli Forestry Bureau of Heilongjiang Province. He had been voted a model worker of Heilongjiang Province and of the Northeast General Bureau of Forest Industry 11 times. After the 1950s, he steadfastly planted over 50,000 trees as a volunteer over a span of 40 years, and went from being a model logger to being a model tree-planter.

At Harbin, for example, the Songhua River silt bed is 4 meters higher than it was in 1932, and that silt in the riverbed is mainly a result of erosion caused by excessive logging upstream. Forests are, in and of themselves, a retention basin. The areas they stood on have now become stretches of bare hills—once it rains, the water all runs off. That's why Jiang Zemin likes to cite these two sentences from Engels's *Dialectics of Nature*: "Let us not, however, flatter ourselves over-much on account of our human conquest over nature. For each such conquest takes its revenge on us."[4] This is well worth pondering over.

When we put new land under cultivation, we chop down all the forests, plant the land, and get a bumper harvest. Once such a place becomes flooded, however, everything is washed away and nothing may be able to grow there. This is nature's way of punishing the human race. That's why last year we were resolved—and this year we are even more firmly resolved—to chop down no more trees no matter what! If there isn't enough wood, we can import it, we can buy it with our forex. This year, even though our finances are very tight, we are allocating RMB 6 billion for projects to protect our forests, and we are prohibiting any more logging. First and foremost, we resolutely and absolutely forbid logging in the upper reaches of the Yangtze and Yellow rivers, that is, in certain parts of Sichuan and Yunnan provinces. Loggers must all become tree planters, and we also expect them to take other jobs to help themselves.

Because our main wood-producing region is in the Northeast, in Heilongjiang, it would be quite difficult to stop logging there entirely, so it must be a gradual process. But I'm afraid the targets for reducing logging proposed by Heilongjiang are a bit too low—you must proceed from the facts. Of course you have to consider the livelihoods of people working in forestry, and you have to give them some subsidies, but you also have to organize them to help themselves by producing. You have to redirect them into various types of businesses so that they cut down fewer trees. You must take the interests of both sides into account and be more determined.

Second, "let the levees[5] be flattened to release floodwaters and let the farmland revert to lakes." That is, we must clear all obstacles from the area within the embankments. "Within the embankments" means the riverbed—you must be clear about this concept. Some people have been building levees inside the embankments, building houses, and planting crops, all of which impede the flow of floodwaters within the levees. Henceforth levees that have been washed

4. See Frederick Engels, *Dialectics of Nature* (www.marxists.org/archive/marx/works/1883/don/ch09.htm).

5. In Hunan, Hubei, and Jiangxi provinces, embankment-like levees were built along rivers and lakes and around houses and fields to keep water out.

away must not be rebuilt—they were flattened by heaven so that they can let the floodwaters pass. The levees that were not washed away this time must be flattened, and there must be no more planting. Farmland must be reverted to lakes. Only half the original areas of Lakes Dongting and Boyang remain, and they are full of shoals and levees that are fighting with the lakes for land. This can't go on. They must be restored so that they can again store water.

I'm not overlooking the fact that reservoirs can be used to control floods. Building reservoirs along the upstream stretches of the main channels and tributaries will allow water to be stored when flooding takes place. But that is a long-term plan—building reservoirs takes a lot of money and must be done gradually. We still have to handle this comprehensively: focus first on preserving soil and stop destroying forested slopes upstream; build reservoirs midstream and embankments downstream. This should be the basic plan for all our water-works construction.

Third, "offer jobs rather than relief aid and move the population to where it can build towns." In order to move people away from within the embankments, the government must allocate a piece of land for them and draw up good plans for new small towns. You have to let them move to a new place or else they'll rebuild their old levees. How should we solve this problem? By offering jobs, not relief funds. The state will put up the money for building new small towns. Let them take these jobs and pay them to do so. If you don't fully subsidize the entire cost of materials for building houses, people will refuse to move and go back to farming within their old levees.

Fourth, "reinforce the embankments and dredge the riverbeds." Embankments along the main channels of the Yangtze and Yellow rivers must be built to standards that enable them to withstand 100-year floods. Right now, both of these have become "rivers in the sky": their beds are higher than the cities and villages along them, and should the embankments ever be breached, a vast area will be submerged. No matter what, we have to reinforce these embankments and learn the lesson of the breach at the Jiu River. An embankment was built there without first doing test drilling. The embankment was built on sand, and once it was hollowed out from below, it collapsed. During construction, no reinforcing bars were used in the concrete. The quality of construction was poor, and it was a mess. The embankment split apart at the first surge of floodwaters. We sank eight boats and poured several thousand tons of flour and soybeans into the breach but still couldn't close it—the water continued to rush through from below. It wasn't until the 27th Engineering Corps of the PLA set up steel scaffolding there and filled it with rocks that the breach was closed.

From now on we have to learn this lesson: we must pass a law on the construction of embankments, and anyone who cuts corners here will be severely

Inspecting flood damage and consoling flood victims at the Horqin Right-Middle Banner, Xing'an League, Inner Mongolia Autonomous Region, on August 29, 1998. (Photograph by Li Xin, Xinhua News Agency)

punished according to law. Otherwise, this will cause enormous harm to others. The approach I have just described can guide us in our post-flood rebuilding. We paid in blood for this and other lessons—we must learn them well.

Lessons for resuming production and building homes. In the effort to resume production and rebuild homes, we should focus on four objectives:

—Strengthen leadership

—Focus on key tasks

—Unify planning

—Implement in phases.

In strengthening leadership, we should—at the appropriate time and at an appropriate pace—shift the emphasis in the work we are leading from combating floods to post-flood resumption and rebuilding. All levels of Party and government should focus on this the way they focused on combating the floods. They should establish responsibility systems and ensure that there is all-round implementation.

We must also focus on key tasks. Homes laid waste by water cannot be restored in two or three years—some might take four or five years. The vital thing for Heilongjiang this year is to get through the winter, not wasting money on the one hand, and ensuring that the people can get through the winter safely on the other. After on-site visits to places ranging from Qiqihar to Harbin on this trip, I sense that the provincial and municipal Party committees and governments have done a great deal of work and that things are much better than we had expected. You've already thought of many issues and done something about them without waiting for the State Council to make concrete arrangements, and some of this was done very well.

Unified planning is equally important. I again stress that planning must be done well. Don't spend money over and over—if something can be resolved by spending money once, don't spread it out over several rounds. After this disaster, we're not just simply going to resume [production] or rebuild homes. Our plans should make even more sense and be even more scientific than previous plans. This time, I'm especially concerned about the rebuilding of schools. They must be our first priority, whereas other things don't have to be built right away. We will revitalize the nation through science and education, so education is extremely important.

It is essential to implement in phases. In the aftermath of a disaster, everything is in ruins, and there are a thousand things waiting to be done. Building on a foundation that focuses on key tasks, you should draw up mid- and long-term plans, implement these in phases, and meet your targets year by year.

September 8, 1998, in Hubei Province

At the moment two things must be done in preparing for the resumption of production and the rebuilding of homes. The first pertains to long-term issues: you should continue to do feasibility studies, make your case, and compare approaches. With the Ministry of Water Resources and other departments concerned in the lead, Hubei Province should carry out careful studies and planning, ascertaining what should and should not be done—this must be determined through scientific means. Plans should be detailed and rigorously thought out; you should listen to views from all sides and take the long view in decisionmaking. In the course of planning, you should free up your minds, absorb new experiences and advanced technologies from abroad, and then make prudent decisions.

The second task is the most urgent one of the moment, which is to help flood victims get through the winter. This must be decided now, action must be taken immediately, and there must be no delay.

A central question for both of these tasks is where will the money come from? This is an important matter to be debated. You've presented me with a bill for RMB 46.3 billion. If this RMB 46.3 billion can solve the problem of flooding in Hubei, then I say it's well worth it. I did some rough calculations for the plan you proposed. The 46.3 billion is to be distributed in four years, which averages to upward of 10 billion a year. Hubei has experienced such a huge flood this year that if we don't support infrastructure construction, the economy won't grow, farmers' incomes won't increase, and society won't be stable.

The central government will first give you RMB 3 billion this year. Hurry up and complete the design, planning, and test drilling for the Yangtze River embankments. The breach of the Jiu River embankments is a lesson on what happens if you don't do test drilling. Embankments also have to be repaired along the Han and the Yangtze rivers, but you can't grow fat by swallowing everything in one mouthful, so you should still start by repairing the main Yangtze embankments, because the flood victims are all located along this line and can provide you with labor. The first projects to tackle should be those for which planning and feasibility studies have been completed, including those requiring repairs because of flood damage.

The most pressing problem right now is how the flood victims will get through the winter. First comes the rebuilding of collapsed houses. In principle, the materials for rebuilding in new locations and for relocating people to build [new] towns should be fully subsidized. Subsidies should be lower for rebuilding in original locations, one-third at most, and [building] standards mustn't be too high. Building that doesn't coincide with plans will not get one penny of subsidies. The Agricultural Bank can offer rural mortgages and loans for building houses, which can then be repaid in installments. Of course there will have to be some procedures for [loan] guarantees, and the national fiscal authorities can subsidize these a bit.

As we move people and build new towns over the next two years, we will generally solve the problem of farmers' incomes by building or repairing waterworks. At the same time, we must come up with new ways for them to make a living—we must develop tertiary industries. This is an extremely arduous task.

How much will home building subsidies amount to? The State Planning Commission has suggested RMB 1.1 billion, but Yu Zhengsheng[6] hopes for a little more. I think that we must even things out somewhat across provinces and can't subsidize on the basis of standards of living. After all, those with higher standards of living can afford to pay a bit more themselves. We also have to be considerate of the Northeast. I visited the three [Northeast] provinces this time and agreed to give them a total of RMB 1 billion. The worst flooding in this area was in Harbin—from the air, you could see wide stretches under water, and losses were very great. We gave Heilongjiang RMB 500 million, of which 400 million is to be used for housing, 85 million for education, and 15 million for hospitals. We gave Jilin 300 million, of which 270 million is to be used for

---

6. Yu Zhengsheng was then Minister of Construction.

housing and 30 million for schools and hospitals. The flooding in Inner Mongolia was slightly less severe so we gave that area RMB 200 million. These three provinces can take action because they received RMB 1 billion between them, which is enough to solve the problem of housing the flood victims.

Overall, the most severe flooding occurred in Hubei, which has the special burden of moving people, building towns, and flattening levees for flood control. Therefore I'm thinking of giving you RMB 1.2 billion. We still have to go to Hunan and Jiangxi, which will definitely be receiving much less. Rather than providing too large a one-time subsidy, I would rather designate more money for projects destroyed by the floods, offer jobs instead of relief aid, and allow farmers to borrow money themselves to build houses and then repay the banks. We should still encourage the farmers to rely on their own efforts to rebuild.

In addition, it will take RMB 1.2 billion to repair facilities destroyed by the floods. Report how large a subsidy you need to the State Planning Commission; this will be considered in conjunction with other waterworks projects. We will simplify procedures and process the documents as quickly as possible. As in other cases, planning for the rebuilding of educational facilities and hospitals should be unified. We'll allocate RMB 100 million to the educational system and 20 million to hospitals—add this 120 million [to your funding request]. The above state subsidies can be given to you any time.

The best way to help flood victims is to offer jobs instead of relief funds. The problem of supplying clothing and blankets to get flood victims through the winter can be completely solved through donations.

There's also the matter of money already spent to combat floods. You've spent RMB 1.19 billion and are asking the central government to subsidize 800 million of this. Jilin says it spent 1.2 billion on combating and preventing floods, while Heilongjiang spent 900 million. The Ministry of Water Resources and the National Office for Combating Floods and Droughts should draw up a unified plan for this money and how it should be evened out. They must summarize the situation in the various provinces: how much is owed, how much the locals can afford, how much more they need from the central government. Finally, I want to stress one thing: all these funds are special funds for special purposes. They absolutely may not be misused for other purposes. Otherwise you will be disciplined and punished.

September 9, 1998, in Jiangxi Province

The work of resettling flood victims in Jiangxi is different from that in other places. Northeast China has a lot of land but few people. The flooded areas are all low-lying lands, so we have no desire to restore them. Their problem can be resolved quite well by generally moving people and building towns. Hubei was flooded along the river's path and the levees nearly all washed away. Now it's going to move the inhabitants away from the levees and build towns. Since the distances involved are not great and Hubei's plans are quite detailed, this problem can be resolved quite well.

As for Jiangxi and Hunan, both face the same types of issues—which are quite difficult to deal with. In the past, parts of lakes were filled in to create farmland. Some people were also in favor of doing this—it was a result of history because at the time we couldn't solve the grain problem. Without filling in lakes to create farmland, there wouldn't have been enough grain to eat. What should we do now? If we look at the problem in that earlier context, filling in lakes to create farmland was a positive contribution then, even though it went against the laws of nature. But now nature is beginning to punish us; it is taking revenge on us. Therefore in light of the new situation, we must revert farmland to lakes. We now have an ample supply of grain; besides, science and technology have been broadly promoted in agriculture, and we no longer have to grow grain inside lakes anymore.

The losses caused by floods these past few years amount to RMB 100 billion annually. We estimate this year's damage to be 160 billion; Hubei alone says it lost 50 billion. Therefore we must think about reverting farmland to lakes, but this is a big problem for Jiangxi. To arrange livelihoods for so many people, you have to take local circumstances into account, make plans for the long term, and implement them in stages. Nevertheless, the goal is to revert farmland to lakes.

The serious flooding this time lasted longer than that in 1954. Although over 100 cities were inundated back then, some of the floodwaters were diverted, and Boyang and Dongting lakes were able to store some of the Yangtze water. Now those lakes can't handle their own levels, let alone take up any of the Yangtze floodwaters, so we now have a prolonged high-water period and a great deal of manpower being wasted. Treating those lakes is the most urgent task at the moment and will require the greatest determination on our part.

How big a step should be taken this year? You've proposed a plan to move 100,000 people away from the vicinity of the lakes. I'm in favor of taking such a step, and you should continue to plan in greater detail. So far, your plan only appears to solve the current problem of recovery, and not the long-term issue of reverting farmland back to lakes. We must give further thought to integrating long-term and immediate [issues]. Your plan would also restore the former approach before the floods, planting as before. Some of the levees would still be diverting floodwaters and would be put to that use for a while when they are needed to store floodwaters. You're planning to move 100,000 people this year. If it were any more than that—several hundred thousand people—I'm afraid it would be very hard to move such a large number and build towns.

Directing work at a breached flood wall, Jiujiang, Jiangxi Province, on August 9, 1998. (Photograph by Zhang Wu, Xinhua News Agency)

We have to give somewhat greater policy support to those who are truly moving inhabitants and building towns. For example, the central fiscal authorities should subsidize the costs of construction materials and provide strong support to infrastructure construction, including the rebuilding of the rural power grid in the newly built towns. These are all things the central fiscal authorities should spend money on. Of course the local governments will have to think about building some roads, water supply facilities, and public utilities, and if they encounter difficulties, the central government can give them appropriate subsidies.

As for how the farmers will make a living after losing their land, this is something you have to think about from all angles. It won't be too hard to solve this problem. During the next few years, the country will be undertaking large infrastructure construction projects, so there will be a way for those farmers to earn a living. They can also grow some vegetables and engage in some aquaculture—there'll be some way to make a living. I must make it clear that the state has no obligation to restore everything that was washed away by the flood back to its pre-flood condition. The state's money is taxpayers' money. Each of us, as taxpayers, should be able to enjoy subsidies from the state in times of difficulty, but not everything can be subsidized, and we can't all eat from the same "big pot." For those rebuilding homes in the original sites, our policy will basically be to let them borrow and repay. Raw materials will be provided on a unified basis, and the state will advance them money, but in the end they must use the money they earn from taking jobs rather than relief funds to repay the costs of building their homes. Of course we can still offer some subsidies to those in exceptional difficulties.

Also, what are your ideas on the safety of the remaining levees during flood periods? It's not realistic to build villages on elevated platforms or to use sand-blowing,[7] and in fact these aren't possible. You'd spend much money to no avail—it would all be washed away again in a big flood. You can think about preparing some areas for storing floodwaters from which people can be evacuated once the need arises. This would mean thinking about evacuation—you have to build roads so that people can be evacuated. In places where evacuation would be difficult, you could build "safe houses" as Hunan did. These wouldn't cost much—you build simple towers four to five stories high that can accommodate several dozen people at the top. Provided the structures can hold out for a dozen hours or so, people can come from elsewhere to rescue those in the towers. The state will subsidize the cost of building several such towers in areas where homes are going to be rebuilt in their original locations.

I think we need to create a model here, a model that can actually move people and build towns and is a permanent solution, so that Boyang Lake will truly become the lake that it used to be, with no shoals or levees blocking the flow of floodwaters—this should be the long-term goal. Of course you mustn't force yourselves to take too large a step. For one thing, there isn't enough money; for another, the people will want to observe things for a while before they can make up their minds to move. You need to construct a model for moving people and building a town. The farmers who move there will find new jobs, their living standards will go up, and they'll be safe during the flood season. Then it'll be a lot easier to get the other several hundred thousand people to move.

September 10, 1998, in Hunan Province

We've already won a decisive victory throughout the country in this struggle to combat flooding. Under the leadership of the provincial Party committee and

---

7. Sand blowing was a technique used to fill in lakes to create farmland. Part of the lake was first encircled with sandbags; a mixture of water and sand from the bottom of the lake was then "blown" by pumps from outside the circle into the encircled area. The water would flow out while the sand would be trapped inside the circle by the sandbags. The encircled area would gradually be filled and become dry land after constant sand blowing.

the provincial government, the soldiers and people of Hunan have made very great sacrifices and paid a very high price. In particular, the PLA and the armed police played a critical, decisive, and irreplaceable role in fighting the floods. It is truly no small victory to keep losses to a minimum in the face of such a massive disaster. The people of Hunan should take pride in the fact that of the 25 PLA officers and men who gave their lives in this struggle, seven were from Hunan. Many fine officials in Hunan—like Luo Diansu, a member of the Yueyang [Party] standing committee and director of its publicity department—did not fear death and served the people with their entire heart and soul.

When the fight against the floods in Hunan was at its tensest, I was unable to take the time to come here and join you in the struggle, but I kept abreast of the flooding and damage, and I believe that your people will be able to overcome this disaster. The purpose of our current visit is to implement the important directives issued by Jiang Zemin on resuming production, rebuilding homes, and developing the economy. Hunan's provincial Party committee and provincial government have already done a great deal of work in this regard, making advance preparations and drawing up plans.

This post-disaster reconstruction must fundamentally be geared toward addressing the threat of flooding. Although our most pressing task at the moment is to ensure that the farmers can get through the winter safely, that they can resume production and rebuild their homes, this work must be integrated with the basic long-term goal of planning to deal with floods. We don't want to spend money for nothing, and we want to adopt measures that will have a permanent effect. Our long-term goal is to restore Dongting Lake to its original appearance, and the basic method will be to greatly improve the ecosystems in the Xiang, Zi, Yuan, and Feng river basins and strengthen anti-erosion work, so that Hunan can truly become a land of verdant hills and clear waters and Dongting Lake can return to its former mighty self. This will not only be a contribution to Hunan, but it will be a contribution to the entire Yangtze River basin.

Dongting Lake is the largest water-storage lake in the Yangtze basin. Therefore some fundamental steps must be taken right away. For example, the work of closing off hills [to farming] and growing forests and the work of tree-planting can hopefully be completed within three to five years. And there must be no more logging. This touches on the question of rural energy sources and must be well planned. I feel that this question can be resolved and there can be alternative energy sources. Slopes at an angle of 25 degrees or more must have their farms reverted back to forests or meadows; this could also apply to slopes under 25 degrees that have serious erosion problems. Don't cultivate those few mu[8] of fields—it is far more important to worry about the punishing acts of nature

8. One mu is equal to 666.7 square meters.

than about that little bit of grain. In any case, China does not lack for that little bit of grain. In some areas where erosion isn't too serious, you can turn "slopes into terraces" and continue planting.

In growing forests, you have to think about combining coniferous and broad-leaf trees. Experts say that it won't do to plant only coniferous trees because they can't stop erosion on their own. You have to combine the coniferous and broadleaf varieties. What's more, there has to be grass cover below if the forest is to be effective in halting erosion. That's why good planning is essential in transforming Hunan's landscape into a truly magnificent one of verdant hills and clear waters. The central government is fully determined to support local governments fiscally and in every other way to complete this task. It's no more than having woodcutters change jobs and resettling them. Besides, some loggers can become foresters and tree planters.

This massive flooding has wrecked many projects and left some levees on shoals. As we rebuild, we have to think about how to restore Dongting Lake to its original appearance and how to allow Yangtze floodwaters to flow freely without any obstacles in their flood channels—this is the long-term goal. Today, when I heard Yang Zhengwu[9] report that you want to restore Dongting Lake to its pre-1949 appearance, I was delighted. This is a job for the ages. It won't be easy to complete, but no matter what, you must strive toward this goal and never waver. It will be very hard to get people to move away from levees that weren't washed away; however, it will also be very hard to restore those that have been destroyed. That means you will have to mobilize those people, get them to move and build homes on another piece of land—the state will give you the necessary support. I feel this is something that can be done, and it will be extremely significant. This is an opportunity that comes along but once in a hundred years—don't pass it up.

Now that these levees have been washed away, don't rebuild them. Instead, I'm proposing this 32-[Chinese] character approach to resuming production and rebuilding homes: "close off hills and plant trees, revert fields to forests; flatten levees to let floodwaters pass and revert farmland to lakes; offer jobs, not relief funds and move people and build towns; strengthen embankments and dredge rivers." This idea has been carefully considered and discussed in a special session by the State Council, which has concluded that we should take this opportunity to remove the existing levees and restore the lake.

Two scenarios can be considered: (a) do no more planting around the levees and use the area entirely for letting floodwaters pass; (b) don't have anyone living within the levees, plant during low-water season, and don't plant during high-water season. Although I said that nobody should be living there, they can

---

9. Yang Zhengwu was then Governor of Hunan Province.

certainly put up simple sheds during the harvest season. There should be no facilities inside the levees, only a single crop under cultivation—if that's submerged, so be it; it won't cause a huge loss. Those are the only two scenarios. Both of them require people to leave, to leave the soil and to leave their homes, but you can make plans to resettle them around the periphery of the enlarged lake and arrange for them to live outside the embankments.

The policy of the central government is to give a home-building subsidy of RMB 15,000 to each household that moves out of a flood path or a river's path. This amount should cover the cost of construction materials for a house of about 100 square meters and will be fully subsidized by the central fiscal authorities. Since all the materials will be provided, all the people concerned need to do is to start building their houses. Subsidy funds will be distributed according to this standard, depending on the number of households you move away from Dongting Lake.

This work can't be done through administrative fiat. Don't force people—work with them by using role models and demonstrations. Since demonstrations aren't yet available, it won't be easy to get farmers to leave their land, move away, and build towns. Start with the people whose levees were washed away this year, and gradually enlarge the scope. As for those whose levees were washed away but who are still very hard to persuade, again don't force them. If they want to go back, let them go back and rebuild their homes. In those cases, the government can only offer a little relief funding, a subsidy of RMB 1,000 per household. We mustn't give a lot of favorable treatment to such people at the policy level. If we did, nobody would be willing to move, and we would never be able to restore the lake.

However, these people are also taxpayers of the People's Republic of China. Now that their homes and their goods have been washed away, we have an obligation to help them a bit and see that they get through the winter safely. For the rest, they will have to rely on jobs instead of relief funds. The government will organize the building of waterworks, and the disaster victims can build their houses through jobs instead of relief. The Agricultural Bank can also provide some funds for loans.

8

A TALK WITH THE PRODUCERS OF *TOPICS IN FOCUS*[1]

October 7, 1998

I'm not sure if I've been the most enthusiastic viewer of *Topics in Focus* ever since it started broadcasting, but at least I'm among your very enthusiastic viewers, and what's more, I've been a strong supporter and volunteer publicist. I often spread the word about the program at different venues. Many ministers haven't been watching it but fear that when they come to meetings I convene, I might just ask them if they watched *Topics in Focus* the night before, so they make sure to do so before the meeting opens.

Topics in Focus is getting better and better and is gaining in public popularity. Those whom it exposes invariably feel quite uncomfortable after watching it—that's why you encounter all sorts of resistance and unpleasant responses in the course of producing and airing this program. While these reactions are all to be expected, the general public is very supportive of you.

I've long wanted to come to CCTV to see you, to express this support, and to thank you all for the great deal of work you've done to publicize the policies of the Party Central Committee and the State Council. It hasn't been easy for you to overcome so many difficulties, so I should offer my thanks to you and also express some hopes for your future work. I've come to CCTV today to talk not just about *Topics in Focus* but also about broadcasting's great and rapid progress. Those on publicity's front lines have played a very important role particularly in the struggle against the recent floods, pulling the entire country together to an unprecedented level and uniting its people as one. As the facts have shown, the broad impact of public opinion has also risen to an unprecedented level. This was fully affirmed by the central leadership at a meeting of the Politburo Standing Committee. Reporters in life jackets were filled with genuine emotion while working in the floodwaters. Soldiers and civilians in the front lines of antiflood work all really liked the reporters. Therefore I should also thank all of you at the forefront of publicity work for the strong support you've been giving to the work of the State Council.

1. On October 7, 1998, Zhu Rongji made an inspection tour of CCTV and spoke to its leading officials as well as the editors and reporters of *Topics in Focus*. This is the main part of his remarks.

Publicity, we've often said, should "primarily report positively and primarily publicize achievements." Although this policy is correct, it also constrains us. What does it mean to report positively? Does it mean 99% of reports should be positive? Won't 98% or 80% be acceptable? I wonder if 51% would also be acceptable. Most programs tend to publicize achievements, but if one or two could point out problems in the course of our progress and mobilize the entire Party to solve them, this would be far better than simply publicizing achievements. Without such programs, the voice of the people won't be heard, so what democracy would there be to speak of? What oversight would there be to speak of?

Now, through the results of its own work and its impact, *Topics in Focus* has demonstrated that its credibility is very high among the people. But instead of bowing their heads and losing heart whenever the program offers criticisms and reports problems, people are accepting these criticisms, improving their work, becoming hopeful about the future, and strengthening their resolve. That's the role *Topics in Focus* has played. Now the *Topics in Focus* phenomenon is becoming more and more widespread. CCTV isn't the only network with such a program—many radio and TV stations have similar programs.

A Half Hour on the Economy, for example, uses similar techniques and seems to have been influenced by *Topics in Focus.* Its report about logging in virgin forests in a certain part of Sichuan has played a very useful role. When I told people to stop cutting down natural forests all across Sichuan and to turn the tree-cutting teams into tree-planting teams, Party and government leaders in Sichuan took this very seriously and were very determined to do something about it. As a result, logging stopped in many areas, but it was still continuing around Mount Emei—which was discovered and reported by journalists. At first, provincial authorities said this was a 1980s project receiving World Bank aid that could not be halted. Later it became clear this was not the case. Although the project was receiving aid from the World Bank, the objective was mainly to help people there plant forests, not cut them down. When the provincial authorities got this feedback, they immediately held a meeting and decided to stop the cutting. The government was very firm in its attitude toward accepting oversight. I think that program was trying to emulate *Topics in Focus,* and to some extent it outdid *Topics in Focus,* with a huge impact.

There's a similar program on Beijing TV. This is a very good thing as it reflects the hardships of the people and exposes the shortcomings of the government so that they can be corrected immediately. To correct mistakes when you make them—that should be the attitude of Communists, and it gives great encouragement to the people. Otherwise, all they would hear about is corruption, and the more they hear of that subject, the less hope they feel. With problems being exposed, people will feel very hopeful after they are corrected, will truly be pulled closer together, and will have confidence. I'm glad that the *Topics*

Inscribing the words "Be the overseer [of government] through public opinion, be the voice of the people, the mirror of the government, and the shock troops of reform" for the Topics in Focus *program during an inspection tour of CCTV on October 7, 1998.*

in Focus phenomenon is spreading: it's giving radio and TV journalists broad vistas in which to use their talents and enables them to play a greater role in promoting our country's reforms and opening up and in promoting the establishment of socialist democracy and the rule of law.

Everyone should get used to this sort of criticism. Come and interview me any day you discover a shortcoming of mine, and I'll be sure to accept your criticism and correct my mistakes. We've made many decisions: all the major decisions of the State Council were issued by me, so it's inevitable that there will be some shortcomings. Look for them, point them out, and correct them.

For *Topics in Focus,* I have four suggestions: "Be the overseer [of government] through public opinion, be the voice of the people, the mirror of the government, and the shock troops of reform." That is how I see your work.

Provide Oversight through Public Opinion

Topics in Focus has fully exercised oversight through public opinion. It covers a broad range of topics and almost every aspect of State Council policies. Every aspect of everything I'm doing falls within the scope of your coverage, and your reports are very helpful to my work. This morning, the State Council held an executive meeting to look into the question of "turning fees into taxes." Right now, there are more fees than taxes, and public discontent is at a boiling point. First of all, we must change to a fee-collection system for highways. This was an insight we gained from your program.

The *Topics in Focus* episode that made the deepest impression on me was titled "Punishments Must Be Meted Out According to the Law," which showed a Shanxi traffic policeman arbitrarily collecting fines—that was a spectacular episode. We can't randomly "turn fees into taxes," and we must start with highway tolls. Therefore the State Council will compile opinions on "turning fees into taxes" and recommend a revision of the "Highway Law." Before the meeting started this morning, I gathered up the relevant reports from *Topics in Focus* and played them for the ministers. After they watched them, it became easier to get this document passed.

Now I can't say that *Topics in Focus* has given me deep insight into every aspect of reform that I'm focusing on, but at least I've gotten many ideas from it. For example, these past few years we've put a lot of effort into reforming the grain purchase-and-sales system, because agriculture is the foundation [of our economy]. The situation today is so good because the grain supply is steadily growing, and "with grain in hand, there's no alarm in the heart." And because there's so much grain, prices are exhibiting negative growth. If we have [enough] grain, the prices of other goods can't possibly go up.

On the other hand, the state is carrying a very heavy burden here. Last year, the central fiscal authorities paid out RMB 50 billion to subsidize grain enterprises, but this money didn't reach the farmers. Most of it wound up in the pockets of crooks. I keep thinking about what we could have done with that RMB 50 billion—for one thing, we could have raised the salaries of all the civil servants in the country by three pay grades!

The management of some grain enterprises is very corrupt. They buy grain cheaply from farmers and sell it at a high price even as they enjoy subsidies from the state. Journalist Cao Hong described a very typical case in an episode titled "[State-]Purchased Grain Shouldn't Wind Up in Private Granaries." When that program was broadcast, the provincial Party secretary and the governor of Hebei Province couldn't sit still. The next day, they sent a telegram saying that they had held a meeting overnight and describing how much work they had done in the past and how they were going to strengthen and improve it. After I read this, I forwarded it to Hu Jintao and Ding Guan'gen and asked them to go have a look. This shows how much impact that episode had—it had a greater impact than anything I said, and it made a major contribution to reform of the grain purchase-and-sale system. It wasn't only the leadership of Hebei Province that watched the show—[those working in] the grain system across the country, as well as all the provincial Party secretaries and governors, learned from it.

The episode's method of presentation was also quite good—it consisted of interviews with a lot of people and let the facts as well as those involved speak for themselves. They went from impressions to concepts, and were able to incorporate the national grain purchase-and-sale policy into a very short program that was strongly policy-oriented and very affecting.

A few months ago, I asked provincial and municipal leaders that I was meeting with to watch *Topics in Focus*. The episode we watched as the meeting progressed was more lively, more forceful, and more persuasive than our speeches. It was the 1996 episode "Stealthy Logging Is Endangering the Great Artery," which reflected a depressing situation. In considering the recent floods, while we recognize that they are of course a natural disaster, we have to admit that in cutting down too many trees we allowed soil to erode and silt up the rivers. In protecting the soil and improving the ecology, we failed to protect the forests very well, and now we saw the seriousness of the issue. In Hubei some people were even taking over the lakes, and what is especially infuriating, some officials righteously claimed that building houses [in the lakes] was the correct thing to do.

In all the areas where you monitor government through public opinion, you have focused on key aspects of current policies, as in the case of the problems surrounding the rural power grid. Without a grid, you can't deliver electricity even if you have it. Even in villages connected to the grid, the cost of electricity is prohibitive. Those who don't have electricity yearn for it, but those who have it are afraid of it. Farmers who've bought washing machines and refrigerators only put them out for show. Furthermore, the power grids that have been built are crude and shabby. They use steel wires for power cables—this wastes a great deal of power, so electricity is incredibly expensive. I gained considerable insight into the problem from watching your program.

The central government is now determined to rebuild the rural power grid and reform rural power prices so that all those on the same grid pay the same price. Urban residents currently pay RMB 0.47 per kilowatt-hour of electricity and soon villages will as well. The state will spend RMB 140 billion to complete the remaking of the rural grid within three years so that farmers can have cheap electricity. Washing machines and refrigerators will sell only if they have electricity; the machinery in factories will operate quickly only if their products sell; production capacity will increase only if the machines are operating, and only then will losses turn to profits at state-owned enterprises. That's why I say that it is extremely important to remake the rural grid and charge the same prices for those on the same grid. After I made this suggestion, the state power companies were pleased and encouraged, the locals were all pleased and encouraged, and the farmers were happier still.

To reiterate, *Topics in Focus* has played a very important role in overseeing [government] through public opinion.

Be the Voice of the People

Your programs relate the words of ordinary people, which is why they are so popular. Now when farmers and ordinary citizens meet up with officials, they say, "Are you listening [to us]? If not, we'll see you on *Topics in Focus*." This shows that *Topics in Focus* has an impact on farmers—they feel there's a place for them to speak out, that there's someone who will speak up for them, and that after they speak, it won't do for the officials to ignore them—[your words] have authority. Everyone should feel pleased that *Topics in Focus* has managed to do this. You've made a major contribution to our country's reforms and development, and you've played a very positive role.

Be a Mirror for the Government

We have truly learned things from *Topics in Focus* that we would not have been able to find out on our own. Your program is like a mirror that reflects whether our policies are really being properly implemented. When we go down [to the grass roots], we are often unable to find out what is really going on. Everything has been prepared ahead of time, so during an inspection we have to go wherever we are told. Then we sit down and listen to reports, but who's going to tell us what they're really thinking?

By contrast, I can see many realities on *Topics in Focus*. I believe that if all levels of government want to truly serve the people, if they want to implement the programs and policies of the Party Central Committee and the State Council, they will gain a great deal from this program. I hope that the greater the difficulties a place is experiencing, the more your editors and reporters will go there, because only at such a time will you obtain the most valuable and accurate materials.

Be the Shock Troops of Reform

Most of the shows on *Topics in Focus* reveal how, in the course of Party and government reforms, policies may be impeded and sometimes cannot be implemented. You are in the forefront, pointing out the various problems of executing policies and prodding all levels of government to implement policies thoroughly. At present, we're reforming the grain purchase-and-sale system. This is easy to talk about but very hard to execute. Today the State Council passed yet another related document. Originally, the Party Central Committee and the State Council issued a policy statement in April, and after half a year of implementation we saw a few results. Then reports came in from all over the country indicating that the State Council's policy was entirely correct, yet in fact it had not truly taken effect. I hope that in the future *Topics in Focus* will continue to play the part of the shock troops of reform and be a good helper to the Party and government.

Your Journalistic Approach

I feel that many of your journalistic techniques on *Topics in Focus* are very good and worth noting. In particular, you let facts and those involved speak for themselves—a very lively approach. Of course we do have to make sure to treat people decently, for the vast majority of officials are good and should be persuaded by reason, moved by emotion, and constrained by law. You have to reason with those who are unreasonable, who refuse to admit mistakes after making them. Reporters should be fully prepared in advance in order to rebut arguments in a sentence or two, then move officials with feeling, making sense and talking reason, so that they will think about losses they have caused the country, their role in increasing farmers' burdens, and any damage they have caused to the environment.

As I just mentioned, officials should also be constrained by law. If they make a mistake, they must correct it. Everything must be done in accordance with the law with absolutely no exceptions. I suggest that you strengthen your follow-up. There should be an outcome for everything you've reported on, and you should see if people have mended their ways—only then can you establish your authoritativeness. Of course the follow-up doesn't necessarily have to be broadcast on *Topics in Focus*. It can be reported with other news. This would also help reinforce public confidence.

Does Topics in Focus *Have Any Shortcomings?*

I truly haven't seen any great shortcomings. There was only one report—about a lawsuit between Tianjin Unicom and the Ministry of Posts and Telecommunications—that wasn't wrong but didn't show how extremely complicated these things are. And you shouldn't take the word of any one side too readily, nor come to a conclusion too soon. The presenter of that episode acted like a referee who had already made up his mind that the Ministry was wrong and Unicom was right—which wasn't necessarily so.

Many things are very intricate and complex. You have to be careful in reaching any conclusions; you have to have an all-round understanding of the origins of the problem, the history of the dispute, and current circumstances. The best thing would be to invite a responsible individual who is familiar with the situation to provide an assessment and act as a referee. The presenter shouldn't be the referee, because people would find that hard to accept.

Finally, on behalf of the Party Central Committee and the State Council, I want to express our heartfelt thanks to the entire staff of CCTV! You've done great work and I thank you!

9

Closing Down Guangdong International Trust and Investment Company Was the Right Thing to Do[1]

October 24, 1998

Why were we able to avoid a financial crisis? Because since 1993, we began to introduce forceful and timely measures to solve prominent problems exposed in our economy. In particular, we put an end to real estate fever and focused on rectifying the financial order as well as preventing and resolving financial risk. The only reasons for the Asian financial crisis were these:

—Economic structures were unsound; countries invested a lot of capital in real estate and built large high-grade buildings, but they had no pillar industries.

—Borrowing from abroad became uncontrolled: if they didn't have money, they would borrow from abroad, and what's more, much of it was short-term foreign debt. Through special relationships, government officials would have banks lend to large enterprise conglomerates, which ruined the banks.

—Governments were corrupt, personal ties were exploited, and officials colluded with businessmen.

We've all learned lessons from these problems. Although the ones that came to light in 1993 have yet to be fully resolved, and although RMB 500 billion to 700 billion—which is all bank money—is still locked up in real estate nationwide, we were ultimately able to prevent these problems from worsening. Furthermore, we kept a firm grip on our forex reserves, which are now the second largest in the world.

At an August 1996 meeting convened by General Secretary Jiang Zemin in Beidaihe, the central leading group on economics and finance studied in depth the issue of financial risk in our country and how to prevent it. In early 1997 the group met again to further study risk prevention and resolution. And in November 1997 the Party Central Committee and the State Council convened a national conference on financial tasks and made comprehensive plans for preventing and resolving financial risk.

---

1. These are some of the remarks made by Zhu Rongji during an inspection tour of Guangdong after listening to work reports by the provincial Party committee and provincial government.

Why did we recently close down the Guangdong International Trust and Investment Company (GITIC)? Some have asked, "Why didn't you rescue it? Why did it have to be closed down?" We felt that if there had been a way, we absolutely would not have closed it down, but there was no way, so we had no choice. After repeated studies by the central authorities and leaders in Guangdong, [we found that] neither the state nor the locals had the money to pay compensation, so, in accordance with international practice, GITIC's only course of action was to apply for bankruptcy. Henceforth we should review the experience of financial institutions that have closed down and implement bankruptcies as required by law. This sort of thing may continue to happen in the future. The overall reaction to this closing down of GITIC has been positive. Hong Kong newspapers remarked: "China really wants to carry out financial reforms, it's really determined, it dares to use a knife to cut out the tumors. This is the only way there'll be hope for China."

I hear that the international trade and investment companies of other provinces and municipalities are now feeling some pressure. Why? Because in the past foreigners all thought that local international trade and investment companies were guaranteed by the state, so they loaned money to these companies arbitrarily. Now they've taken a closer look and see that GITIC has been shut down, that they can't count on [these companies], so they're all pressing for repayment. I think this is a good thing: only by having people press for repayment will [these companies] understand that they shouldn't borrow money so readily. Better to have problems revealed early rather than late. The sooner the lid is taken off, the sooner we'll know what is going on. Even if the difficulties were greater, we'd be able to overcome them. Otherwise, we would sink in deeper and deeper, and it won't do to let things drag on like that.

After studying the closure of GITIC, the central authorities are stressing three points:

—*First, don't associate the closure of GITIC with reform and opening up.* And don't use it as a reason to reject Deng Xiaoping Theory and the path of reform and opening up.

—*Second, don't deny Guangdong's achievements in reform and opening up just because GITIC has been closed down.* Guangdong's achievements are a fact, and we mustn't let the closure of one investment company affect our evaluation of achievements. On the contrary, only by resolving the problems of these companies will we be able to ensure that Guangdong's reforms and opening up can make even better progress.

—*Third, Guangdong is still part of China, and the central government should help out if the province can't solve a problem.* That's why the Standing Committee of the Politburo and the Politburo discussed and approved the closure of GITIC. That was the only path to take, and the correct one. It is also the method that should be used in handling future cases of financial institutions with huge latent financial risks.

In a sense, Guangdong's problems are the price that has to be paid in the course of reform and opening up. Problems will invariably occur, and not just in Guangdong. We absolutely don't think Guangdong's problems are so enormous. Reform and opening up bring many new things. At first, we won't be familiar with or understand them, so problems of one sort or another, perhaps even very serious problems, are bound to occur. These are hard to avoid, but after paying "tuition," we must absorb the lessons, deal with things correctly, and straighten out our thinking. This will enable all our endeavors to develop healthily. We must be of one mind at all levels, work in unison, sum up the lessons of experience, and overcome our difficulties. I believe that Guangdong will now be able to progress even better, more steadily, and more rapidly.

10

A Conversation with Michael D. Eisner, CEO, the Walt Disney Company[1]

October 26, 1998

ZRJ: I've met the head of the Disney Company twice. Was it you I met with last time?

MDE: It was Frank Wells.

ZRJ: I welcome you, your wife, and your colleagues to China. I'm very familiar with the Disney Company. I visited Disneyland in Los Angeles, accompanied by Mrs. [Caroline] Ahmanson.[2] Unfortunately, I've never been to Disney World in Florida. I've also visited the Disneylands in Tokyo and Paris, but I've never paid admission on any of my visits. I've talked to both the former Disney CEOs about building a Disneyland in Shanghai. A piece of land had already been reserved when I was Mayor of Shanghai, and I felt it was the best piece of land. The last time I went to Shanghai, I asked them if they were still reserving it, and they said yes, they've been reserving it for 10 years. But I'm very disappointed that you've announced that you won't build any more Disneylands in Asia—is that true? The Hong Kong papers said that because you weren't interested in Lantau Island, you've lost interest in all of Asia.

MDE: The Hong Kong reports aren't true. First, let me thank you for agreeing to meet with us. Mrs. Ahmanson sends you her regards. I'm very pleased to be here. We've just come from Shanghai, and Shanghai's growth is astonishing. Many skyscrapers are growing in Shanghai like trees, again demonstrating the talent of the Shanghai city leadership. We were very happy to go along the highway from the Beijing airport into the city. My son particularly likes that highway and he's having fun at the Great Wall right now. We hope to engage in various high-quality projects, and at the same time we have in fact started bilateral cooperation with China. We've already invested $1.2 billion to produce consumer goods in China,

1. This conversation between Zhu Rongji and Michael D. Eisner, CEO of the Walt Disney Company, took place at the Hall of Purple Light in Zhongnanhai.
2. Caroline L. Ahmanson was then a board member of the Walt Disney Company and Vice Chairman of the National Committee on U.S.-China Relations.

and we showed the best movie—*Wonders of China*. That was the result of a bilateral agreement facilitated by Mrs. Ahmanson. However, I think this movie needs to be updated to include content on Shanghai. Our project to provide Mickey Mouse cartoons to China from 1986 to 1991 was also very successful.

I came to China for the first time in 1986, and since then China has also achieved great successes in protecting intellectual property and in shared box-office movie distribution. I very much appreciate how we've been having exchanges on a collaborative basis all along, but we made a stupid mistake in releasing *Kundun*.[3] I don't want to go into the details of that film release here. I didn't know anything about the release of that movie, though of course I realize that is no excuse. I learned about it from the *New York Times* and was shocked. Afterward, we released the film in the most passive way, but something unfortunate still happened. This film was a form of insult to our friends and it cost a lot of money, but other than journalists, very few people in the world saw it. The bad news is that the film was made; the good news is that nobody watched it. Here I want to apologize, and in the future we should prevent this sort of thing, which insults our friends, from happening. In short, we're a family entertainment company, a company that uses silly ways to amuse people.

Our strategy is to hope to broadcast Disney children's programs on Chinese TV and to establish a Disney channel and a Disney website to offer various educational programs, with everything linked together by a Disneyland. Everyone hopes to build a theme park in China like the ones in Los Angeles, Tokyo, and Paris. But the cost of building such a theme park is very high, and we will need a lot of people to visit there. If we can't build a high-quality theme park, not many visitors will go there. We also have some questions of expertise, such as on libraries and TV towers. We try to be the best of the best in expertise, and this is also a problem we have to confront. That's why I'd like to first show cartoons like Mickey Mouse and Donald Duck on Chinese TV, offering all kinds of products and information. When there's sufficient demand from the Chinese public for this type of product, then there'll be demand for building a Disneyland.

As for choosing a location for a Disneyland, I'd like to ask for your opinion. In Hong Kong our friends suggested several sites, and we're also very interested in Shanghai. The people in Hong Kong and Guangdong are richer, which would help support a theme park, but the people in Shanghai are also getting richer and richer. We're still considering both these places and would like to hear your views.

ZRJ: I very much admire your courage in correcting mistakes and the efforts you've made to promote Sino-American friendship. This also proves that you're

---

3. *Kundun* was a 1997 film directed by Martin Scorsese. It was a flattering portrayal of the life of the 14th Dalai Lama and a veiled attack on China.

a very far-sighted businessman, and it's also an important factor in ensuring the success of the Disney Company. As for building a Disneyland, if you're going to build one in Asia, you should build it in China, because everyone in the world acknowledges that China is the biggest potential market. Of course, some people are predicting that by 2010, and others predict that by 2030, China's GDP [gross domestic product] will surpass that of the United States. I think it's hard to say. We feel 2010 is impossible; as to whether we can catch up by 2020 or 2030, that will depend on China's own efforts. Even if we catch up in size, we still won't be able to catch up in technology. But no matter what, China will become Asia's largest market and will have a definite place in the world. So as a far-sighted businessman, it's time for you to make a decision.

MDE: Do you think the Disneyland should be built in Hong Kong or in Shanghai, or in both places?

ZRJ: The answer is very clear—Shanghai. I used to be Mayor of Shanghai. Now I'm working in Beijing, but I'm very familiar with Shanghai's position. Shanghai is the largest city in China. Shanghai's economic strength is greater than that of Hong Kong, especially in industry, science, and technology. There are 15 million people in Shanghai itself, and the richest parts of China—Jiangsu and Zhejiang provinces—are adjacent to it. Chinese people all want to visit Shanghai. If there were a Disneyland, even more tourists would go to Shanghai. Shanghai has very convenient land, sea, and air links, and China's first high-speed rail line will run from Beijing to Shanghai. If Disneyland were to be built in Hong Kong, it would be inconvenient for mainlanders to visit. It would be better to build it in Guangdong, in Zhuhai, for instance, because Hong Kong people could still go. But Hong Kong people also like going to Shanghai. They're all too familiar with Guangdong, and don't find it new anymore. If Disneyland were to be built in Shanghai, they would go there for fun, and transportation would be no problem.

In the next 10 to 20 years, Shanghai's growth rate will greatly surpass that of Guangdong, because it has the edge both in science and technology and also in management experience. Shanghai also has the greatest advantage of all: construction costs are very high in Guangdong. In Shanghai, the cost would be a third to a half less than in Guangdong, because Guangdong has learned from Hong Kong, and the cost of land there is extremely high, as are the costs of supporting facilities. It's not the same on the mainland. There are tall buildings everywhere in Shanghai—this is not necessarily a good thing. Many buildings are vacant, so land prices have come down. The Petronas Towers in Malaysia are the tallest in the world, even taller than the tallest structures in the United States, but their economy is still not doing well. The people in Shanghai want to build something even taller. I don't think you have to compete to see who's tallest. I

Meeting Disney Company Chairman and CEO Michael Eisner at the Hall of Purple Light, Zhongnanhai, Beijing, on October 26, 1998.

told them that rather than building the world's tallest building, they'd do better to build a Disneyland.

MDE: I've already been to Shanghai, and my instinct is the same as yours. You're very persuasive. I'd like to point out one difference between us in studying issues. In Hong Kong, the Disney Company's business has been established for a long time. There we have a TV channel and stores, and we're very well known. If we could establish a Disney Channel in mainland China to broadcast children's programs and if we could set up more stores, this would create the same conditions for a Disneyland in Shanghai as in Tokyo and Paris, which would ensure its success. Without such preparations, demand for a Disneyland would diminish over time. Unless 12 million to 15 million people visit it each year, Disneyland would become an empty structure. And we don't want an empty skyscraper.

ZRJ: There are 1.2 billion people in China, so to us, 12 million to 15 million people is not a big deal. China has 800 million farmers, some of whom are very wealthy. Even if we don't count the farmers, we still have 400 million to 500 million city dwellers who would want to have fun in Disneyland, so I can say with certainty that there would be far more mainland tourists than Hong Kong tourists. At the same time, Shanghai will become one of the world's economic centers. More and more foreign businessmen and tourists will be going to Shanghai, no fewer than the number going to Hong Kong.

Disney is already very famous in China—take Donald Duck, for example. The Chinese actor who dubs Donald Duck's voice is more famous than I am, and richer too. *The Lion King* is also very well known, and there aren't many children who haven't seen it. There's no country in the world where as many people have seen *The Lion King* as in China. I think there'll be no problem with Chinese visitors. As for having a TV channel and opening toy stores, these are not impossible, but we'll first have to come to an agreement—first you have to confirm that you'll build a Disneyland in China, and then I'll let you in.

MDE: You're a very good negotiator. We're not saying that all products have to be American. For example, we've produced many cartoons at the Shanghai Animation Film Studio. Besides Mickey Mouse and Donald Duck, we could show Chinese programs. The movie *Mulan* was very successful. We could continue to film a Mulan TV series, and the Chinese side could join in the filming. Mulan could also become part of a China Disneyland, and this would display its multicultural character. And, for example, 3D movies are more educationally meaningful to children and their parents. In Shanghai, we argued about the "chicken or egg" question: that is, should there first be a Disney Channel or a Disneyland. Our view is that once a Disneyland is built, it will attract a lot of Chinese investments, which will advertise on TV. Our hope is that they would advertise on the Disney Channel. The Shanghainese suggested that I bring this question to Beijing because only Premier Zhu can make the decision, so they told me to go to Beijing and negotiate with you.

ZRJ: The power to make the decision now rests with you. Once you decide to build in China, everything is easily open to discussion. If you don't make this decision, nothing can be discussed easily. As long as you make the decision, on the question of whether the chicken or the egg comes first, we can move things along together. Building a Disneyland will take several years, and while the construction is going on, your products can come in. Having both chicken and eggs together makes for a very tasty dish.

As for how to build the theme park, I also have a different opinion. You say your products are very multicultural. I think that Disney should, first and foremost, introduce foreign culture, particularly American culture. If you use Chinese culture to build a Disneyland, nobody would go. They can go to Xi'an to see the Terra Cotta Army, and to the Shanghai Museum to see the bronzes—they don't have to go to Disneyland. The question is very simple—once you make the decision, everything can be discussed, and a feasibility report can be written.

MDE: I agree to basically bring the Disneyland in Anaheim to China—I very much hope to do so. As for management, we will have to study how to establish a management mechanism that can avoid the effects of economic volatility. We will also have to study how to create a good partnership relationship. In Japan, we have very good relations with the Japanese side, and we're sure we will also have similar relations with China.

ZRJ: There's no problem in that regard. I wanted to build a Disneyland even when I was Mayor of Shanghai—I've had that dream for 10 years now. If you build a Disneyland there, there'll be very good cooperation between the two sides. If you use a shareholding system, we can provide land as equity. The cost of land would be lower than in Hong Kong and Guangdong, and of course management would be entirely in your hands.

MDE: During the negotiations in Shanghai, we said that we could operate on the American model, which is for the Disney Company to have full ownership. We could also refer to the European model, which is to create a listed shareholding company. We could even adopt the Japanese model, which is for the local company to have ownership of Disneyland. We would have no ownership rights and only provide copyrights, management methods, and experience. In China, we could also adopt this model: China would have the ownership rights and the two sides would manage jointly. We would provide copyrights, entertainment products, and animations. I hope to use this model.

ZRJ: We can talk about any model.

MDE: This purpose of my trip is to put an end to the problems caused by *Kundun,* and at the same time to introduce Mr. [Bob] Eiger, president of the ABC Company. We hope to cooperate with the Chinese side in reporting on the celebrations of the 50th anniversary of the founding of the People's Republic of China and how China greets the new century, and to introduce Chinese products that will be sold around the world. We are grateful for the results China has achieved in protecting intellectual property rights and hope to release *Mulan* in China. *Mulan* hasn't made much money—it mainly introduces China. I hope our relationship with China can get back on the right track and move further forward on this basis.

ZRJ: Regarding movies, this is Deputy Director Zhao of the State Administration of Radio, Film, and Television, and you can discuss many issues with her.

MDE: Thank you for taking the time out of your busy schedule to meet with us. May we send you a proposal after we get back?

ZRJ: That's a good idea.

11

"Tofu Dreg Projects" Are a Crime against the People[1]

December 3, 1998

An important policy measure adopted by our country to cope with the Asian financial crisis is to issue fiscal bonds to increase funding for infrastructure construction. The key to its success or failure lies in the quality and [economic] benefits of these infrastructure projects. Therefore "tofu dreg projects"[2] are a crime against the people. The Ministry of Transportation should inform the entire country of any quality problems in highway construction that it discovers, and it should expose them so that they come to the attention of Party and government leaders at all levels.

---

1. On November 2, 1998, Minister of Transportation Huang Zhendong submitted "Report on Effectively Controlling Quality in Highway Construction." It noted that the Ministry had organized experts to inspect some key transportation projects, and that while overall quality was good, some problems were also revealed. For example, the Kunming-Luquan highway in Kunming, Yunnan Province, had become a "tofu dreg project." These are Zhu Rongji's comments on the report.

2. Translator's note: "tofu dreg projects" are very flimsy construction projects of extremely poor quality. The dregs left from making tofu are a soft mush that cannot hold its shape.

采取财政发债的方式，增加基础设施建设的投入，是我国应对亚洲金融危机的重大改革措施，而成败的关键在于基础设施建设项目的质量和效益。因此，搞"豆腐渣"工程就是对人民犯罪。交通部应将查出的公路建设质量问题通报全国，公开曝光，引起各级党政领导的注意和重视。

朱镕基
12.5

关于切实抓好公路建设质量的报告

镕基总理：

今年党中央国务院为应对亚洲金融危机，作出了扩大内需、加快基础设施建设的重大决策，公路建设的投资力度比去年提高了 50%。从 1—10 月份统计资料分析是能够完成今年预定目标的，但是公路建设的质量问题必须引起我们高度重视，并要在落实上下功夫。今年

Zhu Rongji's directive regarding the "Report on Effectively Controlling Quality in Highway Construction."

12

Speech at the 1998 Central Economic Work Conference[1]

December 7, 1998

I'd like to share some thoughts on concrete plans for next year's economic work, focusing on six issues.

1. Economic Reforms and Development—A Basic Assessment

After the first session of the Ninth National People's Congress (NPC) last March, I spoke on behalf of the State Council in summarizing economic work for this year as "one assurance, three implementations, and five reforms." The "one assurance" was that we would maintain the economic growth rate at 8%. It now appears that we won't be able to ensure this, as the State Statistical Bureau estimates the rate will be 7.8%. The main reasons are as follows.

First, there is the impact of the Asian financial crisis on our country's economy. Although we had already recognized the crisis would have an adverse effect when we were in Beidaihe[2] last year and made some preparations, we underestimated the depth and breadth of its late-stage impact. However, our fiscal situation last year was relatively good. Besides reducing the deficit by RMB 5 billion, we did not [have to] issue RMB 15 billion of Treasury bonds as planned. Later, after asking for guidance from Jiang Zemin and Li Peng, we issued the entire RMB 15 billion. The purpose of keeping that money for this year was to deal with the Asian financial crisis. Altogether, RMB 18 billion was carried over and was all put into infrastructure construction. By July we could see that the impact of this RMB 18 billion was not nearly enough, so we issued another RMB 100 billion of Treasury bonds, matching them with RMB 100 billion of

1. On December 7–9, 1998, the Party Central Committee and the State Council convened a central economic work conference in Beijing. Participants included leading officials from the provinces, autonomous regions, centrally administered municipalities, cities separately listed in national plans, the Xinjiang Construction Corps, the departments concerned of the Party Central Committee and the State Council and their relevant units, the four main departments of the People's Liberation Army (PLA), and the People's Armed Police. This is the main part of Zhu Rongji's speech there.

2. Translator's note: Beidaihe is a popular summer resort located in Qinhuangdao, Hebei Province.

bank loans. These were also put into infrastructure construction, and only because of that will this year's annual growth rate stay barely above 7%. Where last year's exports increased by 20%, we planned on a 10% increase this year, but looking at things now, never mind 10%—even zero growth would be very good, although I fear there might be negative growth.

Second, no one expected the floods to inflict such enormous losses. They amounted to RMB 200 billion this time, losses suffered by people as well as by the railways, highways, telecoms, and other facilities. The Yangtze River was closed to navigation for a month, which had a huge impact on production. It's not hard to understand why economic growth did not reach the original target. Actually, it would be exceedingly unwise to force it up to 8%. Some in other countries say that China's desire to ensure an 8% economic growth rate means the reforms have come to a halt. This is incorrect and does not fit the facts. Our reforms are continuing to move toward our original goals and have not stopped.

As for the "three implementations," the first entails reform of state-owned enterprises (SOEs), which must resolve their difficulties within three years; the second financial reforms, to be completed within three years; and the third pertains to the streamlining of national government agencies, which must also be completed within three years. The "five reforms" apply to the grain circulation system, the housing system, the health care system, the investment and financing system, and the fiscal and taxation system. The "three implementations" and the "five reforms" are all progressing in accordance with our original plans. Some are moving a bit slower while others are moving even a bit faster and a bit better than expected. To reiterate, they have not come to a halt.

Regarding SOE reforms, "resolving their difficulties" means that the vast majority of large and medium SOEs should move from loss-making to profit-making within about three years. Over a year has passed, and on the whole, because of the effects of the Asian financial crisis and other factors, SOE problems have worsened and returns have fallen below last year's level. However, for the majority of SOEs, particularly the large enterprise groups, operations have not deteriorated so badly.

Two main issues must be addressed in turning enterprise losses into profits. One is redundant construction, which must cease. If such construction continues, products will have no markets; if enterprises cannot operate, they won't be able to turn around their losses. But if enterprises can refrain from starting up new processing projects and refrain from redundant construction for three years, I believe that the situation will change—that existing SOEs will be able to produce at full capacity and will have absolutely no problem turning losses into profits.

The other issue is that SOEs have too many people, as we found at quite a few places in Liaoning on a recent visit. Its nonferrous metals mines, coal mines, the Dazhiqiao magnesium mine, and Yangjiazhangzi molybdenum mine had depleted their natural resources, were without markets for their products, and yet supported several hundred thousand people. The amount of money they're losing every year is almost enough for a one-time resettlement of all these workers. That's why I asked Zhang Wule[3] and Zhang Baoming[4] to go to Liaoning this time. In a bold measure, we decided to shut down all the coal mines in Benxi and Fushun as well as all the nonferrous metal mines in Liaoning, except for a single copper mine. We just have to resettle all the people—that won't cost too much. Otherwise the annual losses will be staggering, which is why reducing staff and increasing productivity are both so important. We can't turn losses around without reducing staff, but in doing so we must resettle people properly.

Great progress occurred in this direction following the national work conference on reemployment convened by the Party Central Committee and the State Council. By the end of last year, over 10 million workers had been laid off, but current studies indicate that by the end of October this year, 99% of these workers had entered reemployment centers and are now receiving basic living expenses. I can't say this figure is completely accurate, but at least upward of 90% of the laid-off workers have entered reemployment centers, and this is a major achievement. Many other reform measures are under way at SOEs, such as reducing the number of cotton spindles and having shareholding enterprises, so you can see that SOE reforms are moving ahead. I continue to believe that the majority of large and medium SOEs will have no problem turning around their losses and will be basically out of difficulty within three years.

Regarding financial reforms, foreign media have said that in order to ensure an 8% economic growth rate, our banks have increased their lending to enterprises, the result being massive nonperforming loans. This argument is baseless. At one time, the banks were widely criticized for being stingy with loans. As I have repeatedly explained, the banks were not being stingy with loans—rather, this was the inevitable result of bank reforms. Banks must have their autonomy, and they must be responsible for their own profits and losses, so they can't be casual about lending. The idea of their being stingy with loans makes no sense. Moreover, banks appear to have improved their controls over nonperforming loans. We are in favor of banks also improving their attitudes toward serving local economic growth, but we can't force them to make loans. When we talk about ensuring the 8%, we've always emphasized striving for a beneficial growth rate, but we can't just produce stockpiles of goods.

In the case of national government agencies, reforms have proceeded far better than we had expected. We've trimmed people in State Council agencies from

---

3. Zhang Wule was then Director of the State Bureau of Nonferrous Metals.
4. Zhang Baoming was then Director of the State Bureau of Coal Industries (State Bureau of Coal Mine Safety).

33,000 to 16,000. The "three determinations"[5] plan has been approved, and new offices have already started operations. Of the 16,000 streamed off, most have been resettled, some are still being retrained, and some have taken early retirement in accordance with the relevant national policies. The fact that the work of persuasion had been handled quite well at the various departments guaranteed the smooth progression of this work.

Recently, both the Standing Committee of the Politburo and the Politburo discussed and passed a plan for reforming local government agencies, and a document to this effect will soon be released. In principle, the central government is proposing these requirements in this regard: first, the departments under provincial, autonomous region, and centrally administered municipal governments should basically correspond to those at the central level, as otherwise it will be hard to ensure that administrative orders are relayed smoothly and that the intent of the higher levels is communicated to the lower levels; and second, the staff of these provincial, autonomous regional, and centrally administered municipal levels should be reduced gradually and in stages by approximately one-half. We have not laid out any requirements for the regional, city, county, or township levels—these should be decided by the various provinces, autonomous regions, and centrally administered municipalities themselves.

As for the five reforms, I won't discuss them individually. Some are already being implemented. For example, there has been more than one conference each on reforms of the grain circulation system, housing system, and health care system. Plans have already been drawn up alongside documents and policies—[these reforms] are already under way. Because the subject is so important, we have to discuss investment and financing reforms carefully and cautiously. Another one with a wide-ranging impact is reform of the fiscal and tax systems, primarily the conversion of "fees into taxes"—our people are burdened with several hundred types of fees. We want to make the conversion of highway "fees into taxes" a breakthrough point. Li Lanqing has been in charge of multiple studies of this issue, and we had originally hoped to implement the idea as of January 1 next year. Because of differing views, however, it looks like it can't be implemented just now, although we still want to actively push this reform forward.

There's another problem: the profusion of fees is placing a very heavy burden on farmers. What's more, the fees "planned by the township and retained by the village" are directly collected by [local] officials, which affects their relations with villagers. Thus if we can incorporate those township-planned and village-retained fees into taxes and not have officials collect them directly, it would greatly improve their relations with villagers and lighten the burden of farmers. Of course, such a move would naturally extend to the collection of the

5. Translator's note: determining the functions, structure, and staffing of each agency.

other hundred-plus types of fees, which would all be folded into the agricultural tax. Many provinces are very interested in this reform and consider it a pressing matter. We hope that several provinces will take the lead next year and gain some experience in this regard. Farmers will be clapping for joy if this policy is handled well; it would also greatly help in the establishment of clean government and in improving relations between the officials and villagers. In sum, our reforms and development have basically achieved the goals we had set for them.

2. Our Overall Expectations for Next Year's Economic Work and Targets for Macroeconomic Controls

I feel that in many respects conditions are favorable for next year's economic work, and that political conditions in particular will be better than they were this year. But in terms of the international macroeconomic environment, things will be worse. Some are even predicting a serious global economic recession. I think it would be best for us to expect the worst. Particularly in light of this situation, we must stay with the policy of not devaluing the renminbi.

Why should we not attempt devaluation? First of all, it's for our own good. The only reason to devalue would be to increase exports, but in fact we might not be able to achieve such an increase. We take our trade relations with the southeastern Asian nations very seriously, of course, but given the situation in those countries right now, our goods cannot be sold there. We currently have a very large trade surplus with Europe and the United States, and if you try to further increase exports there, they'll use all sorts of means to oppose dumping. That's why we won't see much growth in exports to Europe and the United States either. Devaluation would be of little or no use.

If we were to devalue, people's confidence in the renminbi would immediately be shaken, and foreign commentators would rush to say that China is on the verge of collapse. That's why, no matter what, we must not let the renminbi be devalued next year, and our forex reserves must remain steady at $140 billion. We must fully consider what next year's international environment will be like. We expect a sizable drop in foreign trade next year. There was zero growth this year, and there will certainly be negative growth next year, but we hope the drop won't be too large. If it is, and if domestic demand remains as sluggish as it is now, we won't even be able to reach a 7% growth rate.

As I've repeatedly stressed, the current growth target of about 7% is not a prescribed goal. It is based on many factors and is only a projected figure or guideline. Actually it's best not to keep talking about 7% for next year. After all, what we want is economic benefits, not speed. The key is how much taxes will increase, how much profits will increase, whether quality will improve, whether there'll be a greater variety of products, and whether stockpiles will go down.

However, many difficulties will arise if we don't reach a 7% growth rate. Jiang Zemin already talked about this in the morning—for each percentage point below this figure, we will have to find employment for 800,000 to a million people. Below a certain growth rate, workers who are currently laid off will find it hard to increase their incomes, consumer demand won't go up, and social instability will ensue. Thus we don't want to force ourselves to reach a 7% growth rate, yet it would be best if we could do so.

3. We Must Continue to Increase Domestic Demand and Implement a Proactive Fiscal Policy

We cannot produce without demand, nor can we have a 7% growth rate. How, then, can we increase demand? We already have a bit of experience in this regard, namely, through increased infrastructure construction, which will increase production demand, which will then indirectly increase consumption demand. This policy has proved effective in practice. It has already yielded some results this year, although apparently they still aren't good enough. Next year we should continue to increase this demand. It won't work to rely solely on bank loans to increase demand—at the moment, industrial production capacity far exceeds demand, and the banks can no longer find any industrial projects that meet their criteria for lending. That's why the only area in which we can take action is infrastructure construction, although its rate of return is even lower than for industrial projects. As a result, the money must come from the fiscal authorities in the form of relatively long-term loans. That is, the Ministry of Finance will issue bonds to commercial banks, long-term bonds with maturities of 8 or 10 years. Therefore we must continue to implement a proactive fiscal policy next year.

In the coming year, we'll also face several major unusual circumstances. First, since we've already expanded the scale of infrastructure construction this year, relying just on this year's RMB 100 billion of Treasury bonds and RMB 100 billion of [bank] loans won't be enough. Projects were particularly hard hit by the severe flooding this year, and no one can guarantee that floods won't be as extensive during next year's rainy season. We must hurry up and repair these water-damaged projects before its arrival. We must reinforce the embankments along the Yangtze River, the Yellow River, and the other major rivers. Besides using a considerable portion of this year's RMB 100 billion in Treasury bonds for this, we will have to invest at least an additional RMB 30 billion.

The second [unusual circumstance] is that next year the army will have to be compensated for giving up commercial activities, science and education expenditures will have to be increased by the percentages required by law, and we'll also have to give subsidies for reemployment projects, among others. Next year's central fiscal outlays will exceed those of this year by RMB 141.6 billion, and there will be a fiscal shortfall of RMB 183.3 billion in balancing the central government's budget. Hence the central authorities have decided to issue another RMB 140 billion of Treasury bonds next year, and if that isn't enough, we may have to issue more.

Will there be any risk in this? We know that nobody wants to engage in deficit financing because if you keep using this tactic, it may spark inflation in the future. That's why we have said again and again that our long-term fiscal policy will still remain appropriately tight, and this has not changed. We are at present in an unusual period, facing a global financial crisis and excess production all over the world. Under the circumstances, we have no choice but to engage in infrastructure construction, but we can't do so unless the Ministry of Finance comes up with the money. And if the Ministry doesn't have the money, its only recourse is to borrow from the people.

So is there a possibility of inflation? I think the chances of this are very limited because our national strength is much greater in the wake of the macroeconomic adjustments of the past few years. We can first point to the success of our agricultural policies—farmers have become highly motivated, and grain is abundant. If grain prices don't go up, then associated prices, which account for almost 60% of the overall price index, won't be able to rise, and for the remaining 40–50% of consumer goods, supply exceeds demand. As a result, I feel that the conditions for inflation and for price increases do not exist. According to our calculations, the fiscal deficit and cumulative national debt will respectively amount to 1.4% and 10.9% of next year's GDP. These figures are markedly lower than the internationally accepted warning levels of 3% and 60%, and we can handle them.

Of course it's not that bank money is untouchable—it can also be used, for instance, in the rebuilding of the urban and rural power grids, particularly the rural grid. This is a major task that Jiang Zemin emphasized just today. Recently we've been shouting about opening up the rural markets, but how do we open them up? If farmers buy refrigerators and washing machines, they can only put them on display because they have no electricity! And even if they had electricity, the cost per kilowatt-hour is RMB 3, 4, 5, or even 6, so who could afford to use them? The price of urban electricity is only RMB 0.47! In order to open up the rural markets, the first step is to renovate the rural power grid and deliver electricity [to the farmers]. The central authorities have resolved to spend RMB 140 billion to complete this rebuilding within three years. But we have one condition here: first and foremost we must focus on reform. After the grid is completed, power costs must come down so that urban and rural power prices are comparable. This will be extraordinarily significant. Without these measures, there will be no demand, and enterprises won't be able to produce.

Of course we can't rely entirely on production demand, because it is ultimately an indirect demand, with another layer between it and direct consumption demand. That's why we still have to take some measures to increase people's desire and need to consume. In short, we have to increase demand in both production and consumption—only then will we be able to ensure a relatively rapid growth rate and ease our difficulties. We will definitely be extremely cautious about handling the fiscal deficit. The bonds issued must not be used for regular fiscal expenditures, but mainly for infrastructure construction. Once that construction reaches a certain level, once industry has revived, and supply and demand are in balance, we can stop issuing Treasury bonds.

4. Comprehensively Develop Agriculture and the Rural Economy

The 3rd Plenary Session of the 15th Party National Congress has issued a comprehensive document on agriculture and the rural economy that sums up our many years of experience in this area, so I won't go over it again. I just want to discuss two issues, one being the importance of adjusting the composition of agriculture. Right now, we have plenty of grain and cotton, as well as tobacco and other agricultural products. Therefore we need to reduce the production of early indica rice in the south, while spring wheat and corn in the north mustn't increase by much—we have to adjust the area of land under cultivation. Since our grain prices far exceed those in international markets, we also have to adjust the composition of agriculture. In any event, we have to think about growing crops of higher quality that sell better and mustn't promote crops that are already plentiful.

The second issue has to do with the construction of waterworks. I just want to emphasize that these must be built to last for a century, and their quality must be guaranteed. The quality of newly built and repaired embankments, in particular, must be guaranteed. The central government has given very high priority to infrastructure construction, and we hope that local governments will do likewise—don't waste any more money on industrial projects and whatnot.

We recently discovered, however, that locals are not living up to a "gentleman's agreement" whereby the central government would subsidize the cost of construction materials for people in flooded areas to rebuild homes, would turn farmlands over to lakes, resettle people, and build towns, while the locals would pay for infrastructure construction. Some locals are not paying for infrastructure construction but instead using some of the central government's subsidies for this purpose, which only increases the burden on farmers. I raise this subject because the building of waterworks and the repair of flood-damaged projects affect the stability of the rural areas. Local governments must treat this as an extremely important task and be willing to spend money on it.

As for the construction of small cities and towns, we've always asked the Ministry of Construction to strengthen its planning capacities in this regard. Particularly in the flooded areas, it must seize this opportunity to do a good job

Inspecting Granary No. 3 in Dalian, Liaoning Province, in November 1998.

of planning and building small cities and towns. Don't wind up with villages that look like cities and cities that look like villages.

5. Do a Good Job of Preventing and Mitigating Financial Risk

The greatest risk right now is financial risk. The rise in the proportion of non-performing loans is alarming, and what's more, it's growing from month to month. The reason is very simple—too many debts owed to banks have become doubtful loans yet haven't been written off, so all the overdue interest is still kept on the books, turning them into nonperforming loans, which are snowballing. What is the proportion of nonperforming loans right now? Dai Xianglong[6] gave

6. Dai Xianglong was then Governor of the People's Bank of China.

me a figure today: by the end of 1997 it had reach 28.66% at the four state-owned banks, rising to 31.38% in September of this year.

Of course one has to distinguish between nonperforming loans and doubtful or bad loans. The proportion of doubtful loans and bad loans at these four banks is currently 7–8%. Percentagewise, Guangdong has the largest share of nonperforming loans, accounting for 15% of the nationwide total; Liaoning is second, with 7%. At the city level, Hainan is at the top of the list, with 54.28%, or over half of its loans in this category. My old home province of Hunan isn't far behind: it's in second place at 49.63%, Guangxi is third at 46.86%, Heilongjiang is fourth at 43.44%, Hubei fifth at 42.86%, followed by Guizhou at 41.52%, Liaoning at 40.6%, and Guangdong at 40.23%. Whose percentages rose the fastest from January to September of this year? It was Guangdong, Guangxi, and Hainan.

I hope everyone will take note and stop interfering in the operations of financial institutions. The proportion of nonperforming loans at state-owned banks is now so high that they can't even be recovered. How can this be? Still more alarming is the fact that the proportion of nonperforming loans at local financial institutions is even higher. Recently, with the approval of the central authorities, the Guangdong International Trust and Investment Company was shut down. There was no choice in the matter! It couldn't repay original debts amounting to $1.8 billion, which then rose to $1.9 billion, and two days later turned into $2.4 billion. To this day the firm still hasn't figured out exactly how much debt it owes.

The announcement of GITIC's shutdown caused quite a shock, although the reaction was mainly positive as everyone felt this reflected the Chinese government's determination to straighten out the financial order. If we hadn't made this move and taken the opportunity to rectify the financial situation, then what with over 200 international trust and investment companies across the country, we would have faced great financial risk and things could have gotten out of hand. That's why no matter what, we must rectify the financial order and prevent financial risk from escalating.

The main reason that the Central Committee decided to form a Committee on Financial Work last year and to strengthen the Party's leadership over the financial sector was to ensure that the state-owned banks have an environment in which they can operate autonomously. In our reforms this year, we consolidated 30 branches of the People's Bank into 9 regional branches, the purpose of which was also to strengthen oversight—I hope you will understand and appreciate the central authorities' policy measures. We're planning to soon conduct a training seminar on finance for the Party secretaries and governors (or chairmen and mayors) of provinces, autonomous regions, and centrally administered municipalities, because we had previously conducted such a seminar for deputy Party secretaries and vice governors (or vice chairmen and vice mayors) with very good results. We're conducting training seminars in finance for principal leaders because many of them have never done financial work, and if they don't try to understand this work, we will make some major mistakes, the consequences of which will be hard to reverse.

We recently discovered, after converting urban cooperative banks into commercial banks, that municipal Party secretaries and mayors in some locales issued documents ordering all large enterprises to shift their deposits to the commercial banks in their cities. As a result, everyone withdrew their deposits from state-owned banks and put them into urban commercial banks. One city in particular—inasmuch as we had said that urban commercial banks could have shareholding systems—told a power company to buy shares and then asked all the company's enterprises to transfer their deposits to this commercial bank. How could this happen? It is going to create financial risk! It won't do for the government to intervene in the actions of enterprises and banks! Work must be done in accordance with established laws. That's why leading officials need to acquire a bit of financial knowledge.

6. Use Every Means Possible to Increase Exports and Utilize Foreign Investment Effectively

On the one hand, we have to expand domestic demand, but on the other we must use every means possible to increase exports. Increasing exports to Europe and the United States is definitely going to be somewhat difficult because they will instigate a lot of antidumping measures. This requires us to diversify our exports. We should think of ways to export to developing countries, remote places, poor places—provided they have forex. Moreover, I feel that in increasing exports, we can't rely solely on exporting goods. Not long ago, the prime minister of Morocco visited China and discussed with me [the possibility of] our purchasing its phosphate and ammonium phosphate. But its phosphate and ammonium phosphate are incredibly expensive, so we can't possibly afford them! I suggested that instead we set up factories in his country. After all, we in China got our start through the "3 + 1 industries,"[7] which proved very beneficial for us. We can establish "3 + 1 industries" in his country. Whatever consumer goods it wants, we can ship the production equipment over and produce there. That would increase the country's employment, and it could even substitute production for imports and save some forex. It could even export some of the processed goods to other countries. We need to encourage the processing trade to "go out" because our stage of development has already passed that of some

---

7. Translator's note: that is, industries that process imported materials, base their work on imported samples, assemble imported parts, and engage in compensation trade.

developing nations. We can supply the equipment, they can supply the land, and we can have joint-venture operations—this is a workable path.

As for utilizing foreign investment, the point to emphasize is that it must be used effectively—we can't keep bringing in more surplus production capacity to engage in redundant construction. At the moment, foreigners are actively trying to sell us their surplus goods, all the surplus goods in the world. They come here to engage in joint ventures because they want to take over our markets. That's why we must be on our guard at all costs. We must study the markets and keep the overall picture in mind, rather than just consider the interests of one's own locality. I don't want you to engage in joint ventures that produce goods that swamp the market and lead SOEs in other provinces to collapse. That's why in bringing in foreign investment, if it doesn't really introduce new technologies and new product types, you shouldn't engage in any joint ventures—they won't do much good.

Finally, a word on actively implementing the strategy of revitalizing the nation through science and education: I want to stress that enterprises need to pay attention to developing technologies and not simply expand production capacity—they should fund technology development. At the same time, it is essential to attract talented people and work closely with scientific research and educational institutions. Only when we manage to do this will China's industries be able to turn themselves around. Basic scientific research should be part of this effort. On a recent visit, Chinese-American physicist T. D. Lee[8] criticized us for failing to attach great importance to high-energy physics and for underfunding it, whereas Deng Xiaoping fully recognized its value. I think we really do need to strengthen our basic scientific research.

In sum, next year's reform, development, and stability effort will be a very heavy burden. We must keep our spirits up and endeavor with one heart and mind to do even better economic work next year.

8. The Chinese-American physicist T. D. Lee was co-winner with C. N. Yang of the 1957 Nobel Prize in Physics.

13

HAINAN MUST KEEP ITS HILLS GREEN AND ITS WATERS BLUE[1]

December 19, 1998

If Hainan is to develop its economy, the first thing it must focus on is agriculture, as agriculture has very good prospects there. This is an island full of treasures, and protecting its environment is of the utmost importance—it mustn't start any polluting projects. Hainan should be a place of green hills and blue waters, of red bricks, and green roof tiles. With excess industry all over the world and everyone competing for markets, Hainan mustn't engage in any ordinary industries. It must do well in agriculture, and it must do well in tourism.

Yangpu should launch several good, presentable projects, new hi-tech projects with high value added that don't create pollution. Another option is to create a high value-added processing zone, but the problem there is that competition from Southeast Asia is very intense. It would be wonderful if American and Japanese investors were to come to Yangpu and start up processing projects that would sell their products in Southeast Asia, but this would be very hard to do because there aren't many feasible projects right now. Shenzhen has hi-tech enterprise groups. Huawei has the latest technologies, and it has talented people who have mastered these technologies, which is why it has grown so rapidly. Without the talent, how can you expand hi-tech? Over the long term, Hainan will still have to work on high value added, hi-tech, and nonpolluting projects.

Another possibility would be foreign-invested projects. I've never said that no such projects should be agreed to. Provided they don't involve redundant construction and don't require matching funds from our banks, such projects can be arranged. Ethylene projects mustn't be allowed either. There's already a global glut of ethylene, and we absolutely must not start up any more projects of this kind. Yangpu already has a paper pulp project, and it will also be starting up several other projects, including flour milling and optical fibers. You still need to find a few more decent projects. The critical issue for petroleum processing is

---

1. During an inspection trip to Hainan Province on December 18–22, 1998, Zhu Rongji visited Sanya and Haikou. These remarks were made during conversations with provincial Party Secretary Du Qinglin and Governor Wang Xiaofeng.

Inspecting the courtyard economy of a Li farming family in Tianya Township, Sanya, Hainan Province, on December 19, 1998. (Photograph by Liu Jianguo, Xinhua News Agency)

the lack of markets—if there are no markets, they mustn't be started up. Shipbuilding projects should also be prohibited because they cause pollution.

Hainan is integrating the construction of its power grid with reforms of its power management system—this is very good; in fact it is imperative. The power grid must be rebuilt properly to ensure that electricity prices on the same grid are the same for all users. This is hugely important to the revitalization of Hainan. Agricultural development requires electricity, as does any effort to lift areas out of poverty. We must make it possible for more farmers to have access to electricity, that is, to low-cost electricity.

In order to rectify their losses, some enterprises will have to eliminate the causes. If enterprises have no markets, create pollution, and can't support their staff, how can they not shut down? There's more to be gained than lost in shutting down this sort of enterprise.

Hainan's development must follow high standards. Better to do it a bit more slowly than to let it get out of hand. The government must not put its energies into starting up industrial projects, especially those that engage in redundant construction, and it must not focus on projects that have no markets. What the government must concentrate on is improving the investment environment and attracting investors, while also collecting the taxes. Infrastructure construction in Hainan must be done well. Once there is a good environment, foreigners will come, and the talent will come—under no circumstances should you sacrifice core interests for peripheral gains. Infrastructure must be built to last a hundred years and must be scientifically planned. Hainan is now the only island of treasures we have left—it is far too precious. This is a very special place, a very precious place—you must develop this island of treasures well.

Cities like Sanya cannot be in charge of their own city planning. It won't do for city planning not to be controlled by the province. What I'm worried about in Sanya's urban development is the haphazard construction of buildings. With such a fine climate, fine conditions, fine environment—how can we not manage its planning well? The provincial government must handle urban planning well. Moreover it must strengthen oversight. The city government should mainly implement the plan. The provincial government must pay more attention to the infrastructure construction of the entire province—where ports should be built, where highways should be built—and the provincial governor must have firm control over the overall plan. I hope you'll remember this word of warning: don't build cities that look like villages, and don't build villages that look like cities.

14

Ensure Construction Quality of the Three Gorges Project and Properly Resettle the Area's Inhabitants[1]

December 30, 1998

My main purpose in coming to the Three Gorges at this time is to inspect the quality of the engineering work and the resettlement of the residents from the area around the reservoir, in order to prepare for next year's conference on resettlement work. The Three Gorges Project is an exceptionally large project of global significance not only for the new millennium but also for the ages. Indeed, the whole world is watching. The Party Central Committee and State Council attach great importance to it and have made many decisions [about it]. We must abide by the decisions and directives of the central authorities and employ effective measures and every means possible to ensure the quality of the project—we must not slacken up in the least.

The Three Gorges project is currently at a critical stage of its Phase 2 construction. We should carefully review our experiences thus far, refine policies, properly resettle the people displaced from the reservoir area, and improve the ecological environment. The impact of this work will be felt for a thousand years and will have bearing on the future of the nation—it is a major task that we must handle well. I recently looked at some materials on the construction of the Three Gorges project; in the past few days I also visited sites to inspect construction quality and to better understand the circumstances of the resettlement work. Now I'd like to discuss several thoughts.

The Quality of the Three Gorges Project Requires Close Attention

On the whole, the quality of project construction across the country has been quite good over the past few years. However, some regions, departments, and units have experienced very grave accidents caused by the neglect of quality,

---

1. On December 28–30, 1998, Zhu Rongji went on an inspection tour of the Three Gorges Dam project and its reservoir site. He also made inspection visits to Chongqing and Yichang. These are the remarks he made at the reservoir site after listening to Hubei Province reports on the resettlement of displaced people and on dam construction.

Visiting technicians on-site at the Three Gorges Project on December 29, 1998. (Photograph by Wang Xinqing, Xinhua News Agency)

violations of construction procedures, lax enforcement and oversight, chaos in the construction markets, and serious corruption. The country's interests and the lives and property of its people have suffered great losses as a result. We must employ powerful measures to solve these problems in earnest.

The Three Gorges Project has the potential to rank as the world's largest hydropower project, and its success or failure will be determined by its quality. Technically speaking, the project has no insurmountable difficulties, but even "a thousand-mile-long embankment can collapse because of ant holes." Provided we focus firmly on its quality, the Three Gorges Project will succeed. Quality is its lifeblood, and responsibility for quality is greater than Mount Tai: the slightest carelessness will bring disaster to future generations. To add to the importance of ensuring its construction quality, any quality problem with the main dam will render it unsalvageable. The main dam is being built with poured concrete, so flaws may not be visible on the outside. If [internal] gaps were to occur, turning it into a "tofu dreg project," and if they are not discovered in a timely fashion, then the hidden dangers would cause irrecoverable losses. Therefore we must pay utmost attention to the quality of construction.

The current Phase 2 of the construction is extremely important. Each and every person involved in the building of the Three Gorges Project must have a sense of historical responsibility, must have a spirit of being highly responsible to the country, to the people, and to future generations, and must be thoroughly imbued with the idea that "quality is the number-one priority" so as to ensure that the quality of the Three Gorges Project is first-rate. There must be all-round and effective controls at every link throughout the entire process, beginning with the quality of the designs, equipment, raw materials, and work. Every step of the project must be fully prepared for, carefully organized, meticulously executed, and strictly monitored. Not a single screw should be overlooked, and we must make sure that there are absolutely no mistakes, that we are not creating any hidden dangers.

To ensure the quality of the Three Gorges Project, we must seriously implement a system of having legal persons do the project bidding, project oversight, and contract management. In other words, quality must be managed under a standardized, institutionalized, and law-based system.

1. The Legal Person in Charge of the Project. This legal person must have a strong sense of responsibility and must assume full responsibility. The head office of the China Three Gorges Project Corporation is the legal person for the Three Gorges project. The central government has entrusted you with this project, and you are responsible for its planning and construction. Yours is a major task— you must be responsible to the Party Central Committee, to the State Council, to history, and to future generations, and you must ensure the quality and on-time completion of the project.

First of all, the leading officials at all levels of the head office must have a strong sense of responsibility and a strong sense of historic mission. You must start with a broad political perspective, must see the big picture, must take your responsibilities seriously, and handle all the various tasks of the project well. And you must pay attention a hundredfold or a thousandfold to the quality of construction without the slightest slacking off.

Second, you must continually raise the overall caliber of the entire construction corps. The quality of the project's construction will be determined by the caliber of the construction corps. You must step up education and training of the staff and strengthen political and technical studies to ensure that you can provide reliable organization and talented people for top-quality construction of the Three Gorges Project.

Third, you must strengthen inspections and management of the construction and supervising units as well as other units involved in the project. If any rules are violated, if supervising units indulge in fakery or favoritism, such actions must be rigorously investigated and punished; if the offenses are serious and violate criminal laws, they must be punished as required by law. You must also strengthen oversight of other related units and prevent corruption.

Fourth, you must keep strict watch over the quality of equipment and materials. The construction materials and equipment provided to the Three Gorges Project should be the best in our country. If any unit involved in the project commits fraud and causes a major quality-related accident, the persons responsible in that unit should be severely punished as required by law. The project's quality directly affects the safety of the people's lives and property! When we protected the embankments along the Jing River this year, we were protecting the lives and property of the million or more people in the Hong Lake area and of the 8 million or more living in the Jianghan plain. If any quality-related accident were to occur at the Three Gorges dam, the consequences would be unthinkable. That's why each and every unit, each and every person who participates in the Three Gorges Project must, even if they are only making a single screw, be responsible to our country and to our people. This is your duty, and it is your honor. If the Three Gorges Project is well built, it will demonstrate not only the general technical and management standards of China, but to some degree also the general technical standards of the world. The equipment used for the Three Gorges Project was purchased from around the world through international bidding. Even if we don't dare claim that it is the world's best, we can at least say it's quite good.

2. *Project Supervision.* You must strengthen the supervision of project construction. The companies you select for this purpose must be well qualified, careful, responsible, and strict in enforcing laws so they will be able to comprehensively supervise and inspect the quality and progress of project construction without regard for sentiment or face. For certain key parts of the project, you can engage internationally renowned, reputable, and experienced supervision companies to help with this task. They are more experienced than we are, they have a strong sense of responsibility, and they don't worry about sentiment and face. Of course we must rely principally on supervisors trained from our own ranks and rely on our own abilities to strengthen supervisory work. Project supervisors must be true to their professional ethics, execute their duties carefully, and discharge their obligations to the project solidly.

We must also institute a system of on-site supervision; each step of the project must be supervised, and we cannot be lax at any point. Work must proceed under standardized and strict systems with a legal base to ensure that everything is error-free. I am the backstop for the supervisors of this project—if you have any problems, you may write to me directly. I believe that whatever foreigners can do, we, too, can do, provided we take it seriously.

3. *Bidding System.* You must insist on using the bidding and contract system. The state has now clearly mandated open bidding for survey and design work, construction, and purchases of major equipment and materials for construction projects. When it is truly necessary to have tenders made through invitation or negotiation, these must be approved by the department or the local government having jurisdiction over the project. Bidding and tenders must be handled

strictly in accordance with the relevant national regulations and demonstrate the principles of openness, fairness, impartiality, honesty, and selection of the best qualified. In cases where open bidding departs from the regulations, or where invitations to bid or to negotiate tenders are unauthorized, the local governments and departments concerned must not permit work to begin. The units supervising the project should also be chosen through competition to ascertain who is best qualified. The Three Gorges Project must strictly abide by national rules on bidding and absolutely must not engage in fake bidding or tendering.

Late last year, the Kunming-Luquan highway in Yunnan ran into problems because of this. In order to serve local interests, they conducted fake bidding and allowed a company with no experience whatsoever in building highways of Grade 2 or above to "win" the bid, so ended up with a "tofu dreg project." Henceforth, if we uncover such a problem in any locations, all project funding will be cut off, no projects from that locale will be accepted for review, and the incident will be publicized. We absolutely must not waste our country's taxpayers' money as if it were the "flesh of Monk Xuanzang of the Tang."[2] If we did so, we would be letting both the country and the people down.

You must also implement a system of contract management. Contracts must be signed in accordance with the laws for project surveying and designing, construction, equipment and materials purchase, and supervision. Each type of contract must have explicit requirements for quality, for performance guarantees, and for fines should the contract be violated. Violating parties must assume the associated legal and economic liabilities.

Resettlement of the Population from the Reservoir Area Must Also Be Handled Well

Over the past few years, the work of resettling people from the reservoir area has been carefully conducted according to the principle of the central authorities regarding the "double-contracting outs"[3] for funds and tasks. This approach has achieved a great deal, provided some useful experience, allowed the first phase of resettlement to be completed, and ensured that the river flow could be cut off as scheduled. The period from 1998 to 2003 will be the most difficult stage of the second phase of resettlement. 550,000 [urban and rural] people will have to be moved and resettled to ensure that the water storage, power generation, and

2. Translator's note: This refers to an episode in the classical novel *Journey to the West*. Various demons and devils wanted to eat the flesh of Monk Xuanzang, believing that this would make them immortal. The term is now used as an allusion to something that, because it confers great benefits, is sought after by many at all costs.

3. The "double-contracting outs" are the contracting out of the relocation of residents and the contracting out of the investing of funds for compensating those who are relocated.

navigation can be completed by 2003. Time is very tight, and the work is even more onerous and difficult now. You must shore up your confidence, strengthen leadership, broaden your vistas, refine your measures, and make sure that the resettlement target is reached.

What means should we use to resettle the 405,000 villagers from the reservoir area? What new means of livelihood can we develop for them? We have now accumulated considerable successful experience in this regard, and also learned many instructive lessons, and uncovered many inadequacies. The Three Gorges Reservoir area exemplifies the sharp contradiction between having too many people and little land. In resettling, we must avoid causing new soil erosion, and must restore the green hills and blue waters along the banks of the Yangtze. We must adopt effective measures so that after the villagers have migrated, they will have a means of production, their standard of living will not decline, and there will be ways they can gradually become rich. In a word, we must make it possible for the migrating villagers to move out, to enjoy stable lives, and to grow richer.

That's why we must steadfastly maintain a policy of using diverse methods to resettle these villagers. We must adapt to the terrain and combine local and outward relocation, concentrated and dispersed placement, government and self-placement. In particular, we have to come up with policies that encourage outward migration, which should preferably be resolved by this province and this municipality, and should encourage farmers to turn to their own friends and relatives. Of course the government must use macroeconomic controls to manage this. Those migrants who turn to friends and relatives in other places should be enthusiastically accommodated by the local governments; those who move en masse beyond this region or this province should be warmly welcomed by the local governments, which should help them settle down and develop livelihoods—they must not levy one fee after another.

En masse migrations should be organized and planned and must not turn into blind flows [of people] that could disrupt social order. Governments receiving them must be supportive—these are called "migrants with capital": they come with money and should be welcomed by any locale. Some of the migrants might be placed in Xinjiang and Heilongjiang, for example, but this must be carefully considered and meticulously arranged—there must be no coercion.

When I talk about encouraging outward migration, it doesn't mean I don't attach importance to migrating nearby. It's just that most migrating farmers will want to settle down nearby—they know the area and the people, and find this easier to accept—but there has to be a major precondition: namely, there must be no further destruction to the environment, to the hills and forests or to the water and soil. The state has invested money in the reservoir area to build roads, plant forests, construct infrastructure, and protect the slopes and riverbanks.

The purpose of these projects is to protect the environment, and they can also absorb a great deal of rural labor, allowing a portion of the migrants to settle locally. Governments at all levels in the reservoir area must think of more methods along these lines; they must come up with more ways to both properly resettle the migrants and yet not destroy the natural environment.

Plan Relocation and Build New Towns Sensibly and Proceed According to Ability and in Stages

The size of new towns can't be expanded at will and go beyond what the plans call for. According to the relocation and building plans drawn up by the Yangtze River Water Resources Commission of the Ministry of Waterworks and approved by Hubei Province and Chongqing Municipality, new county seats will, on average, be 2.4 times larger than the present seats. Even at this scale of construction, the work must be done in steps and be gradually phased in. However, some locales did not build new county towns that complied with the planned scale. Rather, they drew up their own plans and made the new county towns four or five times larger than the old ones. The planned scale of the new towns is already quite generous. To increase it at will during actual operations would be committing a historic mistake, which must be resolutely corrected. Increasing the size of new county towns at will not only creates a fiscal burden that will be hard to cope with, but it also has the potential to cause endless ecological harm along both banks of the Yangtze.

The related rules stipulate that on slopes exceeding 25 degrees no new land may be put under cultivation, no forests may be destroyed to create farmland, and land already under cultivation must be reverted to forests in a planned and orderly manner; farmland on slopes below 25 degrees must be remade into high-standard terraced fields that prevent soil erosion. This means there isn't much land left in the reservoir area for new towns. How many places are left that meet the conditions for expanding the scale of new towns? If localities ignore realities, pursue only projects that are large and all-inclusive, and enlarge the scale of new towns at will, they will occupy more farmland, dig up mountains, destroy forests, destroy planted slopes, and cause erosion.

That's why I say again: the moving of migrants and construction in the reservoir area must be planned sensibly, must proceed according to capacity, absolutely must not be detached from the realities of the reservoir area, must not blindly set high standards regardless of fiscal and material limits, and must not arbitrarily expand in scale. All levels of government in the reservoir area must treat this as a key task. Plans for new towns that exceed the required scale and standards must be resolutely amended. Even construction that accords with plans must be implemented in steps and be put in place year by year—don't

In conversation with a migrant family at the Yinxingtuo New Migrants Village in the new county seat of Zigui County, Hubei Province, on December 30, 1998. (Photograph by Wang Xinqing, Xinhua News Agency)

rush to get results, and don't try to do at once things that should be done years from now.

Decisions on building their new homes should be made by migrant farmers on the basis of their own economic capacities. The government must plan meticulously but must not force farmers to build according to a single standard, or require homes to have a certain number of stories or a certain external appearance. You can delineate zones for farmers' residences and you can have a master plan designating where each family is allowed to build; you can also forbid people to build wherever they please. Don't guide them into using all their money for building homes; rather, guide them in developing production.

Before building new towns and launching the various resettlement projects in the Three Gorges reservoir area, we must do solid studies and assessments of the geological environment, do better geological surveys, and make sure geological disasters do not occur. We have to maintain a well-balanced relationship between construction for resettlement and environmental protection, and we have to work hard to coordinate economic construction, placement of migrants, and environmental development, so that we may leave green hills and blue waters for the Chinese people, and at the same time transform the reservoir area into a new type of economic zone with a thriving economy and a beautiful environment where people can live and work happily.

Enterprises in the Reservoir Area Should Not Be Relocated As Is, and Should be Closely Integrated with Adjustments to the Post-Migration Economic Structure and with the Enterprise Structure

In moving industrial and mining enterprises out of the area to be submerged by the Three Gorges reservoir, we must resolve to eliminate those enterprises with obsolete products and aging equipment, those that pollute the environment and destroy [natural] resources, or those whose debts outweigh assets—these must not be relocated as is. Otherwise, they will generate new losses and pollution. At the same time, given that production capacity exceeds demand for industrial products nationwide, enterprises should not be relocated or rebuilt unless they manufacture famous brands or outstanding and truly competitive products.

The Three Gorges project is providing a rare opportunity—one that comes but once a millennium—to restructure enterprises in the reservoir area. We must seize this opportunity and put our energies into adjusting the structure of the economy, seeking out new economic growth points, and increasing overall economic benefits. There are good enterprises in the reservoir area but not many of them. The vast majority have outdated products, backward technology, weak management, and serious losses. They are a burden on the state and should be shut down, suspended, merged, or transferred. If we don't seize this chance to restructure and instead move and rebuild the small cement factories, chemical factories, and paper mills as is, they will continue to pollute, destroy resources, and do no good for the country. All levels of government in the reservoir area must integrate the moving of industrial and mining enterprises with adjustments to the economic structure and enterprise organization.

Use this opportunity to shut down a batch of the "five small enterprises."[4] Only by doing so will you avoid redundant construction and make the economic structure of the reservoir area more rational; only then will you stop discharging industrial waste water into the Yangtze, effectively protect the ecology of the reservoir area, and promote sustainable and healthy economic development there.

At present, the national markets are a buyer's market: supply exceeds demand, and there is a surplus of most industrial products. The State Council is no longer approving any new industrial construction projects. The entire country should focus on adjusting the economic structure, even more so in the reservoir area. This is the only way out. The state is investing a large sum of money in the Three Gorges reservoir area. If you don't focus on structural adjustment and

---

4. The "five small enterprises" are the small oil refineries, thermal power plants, steel mills, glass factories, and cement factories that rely on outmoded technologies, waste resources, manufacture poor-quality products, pollute the environment, and fail to meet production safety regulations.

if the reservoir area enterprises are simply moved as is, you will immediately be burdened with new losses. Such an attitude would shirk one's responsibility to the country, to the people, and to future generations, and is impermissible. This matter demands the utmost attention from all levels of government.

Strengthen Supervision of Funds for Project Construction and Resettlement

The funds for the Three Gorges project and for settlement were not easy to come by. Every penny must be spent on project construction and on the migrants and must absolutely not be misused or eaten up level by level. We must strengthen supervision and auditing of the way these funds are spent and utilize them more effectively. State auditing agencies and the Bureau of Supervision of the Three Gorges Project Construction Commission must inspect more forcefully and audit every single level. We must send a team of upright and selfless comrades to audit constantly and to deal strictly with problems uncovered through their audits. We must increase transparency and inform the public of major problems.

Some individual officials have total disregard for Party discipline and national laws, and their corruption is astounding. They must be dealt with strictly. Some cases of corruption have already surfaced in the China Three Gorges Project Corporation, which is under the supervision of Three Gorges Project Relocation and Development Bureau. These must receive strict and serious attention. Henceforth the relocation and development bureaus at all levels will not be allowed to run companies and must delink themselves as soon as possible from companies they have already set up. As a government agency designated the highest leadership agency for construction of the Three Gorges project, it should be focusing on implementing plans and policies and on performing audits—it must not run enterprises.

We must establish a rigorous auditing system that employs standardized and institutionalized methods. In accordance with the principle of contracting for quotas, we should strengthen the management of funds, increase transparency in their use, and ensure that special funds fulfill their designated purposes. By comparison, money for resettling migrants is to be used in a more diffuse way and at many more levels. Problems are more likely to occur here than with project construction funds, so the management of this money needs to be handled even more carefully and seriously. We must strictly forbid the contracting out, level by level, of projects to move and rebuild for migrants, and we must strictly forbid the sale of land designated for [such] construction. We must absolutely not allow resettlement money to be squandered in disguised forms.

15

A Conversation with Alan Greenspan, Chairman, U.S. Federal Reserve[1]

January 12, 1999

ZRJ: Mr. Greenspan, your role in the U.S. economy is becoming greater and greater, and you've already gone from a human being to a god. Last December, the U.K. *Financial Times* published an article saying that you're allowing the U.S. stock market bubble to continue growing, and it pointed out that short-term success may lead to a major collapse of the financial markets in the future. Do you have any thoughts on this?

AG: The Chinese economy has benefited from your tireless efforts. It is developing very successfully and has achieved a rather high growth rate. The American economic growth momentum is also very good. China has now already become one of the world's pivotal nations. If China maintains its present growth momentum, it will not only become a major cultural and political world power in the 21st century, it will also become a major economic power.

The past two years have been relatively difficult ones for all the countries of the world. The economic growth of some of the countries around China has not been good because of the effects of the financial crisis. This has had a negative effect on China's economic growth; China's economic performance has also had an effect on America's economic growth. This situation has forced us to undertake reforms of the international financial system. Yesterday, I, Governor Dai Xianglong, and some central bank presidents were in Hong Kong attending a special meeting of heads of international clearing banks. We explored many issues, including what measures to take to stabilize the international financial order and how to establish a stable global financial system that is oriented toward the 21st century.

The development of science and technology not only makes the relations between many economic sectors closer, it also has a major impact on the international financial system that is revolutionary. In the United States, the rapid development of technologies like computers and telecommunications has

---

1. This conversation between Zhu Rongji and U.S. Federal Reserve Chairman Alan Greenspan took place at the Hall of Purple Light in Zhongnanhai.

resulted in a revolution within the financial system; it has raised productivity, improved the effective use of capital, and raised the living standards of the people. The rapid changes in scientific and technological developments have exceeded levels that we could not have anticipated a few years ago. At the same time, the scientific and technological factors that have affected the United States have also affected other countries. Financial institutions and financial products are growing rapidly, and capital can shift in the most optimal way from products that consumers don't need to products that they do need. Even as the complex international financial system brings people benefits, it also brings potential crises.

Right now the United States very much wants to clearly understand this question: considering how the Southeast Asian countries were able to achieve high growth rates for the last 20 to 30 years, how is it that as soon as the financial crisis occurred, these countries were unable to deal with it, causing their economies to be on the verge of collapse? We feel that this is related to the current international financial system. At present, quite a few countries in the world are too dependent on banking systems. They finance systematically only through the banking system, and banks have become the sole source of financing in these countries. This is an inflexible system that is unable to resolve crises when they arise, as is the case in Russia right now. The situation in the United States is different from that in other countries. Because there are alternative forms of financing other than the banking system, when a financial crisis occurs it can be tackled and resolved well.

The present American economic situation is very good, better than the American economy—which I've been observing daily—has been at any time for the past 50 years, but we have to be cautious because we can't be sure if this good economic situation can continue. The Fed is paying close attention to the changes brought about by high-tech and to whether or not we can control the new financial products created by technological forces. Hi-tech will continue to have an important impact on the financial system, manufacturing, and services. The United States will try to gain an in-depth understanding of the forces of science and technology, of the impact they are having and of their effect on global economic stability.

ZRJ: The whole world is paying attention to the state of the U.S. economy, as it is the locomotive of the world economy. At present the U.S. economic situation is very good—it couldn't possibly be better. Some feel that U.S. stock prices are greatly overvalued, that the Dow Jones index may break through 10,000 this year and then be followed by a great recession. You've stated your views on the U.S. economy on many occasions, and I'd like to ask you now to tell me, face to face, your views on this subject.

Meeting with U.S. Federal Reserve Chairman Alan Greenspan at the Hall of Purple Light, Zhongnanhai, Beijing, on January 12, 1999. (Photograph by Liu Jiansheng, Xinhua News Agency)

AG: Right now it's hard to say whether the outstanding performance of the stock market and the unusual rise in stock prices truly reflect the realities of the American economy or whether they are signs of a bubble. In Japan, the bubble burst in 1996 after the stock markets peaked. Some people are overoptimistic in assessing the potential benefits of technological developments. They think that technical advances like computers and the Internet have greatly increased the productivity of both labor and capital and have raised the revenues and potential values of companies. The optimists think that because of technological progress, America's economic development has already risen to a new level and that the stock markets are in fact reflecting this reality, reflecting the rather good results of the companies. Personally, I am skeptical about this and think it's better to be a bit more cautious.

Judging from historical experience, the current situation in the stock markets is not a normal phenomenon. It is an unusual phenomenon that does not reflect the realities of America's economic growth and is not a normal phenomenon. Judging by conventional standards, compared with corporate results and prospects for future results, current stock prices are already too high. Nevertheless, I personally feel that if stock prices are overestimated, there will be an adjustment in these prices later, but if there is a slowdown in the rate of increase of American stock prices or if the prices fall to a certain extent, it would not necessarily mean that the American economy has entered a downturn; it would only show that the rate of America's economic growth has slowed down or decreased.

ZRJ: Last year Hong Kong came under attack by some international hedge funds. The Hong Kong government initially raised interest rates to fend off these attacks but suffered large losses. Later they had no choice but to use their forex reserves to prop up the market. At the time you were critical of this, and Joseph Yam[2] said he would have to explain it to you personally. What kind of explanation did he give you this time when you met with him? And what do you think? Does the United States plan any regulatory strengthening to address the harm caused by large flows of speculative capital into the international financial markets, and [if so] what regulatory measures do you plan to adopt? I just met with the Australian ambassador to China. He handed me a letter written personally by Prime Minister [John] Howard in which he proposes a meeting of 20 parties[3] to study how to regulate the international financial markets. What do you think of this?

AG: Joseph Yam and I had a very good conversation in Hong Kong. We both feel that short-term capital flows bring both advantages and disadvantages, but Joseph Yam is more concerned about the disadvantages created by short-term capital flows. I once said that I was opposed to the Hong Kong government's use of forex reserves to support stock prices. I feel that doing this is effective in the short run, but over the long term it creates price distortions and stands in the way of rational operations of capital markets. The value of a listed company is not determined by who owns the company or by how much money people spend to buy its stock—it's determined by its productivity. The result of the intervention is that the Hong Kong Monetary Authority is holding shares in many companies and this is very disadvantageous for the effective allocation of capital. Joseph Yam feels that an economy that is functioning well should not be faced with this sort of investment-driven capital-flow problem.

The attack on Hong Kong by short-term capital flows caused us to think about many issues in the international financial system. The present international financial system is already completely different from what it was 10 or 15 years ago. The current international financial system is more complex, touches on more areas, and is more sensitive; the speed of information transmission is greater, and at the same time inaccurate information is also transmitted more quickly. The problem is how to enable the strengths of the international financial system to play a greater role and how to minimize its complex disadvantages.

2. Joseph Yam Chi-kwong, then Chief Executive of the Hong Kong Monetary Authority.
3. The meeting of 20 parties, also known as the G-20 meeting. Participants include Argentina, Australia, Brazil, Canada, China, France, Germany, India, Indonesia, Italy, Japan, Republic of Korea, Mexico, Russia, Saudi Arabia, South Africa, Turkey, the United Kingdom, the United States, and the European Union.

The main problem has two aspects. The first is that many countries or territories borrow from international financial markets but have not taken necessary measures to prevent exchange-rate risk, so they suffer losses when the markets are volatile. The second is that we must identify those financial institutions whose lending has been counterproductive for financial stability and then exercise the necessary monitoring over them. One of the main questions currently being debated is that since the financial crisis has made people more cautious, what measures should be taken to monitor the international financial system? I expect that over the next year or two, we will carefully review and study the international financial system's course of development and its strengths and weaknesses, and undertake to reform it.

I personally feel that if we can get through this current crisis—and in fact we've already basically gotten through it—then it's highly unlikely there will be even greater crisis factors in the next year or two. If we don't do this work well now, should a crisis occur again after four or five years, it might be even more powerful and be even greater and broader in scope. I feel that the central banks of all countries should be working toward this goal. I hope that China will also be prudent as it exercises even stricter oversight of its financial institutions, so as not to obstruct positive growth of its capital markets.

ZRJ: China is taking note of American experiences and methods in banking reform. We've already changed the organization of our central bank from one with a provincial-level branch in each province to one with nine major regional branches. The goal is to strengthen oversight by the central bank and to eliminate inappropriate administrative interventions by local governments. We are conducting reforms of our commercial banks in accordance with the principles of commercial credit lending. China's problem is that the ratio of nonperforming loans at the banks is quite high—this is a legacy problem that originated during the period of economic overheating in 1992–93. At that time, real estate was overheated and too many development zones were being set up everywhere, all with money borrowed from the banks that now can't be repaid. That's why China wants to draw on U.S. experiences and methods in establishing asset management companies. [We want to] establish financial asset management companies and first hive off nonperforming assets from the commercial banks, then reform the commercial banks so that they can operate better. Do you think there is value in China's drawing on the U.S. experiences in this area?

AG: When commercial banks have many nonperforming loans, the ability of banks to promote economic growth through effective operations is greatly restricted. Japan's problem is that large numbers of nonperforming loans have caused a contraction of the banking business, and the effects have been felt even globally. Now the cost to Japan of raising capital in the European markets is quite high. Nonperforming loans make it hard for banks to obtain capital from the private sector, and even if they can obtain it, they will have to pay a higher price. Banks will be able to play a better role and promote an economic recovery only after this problem is resolved.

The structural changes at the People's Bank of China and the reforms of the commercial banks are extremely important. Right now China's commercial banks don't need to raise funds directly from the market, and they only take deposits and make loans; however, once they develop to a certain stage and need to raise funds from the market, nonperforming loans will be a serious problem. Before taking this step, China should first establish asset management companies to resolve the problem of bad assets at the commercial banks—this would be very useful. I think it's a good method. Our present understanding of the negative effects of nonperforming loans on bank operations is greater than our understanding of 10 years ago.

ZRJ: The U.S. ambassador to China isn't here today, but the chargé d'affaires is. I now want to discuss a problem not addressed to you, Mr. Greenspan, but to the U.S. chargé. There has recently been an upsurge of anti-China comments and opinions within the United States, some attacking China's human rights situation, and some spreading rumors about China stealing American military secrets. I don't intend to speak about these separately here. I just want to talk about the trade deficit between the United States and China.

The figures published by the United States indicate that in 1997 the United States had a trade deficit of $50 billion with China, and this rose to $60 billion in 1998. These figures show that the United States understands far too little about the situation in China. Last year, China's total exports to the whole world amounted to $180 billion, of which 60% came from the processing trade. That is to say, about $110 billion came from exports to countries, including the United States, by foreign-invested enterprises in China, including Sino-American joint ventures. Moreover, that $110 billion of exports required about $90 billion of raw materials imported from other countries, including the United States. That is, China only has a trade surplus of $20 billion. However, even this $20 billion isn't in Chinese hands, it's in the hands of China's foreign-invested enterprises, including American-invested enterprises.

Because of various trade restrictions and protectionist measures, China's exports, after deducting processing trade exports, amounted to only $70 billion—there couldn't have been more exports. If you say that the 1998 U.S. trade deficit with China was $60 billion, then China would have exported only $10 billion to all the other countries in the world, which is absolutely impossible. I feel that we have to look reasonably at the existing trade problems between China and the United States. In reality, China's surplus with the United States is only $20 billion. I say all of this with the intention of maintaining friendly Sino-American relations. Any words or deeds that damage Sino-American relations do China no good and do the United States no good. The China trade-deficit figures published by the United States are completely baseless, and they also do not fit the facts.

At President [Bill] Clinton's invitation, I'll be visiting the United States in April of this year. I hope that during my visit, our two countries will be able to reach an agreement on China's accession to the World Trade Organization (WTO). I've already asked Minister Shi Guangsheng of the Ministry of Foreign Trade and Economic Relations to conduct negotiations with U.S. Trade Representative Charlene Barshefsky. If the conditions laid out by Ambassador Barshefsky are reasonable, we will accept them, but there must be a timetable. I say there must be a timetable, but that's not to drag things out. The idea of a timetable might be one year or it might be three, not exceeding five years at the most. The toughest issues—for example, completely opening up the capital markets—will require five years. The lesson that the Asian financial crisis has taught us is that no good comes out of opening up financial markets quickly. The full opening of financial markets must be done gradually, the conditions must be mature, and regulatory capacities must be able to keep up. [Turning to Mr. Greenspan] I'm very sorry to talk about things unrelated to you while I'm meeting with you.

AG: On the contrary, what you said just now is very relevant to me. I'm looking forward to your visit to the United States this year. You're a very good speaker and will certainly be able to thoroughly explain China's policies in your speeches. Because China is an important member of the great international economic family as well as an important member of the international political sector, the U.S. government feels that the accession of China to the WTO is of great importance to the United States. Members of American economic circles, including myself, also hope that China will join the WTO as soon as possible.

I agree with your view that the Southeast Asian nations opened up their financial markets before they were fully prepared, and they also were not fully prepared to deal with the increasingly complex and changing challenges of the international financial markets. Your thoughts on U.S.-China trade are as perceptive as your thoughts on financial issues. These thoughts offer a great deal of inspiration to us, and we need this kind of insight.

ZRJ: I'm very delighted to meet with you again. I always gain something each time you meet with me. I hope you'll visit China more often.

16

A CONVERSATION WITH AN AMERICAN CONGRESSIONAL DELEGATION[1]

March 31, 1999

ZRJ: First, I want to apologize for having kept you waiting for 10 minutes. It was because the delegation I had just been meeting with was also an American congressional delegation. They were fewer in number than you, but the arguments were very spirited, so we couldn't control the time—I'm sorry. This is the first time I've received such a large American congressional delegation, but you won't break my record of meeting with 24 members of Congress in a single day. In May of 1990, when I visited the United States as a member of a delegation of Chinese mayors at the invitation of David M. Lampton,[2] and in my capacity as Mayor of Shanghai, I met with 24 members of Congress on one day—that was my highest record. I originally heard that you had 11 members of Congress and 10 senators, but now only 6 senators have come. There were 3 members of Congress in the delegation I just met with. Originally there were to have been 4, so all together there have only been 20 members of Congress [today]—my record hasn't been broken yet.

There's an upsurge of anti-China sentiment in the United States right now. To have so many members of Congress overcome difficulties to visit China at a time like this causes me to consider you to be true friends. I very much appreciate your coming and am very willing to listen to your views. I regard you as envoys of the American people. This visit of yours will help the Chinese and American peoples have a greater flow of information and promote exchanges. Therefore if you have any questions, please raise them. I can answer any questions you raise, and I can accept any valid views of yours, so I invite you to speak first, and then I'll respond. Basically, I hope you'll hear more and see more, and I believe that you'll conclude that China is not a potential adversary and enemy of the United States, that China is a friend of the United States.

Senator William Roth: Mr. Premier, first of all I'd like to thank you for taking the time today to meet with such a large delegation. Today should be "U.S. Congress

---

1. This is a major part of a conversation between Zhu Rongji and a delegation of members of the U.S. Congress.
2. David M. Lampton, then President of the National Committee on U.S.-China Relations.

Day" in Beijing, and we're very honored that you can meet with our delegation. The U.S.-China relationship is the most important bilateral relationship in the world, and we've come at a time when there are both great challenges and opportunities. I say "great challenges" because the relations between the two countries have unfortunately deteriorated due to certain events. But at the same time there are opportunities; that is, we will be discussing some interesting things such as the question of China's accession to the World Trade Organization (WTO). We're very interested in and also willing to discuss these issues with you. Under your leadership, the negotiations on China's accession to the WTO have already made great progress, but in order to achieve final success, we still have to make more progress. Now I'd like to leave some opportunity for my colleagues to ask questions.

Representative Jim Oberstadt: I'm very glad to see you again. The last time we met, you were still the Mayor of Shanghai. You've gone much farther than I have and you've already risen higher, whereas I'm still in the same place. Our main purpose in coming this time is to better understand the situation in China, to engage in discussions with American and Chinese scholars, to understand the economic situation in China and the forces that are pushing China forward. We also hope to visit the Three Gorges Hydropower Plant, the world's largest hydropower plant. Our two countries are currently negotiating the renewal of our bilateral civil aviation agreement. I hope that during the upcoming negotiations, the Chinese side will designate an American airline—of course I would even hope for two. This way there could be more services and more American flights between the United States and China. At the same time, I hope the Chinese side will allow other, nondesignated airlines to establish representative offices in the cities of their choice. I hope you can facilitate this process as it would strengthen the understanding and communication between the American and Chinese peoples.

ZRJ: We're willing to give positive consideration to your views and to give you a positive response. I hope there'll be a better outcome.

Senator Paul Sarbanes: Mr. Premier, I'm delighted to have the chance to meet you. I'm visiting China this time because I'm interested in U.S.-China relations. Can you tell us which issues are making this relationship more complex and difficult? What do you feel are the difficult problems in U.S.-China dealings?

ZRJ: This problem does not lie with China. There are very good conditions for China and the United States to work toward building a constructive strategic partnership. Many issues are peripheral ones, and to mistake them for the mainstream would obstruct the development of Sino-American relations. If we both proceed from the big picture of Sino-American relations and the global situation, Sino-American relations will develop smoothly.

Senator Sarbanes: I feel that the way Americans view U.S.-China relations is greatly influenced by the issue of human rights. Any movement forward or backward by China on the human rights issue will have a great impact on American public opinion, and it will likewise affect Congress.

ZRJ: I feel that there's quite a large gap between American media reports on human rights in China and the actual situation. In human rights, China is progressing by the day. China has a population of nearly 1.3 billion, and the arrests of a few criminal elements are unrelated to the question of human rights and should not become an issue that affects the development of Sino-American relations. I regret the current developments. We're willing to engage in dialogue on human rights and to narrow the differences. We don't want to become adversarial. The more adversarial we are, the more it will affect the big picture of Sino-American relations.

Representative Doug Bereuter: Thank you very much for taking the time to meet with us. I'm looking forward to your visit to the Hill in two weeks' time. Two months ago, I and 50 other members of Congress wrote a letter to President Clinton asking that the agreement he reaches with China on China's accession to the WTO not be a politically motivated agreement, but rather one that has real commercial meaning. Right now the U.S. trade deficit with China is increasing by $1 billion a week, which has led to dissatisfaction in American business and agricultural circles. I'm the Vice Chairman of the House Committee on Foreign Relations. After China joins the WTO on a commercially meaningful basis, I would be willing to promote the process of giving China permanent trading relations status. We feel that in this regard China needs to further open up its financial markets and give investors in banking and insurance greater market access. We hope there can be greater openness in market access. As we see it, in order for China to join the WTO on a commercially meaningful basis, it will have to lower its tariffs within a fairly short time. This would not only be helpful for the domestic reforms that you are leading, but it would also be helpful for China in the new round of talks in Seattle on accession to the WTO. Could you talk about how important it is to China for it to join the WTO?

ZRJ: Since the second half of last year, great difficulties have emerged in Sino-American relations, mainly because many Americans have major misunderstandings of many issues. I'd like, through your visit, to explain the actual circumstances to the American people, so that they may have a correct understanding of Sino-American relations. China has made very great concessions in the negotiations on China's return to GATT [General Agreement on Tariffs and Trade] and accession to the WTO. Even the U.S. Trade Representative feels that these concessions would have been unthinkable three or five years ago. China has been negotiating to join the WTO for 13 years. To the U.S. Trade Representative, these concessions are already sufficient and considered acceptable. But they've come under pressure from Congress, which has accused them of bartering away their principles, so they've become very tough, and the talks have become increasingly difficult. As we say in Chinese, "You give them an inch and they take a foot." Therefore, it isn't the Chinese side but the American side that has turned economic issues into political ones, so it's very hard to reach an agreement.

Your lead negotiator, Ms. [Charlene] Barshefsky, has the rank of a Cabinet Secretary, whereas Ms. Wu Yi, who represents us in the negotiations, is the equivalent of a Vice Premier. Within a few short days, I met twice with Ms. Barshefsky, and each time we talked for over two hours. I very seldom meet with a delegation for as long as two hours, and even as important a delegation as yours won't be talking with me for over two hours. Yesterday, I spent the afternoon talking with Ms. Barshefsky. I originally thought we would reach an agreement very soon, but yesterday afternoon her tone changed and she again became very tough. Why? I think it's because you in Congress are putting too much pressure on her. Our side has already made very major concessions on market access and on agricultural issues like quarantine inspections for TCK [*Tilletia controversa Kuhn*]-affected wheat, citrus, and meats. Your negotiators also feel these concessions are already sufficient, but they still refuse to sign this agreement. I'm 70 years old this year and have met with countless foreign guests, but never before have I come up against such a difficult negotiating counterpart.

I feel this is no longer a negotiation about economics; it's about politics. I hope the American people won't think that China can't survive if it doesn't join the WTO—don't think like that. We've been negotiating for 13 years. China has done well and is doing better and better. If we fail to reach an agreement this time, China will bid farewell to the WTO for 3 to 5 years. This won't have much of an impact on China, because we'll continue to develop bilateral trade relations with countries all over the world, but the United States would be passing up a great opportunity. On agricultural issues, we used to distinguish between TCK-affected and TCK-free wheat-producing areas, and now we've done away with that distinction. This is a very great concession, and we've already run a very great risk in making it.

In the past, our telecom industry was basically not open, and now we're opening it, with only some restrictions on investment ratios. Even many industries in the United States, such as civil aviation, have such restrictions on investment ratios and don't allow foreign companies to have controlling interests. In the communications sector, China has agreed to adopt the American CDMA[3] standard. You all know that most countries around the world are using the GSM[4] standard and only a few countries use the CDMA standard, but we still agreed to adopt it. There's hundreds of billions of dollars of business in cooperation in these areas as well as several others, including environmental protection, energy, and information technology. If these were opened up, it would solve America's trade deficit with China.

If the United States did not impose restrictions on exports, the present situation would be different, and there would be a great change in the Sino-American trade situation. Perhaps you're wondering why China would make such great concessions. Didn't I say that China could survive even without joining the WTO? The reason is that we realize that cooperation between two big countries like China and the United States is good for world peace and development, and we're willing to make sacrifices for it.

The United States calculates that its trade deficit with China last year was $57 billion. I'm not interested in arguing about whether or not this figure is accurate, [because] our countries use different methods of calculation. I just want to make two points. First, most of the goods exported by China to the United States are labor-intensive and resource-intensive consumer goods. The United States stopped producing such goods 15 years ago, [so] importing these goods is helpful for the restructuring of American industries. If you don't import them from China, you'd still have to import them from other countries; otherwise American consumers wouldn't be able to buy quality products at low prices, and you'd have inflation. Suppose you no longer imported textiles from China, and imported them from Mexico instead. The more you import, the more ordinary Americans would have to pay. Second, 60% of China's exports are processing-trade products. That is, foreign businessmen, including American businessmen, set up factories in China, import raw materials, process these into finished goods, and export them.

Importing raw materials requires large sums of foreign exchange, and China only gets a small portion of the foreign exchange from the exported goods—it doesn't benefit all that much. If all [the foreign exchange earned from exports] were attributed to China, then China's forex reserves would be over $300 billion at year's end—which would be the largest in the world—and not $145 billion. But last year I didn't even get a single dollar. The money all went into the pockets of the businessmen from Japan, South Korea, and the United States. So the U.S. foreign trade deficit is not much changed at $169 billion. It has decreased

3. Code division multiple access cellular technology.
4. Global system for mobile communications cellular technology.

against South Korea and Japan, and increased against us. This in fact is transferring the trade surpluses of those countries over to us.

That's why I feel that resolving the trade-deficit problem would be good for both sides, and the way to resolve it is for China and the United States to engage in cooperation in the broad sectors of information, energy, and environmental protection. There's hundreds of billions of dollars' worth of business there. If the United States were to relax its export controls, the Sino-American trade-deficit problem would be resolved very quickly.

Representative Marge Roukema: Representative Bereuter and I have the same question. We're paying great attention to China's negotiations with Ms. Barshefsky and hope you can talk specifically about the issues of trade and tariff barriers and the dumping of goods. Most members of Congress want Ms. Barshefsky to propose concrete ways to solve the U.S. trade deficit with China, but so far we haven't seen any proof that this problem can be solved.

ZRJ: That's because they haven't announced the details of the negotiations to you; they've only given you some hints and haven't told you what major concessions we've made. If only the details of the negotiations were to be made public, the American people would be very pleased.

Senator Roth: Mr. Premier, there isn't much time left. You've made many contributions to the negotiations. I'd like to state some of my views on the importance of the negotiations. I think that you've made great contributions to promoting the negotiations on China's accession to the WTO. What the United States wants is for the degree of market access of American goods in China to be the same as the degree of market access for Chinese goods in the United States. The negotiations between us are very complex and cover many areas, including agriculture, telecommunications, and information industries. A very important point is that we hope these negotiations will continue under your leadership so that they continue to make progress—we hope there will be even greater progress. Once an agreement is finally reached, business circles and unions in the United States will carefully go over each and every clause. I think that the forthcoming negotiations will make further progress and ultimately succeed, and China will join the WTO. This is in the interest of both sides.

Representative Howard Berman: Just now you said that the negotiations between the two sides are on economic and not political issues, but that these have become political issues in the American Congress—you are right. The negotiations are for achieving an agreement on economic matters, but many in Congress think about normal trading relations or MFN [most favored nation] status comprehensively together with other issues like nuclear nonproliferation, human rights, and geopolitics, so that will affect the MFN issue. It will be a tough fight to get Congress to give China permanent trading relations. That's why I cannot possibly overstate the importance of your trip to the United States. Most Americans don't consider China to be a potential adversary and don't feel we should be antagonistic toward China, but they really are very concerned about these practical matters.

ZRJ: I agree with you. Your Congress has turned economic issues into political ones. China also has people; it also has a Congress. The sentiments of the Chinese people have been inflamed by America's use of force in Yugoslavia over the Kosovo question and its tabling of an anti-China resolution at the U.N. Human Rights Council, and they're all asking me not to visit the United States. I don't agree with some of the people in your Congress who link up human rights and nuclear nonproliferation with the WTO and normal trade relations. That goes against the tide of world peace and cooperation.

17

REMARKS AT PRESIDENT BILL CLINTON'S WELCOMING CEREMONY[1]

April 8, 1999

President Clinton, Mrs. Clinton, Ladies, and Gentlemen,

In this sun-drenched spring and at President Clinton's invitation, I'm very pleased that the delegation of the People's Republic of China is making this friendly official visit to your beautiful country. At President Jiang Zemin's behest, and exhorted by the 1.25 billion people of China, we bring to the great American people their warmest regards and their best wishes.

Over the past 18 months, Presidents Jiang and Clinton have conducted successful mutual visits and have resolved to work toward building a constructive strategic partnership. This type of friendly cooperative relationship is in the interest of the people of both China and the United States, it is in the interest of the people of the world, and it is in the interest of world peace and international cooperation. The Chinese people will unswervingly strengthen and develop this relationship and work toward it unremittingly for generations to come.

The United States is the world's largest developed country, and China is the world's largest developing country. We are both members of the U.N. Security Council, and cooperation between our countries will lay a solid foundation for maintaining world peace, preventing war, and resolving disputes. The United States is the most prosperous and most powerful nation in the world, and China is the world's biggest potential market. Close cooperation between our countries in economics, trade, science, and technology will bring wonderful hope for the unity and cooperation of the people of the world, and for prosperity on our earth. The United States is a freedom-loving, open, self-made, and dynamic country, and China is a country that is peace-loving, hard-working, wise, trustworthy, and self-reliant. The friendship that we have built based on the three

---

1. At the invitation of President William J. Clinton, Premier Zhu Rongji of the People's Republic of China made an official visit to the United States on April 6–14, 1999. On April 8, President Clinton held a welcoming ceremony on the South Lawn of the White House. These are Zhu Rongji's remarks at the welcoming ceremony.

139

Speaking at President Bill Clinton's welcoming ceremony on April 8, 1999.

joint communiqués[2] and the mutual solemn promises of our governments' joint statement[3] are unshakable, and no one can drive a wedge between us. Between China and the United States, there is no question that cannot be resolved through friendly discussions. We will have differences of opinion, but only friends who can voice different opinions are the best friends, and only friends who speak truthfully are true friends.

Spring is a season for planting; it is the season of hope. When we arrived in Los Angeles, your "City of Sunshine," the spring rains were drizzling; when we departed Los Angeles, the rains had passed, and the skies were clearing; when we arrived in Washington, the sun was shining brightly. As we again plant the seeds of Sino-American friendship in this beautiful and fertile soil, we cannot help remembering those pioneers of friendly Sino-American relations, those Chinese and American pioneers. Some of them have already left us, and some are still with us. I cannot help expressing my highest respects and warmest feelings to them for their historic vision, their decisiveness, and their unstinting efforts.

I love the Chinese people, and I love the American people. Thank you.

2. The "three joint communiqués" are the "Joint Communiqué of the People's Republic of China and the United States of America," signed on February 28, 1972; the "Joint Communiqué on the Establishment of Diplomatic Relations between the People's Republic of China and the United States of America," issued on December 15, 1978; and the "Joint Communiqué of the People's Republic of China and the United States of America," signed on August 17, 1982.

3. This refers to the China-U.S. Joint Statement issued in October, 1997.

18

ADDRESS AT A WELCOMING DINNER HOSTED BY PRESIDENT BILL CLINTON

April 8, 1999

Mr. President, Mrs. Clinton, Ladies, and Gentlemen,

My wife, my colleagues, and I are deeply grateful to President and Mrs. Clinton for hosting such a lovely dinner for us. At the same time, I want to take this opportunity to express heartfelt thanks to the American government and the American people for their generous hospitality toward us, and especially to my old friends in the United States for their warm support.

This year marks the 20th anniversary of the establishment of diplomatic relations between China and the United States, and the relations between our countries have come through these 20 years with ups and downs. However, I've always felt that the friendly cooperative relations between us are becoming deeper in depth, broader in scope, and higher in quality. Particularly since Presidents Clinton and Jiang Zemin successfully exchanged historic visits, our two countries have been working to establish a constructive strategic partnership. This relationship is in the interest of the Chinese and American people, and it is also in the interest of the people of the world, and we must persist in it without wavering. There will be differences of opinion between any friends, but I believe that any issues between China and the United States can be resolved through friendly consultations. It is our duty to promote mutual understanding and to strengthen the exchanges between us. That way, we can make the friendship between China and the United States develop better.

Just now, President Clinton mentioned Chinese civilization. Today at the White House I learned a lot about American civilization. Today I visited President Lincoln's bedroom and saw the Gettysburg Address. I had studied that in high school and could even recite it. Now I can no longer recite it, but I can still recite "of the people, by the people and for the people." At the same time, I also saw the place where President [Franklin] Roosevelt gave his fireside chats. During World War II, I was very glad to be able to read his famous fireside chats.

I especially liked the welcoming ceremony at the South Lawn of the White House. This ceremony, which was held before dinner, was both solemn and cordial, but I also must say something frankly. President Clinton said just now that

142

Speaking at a welcoming dinner hosted by President Bill Clinton on April 8, 1999.

I like to speak frankly. When I was standing there shaking hands with everyone, I stood until I could no longer move my legs—it just tired me out! But I've always felt that this sort of hand-shaking ceremony is very good and can promote closeness between each visitor and the guests. Actually, I said I was tired out because I'm already 70 years old; I'm not as young as President Clinton. President Clinton said just now that I wanted to take a nap while I was watching the

In talks with President Bill Clinton on April 8, 1999.

opera—let me offer a few words of explanation. Please do not misunderstand and think that I was napping during the opera. I absolutely was not napping, I only said I "wanted to take a nap." Not only did I not nap, I even applauded extra vigorously, and I'm afraid I might even have clapped at some places where I shouldn't have clapped. That's why I feel that strengthening cultural exchanges between China and the United States is a necessary path for us to take as we establish a lasting friendship.

I can tell you all that I had very friendly, frank, constructive, and productive talks with President Clinton and his colleagues. We reached a consensus on many issues, and on many issues where we had differences of opinion, we achieved a certain mutual understanding. We reached agreements in those areas where agreements could be reached. For example, we will be issuing a joint communiqué on China's entry to the World Trade Organization. At the same time, we have to sign an agreement on part of these negotiations, that is, on agriculture. I believe that this agreement will definitely be welcomed by all of you here, but I feel that the most important aspect of my visit lies in the fact that I will be visiting quite a few of your cities in order to have direct contacts with the American people and to strengthen the friendship between China and the United States.

I should heed President Clinton's warning. He told me that after making a two-hour speech, one of your former presidents fell ill and passed away. Therefore, I mustn't go on any longer. I still haven't done a good job of learning from

President Lincoln. His shortest speech, which was the Gettysburg Address, lasted only two and a half minutes but is widely remembered to this very day. I believe that in the future people all around the world will continue to remember his speech.

Lastly, I would like to propose a toast:

To the friendship between the Chinese and American peoples,
To the health of President and Mrs. Clinton, and
To the health of everyone here,
Cheers!

19

THE FUTURE OF SCIENCE LIES
WITH YOUNG PEOPLE[1]

June 10, 1999

Since its founding in 1994, the National Science Fund for Distinguished Young Scholars has achieved great results. It has supported over 400 outstanding young scientists, of whom 80% returned home after studies abroad. These scientists have already matured to become leaders in science, and some have become members of the Chinese Academy of Sciences or the Chinese Academy of Engineering. I feel very pleased by all this. It proves that a science endowment system can play a very great role in selecting, cultivating, and attracting scientists and in stabilizing their ranks. The endowment system is a major result of reforms in our country's science and technology systems. The speeches by several young scientists that I listened to show that a new generation of scientists has matured quickly and well, and we find this very encouraging. In you, we can see China's hopes, the hopes of the Chinese people.

At present, the greatest gap between our country and the developed ones lies in our science and technology being relatively backward. If we want to revitalize China and refuse to remain behind, we will have to improve our science and technology as quickly as possible, and in order to significantly improve science and technology, we must be able to cultivate some outstanding leaders who can be on the cutting edge of world science and technology. Education is the foundation for developing science and technology, so in the final analysis we have to develop education. We must improve the quality of education—science and technology will develop only on a foundation where the caliber of education is improved across the board.

The central authorities will soon be convening the third national conference on education and making important plans for reforming and developing

---

1. These remarks were made by Zhu Rongji at a seminar marking the fifth anniversary of the establishment of the National Science Fund for Distinguished Young Scholars. The fund was created in 1994 with the approval of the State Council. Its mission is to promote the development of talented young people in science and technology, to encourage Chinese scholars studying abroad to return to China to work, and to cultivate a group of scholarly pacesetters who are in the forefront of world science and technology. In 1998 the fund was augmented by the Joint Research Fund for Overseas Chinese Scholars and the Joint Research Fund for Young Scholars in Hong Kong.

In conversation with teachers of the Fengting Linshan Primary School, Xianyou County, Putian, Fujian Province, on January 18, 1999.

education in the new century, and have decided to increase investment in education. In the five years from 1998 to 2002, the percentage of education expenditures in central-level fiscal outlays will be increased by one percentage point each year. This increase in funding is not insignificant, and it must be used well. At the same time, we must mobilize society's resources to develop private noncompulsory education in order to raise the caliber of our nation's population.

A science endowment is an excellent approach that helps attract and cultivate talent. A couple of days ago, I received a letter from the public saying that our country is losing a large number of "technology emigrants," that many undergraduates, M.A.'s, and Ph.D.'s are all going off to other countries because wages there are higher! Therefore [the letter writer] proposed that we levy a RMB 500,000 training fee on each "technology emigrant" who goes abroad. I think this proposal is well intentioned, but it wouldn't necessarily be effective. Even if you charge [a "technology emigrant"] RMB 500,000, he's still going to leave— he's not going to not leave just because he has to pay this RMB 500,000.

The [more] positive approach is to create a mechanism that makes talented people stay at home. After all, they aren't necessarily pursuing a standard of living as high as that in the United States. What they're pursuing is still primarily their vocation. We should make it possible for them to do good work with adequate funding and other working conditions so that they can play to their strengths; of course we should also guarantee them a certain standard of living, one that is at least higher than the average domestic standard of living.

We should be able to do this much, because only then will we be able to keep our talent, and only then will China be able to develop. China's development requires talent, and in many areas we have to import talent, yet we ourselves have so many talented people but don't cultivate them, don't let them play a role. How can this work? That's why I feel we ought to have ways to attract, stabilize, and cultivate talent, and the National Science Fund for Distinguished Young Scholars has created this sort of experience.

I very much agree with T. D. Lee's[2] conclusion that scientific achievements come from young people. He himself won the Nobel Prize in Physics when he was 31! Einstein was only 26 when he published his first paper on relativity. A great many facts demonstrate that scientists all make their marks when they are young, especially in physics. Of course we will also depend on young people to solve the major questions of 21st-century science and technology. The future of science lies with the young, and our hopes for prosperity and development lie in the growth and maturation of the younger generation.

The Party and government place high hopes in young scientists. You must all have a strong sense of responsibility and of mission. You must do your best to be on the cutting edge of world science: you must dare to innovate, to bring together the best of everything, and to raise standards of scholarship. You must firmly remember and carry on the spirit of "dedication, innovation, fact-seeking, and collaboration" of our older generation of scientists, make greater contributions to our country's science and technology, and mature into outstanding scientists of the new century. I hope you will make something of yourselves, have high aspirations, continually improve yourselves, and act as role models for all young people in our country working in science and technology. At present major issues in many areas of our nation's social and economic development need research and breakthroughs, and this is a fine opportunity for talented people in science and technology to show what they can do.

Just now, some committee members of the National Natural Science Foundation of China made a request—they are hoping we will add some funds to the National Science Fund for Distinguished Young Scholars. They said that at present the National Science Fund for Distinguished Young Scholars has RMB 70 million a year at its disposal, and they would like that to be increased to RMB 110 million. We agree in principle, but I'm worried that you won't be able to use this [extra] money. Don't lower your standards for talent just because you have more money—that would be awful and would mean that my money is being wasted! You still must keep up your standards. General Secretary Jiang Zemin said that we must have long-term vision, plan for the future, look at the

---

2. The Chinese-American physicist T. D. Lee was co-winner with C. N. Yang of the 1957 Nobel Prize in Physics.

big picture, focus on key areas, and know what to do and what not to do. We must act in accordance with his directive and the fund must do a good job of selecting people.

Finally, I want to congratulate those outstanding young scientists who have previously won awards! May all young scientists achieve more sooner, may the National Science Fund for Distinguished Young Scholars become better and better, and may it make ever greater contributions to the work of modernizing China and to the revitalization of the Chinese nation!

20

WE MUST BE SELECTIVE IN SUPPORTING SMALL AND MEDIUM ENTERPRISES[1]

June 24, 1999

In supporting small and medium enterprises, we have to be clear about what we're supporting and what goals we hope to achieve—this is an extremely important issue. Right now many of our small and medium enterprises are township and village enterprises. They surged into existence all at once when there were markets for their products, but now many of their products have no markets. Even goods from state-owned enterprises (SOEs) can't be sold. If we try to support these small and medium enterprises now, we won't be able to succeed.

The other day I was watching a TV report about Zhejiang Province's capacity to produce 43 million tons of cement. Obviously there isn't such a large market for this, and what's more all the producers are small enterprises that pollute their environment terribly. I remember being in Jinhua when I visited Zhejiang in 1995, and the entire route was foul: the green hills and blue waters had changed color because of the cement factories. Those were also small and medium enterprises—can you support them? No, you cannot!

You can build Phase 2 of the Jiaxing Power Plant, but you must clamp down on small power plants. The latter create long-term environmental pollution, operate with low efficiency, and consume a high level of coal—they must not be supported either. Can small chemical plants and small paper mills be supported? They, too, create massive pollution and have low productivity, so lending money to them would be for naught. That's why talking in generalities about supporting small and medium enterprises doesn't provide much guidance: it's too abstract and too general. You have to be selective in supporting small and medium enterprises, you have to develop with a view to becoming a knowledge-based economy, you have to have new products and new production techniques, you have to be able to improve quality and productivity and meet some market needs.

The development of knowledge-based and science- and technology-based small and medium enterprises should be encouraged. India and other countries

---

1. These comments were made by Zhu Rongji as he was listening to work reports by the provincial Party committee and the provincial government during an inspection tour of Zhejiang Province.

have many policies to encourage the development of information and software enterprises. These are in fact a type of knowledge-based enterprise; they don't require a lot of equipment but once they're started up, they have very good prospects. I've now asked the four big state-owned banks to establish departments to lend to small and medium enterprises, that is, to support small and medium enterprises. But we have to be very clear on one point, namely that we want to support knowledge-based and science- and technology-based small and medium enterprises, and we don't want to support township and village enterprises in establishing small and medium enterprises the way we did in the past.

In light of the current circumstances, at a time when the entire economic structure is undergoing major adjustments, the question of how to support small and medium enterprises requires careful study and needs to be treated in more specific terms. Banks must also think it through. If a small or medium enterprise established by a few people really possesses technology and really understands the market, then even if it doesn't have any assets to use as collateral, you should risk supporting it. Of course bank interest rates can vary and can rise when the risk is very high. Small and medium enterprises that have the talent may be willing to pay that high interest, and once they succeed, their returns will be adequate to cover the banks' high interest. This issue merits close examination, particularly because Zhejiang Province got its start from small and medium enterprises. It doesn't have many large enterprises—only 10% are SOEs. I feel that the provincial Party committee and the provincial government can organize the banks to join them in looking into how to support small and medium enterprises, as you need to make some breakthroughs here.

21

TO TAME THE YELLOW RIVER, WE MUST CONSERVE SOIL AND WATER IN ITS MIDDLE AND UPPER REACHES[1]

August 6, 1999

Our purpose in coming to Shaanxi this time is to carry out General Secretary Jiang Zemin's directive on doing good work in taming the Yellow River, and to join all of you in studying how to do this. The Yellow River is the hardest river in China to tame, yet our experience and our wherewithal for taming it are better than in the case of the Yangtze River. Putting aside how it was done earlier, ever since the Qing Dynasty [1644–1911] the work of taming the Yellow River has been under unified leadership, and this is much better than the way the Yangtze is tamed, where "each railway policeman patrols his own section of track." Remember that "a thousand-mile-long embankment can collapse because of ant-holes."

Each section of the Yangtze is separately managed, and the management standards differ—there are a lot of problems with this. I had a look at the Yangtze last month and came away with many [mixed] feelings—I think that it's very dangerous in some places. Its management system is a great problem—there's no unified management, and each section is managed separately. Since last year, we've put in several tens of billions of renminbi into reinforcing the Yangtze embankments—this was unprecedented. But the way Hubei is doing it—dividing it into kilometer-long sections and then contracting each section out to a unit or individual—that's extremely dangerous, and how can they guarantee the quality of the Yangtze embankments?

Then I went to Jiujiang in Jiangxi Province and saw the section of embankment that was breached last year and subsequently repaired by the Gezhouba Engineering Bureau of the China Water Resources and Hydropower Corporation. I was very pleased and felt this was a model project done by a large

---

1. On August 5–9, 1999, Zhu Rongji visited Henan and Shaanxi provinces to inspect work on combating erosion of the loess plateau and flood prevention along the Yellow River. During his stay in Shaanxi, he visited Yan'an and the Yangling agricultural hi-tech demonstration zones. These are the main remarks he made after listening to work reports by the Yellow River Conservancy Commission of the Ministry of Water Resources and by the Yan'an municipal Party committee and municipal government.

mechanized team. It was designed by the Yangtze Waterworks Commission of
the Ministry of Water Resources, and the construction unit was selected through
bidding, so I had no worries.

After I returned to Beijing, many major leaks appeared along the [embankments of the] Yong'an section of Jiujiang in Jiangxi, not far from the site that I
had been so pleased about. We managed to prevent a breaching of the embankments only by sending in several thousand People's Liberation Army troops—
this happened very recently. So who repaired this section? The Gezhouba Engineering Bureau had asked a team from one of its subsidiaries to carry out the
repairs, but this team didn't even have any engineering credentials. As a result,
the places it had repaired began leaking. It pained me to hear that this incident
happened at the Gezhouba Engineering Bureau, which I had just praised.

This Yangtze management system just won't do; sooner or later major chaos
will occur. No matter how much money you give them, everyone will come to
"eat some of the flesh of Monk Xuanzang of the Tang."[2] How can this be? How
much money will really be used to repair embankments? How much of it will be
misused? There's no guarantee of embankment quality. The Yellow River is a bit
better: it has centralized management. But centralized management also has its
drawbacks. If there's a small breach somewhere, it can be repaired in a hurry, but
if the Yellow River Waterworks Commission of the Ministry of Water Resources
has a poor sense of responsibility, there could be breaches everywhere, and that
would be even harder to deal with.

Efforts to tame the Yellow River have a very long history. Since the founding
of New China, everyone from the Administrative Council[3] to the State Council
has attached great importance to this task. Today we have to work harder, invest
more effectively, and do an even better job of it. However, I'm afraid we need to
adjust the thinking that guides us in taming the Yellow River. That is to say, if
we don't improve soil and water conservation in the middle and upper reaches
of the Yellow River, if the ecological environment isn't improved, and if erosion continues, there won't be any results no matter how many waterworks we
build downstream. Or, to put it another way, even if there are results, it will take
twice the effort to achieve half the results. That is, you'll keep building "sand
reservoirs" because your reservoirs are in fact "sand reservoirs." These provide

2. Translator's note: this refers to an episode in the classical novel *Journey to the West*. Various
demons and devils wanted to eat the flesh of Monk Xuanzang, believing that this would make them
immortal. The term is now used as an allusion to something that, because it confers great benefits,
is sought after by many at all costs.

3. The Administrative Council was the precursor of the State Council of the People's Republic
of China. It was the highest executive agency for state affairs of the People's Republic of China from
October 21, 1949, to September 27, 1954.

Inspecting the Xiaolangdi Waterworks, Henan Province, on August 9, 1999.

an opening for the upstream silt to come in, so it keeps rushing in and makes a mess of the loess plateau.

True, by bringing in the silt you are avoiding floods, but how much do you have to spend? You keep building such "sand reservoirs"; then build some more when they're silted up, and after they're built they'll silt up again. This method amounts to an emergency rescue because right now there's still no way to properly conserve upstream soil and water within a short period—who knows how many years it will take before there's no more silting? Hence it won't do not to build reservoirs. However, if we don't turn our attention to the fundamental problem, to the question of managing upstream erosion, then twice the effort will yield half the results, our people will be exhausted, and our money depleted! People can't live upstream because of erosion there, while downstream silting creates a danger of flooding. That's why in coming here this time, I want to further emphasize that we must devote more of our energies to improving the ecological environment of the middle and upper reaches of the Yangtze and Yellow Rivers and to conserving soil and water.

In northern Shaanxi, several tens of thousands of troops of the Chinese Communist Party once lived off these little gullies, and they were ultimately victorious across all of China. But an army has to eat—if it doesn't eat, how can it conduct a revolution? So they had to put new land under cultivation, and they had to cut down trees and burn them for fuel. The people of northern Shaanxi

Inspecting comprehensive ecological management measures in Yan'an, Shaanxi Province, on August 6, 1999. (Photograph by Hui Huaijie)

made an enormous contribution to winning the nationwide victory. Now look around—all the hills are barren. Doesn't it make you feel bad to see this?

Today we went on an inspection tour of the outlying areas of Yan'an. The entire hill is bare [of trees] right where there's a turn to go up the hill, and some slopes are even planted with crops. This won't do! I ask: if you can't do anything else, can you at least turn this little patch of land green? Can you turn this outlying area green? Can you do that much? I'll let you be in charge of the whole thing, and I'll send you the money. Do you have any laid-off workers here? If you do, let them plant trees. This is honorable work, and this is revolution.

En route we saw that some trees are indeed growing quite well—these were irrigated forests. But there are also some hilltops where land is still being cleared for cultivation. You get quite a bit of rainfall here, but all the water is lost soon after it rains. Ultimately you will have to plant trees. It will take tree planting to make the hills and streams beautiful, and there must be no more crop cultivation on the hills. I don't want you to keep planting crops because we already have way too much grain nationwide—it's all stored in granaries and about to grow moldy. The cost of growing crops downstream along the Yellow River is much lower than it is here, and the benefits are much greater. That's why I say I hope you won't keep growing grain.

Instead my hope for you is to have beautiful hills and streams: if the silt from the middle and upper reaches doesn't flow downstream, grain production downstream will be much greater than what you can grow. I'm speaking frankly—isn't your grain yield no more than 100–200 jin[4] per mu?[5] It can reach

4. One jin is equal to 0.5 kilogram.
5. One mu is equal to 666.7 square meters.

several hundred jin downstream. I was originally very worried that these hills would have no water and that you wouldn't be able to plant trees. But according to Wang Shucheng,[6] trees planted during the rainy season can survive—isn't that a fine thing? I think you could also try planting aerially, and replant in places where the trees failed to take root. This is an essential measure for managing the Yangtze and Yellow rivers and for creating a new China with beautiful hills and streams for future generations.

Building a few reservoirs that act like "sand reservoirs" won't solve the problems of these rivers. I'm not saying you shouldn't build reservoirs—you still have to build them before the trees are fully grown, but that isn't a fundamental solution. At the moment Yan'an still lacks water. If you plant trees on the hills, you could also build a reservoir to trap the water. My heart ached to see that the Yan River had stopped flowing. There's a song "The Rolling Waters of the Yan River" in the movie *The Fires of War by the Yan River*, but now those waters don't "roll" any more. [The river] looks like a little gully with a bit of dirty water in it. That's why it will be quite unacceptable if you don't build up the environment, if you don't manage erosion, and if you don't plant trees. I hope that from now on, you will draw up good plans for soil and water conservation and for environmental protection in northern Shaanxi. The better your plans, the faster I'll send money to you.

I've used a 16-character expression in this regard: "Revert farmland to forests (or grasslands), close off hills and make them green, offer grain instead of relief funds, and let individuals subcontract." Most of the land in China should be covered with green forests—it shouldn't all be planted. If we keep planting, it will all turn into desert. We still have a lot of potential to increase yields of farmed land [so] we don't need you to grow crops on your land. According to aerial surveys, you have eight mu of land per capita here. What do you want with so much land? In the south a few fen[7] is enough to support a family—what will you do with eight mu? Most of it should be planted with trees. Many types of livelihoods can be derived from forestry after you plant trees, so you should adjust your economic structure.

You should also close off hills to grow forests—stop going up the hills to clear new land. Up on the hill today, I talked about turning *Brother and Sister Clearing the Land*[8] into *Brother and Sister Planting a Forest*. People in the field of literature in Yan'an could even write a script to guide us as we transform the spirit

6. Wang Shucheng was then Minister of Water Resources.

7. One fen is equal to 66.67 square meters.

8. *Brother and Sister Clearing the Land* was a *yangge* dance drama produced in February 1940 during the *yangge* movement in Yan'an, after the Party Central Committee called for the launch of a major production campaign in Yan'an. (Translator's note: *yangge* is a traditional form of dancing and singing very popular in northern China.)

of *Brother and Sister Clearing the Land* from the revolutionary war years into the spirit of *Brother and Sister Planting a Forest* as we turn barren hills green. What should you do if your people have no grain to eat? I'll send you some from the granaries. Aren't you only 2 million people? How many million jin of grain could you eat in a year? I'll send it to you and give you grain instead of charity. Provided you plant trees, I'll give you books of grain coupons. You can claim your grain with these and you won't have to pay.

As for "individual subcontracting," it means I can contract this piece of forest to you. You'll have to conserve and protect this piece of forest, and in the future you'll be able to engage in some secondary agricultural activities around it, but you may not cut down the trees—this is absolutely forbidden. Some fast-growing forests may be logged intermittently, but we have to set some rules for this. I'm going to ask Wang Zhibao[9] to be in charge of drawing up a plan to control soil and water erosion in northern Shaanxi. He should flesh out the details of some of these methods and consult with the locals.

The State Planning Commission, the Ministry of Finance, and the State Bureau of Forestry must work together closely and come up with this plan in the shortest time possible. This is a master plan, not just one for the Yan'an region. However, the Yan'an region is a focal point. You must start taking action as soon as possible and make the first move, becoming a pilot program for the entire country. We need to have a master plan, a plan that covers 10 or 20 years, with estimates of how much money must be spent to turn all the barren hills green. We must maintain investment at a relatively high level. When it comes to conserving soil and water, turning barren hills green, and building ecological projects, we must invest, and we must guarantee that we first turn the outlying areas of Yan'an green. I hope that when I come back in three years' time, there will be no more bare hills. Can you guarantee that trees will be planted on all the hills three years from now? Surely this is not too much to expect.

I visited Yan'an in 1992. I could see on this visit that it has made great progress: the environment is vastly improved, production is developing well, and people's living standards have risen sharply. I want to thank you and to fully affirm your achievements, and hope you continue to do better than ever.

9. Wang Zhibao was then Director of the State Forestry Administration.

22

WE MUST BE DETERMINED TO STOP LOGGING IN NATURAL FORESTS[1]

August 14, 1999

On this visit to Lijiang, I can sense great changes. Since the earthquake,[2] Lijiang looks very different from the way it did several years ago. This has been achieved with the support of the entire country, including our compatriots living abroad, but it was mainly through your own efforts. This proves that provided that our Party's programs and policies are correct, many things can be accomplished when our people are fully mobilized.

One endeavor that now needs support is the protection of natural forests. Logging in natural forests has reached a point where stopping it is of the greatest urgency—there is not a moment to lose. If it is delayed any longer, the disasters suffered by the country because of the Yangtze and Yellow rivers will be worse than ever. The time has come for a determined effort to thoroughly halt logging in natural forests! However, such action will create a series of contradictions, the main one being the question of how we will have to adjust the economic structure.

At present, our country is entering a stage where the economic structure is heading for major adjustments, with deepening economic reforms. Unless our economic structure undergoes a major strategic adjustment, we won't be able to sustain a strong growth rate. If Yunnan is to develop further, it, too, will have to make major adjustments to its economic structure. It can't continue to rely entirely on "tobacco finances" and even less on "lumber finances"; rather, it must adjust by playing to its own strengths.

Last year the State Council decided to halt logging in natural forests, but has it really all stopped as you claim? I absolutely don't believe that it has all stopped. It's not that I don't believe you, but isn't what you claim also based on

---

1. On August 11–16, 1999, Zhu Rongji visited Kunming, Lijiang, and Dali during an inspection tour of Yunnan Province. This is the main part of remarks he made in Lijiang after listening to work reports by some of the leading officials from the local prefectures.

2. There was a powerful 7-point magnitude earthquake in Lijiang on February 3, 1996. Nine counties and 51 townships within the 4 prefectures of Lijiang, Dali, Diqing, and Nujiang were severely affected, with 309 dead, 3,925 seriously wounded, and over RMB 4 billion in direct economic losses.

Inspecting new villages rebuilt after an earthquake in Lijiang Prefecture, Yunnan Province, on August 13, 1999.

reports that came up to you level by level? According to your report, a number of problems have yet to be resolved, so how could it have stopped? No matter what, don't say, "We are very resolute in implementing the State Council's decision and have already stopped all logging in natural forests." I've never believed that because [even] I wouldn't be able to resolve all those problems. I can only believe that logging in natural forests has been greatly reduced but has not stopped.

Some of my colleagues went to see the "first bend of the Yangtze" today. On the way there, they encountered 6 large trucks of the type used for hauling lumber that were loaded with very large logs. On the way back they encountered another 6 trucks, also hauling very large logs. In one day they encountered 12 trucks. It's been over a year since logging was supposed to have stopped—why, then, hasn't the hauling finished? It would be strange if they were not logging anymore! That's why I absolutely can't believe it when you say that logging in natural forests has stopped. I hope you can do some solid work that digs a bit deeper and does not simply accept the reports of officials from one level to the next.

Instead, you have to look deep into the forests, the tree farms, and the lumber markets, and under no circumstances should you underestimate this problem. That's why I will say again that protecting forest resources requires the spirit of the "Foolish Old Man Who Moved the Mountain,"[3] and this protection must be carried on by generations to come.

We've already inspected a great many places and come up with some policy ideas for protecting the environment. In fact, these have already been tried out in some places since last year, but this isn't enough, and now we have to revise these policies. On this trip, we've come to discuss with all of you how best to revise these policies. I have some tentative ideas to discuss with you; and depending on your views, they will be unveiled as soon as possible after they are revised.

1. The Most Important Thing Is to Rouse the Enthusiasm of Officials

Some places rely on "lumber finances," so they will feel a great fiscal impact if logging in natural forests is stopped. Without a certain level of subsidies, these places will have no desire to stop logging. The central fiscal authorities must give them certain subsidies, the amounts to be determined by the province. For prefectures and counties that will really feel a major fiscal impact, with revenues plummeting after a ban on logging, we must provide a certain level of subsidies. However, we can't fully subsidize everyone, so some prefectures and counties will have to pay a certain price. They'll have to streamline their agencies and trim expenses.

After logging ends, they'll still have to pay a definite price in order to adjust their economic structure and improve returns, and for the sake of long-term development. There's no way for us to assess each and every county and prefecture on this issue, and we'll have to accept the numbers from the provincial government. Subsidies from the central fiscal authorities will be rebated to the locals through transfer payments. In short, without paying this price, we won't have green hills and blue waters. However, I've already told your provincial Party secretary and your governor that at a time like this, you mustn't try to "plunder a burning house" because the central fiscal authorities are also experiencing difficulties. You must all seek truth from the facts and not try to solve all your problems using this opportunity—they can't be resolved this way.

2. You Must Implement the 16-Character Expression

I used this expression while inspecting in Shaanxi: "Revert farmland to forests (or grasslands), close off hills and make them green, offer grain instead of relief,

---

3. Translator's note: this refers to an old Chinese fable about an old man called The Foolish One, whose house was obstructed by two large mountains. He was determined to level these mountains but was mocked by others who felt that it was silly of him to attempt such an impossible task. He replied, "After I die, my descendants will continue to carry on. These mountains will not get any higher, and one day, they will be flattened." This expression is now used to describe someone who perseveres and is undaunted by difficulties.

Planting a tree in the Evergreen Garden of the China '99 World Horticultural Expo in Kunming, Yunnan Province, on August 12, 1999.

and subcontract with individuals." You must close off the mountains—it won't do for you not to close them off. You used to cut forests down in order to grow grain, but it costs far too much to grow grain on such high mountains. In any case, we have a nationwide grain surplus at the moment, so why must you grow it on the mountains? Instead you must let the farmland on the slopes revert to forests, and the state will give you, without charge, however much grain you were harvesting there. We must abide by this policy in order to revert farmland to forests. Otherwise, if we just force the farmers to stop farming, what will they do when they have nothing to eat?

The policy that must be implemented now prohibits the cutting down of forests. Since we will be giving grain without compensation, farmers who stop farming must also plant trees without compensation. The state will provide the seedlings and fertilizer or plant aerially and only asks that they care for the trees. No harm will come to farmers' interests. Based on the assessed output per mu[4] of land, once we verify how much land has reverted and how many trees have been planted, we will give you the grain based on average standards—this is called "offering grain instead of relief." I believe that the farmers are willing to implement this policy because they will have the grain, and once the forest has grown they will gain other benefits as well. This way, the hills will turn green

---

4. One mu is equal to 666.7 square meters.

and the waters blue, the soil and water will be conserved, and grain production in flatlands and along slopes will increase.

But we must insist on individual subcontracting. This is no longer the past, when even having enough to eat was a problem. With the success of the Party's agricultural policies and rise in agriculture's technology standards, food supplies will not be a problem from now on. Of course I'm not saying that we should be lax about grain production or that grain is unimportant, only that the situation has changed greatly. Once the ecological environment is improved, this will promote the development of agriculture, and grain will be even less of a problem. This is what we mean by adjusting the economic structure.

However, we have to be more specific about the methods to be used to implement this policy. That is to say, how will we get the grain into the hands of those who plant trees? How will individual subcontracting work? How will grain take the place of relief? How will we inspect? How can we plant aerially? How is a mountain to be closed off? A host of questions need to be explored here. The provincial government must send many people out to investigate these questions, to study how to set standards and how to ascertain that money and grain are received by individuals. How will the employees in forestry enterprises shift from cutting trees down to planting them? These enterprises must undergo adjustments as well and mustn't say that once they stop cutting down forests they'll still have to support all their employees—that won't do. Forestry enterprises also have to lay people off and reassign them, they have to reduce staffing and increase efficiency, and then create means of livelihood for them. Laid-off forestry workers will no longer have any income but you'll still have to feed them—the policy of supplying grain without charge also applies to them.

At the same time, you must turn the loggers into tree planters, you must pay for their work—this is the cost of planting a forest—and it must be reasonably assessed. The provincial authorities can propose a figure, and we will go down to inspect whether such a standard is appropriate. This funding for planting forests will provide forestry enterprises with a way to survive.

In its report, a prefecture has just said it wants to set up stations in the managed forest area and do infrastructure construction. Just when we've relieved the forestry enterprises of a large burden in order to protect the natural forests, this is going to place a new burden on them! How can we let that happen? We must still insist on individual subcontracting. The mountains must be closed off, and once closed, no parts may be used at will any longer, particularly for logging. To support several people and to set up so many stations will serve absolutely no purpose! It's impossible to try to keep supporting all the people who were working in forestry enterprises. You still have to use layoffs and streaming, allowing extra staff to gradually develop other occupations and gradually be reemployed, but you must guarantee their basic livelihoods.

Furthermore, the debts of forestry enterprises can't be written off right away. After we go back, we'll have to discuss this with the banks and draw up a series of policies to first allow them to owe the money without further accumulating interest, and then to inventory and liquidate their assets. In the end, these debts will have to be canceled. If they aren't allowed to cut down trees, will they be able to repay the money? No, they won't.

Forestry enterprises mustn't casually go into other businesses. It's extremely hard to develop a new industry or a new product. If they went into other businesses now, what would they do? They don't have the skills or the knowledge. How, then, would you adjust the economic structure? That's why I feel that it will take time to go into other businesses. It will take money and it will take effort. Don't be in a rush to designate some conversion projects; otherwise these will all turn into burdens, and the next leaders will have to clean up the mess.

3. One Other Issue: The Protection of Forestry Resources

Regarding factories that use timber for raw materials, I agree with your proposal to shut down those four little paper mills. Their enterprise debts should be included in their bankruptcy plans and written off in accordance with bankruptcy procedures. As for the 7-ton Simao Paper Mill and the 3-ton Dali Paper Mill—and I suspect there aren't just these two, there may also be some in other provinces—the State Planning Commission and the State Economic and Trade Commission should take the lead, and the State Forestry Bureau, the International Engineering Consulting Company, and the State Bureau of Light Industry should all participate in organizing a team to investigate and then determine how these should be handled. Is it really possible to develop fast-growing forests? Is it really possible to guarantee a supply of raw materials? They also have to consider costs and benefits and ultimately decide whether they should keep operating or be shut down.

Do you agree that we should continue to halt logging in natural forests and revert farmland to forests? What other policies are needed? I think I may have figured it all out for you:

—First, the central fiscal authorities will provide subsidies, with amounts to be determined by the provincial government. You mustn't report false figures, nor can 100% of everything be subsidized—this we cannot do.

—Second, as farmers revert farmland to forests, I guarantee to provide them with grain at no cost.

—Third, when forestry enterprises convert from logging to tree planting, you have to pay them a fee for managing [the forests] and for planting trees, and you have to give them grain.

—Fourth, excess staff should be laid off and reassigned, and gradually shifted into other occupations in the future.

23

SOME THOUGHTS ON SPEEDING UP DEVELOPMENT IN ETHNIC MINORITY AREAS[1]

October 3, 1999

It is essential to speed up the development of ethnic minority areas, especially to improve their economy. This will have deep and far-reaching significance for narrowing differences between regions, promoting the revitalization and development of the national economy, achieving common prosperity for all ethnic groups in the country, and reinforcing and fostering ethnic unity.

Although we must have a strong sense of historical responsibility as well as urgency in speeding up the development of minority areas, we must also proceed from realities and abide by objective rules. From now on, a prime concern must be to study circumstances in these areas, draw up plans, adopt more forceful measures, implement these in a planned and orderly manner, and achieve our goals in stages. I'd like to discuss a few thoughts along these lines.

Step Up Infrastructure Construction in Ethnic Minority Areas

Backward infrastructure is a major factor constraining the development of minority areas. The central authorities have always attached great importance to infrastructure in these areas and over many years have completed a succession of major projects there. For example, the Lanzhou-Xinjiang railroad, the Chengdu-Kunming railroad, and the Qinghai-Tibet highway were completed even before reforms and opening up began. Since reforms and opening up, we have completed the Nanning-Kunming railroad, Tarim Oilfield in Xinjiang, Lhasa Airport in Tibet, and the Lanzhou-Xining-Lhasa optical cable project. In the past two years, in the course of increasing domestic demand and adopting

1. On September 29–October 3, 1999, the Central Minorities Work Conference and the State Council's Third National Conference for Commending Ethnic Unity and Progress were held in Beijing. Attendees included leading representatives from the various provinces, autonomous regions, and centrally administered municipalities, responsible members from the central Party and government agencies concerned, representatives of the model collectives, and individuals receiving awards. This is part of Zhu Rongji's speech at the closing ceremony.

a proactive fiscal policy, the state has quite significantly increased infrastructure investment in central and western China, especially in minority areas.

At present, a batch of major national projects are also under way, among them the Neijiang-Kunming railroad, the Sichuan-Tibet highway, a project to alleviate poverty in Ningxia by pumping water from the Yellow River for irrigation, and a project to channel water from the Ertix River in Xinjiang. These endeavors are playing a major role in the development of western China and will continue to do so. Infrastructure construction in western China and in ethnic minority areas requires very large investments. Although it will take time for many of these projects to reap economic benefits, they still must be undertaken. Without infrastructure construction there can be no development in minority areas. Therefore we must put even greater effort into infrastructure construction in minority areas, as follows:

—First, accelerate construction of the transportation system, including railroad construction in Xinjiang, Tibet, and the border regions in southwestern and northeastern China; extension of the major east-west and north-south trunk roads of the national highway system into more ethnic minority areas; and development of water, air, and pipe transportation where the terrain permits.

—Second, continue to give priority to the development and comprehensive use of water resources, focusing in particular on alleviating the shortages of potable water for people and livestock in farming and grazing areas.

—Third, continue to step up construction in energy, particularly in electricity.

—Fourth, accelerate construction of communications and promote the adoption of information technology in minority areas.

These measures will not only assist in the current economic development of minority areas, but they will also create conditions for long-term development.

Speed Up Industrial Restructuring and Develop
Economies with Distinctive Ethnic Features

My visits to ethnic minority areas over the past few years have left me with a deep impression of the richness of their natural resources. Some areas straddle several climate zones and thus have many types of biological resources. A great deal can be done to develop regional economies with special characteristics of their own. We must insist that development be market-guided, that it use local resources to full advantage, play to strengths while avoiding weaknesses, and undertake industrial adjustment and optimization, as follows:

—First, make major changes in crop composition, taking full advantage of our diverse biological resources to develop high-yield, high-quality, and high-efficiency eco-agriculture and adapt to the terrain in developing various types of cash crops.

—Second, speed up the development of pastures, giving the development of grasslands equal priority with agricultural infrastructure and changing the fundamental practice of favoring agriculture over herding, of favoring grain over grass; also promote the coordinated development of agriculture and animal husbandry.

—Third, take full advantage of our wealth of mineral resources and build a batch of national production bases for energy, nonferrous metals, rare earths, and petrochemicals.

—Fourth, make an all-out effort to expand tourism and other tertiary industries.

In short, all areas must proceed from actual conditions and put their energies into nurturing various types of industries, especially pillar industries that can take advantage of their local strengths and become new economic growth points.

Focus on Projects to Protect Natural Forests and Develop the Eco-Environment

This is an important strategic decision of the central authorities based on their overall picture of modernization and sustainable development in our country. In the past few years, parts of southern China have been subjected to frequent flooding, a danger that is worsening. Apart from climate change, this has mainly been due to unrestrained logging in forests in the upper and middle reaches of the Yangtze and Yellow rivers. Ground cover has thus been destroyed, resulting in serious erosion. Therefore we won't be able to control flooding at all unless we do a good job of protecting the natural forests in the upper and middle reaches, and unless we revive the ecosystem and conserve soil and water by planting trees and creating forests. Nor will we be able to effectively deal with the aridity and desertification in northwestern China, which are worsening by the day.

After the extreme flooding in the Yangtze basin last year, the central authorities resolved to halt logging in natural forests in the upper and middle reaches of the Yangtze and Yellow rivers, and to prevent soil and water loss by planting trees and growing grass. Since the beginning of this year, I've repeatedly emphasized this issue during my several visits to some places in southwestern and northwestern China. Forest protection and environmental restoration are important steps in implementing the strategy of the great development of the west and of speeding up development of ethnic minority areas.

We must make comprehensive and integrated plans to address both the symptoms and the root causes. In dealing with erosion in the upper and middle reaches of the Yangtze and Yellow rivers and in implementing forest protections, we must "revert farmland to forests (or grasslands), close off hills and make them green, provide grain instead of relief funds, and subcontract with individuals " so as to revive the forests and ground cover. [The future of] farming in areas that

Speaking at the Central Minorities Work Conference and the the State Council's Third National Conference for Commending Ethnic Unity and Progress on October 3, 1999. On the right is Politburo Standing Committee member and Chairman of the Chinese People's Political Consultative Conference Li Ruihuan. (Photograph by Liu Jianguo, Xinhua News Agency)

are half farmland and half pasture should be determined by water—if there is no guarantee of a water supply, farmland must be returned to grasslands.

After logging in natural forests is banned and farmlands revert to grasslands, fiscal authorities at the central and provincial levels will have to provide proper compensation or subsidies for the people in the affected areas. Our total grain supply now exceeds demand: 550 billion jin[2] are stored in granaries across the country, and if you add the grain held by the farmers, we have over 1 trillion jin in the country as a whole, which is equal to a year's production. This is the best time to exchange grain for forests and grasslands—we must seize this historic opportunity and not let it slip by.

The departments and regions concerned must be even more determined— they must focus on drawing up and implementing effective policy measures and persevere in keeping a tight, solid, and good grip on the work of protecting our natural forests. Planting trees to create forests and reviving the ecosystem will require the long-term efforts of generations to come, but even now there is not a moment to lose: "It takes ten years to grow a tree." After some years, the forests will have grown up and our country's natural environment will look

2. One jin is equal to 0.5 kilogram.

very different, and that will create very important conditions for the sustainable development of our national economy.

Concentrate on Forcefully Tackling the Hard Issues in Alleviating Poverty

These past few years, great results have been achieved in alleviating poverty in ethnic minority areas. From 1994 to 1998, subsistence was no longer a concern for 8.5 million people in minority areas. Now we've entered a critical stage in tackling the tough issues in poverty alleviation. About 40 million people in our country's rural areas remain poor, mainly in the minority areas of southwestern and northwestern China. We must approach this problem with the big picture as well as politics in mind, and we must attack poverty in minority areas with greater force. We must persevere in making subsistence the central objective and must view impoverished villages as the main battlefield. Our emphasis should be on improving their basic conditions for production and for living, on helping them grow crops and raise animals, and on investing more in poverty alleviation through a variety of channels. The goal of tackling these tough poverty issues and implementing measures to resolve them must apply to every poor village and poor family. Special policy measures must be instituted to enable poor people to achieve subsistence, especially in disaster-prone areas, in poor ecological environments, and in pasturelands.

Just now I said that projects to protect natural forests will help minority groups rise above poverty and move toward prosperity. Ethnic minorities living in mountainous areas have to walk great distances into the mountains to farm, and often the grain they harvest isn't enough to support their families. By reverting farmland to forests (or grasslands), by providing grain instead of charity and subcontracting with individuals, by supplying them with grain at no charge and encouraging them to plant trees and grow grass, we can rapidly solve their subsistence problems as well as improve the environment, attract many tourists, and develop tourism and other tertiary industries. Many benefits will ensue from one action.

Revitalize the Nation through Science and Education and Promote Coordinated Economic and Social Development in Ethnic Minority Areas

If development in minority areas is to proceed from a higher starting point and forge a new path, science and education must lead the way. We must increase investment in science and technology in minority areas, promote the transfer of scientific and technical advances to these areas, and improve their ability to apply scientific and technical results and to devise innovative approaches in science and technology.

Minority areas face a huge educational problem right now—it's very hard for students in these and impoverished areas to attend senior high school and university, in large part because they can't afford the tuition. If young people in minority areas can't go to school and can't acquire knowledge, then they won't have the necessary means to overcome their backward conditions. The State Council is already devoting special attention to this topic and is studying ways to handle it.

A variety of measures could speed up the development of education in minority areas:

—Explore school systems and formats suited to the special characteristics of minority areas.

—Encourage and advocate the mixed [government and nongovernment] operation of schools using many methods.

—Find substantive solutions to the difficulties of running and attending schools in some minority areas.

In addition, we must accelerate the development of health care and raise the health standards of minority groups. We must do a good job of family planning and mother-and-child care, taking into account the realities of ethnic minority groups. And we must actively develop ethnic minority cultures, protect and develop their cultural resources, and help them maintain their outstanding cultural traditions while integrating them with the spirit of the times.

In order to accelerate development in ethnic minority areas, we must continue to cultivate high-caliber ethnic minority talent of all types and at all levels. We have to work hard to build up the ranks of ethnic minority officials who are of good character and highly talented. While we must pay attention to increasing their numbers, we must pay even more attention to improving their caliber and their composition. At the same time, we have to work hard to bring in talented people. Only by "combining talent with science and technology" will we be able to turn our advantages in natural resources into advantages in economic development. We have to establish a system of rewards that will draw talent of all sorts to jobs in minority areas. The state must undertake related measures to encourage graduates of tertiary institutions to work in western China and in ethnic minority areas. The minority areas must also work to create conditions that will attract diverse kinds of talent. Only then will people be willing to come, to stay, and to put down roots.

24

Three Main Approaches for the Development of Western China[1]

October 29, 1999

On this visit to the northwest, I've been to Gansu, Qinghai, and Ningxia. I had previously visited several other provinces, including Shaanxi, Yunnan, and Sichuan. My main purpose is to implement the grand concept of the "great development of western China" proposed by General Secretary Jiang Zemin. After many investigations and studies, I believe that we will mainly have to use three approaches to develop western China.

1. Strengthen Infrastructure Construction in the West

This is the foundation for western China, which is full of mountainous and arid areas. If transportation isn't expanded, if we don't first solve this problem, then there won't be any way to keep up with the progress of the country at large. On this visit to the west—I've traveled all the way from Gansu and Qinghai to Ningxia—I've been stressing that we first build roads to reach every village, every township, and every county. However, the surface grade, whether grade 3, 2, 1, or expressway, should depend on actual conditions in each locale. That's why since arriving in Ningxia, I've also asked Mao Rubai[2] and Ma Qizhi[3] to draw up plans as soon as possible. The state will treat road transport in the west as a special project and give it support, [so] you should hurry up and complete the roads.

After I go back, I'll tell Huang Zhendong[4] I hope the Ministry of Transportation will pay special attention to road construction in the west and ask him

---

1. On October 21–30, Zhu Rongji made inspection tours of Gansu and Qinghai provinces and the Ningxia Hui Autonomous Region. During his stay in Ningxia, he visited the water-pumping station, irrigation zone, and resettlement areas of the project pumping water from the Yellow River for irrigation in impoverished areas. This is the main part of the remarks he made after listening to work reports by the autonomous region Party committee and government.

2. Mao Rubai was then Party Secretary of the Ningxia Hui Autonomous Region Party Committee.

3. Ma Qizhi was then Chairman of the Ningxia Hui Autonomous Region Government.

4. Huang Zhendong was then Minister of Transportation.

to inspect the plans proposed by all the provinces, autonomous regions, and municipalities in the region. The Ministry of Transportation must consider this matter in terms of not only the north-south and east-west road system and the national highways, but also the roads that would provide accessibility to every village, township, and county. In Ningxia, especially in southern Ningxia, this is a key aspect of poverty alleviation. Without roads, even if you have grain you wouldn't be able to ship it [to these areas], so you should come up with a plan as quickly as possible.

You suggested just now that we build a Zhongwei-Taiyuan railroad. I support this and will ask the Ministry of Railways to step up the preliminary work. The state is also very determined to build the rural power grid and make electricity available to every village. We started preparing for this last year, and I had originally said it would take RMB 180 billion—now I'm afraid it will take RMB 260 billion. Within three years, every village in the country must have access to electricity, and the rural grid must be rebuilt. If you don't even have electricity, how will you be able to open up rural markets? How will farmers lift themselves out of poverty?

Now I'd like to ask how Ningxia's development is coming along. [Li Rongrong remarks,[5] "It's less than ideal."] Less than ideal! I hope you'll really focus on this. You must establish a small leading group, and you must have unified leadership; otherwise it will be very hard to move this work forward. You can't let things happen on their own or they will happen very slowly. This infrastructure construction is very important, and I hope you can turn your present less-than-ideal situation into a somewhat better one. An effort is also under way to make TV and radio accessible in every village. This is not only building civilization physically, but is also making cultural progress.

I might just ask, do all your cities and counties have TV stations? [Ma Qizhi responds: No, only in Yinchuan.] I've said very explicitly that apart from the provinces, other prefectures, cities, and counties must not set up their own TV stations. What would you do that for? Isn't it enough for you to rebroadcast programs from CCTV and the [Ningxia Hui] Autonomous Zone TV station? I suspect that you could produce only two kinds of programs: one would glorify the county heads and mayors, reporting from morning to night on where they went today to carry out an inspection and where they will go tomorrow for a ribbon-cutting; the other would be programs from Hong Kong and foreign countries that are full of violence and rabble rousing. If it's just to rebroadcast such movies, why would you set up a TV station? It would burden your people and deplete your funds, and it would especially do the younger generation no good.

5. Li Rongrong was then Vice Chairman of the State Development Planning Commission.

2. Improve the Ecological Environment

We have a policy of improving the ecological environment and reverting farmland to forests or grasslands. Environmental degradation is a very serious and quite frightening problem in western China. Without improving the eco-environment, how can we talk about the great development of western China? Talented people won't come! Therefore we have to seriously implement the central authorities' policy of reverting farmland to forests. We must improve the environment, conserve soil and water, not let the silt be carried downstream, and control loess erosion—this is for the benefit of the people of the entire country!

Yesterday I visited the project pumping water from the Yellow River for irrigation in impoverished areas. This project is already very different from what it was when we decided to start it up. At that time, there wasn't enough to eat, and we wanted grain. That's why it was a good thing to have poor farmers from other places in the Xihaigu area move here and grow grain. However, it now appears that we can't afford to keep planting here because this project has become a huge burden. This is not to deny the value of past activities; rather, it's a historical assessment. We did some tentative calculations yesterday: just the electricity needed to pump water alone costs tens of millions of renminbi a year. You've spent RMB 3 billion for just 2 million mu[6] of land. Is 1 mu worth RMB 1,500? The water costs several tens of millions a year, yet the grain harvested isn't worth that much, and it can't be sold—it can only be stored in granaries. Ningxia is self-sufficient in grain with some to spare. If you have still more grain, you won't be able to sell it—what do you think should be done? In the future, this irrigation won't be sustainable without fiscal subsidies from the government. It now seems, as Ma Qizhi pointed out yesterday, that we can no longer afford migrations like this. Well, if you can't afford it, then stop migrating.

Why is the Xihaigu area poor? Because it lacks water, so grain production is very low. Then stop growing it—ship grain there and let the farmers eat it at no cost. Isn't that poverty alleviation? Then ask them to revert the farmland to forests, to plant grasses and trees, or to combine trees, grasses, and shrubs in order to improve the environment there. Although there is little rainfall, [the soil] can still retain a bit of water. Also, we must control loess erosion. I asked just now [and learned that] the silt in the Yellow River here comes mainly from the Xihaigu area, so it would be a fine thing if you could stabilize the sand. If you plant trees and stabilize the loess, you'll be able to build reservoirs, and grain production in the flatlands can increase. Moreover, the increased grain production will be much greater than the amount of grain produced in the mountains—this is called swapping grain for forests.

---

6. One mu is equal to 666.7 square meters.

Hearing about the working and living conditions of a family of relocated migrants in the Hongsibao Irrigation Area of the Yellow River Anti-Poverty Irrigation Project in the Ningxia Hui Autonomous Region on October 28, 1999.

There is a scientific basis for what I'm saying. Grain is really plentiful now—a nationwide surplus of several tens of billions of jin[7] a year. Besides, it won't decrease in the future because after the environment is improved, grain production in midstream and downstream areas will grow and grow. Meanwhile, because you've improved the environment here upstream, grain production will also increase in the flatlands. That's why it's entirely acceptable not to plant grain on slopes—it absolutely won't lead to grain shortages. We had originally thought we would provide grain at no cost for five years to the farmers who revert their farmland to forests. Now we can be bolder and say that we can provide it at no cost for however long it takes: 8, 10, or even 20 years. Duan Yingbi[8] put it very graphically just now: "You're now saying you'll provide grain at no cost for five years. If, five years from now, the farmers' lives haven't improved and their incomes haven't increased but you stop providing grain, won't they just cut down the trees and turn the forests back into farmland?" That's why we must wait until the farmers' forests have grown so that they can develop various income-producing sidelines and businesses.

7. One jin is equal to 0.5 kilogram.
8. Duan Yingbi was then Vice Director of the general office of the Central Leading Group on Financial and Economic Affairs.

At that point, we can change the policy of providing grain at no cost and ask them to buy grain. If this takes five years, it will be five years; if it takes six years, it will be six years; if it takes ten years, it will be ten years; or perhaps it might take even longer. We are certain not only that we can provide grain at no cost, but also that we can afford to do so in terms of our national finances. That's why this policy kills two birds with one stone—it will improve both the environment and the balance of grain.

The extent to which farmland can be converted to forests will depend on the terrain. All local governments must do research and come up with policies that are suited to local conditions. If [the terrain] is suited for forests, grow forests, and if it's suited for grass, grow grass. I'm not saying grain should not be grown anywhere. Production is very high in the flatlands where you can get 700–800 jin per mu, so why would we not grow grain there? I'm talking about mountainous slopes—farmland there can be restored to forests whether the slope is 25 degrees or 15 degrees. However, you still have to carefully study what to plant there during the conversion, and you also have to respect the wishes of the farmers. The state will pay for saplings, which will be provided at no cost by our forestry agencies.

This policy can be put into action once the farmers understand it, but you must begin at a steady pace. Don't try to do too much at the outset. You've suggested converting 500,000 mu of farmland a year—don't do so much, even 100,000 or 200,000 mu would be quite a lot because the farmers don't understand your policies yet and still don't have confidence in you; moreover, a system is not yet in place [to ensure] that you'll provide them with grain. We also need to have an inspection system—it won't do for farmers to take the grain but not plant the trees. If you're in too much of a rush to act before such a system is established, it might be all too easy for people in the middle to misuse or take [allotments] away, or for officials to withhold grain from farmers—that's what I'm afraid of. That's why at the very beginning you should select locales where officials are of higher caliber, farmers have a better understanding [of policy], and the soil is more fertile, so that they can be role models. Better to start a bit slower than to move too quickly and fail—this would give the policy a bad name.

Another thing—the reversion of farmland to forests need not be restricted to mountainous areas. I traveled several hundred kilometers yesterday and felt that you're still not planting enough trees in Ningxia—after all, you can also plant a lot of trees along highways and railroads! Every family and every household should plant trees in front of and behind its house. Cities aren't planting enough trees either—you should make them greener. To change the ecology, the entire population of the northwest must be mobilized. You should start a campaign to make things green and get everyone to take part in tree planting. It isn't just a matter of changing farmland back to forests—you have to be very clear about this concept.

After we go back, we'll immediately convene a State Council meeting to discuss this policy of "reverting farmland to forests and offering grain instead of relief funds." At the same time, I hope you'll report your views and your concrete plans to us as soon as possible. After the State Council discusses a plan, it still has to be presented to the Politburo Standing Committee and receive its approval—I think we should be able to issue an official document around the end of this year. That way, you'll be able to start reverting farmland to forests by next year's spring planting.

3. Adjust Your Economic Structure

This is a decisive period for economic restructuring. All the provinces, autonomous regions, and municipalities in western China must adjust their own economic structures and establish industrial structures with their own distinct features based on their own climates, resources, and markets. If you don't adjust, you're just waiting to die! This morning we held a discussion with Ningxia state-owned enterprises. A company like the Ningxia Petrochemical Plant has very good conditions for development—it has natural gas, a foundation of good management and public utilities, and should develop further. But your report states you want to produce high-density polyethylene and polypropylene. Don't make these—why don't you make chemical fertilizers instead? These products won't improve your competitiveness and the routing of raw materials also won't work; your strength really lies in making chemical fertilizer. You should integrate your advantage in resources [with production] and develop some new kinds of industries. This is a major subject and it really needs to be studied very carefully. Don't casually start any projects before you have a clear understanding of the market.

As for enterprises that are losing money and have no hope of a turnaround, it's better to let them go bankrupt than to rescue them. You would be assuming a new burden if you were to start up another project and invest several hundred million renminbi—not only would you fail to save [the enterprise], but your burden would grow even heavier. So you should shut it down and just resettle the workers properly. Concentrate your energies on developing a few new industries, industries with market demand.

Economic adjustment could also include tourism. The Chinese people originated in the northwest—it is full of historic sites and relics that are well worth visiting and that also have special educational significance for the next generation. Yesterday, I visited the Xixia Museum and received a very lively historical and traditional lesson in patriotic education. Hence there is a lot of room for growth in this area.

25

THE IRON AND STEEL INDUSTRY MUST CONTROL
TOTAL OUTPUT AND RESTRUCTURE[1]

December 6, 1999

I completely agree with [Wu] Bangguo's opinion [on controlling total volume], and we should carry it out in earnest. These past two years, we have been producing 110 million to 120 million tons of steel a year and importing another 10 million or more tons—I cannot believe we're using it all up. The steel industry should curb its tendency to value quantity more than quality and benefits. At its present stage, the industry should not take on any more large projects, and technical upgrading should focus on quality and management—spend less and get more done.

We have been doing import substitution for many years now, yet more and more steel products are being imported. It's time to examine the lessons of this experience. The key lesson is that product variety, quality, and technical standards have to reach the advanced levels of foreign countries. Costs, in particular, have to be lower than for imports; otherwise we won't be able to substitute even if we want to. As for quantity, not all needs have to be met by domestic production; otherwise there would be no business for the foreign trade sector.

An important reason why project investments can't be recouped and why costs can't come down is that demand is often overestimated. This is also an old shortcoming of our planned economy and should be corrected. I've gone on at length because Baosteel has "great riches," and I hope it will beware of "speaking loudly."[2]

Zhu Rongji
December 6, 1999

---

1. Zhu Rongji wrote several comments on the need for the steel industry to control total output and to restructure (on December 6, 1999, February 27, 2000, and April 8, 2000, respectively). This one was his comment on "A Report on Implementation of Instructions from the State Council to the Baogang Steel Works," submitted by Wang Wanbin, Vice Chairman of the State Economic and Trade Commission, and Pu Haiqing, Director of the State Bureau of Metallurgical Industries.

2. Translator's note: the Chinese saying, "As people get richer, their voices get louder," is used to describe people who become domineering when they get rich.

请培炎、华仁、怀诚、相龙阅后阅。

大厂优少，小厂增多这不符合产业结构调整
的精神。财政、银行应该支持冶金工业部门
的调整工作，支持地方关停小企业，对消耗高能
量不合格、钢材滞销的产品应以信息贷款予以限
贷、停贷。（抄报国务院领导同志，抄送各商业
银行总行等。）

2/4月

邦国副总理并镕基总理：

4.8.

　　去年钢铁工业未能实现较上年减产 10% 的目标，钢产量由
1998 年的 1.14 亿吨增加到 1.24 亿吨，钢材价格平均每吨下
滑 150 元。根据镕基总理和邦国副总理的指示精神，国家经贸
委把钢铁作为今年总量控制、结构调整的重点，力争钢产量控
制在 1.1 亿吨，钢材产量 1 亿吨以内。

　　从 1 月份总量控制实施结果来看，钢产量增长过快的势头
有所遏制，大企业控制产量目标完成较好，但仍有一些地区和
企业超过控制目标，其中河北、山西、江苏、浙江四省超过目
标 8% 以上。根据经贸委党组决定，我们于 2 月 28 日主持召开
了这四个省副省长、经贸委和冶金主管部门负责人参加的座谈
会，要求明确责任，制订措施，确实做好总量控制工作。从 3
月 22 日开始，我们用了近 10 天的时间，又到浙江、江苏两省

Zhu Rongji's directive on reducing production of iron and steel.

26

LET OUTSTANDING ARTS AND CULTURE BE PASSED DOWN FROM ONE GENERATION TO THE NEXT[1]

February 13, 2000

The Chinese people have a magnificent culture with a long history that we should greatly cherish and love. I've visited the Sanxingdui site in Sichuan, for example, and found it truly breathtaking. Cultural relics such as this must be conserved and managed well. They are not only classrooms for our people's patriotic education but also potential centers of culture and tourism showcasing Chinese civilization; they can yield great social and economic benefits. In short, work involving cultural relics is very important and must be handled well.

At present, we are studying and drawing up the 10th Five-Year Plan for all-round national economic and social development, which includes cultural work. Many people rave about the museums they visit in Egypt. Some museums in China, such as the Shaanxi History Museum and the Shanghai Museum, are also very well run—although not very large, they have their own distinctive features. Our country has a great many cultural artifacts, and there should be a place where they can be displayed together. The existing Museum of Chinese History, Museum of the Chinese Revolution, and the Palace Museum alone are not enough, and we should consider building a national museum to display our 5,000 years of magnificent civilization. The preparatory work must be done during this administration. We must engage the world's top designers (including Chinese designers) to plan it. We've already started construction of the National Center for the Performing Arts, but construction of a National Museum would have even greater significance.

Right now, the smuggling and piracy of audio-video products is very serious and crackdowns aren't forceful enough. The departments concerned need to coordinate well and concentrate their forces on combating smuggling and piracy. At the same time, through the media we must vigorously show the world that we stand behind the protection of intellectual property; otherwise, it would be very bad for our country's image and make it difficult to turn social mores around. Many pornographic, crass, and vulgar elements enter [China] through

---

1. These remarks were made by Zhu Rongji after listening to a work report by Sun Jiazheng, Minister of Culture.

Central leaders Jiang Zemin, Zhu Rongji, Li Ruihuan, Hu Jintao, and Wei Jianxing with cast members after a New Year Peking Opera performance in Zhongnanhai, Beijing, on December 30, 1999. (Photograph by Rao Aimin, Xinhua News Agency)

smuggling and piracy—we must not let these things poison social mores and affect the building of a socialist moral culture. Some people think that piracy can reduce the cost of bringing in foreign science and technology, but that's a very short-sighted view. A country that does not protect intellectual property cannot produce innovative ideas.

We must be determined to help all types of art to flourish and mustn't keep flocking to organize evening extravaganzas. Some variety shows use a mixed-bag format imported from abroad with strong commercial overtones, and we should not be imitating them. Before the Spring Festival, the Politburo Standing Committee watched an evening gala presented by the Political Department of the People's Liberation Army. It was a departure from the usual practice of songs being accompanied by dance or dance being accompanied by songs; there was generally just dancing or singing alone, which allowed the audience to focus on each art and thus appreciate it better. Of course combining songs and dances is also a way of performing, and there's nothing wrong with it, but it shouldn't become a fad—why must a dance always take place with a song?

If I had to name a shortcoming, it would be that often too many performers appear onstage, causing spectacular artistry to be lost amid dizzying numbers of people. Of course I'm not saying that absolutely no extravaganzas should be presented. For example, it was essential to have some large ones during last year's celebration of the 50th anniversary of the People's Republic, and they created a very exciting atmosphere. The problem now is the profusion of extravaganzas. Veteran performers are very popular with the audience, but you can't always just have the same old faces. Art requires innovation, and you have to keep producing new talent.

We are still in a period of arduous construction, and arts and culture should inspire everyone to be of one heart and one mind as we fight for the prosperity of the nation and revitalization of the people. Cultural activities should exemplify the spirit of diligence and frugality, championing a style that is fresh and simple as opposed to the trend of pomp and lavishness. Some current social mores are unhealthy, and the people detest these manifestations of corruption. You must help all the arts to truly flourish, and you should guide and encourage cultural workers to create more outstanding works that are truly full of feeling, reflect the times, convey noble sentiments, reverse social mores, and stir the people's spirits. Although opinions differ about the TV series *Yearning* and *Sins of the Fathers,* they reflected the social contradictions of that era, portrayed some very typical people, evoked genuine emotional responses from the audience, and really were very touching.

Cultural work must not only emphasize professional cultural creativity, but it must also show concern for the cultural life of the people and must not just keep its sights set on the cities—it must care about rural areas and about the lives of farmers. Rural movie projection teams are very important—they're popular with the farmers and should be managed well. Movie distribution and screenings are both under the aegis of cultural institutions, and cultural departments and the State Administration of Radio, Film, and Television should work together closely to handle them well. In short, we must enrich the lives of people at the grass roots, and we must stir their spirits, imbuing them with ideals and passion as they go about building their new lives.

I approve of the general approach to cultural exchanges with other countries over the past two years. We should bring in some high-quality arts and culture so that people can understand the world's outstanding cultures; at the same time, we must put a lot of effort into enabling our own national arts to flourish and to introduce our truly outstanding talents to the whole world. Take Peking Opera, for instance. We should introduce classic operas and outstanding melodies to other countries and not just keep performing *The Fork in the Road.*[2] Moreover, we mustn't give foreign audiences the mistaken impression that Peking Opera is just acrobatics or a sideshow.

---

2. Translator's note: *The Fork in the Road* (*Sanchakou*) is a frequently performed opera episode featuring mime and martial arts, with minimal singing.

With the cast of celebrated artists after a performance of famous Peking Opera excerpts on September 15, 1996. Present were Politburo Standing Committee member and Chairman of the National People's Congress Qiao Shi, Zhu Rongji, Politburo member and director of the Central Committee Publicity Department Ding Guan'gen (first row, second from left), Deputy Chairman of the National People's Congress Wang Guangying (first row, second from right), and former Vice Chairman of the Chinese People's Political Consultative Conference Gu Mu (first row, first from right).

Of course art must be innovative—it should introduce new performing techniques and enhance expressiveness through hi-tech methods and a multitude of stage effects—but under no circumstances should outstanding traditions be lost. If Peking Opera doesn't innovate, young people will find it very hard to appreciate, yet if you change it too much, it will no longer be Peking Opera. For example, if accompanied by an orchestra rather than by the *jinghu*,[3] it won't resemble Peking Opera very much. Peking Opera should emphasize singing. Some middle-aged and older audiences in particular like to listen to the singing in Peking Opera, which is why they often say they "listen to Peking Opera" rather than "watch Peking Opera." I see no contradiction in innovation alongside preservation of the traditions and the best of our national arts.

You should introduce outstanding traditional culture to young people. For example, having them learn some classical Chinese and read some ancient poetry will help them understand history, enrich their knowledge, and make them more cultivated. Chinese proverbs and [historical] allusions are concise in words but rich in meaning; they are precise, vivid, and lively, and fully embody

3. The *jinghu* is a traditional, stringed Chinese instrument with a long neck, one well-known version of which is the erhu.

the beauty of our language—young people should be better educated about them. If we don't pay attention to carrying on and enriching our cultural traditions, then the spiritual bonds and cohesiveness that have held the Chinese people together for 5,000 years will be weakened.

Much effort should be devoted to running national academies of arts well. The fiscal authorities should come up with some money for this. We will provide RMB 20 million a year to support cultural creativity, outstanding works, and all that is best in our national culture—if this money is used well, it will be worth it. And we can save some money by not putting on those variety shows, instead using it to support true artistic creation. We must help improve conditions for arts academies and companies while encouraging them to reform boldly and be more market-oriented. In this regard, the State Council supports you.

We must also care about and cherish our veteran artists. Artists as well as scientists are precious treasures of the country and the people. They should be allowed to play a role in transmitting and mentoring so that outstanding arts and culture are passed down from one generation to the next. At the same time, we must consider the needs of daily life and provide appropriate subsidies to various types of veteran artists—the Ministry of Culture should draw up concrete plans for doing this. It is very important to develop culture. Cultural enterprises have very little money to begin with, so it's only right to give them a bit more. I approve of this in principle, and you can apply for support in accordance with standard procedures.

27

Customs Must Regain Its Former Stature[1]

February 20, 2000

The General Administration of Customs is currently holding a meeting of nationwide Customs directors. Generally, we State Council leaders don't attend the working meetings of departments—this is one of our rules. However, Customs is facing an extremely difficult situation: some serious problems have been exposed in the way Customs is cracking down on smuggling, for which it is being criticized in many quarters. Thus you are now burdened with the task of trying to keep your spirits up as you forge ahead with Customs work.

Leaders from the State Council are having this informal heart-to-heart discussion today to demonstrate to you all that the State Council trusts you, that we recognize your achievements, and that we have a correct assessment of the shortcomings in your work. We hope that you will return to your former greatness, reach new heights, do even better work at Customs, and fulfill your mission of acting as the nation's gatekeeper. I'd like to discuss the problems that have been exposed and measures to combat them.

Problems That Have Been Exposed

By 1998 smuggling had become a brazen activity in China, was directly affecting the growth of the national economy, and was creating major financial losses. According to our estimates, direct losses might have amounted to several hundred billion renminbi a year. In the first half of 1998, we had a foreign trade surplus of $43.5 billion, yet only $4.7 billion was settled and sent back—almost $30 billion was lost. Perhaps the actual amount is not quite so high because of some false export reporting, but large sums of export rebates were clearly obtained fraudulently.

In the second half of 1998, we cracked down on smuggling with much fanfare, and things improved greatly, as reflected in the situation from 1999 on. The 1999 trade surplus, for instance, was $29.3 billion and $23.5 billion was actually

---

1. On February 20–23, 2000, the General Administration of Customs convened a national meeting of Customs directors in Beijing. This is the speech Zhu Rongji gave during a discussion with some of the attendees.

183

Addressing some of the delegates attending a national conference of Customs directors in Zhongnanhai, Beijing, on February 20, 2000, with Politburo Standing Committee member and Vice Premier Li Lanqing (first from right), State Councillor and Secretary of the Central Political and Legal Affairs Committee Luo Gan (third from right), and State Councillor and Secretary of the State Council Wang Zhongyu (fourth from right). (Photograph by Wang Xinqing, Xinhua News Agency)

settled, so the two figures are much closer. This demonstrates that the crackdown on smuggling has achieved a great deal, but also how serious the problem was previously—a hundred if not hundreds of billions of renminbi in state-owned assets were lost for nothing. I hope you'll go over these calculations carefully when you review your experiences to determine whether they are correct.

Back in 1995 Jiang Zemin asked me to have a talk with Xie Fei and Zhu Senlin[2] just after we had conducted a major check on our forex. Our original impression was that Guangdong Province was a major earner of forex, but our review showed that Guangdong was actually a major user of forex—its forex deficit had reach $5.5 billion in just half a year. It was not only failing to earn forex, but it was even cheating the country out of these funds. Both men were shocked by the news of this problem, but they also said that Customs as well as the State Administration of Foreign Exchange were controlled by the central government, so there was nothing they could do. And in fact, in 1996 and 1997 the problem only grew worse. Indeed, if the central government doesn't crack down hard on smuggling, there's no way for locals to combat it.

After the forceful crackdown in 1998, Guangdong had a $6 billion surplus in 1999. This is an enormous change, going from a deficit of nearly $6 billion to a

---

2. Xie Fei was then the Provincial Party Secretary of Guangdong Province. Zhu Senlin was then Governor of Guangdong Province.

surplus of $6 billion—you can see the importance of cracking down on smuggling. However, an even more serious problem has now been exposed: a smuggling chain, or rather, a smuggling network is now in operation. If only a single link in this chain dared to act in a principled way, the smuggling would fail. But in light of the situations in Zhanjiang and Xiamen, [we can see] how serious the problem is: the smugglers have been able to buy their way through every single link in the chain and persuade people at each point to fall in with them, so that smuggling can be carried out unimpeded. This is truly alarming.

When smuggled goods come in, they first have to go through transportation links and port handling—this is the work of the Ministry of Transportation and provides a very important checkpoint. If a ship is clearly carrying 10,000 tons of steel but this is reported as 1,000 tons, isn't that smuggling? Next there's commercial inspection, which was originally the job of the Ministry of Foreign Trade but is now handled by Customs. The Customs people responsible for the "three inspections"[3] have all been bought off, so when they board a ship, they keep one eye open and the other shut, and the inspection is quickly over. Then we have tax departments that are supposed to get value-added tax (VAT) receipts—the receipts are fakes! Next they go to the Bank of China to obtain forex fraudulently. The State Administration of Foreign Exchange isn't a link they must go through so things are slightly better there, although that doesn't necessarily mean they have no problems. Finally, we have the industrial and commercial departments, which issue fake invoices. If in this entire chain a single link, a single person was good, then [smugglers] wouldn't be able to buy them off. With bad people throughout the chain, [smugglers] will simply buy them all off. This is a profound lesson—it is a very typical example of corruption, and we have to be on high alert against it!

How extensive is this corruption? Quite extensive. To judge by the problems at the ports of Zhanjiang and Xiamen, about 20% or more of the people there have been corrupted, and this has created huge losses. Doesn't this deserve a high alert among our staff at Customs? We have to recognize the seriousness of the problem, deal with it correctly, and absorb our lessons. If we persist in not cracking down and not taking charge, then, as General Secretary Jiang Zemin has said, it will bring about the ruin of our Party, not to mention our country.

Measures to Combat the Problems

The Party Central Committee and the State Council have adopted a series of measures to crack down on the crimes of smuggling and corruption. When in

---

3. The inspections of goods, animal and plant quarantine inspections, and health quarantine inspections.

1998 we saw that the problem was becoming more and more serious, the Party Central Committee and the State Council convened a national antismuggling conference in Beijing. On July 13, on the morning of the first day, General Secretary Jiang Zemin made an extremely important and impassioned speech pointing out that the fight against smuggling is a major economic as well as political struggle. He asked that we crack down on the crimes of smuggling and corruption in accordance with the law and with great resolve, quick actions, tough measures, and severe penalties. He stressed in particular that the armed forces, the armed police, and the legal departments must halt all commercial activities.

That afternoon, Wu Yi spoke, and after the conference ended on the afternoon of July 15, I spoke,[4] and with strong leadership and organization from the Party Central Committee and the State Council, the national fight against smuggling unfolded rapidly. At the time, I compared the momentum of the fight against smuggling to "splitting bamboo,"[5] as one case after another became exposed. Through a unified command, joint action, and competent performance, we made sure not to overlook even the smallest problems and arrested all those who had broken the law. If it hadn't been for that "clean government hurricane," who knows how serious the problem would be today! And we could not possibly have achieved the good economic results at present. Last year alone, Customs tariffs grew by RMB 71.1 billion, an almost twofold increase. This is a tremendous boost for our fiscal revenues and our economic growth. That's why we should look at this problem comprehensively and correctly.

1. Recognize the Gravity of the Problems. The problems at Customs that we have exposed are very serious, and those at each link of the chain are also very serious.

2. Affirm the Good Work of Customs. Despite the seriousness of the problems it faces, Customs has persevered in its work, continued its fight, and achieved great results—this is something that must be fully affirmed. We went all out to get to the bottom of cases and to arrest offenders. This shows that the majority of those in Customs are good people. Under intense political pressure, you persevered in your work and collected the tariffs, all of which is outstanding. We must look at things dialectically, from both sides. You must transform the ideological pressure on you into a driving force that will help you continue to do the work of Customs well.

---

4. See chapter 6 in this volume.

5. Translator's note: when one end of a bamboo is cleaved, the entire stalk splits open readily. This expression is used to describe an action that progresses rapidly and smoothly, meeting little resistance.

3. *Do Not Let Up in the Fight.* We must continue to investigate the major and important Customs cases and thoroughly smash the smuggling network and smuggling links, showing no mercy and with absolutely no letup. We must not ease up! There will still be problems, and even greater problems may still occur. I must ask all you Customs directors to make this task your highest priority. You must get to the bottom of each case—this is a matter that affects the very life and death of our country and our people, and if we were to ease up, there would be no end to our future troubles! Don't feel demoralized, and don't be listless! You should stand up, stand a bit straighter, perk up, be confident that you are right, and be resolved to keep investigating those major and important cases.

To do this job properly, we must win over the majority, focus our strength on going after the main culprits and investigating them until we are totally clear about their crimes. For their accomplices, we should follow policy. If they confess to everything honestly, they should receive more lenient punishment; if they not only confess honestly but also expose others, they will have done something of value and can be spared punishment. Some are first offenders. If a Customs director was threatened or tempted into committing an error, this of course should not have happened, but we also have to take into account the specific historical circumstances and conditions of the time, so if he shows remorse and makes a contribution, we should immediately let him go. There's one thing we must pay particular attention to: don't suspect everybody and make your own circle very small—that approach won't lead you to a clear understanding of the problems. But don't shirk self-investigations either. You must go after the main culprit and break the case wide open. Otherwise, self-investigations cannot be thorough. If you don't have a clear understanding of the problem and haven't yet uncovered the main culprit, the accomplices will certainly not thoroughly expose others. Only after the facts of the case are clearly established and you have arrested the main culprit can you release the great majority.

I think we will have to ask the Central Commission for Discipline Inspection, the Central Political and Legal Affairs Committee, and the General Administration of Customs to study this jointly and draw up a clear policy on the matter. You said just now that in fact this is already being done and that the might of this policy is already being demonstrated. However, we must make the policy a bit clearer still; otherwise we won't be able to rally the great majority. It won't do to be too suspicious, nor can we be too lax. Once the policy is clear, you can be confident in your work, and you won't get things wrong.

4. *Strengthen Customs through Ideological Means.* We have to build up Customs using laws, institutions, political ideology, and technical means. First, we must ensure that the leadership is incorruptible and self-disciplined and must strengthen its ideological work—this is extremely important. The problems

exposed in Customs are a reflection of weak ideological work on our part—we put operations first, not politics. We don't seem to talk much about putting politics foremost nowadays, but I think this is something we still need to talk about. The first of the "three emphases"[6] is an emphasis on politics.

The most important concern here is that an official in a leadership position be incorruptible and self-disciplined. When leading officials like ourselves originally joined the Chinese Communist Party, we had already affirmed our proletarian worldview and philosophy of life. We all swore to fight for the liberation of the proletariat and of all humanity and to fight for the realization of communism. Other than this, what goals could we possibly have? The most exotic delicacies? You can only eat three meals a day. A fancy hotel room? It's still no more than a bed at night. What exactly are you aspiring to now? Someone said just now that we are being ruined by our mouths, eating and drinking day and night. Comrades, that kind of eating and drinking will harden your arteries.

I recently read a description in a Taiwan newspaper about how Wang Yung-ching[7] stays healthy. He said that simplicity is the way to stay healthy—the more complications, the shorter the life. At mealtimes, he doesn't eat delicacies, mainly just simple dishes. Occasionally he'll have a fish head, a few slices of lotus root, and a bowl of porridge. What good can come out of going to one banquet after another all day long? You'd just be making trouble for yourself and hastening your own death!

Comrades, unshackle your minds and come back to our proletarian worldview and philosophy of life. There's a saying, "When you're born naked and you die naked, you don't have a care in the world." You were naked when you were born, and won't you be naked when you leave this world? What could you take with you? It's only when you're fighting for your Communist ideals that you really sense the meaning of life. Right now, people will talk about you behind your back no matter what you do; never mind if you did something bad, they'll talk even if you did something the least bit inappropriate. And it doesn't matter if you're some leading official or other; there'll always be people critiquing you behind your back, judging whether your actions were right or wrong, good or bad. Don't think that they can't see clearly—if you do something you shouldn't have done, what you'll get is a whole pile of invective.

What are you doing? I think that as Communist Party members, we should correct our worldview and philosophy of life. In particular, those of us who are public servants should always be thinking of ways to do something for the people, to bring some benefit to the nation. As for whether we get a little more remuneration or a little less, whether we are promoted a bit more quickly or a

6. Emphasizing study, emphasizing politics, and emphasizing a sense of what is right.
7. Wang Yung-ching was the founder of the Formosa Plastics Group.

bit more slowly—what's the point? As top Party and government decisionmakers, provided you correct your worldview and your philosophy of life and take a firm stand, you won't become corrupt, or at least serious problems won't occur. This is the most important point. That's why I feel that Customs should greatly strengthen its ideological work.

Some people have been unseated during this major rectification of Customs, and I'm afraid we should work very hard to recruit some officials. During this fight, quite a few people have stood firm and passed the test—promotions should come from among these young people, especially the ones in operations. But even this won't be enough. We can't just consider operations officials; we also have to select some officials from outside who are outstanding, who are ideologically quite sound, and who are tried and true, and let them become mainstays at Customs. Initially they can focus on doing ideological work and serve as deputy Customs directors or deputy Party secretaries. After they gradually learn the profession, they can be promoted or rotated. I think this is very important, and we should take action promptly. All departments should send some people here to support Customs.

5. Help Customs Officials Avoid Mistakes through Laws and Institutional Means.
One way to avoid mistakes is to establish a system of checks, among other institutional devices. Before the founding of the People's Republic, banks had a checking system, but now that they use computers, they no longer check—that won't do. We used to talk about the "three ironclads": ironclad account books, ironclad abacuses,[8] and ironclad rules. I've repeatedly asked the banks to keep this fine tradition. Nowadays they don't emphasize them nearly enough, and they've never really taken this issue very seriously. Even some leading officials don't know what the "three ironclads" are. Now there are many fake accounts, which are signs of corruption. If a bank president has the means at hand to arbitrarily deploy large sums of money, if he doesn't have to enter these in the books, and if his every wish is a command, isn't this going to corrupt him?

I recently read a funny story on the Internet about something that happened at the Hangzhou branch of the Agricultural Bank of China, which turned out to be true. A worker deposited several hundred renminbi at this branch using a credit card. When he looked, the card indicated a balance of RMB 620,000,000. He wondered, "Is this for real? Let me give it a try." First he tried to withdraw several hundred renminbi, and sure enough he was able to do so. So then he started buying gold jewelry and other valuables, which of course was subsequently discovered. How did it happen? The procedure for using the credit card was to first enter the account number on a keypad and then the sum of money.

8. Translator's note: an ironclad abacus is an extremely accurate one.

Although the bank employee correctly entered the account number first, he then punched the same number again. The account number was something like 620,000,000, and he never checked. This shows that we cannot do without a system of reviews.

To give you another example, recently the Hong Kong Stock Exchange lost power for 20 minutes, which resulted in the loss of several tens of billions of Hong Kong dollars. What caused this? In the event of a power failure, its system was supposed to automatically switch power sources from the main power supply to a backup supply, but the operator had not read the instruction manual carefully enough. When the power failed, he immediately pressed the button that turned the automatic switching off completely, so no switching occurred. That's why they lost power for such a long time. The newspapers said this was a great humiliation for Hong Kong—a world-class economic center, whose staff couldn't even read an instruction manual properly. Later it instituted a new system: two people had to be present before the button was to be pressed; one person alone could no longer do it. Shouldn't Customs also have a checking system like this? You should always have someone on hand to supervise, you should have two people checking on each other, and only then will you commit fewer mistakes.

Furthermore, I think we must keep using a system of end-of-term audits. Recently the presidents of the four major state-owned banks started rotating and changing places, and the average age of their officials was lowered considerably. This is one way to help them prevent errors. When a leading official has been in the same office for too long, he will be surrounded by too many "palanquin bearers" and thus be more likely to make mistakes. For those who will be reassigned this time, we should conduct thorough end-of-term audits. This is not a question of not trusting a person—it is one of our country's systems, and we must abide by it.

I've already asked the People's Bank to hurry and come up with a set of evaluation criteria for commercial banks. From now on we will start evaluating the performance of bank presidents and use these criteria to determine who is doing a good job and who isn't. Then nobody will be able to create fake accounts. We must explicitly tell these bank presidents that they have to work with the State Audit Administration and perform good audits on the outgoing presidents. If you don't do so, then in the future all your predecessor's problems will be attributed to you—we must make this clear. This is absolutely not a question of whom we trust and whom we mistrust. You audit the books of your predecessor, and your former unit will audit you—everyone has to be audited. Only then can we institutionally guarantee that you will not make mistakes, or at least make fewer of them. We must be sure to keep using this system.

The State Audit Administration should concentrate on achieving some breakthroughs instead of spreading itself too thin. If you try to audit tens of thousands of units all at once, you might be able to uncover a few irregularities, but it won't solve the problem, and it won't be as significant [as making some breakthroughs]. We must thoroughly audit leading officials at the end of their term, especially leading officials who are exceptionally influential—this is one of our country's important systems and it must apply to the Minister of Customs and the deputy ministers as well. The audit will not be restricted to the highest-ranking official of each unit, either; nor will we say that the higher ranking the officials, the less the need for audits. Henceforth end-of-term audits must be carried out for every single leading official, especially for those of vice ministerial rank or above. This is very important—otherwise responsibilities won't be clear. This measure will, through laws and institutions, help leading officials avoid making mistakes or at least make fewer of them. Of course leading officials must first improve their own awareness, ideological level, and self-cultivation, and must be incorruptible and self-disciplined. This is the only way to ensure the purity and incorruptibility of our ranks.

In addition, we have to strengthen every aspect of our work in cracking down on smuggling. For example, the antismuggling police of Customs need to work closely with public security departments on major and important cases, but how? We have to think of institutional approaches. So many people have been arrested in the antismuggling crackdown—the forces of Customs aren't large enough, and without the cooperation of public security departments, they couldn't have achieved such great results.

The major areas of corruption that need close attention at present are smuggling, financial crimes at banks, and tax-related crimes. The measures we employ to deal with these areas must be effective. For example, the Customs Administration's antismuggling police should be reinforced with people performing compulsory military service, and they can be rotated. This is a rather good method that can institutionally maintain the fighting spirit of the antismuggling police. Whereas in the past very few people were arrested for smuggling, last year the 3,000 antismuggling police arrested 3,000 smugglers—this is an outstanding achievement.

6. Strengthen Technical Measures. While I was in Guangzhou in 1998, I saw its network—a network jointly operated by Customs, the Ministry of Foreign Economic Relations and Trade, and the State Administration of Foreign Exchange. As soon as a Customs declaration is checked [on the network], you know immediately if it's real or fake. I hear that you're studying even more advanced computer systems and networks. This will require a breakthrough—sometimes problems are difficult to uncover or check on if you depend entirely on people, so we have to rely on the most advanced technologies. The fake Customs declarations discovered in the first half of 1998 were worth US$11 billion. After the current network was put in place, the detection rate increased greatly, and many problems disappeared before they became crimes. That's why Customs must use advanced technology to build a hi-tech and very secure computer system—you must bring in some talent that understands this technology. Only by combining advanced methods with people who understand them can the work of Customs be done well.

The equipment used by Customs to scan containers was made by the Tsinghua Tongfang Company—we developed and made it ourselves. You can give them suggestions for improvements and should offer them some incentives in the future. Once cars are examined by these scanners, we can see right away if they contain anything inappropriate, including handguns and drugs. Nowadays the paperwork is correct when goods leave the port in Hong Kong because it's harder to fool Hong Kong Customs; but once they get to our shores everything changes, and 10,000 tons easily becomes 1,000 tons. That's why we must cross-check with Hong Kong Customs. Once we're networked, won't the problem be solved? [The exercise of sovereignty over] Hong Kong has already returned to us, so many issues can be resolved through technical means.

Finally, I sincerely hope that all of you at Customs, especially the leaders, will keep your spirits high, return to your former greatness, reach new heights, and elevate the work of Customs to new standards. The Party Central Committee and the State Council trust you! We believe that the team at Customs can stand up to the test, and even though serious mistakes have been made, most of you are good; the majority of leaders are absolutely firm in their stands and are incorruptible. There may have been some termites and some lawbreakers, but now they've been arrested, and Customs is cleaner than ever. We must not deny the achievements of reform and opening up just because there have been some serious cases of smuggling. Such problems will occur in every country. We're very fortunate to have discovered them quite quickly and to have resolved them. We mustn't criticize the open policies of the special economic zones because a major smuggling case occurred in Xiamen; nor should we disparage the entire Customs team because of a few termites and lawbreakers. The majority of the Customs team is good.

Comrades, I hope you will perk up, hold your heads high, stand firm, and focus on your work. I want to thank you for the economic results and economic benefits that you have achieved cracking down on smuggling during the past year. You must persevere in your work and not let up. I hear that because you're now under heavy pressure and you are being criticized, some of you feel much put upon, your service attitudes have worsened, and you lose your temper when dealing with clients and with people going through our ports. That's not good—you should take pains to stamp out such sentiments and help these people become more positive so that they don't feel put upon. The central authorities follow policy and are judged by the punishments they mete out to those who have made mistakes. The main culprits who should be shot must be shot; accomplices who confess honestly will be dealt with leniently; those who contribute by exposing others will be spared punishment. I hope you will all raise your spirits, absorb these lessons, unite everyone at Customs, do your work well, and together complete the task entrusted to you by the Party Central Committee and the State Council.

28

A Conversation with Pascal Lamy, EU Commissioner for Trade[1]

March 29, 2000

ZRJ: Mr. Lamy, I'm delighted to meet you. I had previously dealt with Lord Brittan[2] for many years, and now I'm meeting you. I think that we're negotiating counterparties as well as partners in cooperation, and at the same time we will also become close friends.

The moment I saw you I knew you would be a tough negotiating counterparty, because you're just like our Minister Shi,[3] who has lost all his hair in his negotiations. This suggests that you'll be a bit tougher than Leon Brittan, but I think that the more this is so, the better friends we'll become.

I'd like to first say a few words to relax the atmosphere, and then we can conduct intense negotiations.

PL: Mr. Premier, thank you for your friendly words, and also for taking the time to meet with us.

You mentioned my predecessor, Lord Brittan. I must say that he has done a lot of work to make it possible for China to join the World Trade Organization, and in this regard I want to express my respect for him. If he had not personally made such efforts in those years past, we would not be where we are today.

ZRJ: May I interrupt for a moment—you've put it very well. I was only trying to tell a joke and didn't mention Lord Brittan's contributions. I entirely agree with you and was only joking.

PL: Mr. Premier, I think we're already very close to a direction that will lead us to the right place. Coming back to China after two years, I can see that everything here is flourishing, and there is ample confidence. This is an excellent sign that shows that you can play a very good leadership role. We can see how the internal

---

1. This conversation between Zhu Rongji and Commissioner Lamy took place in the Hall of Purple Light in Zhongnanhai.

2. Leon Brittan was a former Vice President and Trade Commissioner of the European Union.

3. Shi Guangsheng was then Minister of Foreign Trade and Economic Relations.

Meeting with European Union Trade Commissioner Pascal Lamy at the Hall of Purple Light, Zhongnanhai, Beijing, on March 29, 2000. (Photograph by Wang Xinqing, Xinhua News Agency)

policies formulated in China can bring people together, and at the same time we have seen the role you have played for joining the WTO.

As you know, there are still some issues that need to be resolved in our bilateral negotiations. I'd like to give you a simple description of the spirit of the talks. We very much hope that China will join the WTO. Because of the reasons I mentioned, we will still have to conduct many rounds of negotiations. Your reaching a bilateral agreement with the United States last November got this process off to a good start. We very much welcome this agreement because it will greatly help things develop. But there are still some problems between us that require a joint solution. As far as we are concerned, your bilateral agreement with the United States should not be the only point of reference.

This is mainly due to two reasons: one is political; the other is technical. The political reason is based on a mutual understanding between China and the European Union about what the world political system should be like, that the world should be multipolar, and China's relations with the European Union are different from China's relations with the United States. To the member nations of the European Union and to public opinion in the EU countries, these are not the same. We are moving forward in this direction also because there are even more technical questions. It's precisely because of this basic fact: some issues that were important in your negotiations with the United States are not so important to us.

In the negotiations, the Chinese side agreed to let the United States keep its protectionist measures for a longer period of time, but for us, we don't need such a long time. The balance you have reached with the United States affects us, and this kind of balance is not very convenient for us. In some specific areas, we also understand that in the course of events China will need to gradually introduce some things and gradually abolish some things, primarily [restrictions on] automobiles, telecommunications, insurance, and state-sponsored trade. I'm prepared to show some flexibility on these matters to accommodate China's concerns, that is, to gradually abolish or to gradually open up.

Mr. Premier, if you agree, I could meet with you or with Minister Shi in the afternoon to jointly explore ways to resolve the problems. I leave it to you as to whether we should talk now or talk later, or whether I should talk this afternoon with Minister Shi. As for the resolution of the remaining problems, I have some ideas.

ZRJ: We have to conduct bilateral negotiations with 37 members over China's joining the WTO. As of now, we still haven't reached an agreement with 8 members, and of these, we're close to signing with 5. The European Union is one of the major ones of the remaining 3 with which negotiations are not about to be concluded.

Because the European Union, like the United States, is one of our largest trading partners, we hope that it will not be the last to conclude negotiations with us, or be unwilling to sign an agreement. That's why although our negotiations with the European Union are very intense, they're also very friendly.

I agree with your thought that the agreement between China and the United States should not be taken as the sole point of reference. We know that the issues the European Union is concerned about are not the same as the ones the United States is concerned about, and you each have your own distinctive points. For example, the United States is concerned about exports of wheat and citrus fruits, while you're probably concerned about exports of grape wines and olive oil. Isn't that so? Is there anything else?

We fully understand the composition of EU membership and have made very great concessions. Minister Shi says that we've already made great improvements to 125 of 150 tariff numbers, and have made many concessions on lowering tariffs. We haven't made such concessions to the United States. Of course I must also add something to your comments. Although each country has its own distinctive points, every concession we make to one country is a concession to all countries. That is, a concession to the United States is also a concession to you, and the concessions we make to you today are also concessions to the United States. We cannot allow two types of policy to appear.

You mentioned auto tariffs and the proportion of controlling interests in telecoms and insurance. Since these are issues you raised today as well as issues we argued about most intensely with the United States, I don't see any differences between you.

I remember that last year's agreement with the United States was reached almost at the very brink. During the last round of negotiations, they changed their air tickets and checked out of their rooms four times. I don't know if they really would have left, but they indeed changed their air tickets and checked out of their rooms four times. The last time, which is when we reached an agreement, they told us in the morning that they had to leave at 10 a.m., so I had to rush over to the negotiation venue at 9 a.m.

The several issues they were insistent about were the ones you're insisting about today: auto tariffs, shareholding percentages in telecoms, shareholding percentages in insurance, and eight products traded exclusively by the state. Now you're insistent about four products, while the United States was insistent about eight. On the day they were to leave, I went to the venue at 9 a.m. to negotiate with Ms. [Charlene] Barshefsky and Mr. [Gene] Sperling, and I made no concessions on these four issues. What did I make concessions on? It was the provisions on special safeguards and antidumping—we agreed to extend these by several years. But on these four issues, I did not make any concessions.

This was because it was the consensus of all our departments and of our entire nation that we should hold firm on these, so I could not make concessions. Mr. Lamy, permit me to make a joke—even if you were to change your air tickets five times and check out of your rooms five times, I would still make no concessions!

PL: But I'm not that sort of person.

ZRJ: You spoke before I had finished, and you said what I was going to say. As a European, your character is entirely different from that of the Americans, and you wouldn't do such a thing. I was just joking.

But I do want to make one thing clear—it's not that we will never make concessions on these four issues, but you must give us a transition period. That is to say, once our oversight capabilities are in place and once China's own enterprises have a certain degree of competitiveness, we will certainly make concessions on these issues. Personally, I feel that it's entirely possible for us to make greater concessions on these four issues after a period of time and that won't pose any threat to China. But at present we can only do so much, and this is the limit of what the Chinese people can accept. Please give me time and don't demand that I do this immediately. If you must demand that I do this, then we'll get stuck on this question. This is what I said to Ms. Barshefsky on November

15, 1999: "Why should we let Sino-American relations and the negotiations over China's joining the WTO end so unhappily over these few issues?" We all have to keep the big picture in mind. These four issues are not such a big deal; it's only a matter of time.

For my sake, please consider this: at that time we made no concessions to the United States. These issues are not like those of grape wine and olive oil. If we were to make concessions to you today, wouldn't that be slapping ourselves in the face?

Don't view these issues too seriously—they're basically not questions like grape wine and olive oil. I can say that these issues are general ones that any country would be equally concerned about and would take equally seriously, and on which there cannot be any new openings. We can make concessions on other issues and have authorized Minister Shi to negotiate with you. We must keep the big picture in mind! Please say something about the other areas we need to talk about.

PL: Mr. Premier, Thank you for your explanation. I have two comments.

First, these four issues are highly political ones. China cannot make any concessions on these four issues because the United States has made no concessions, but politically we cannot accept this reason. As we see it, the relationship between the European Union and China is not this type of relationship. We have already fully considered the difficulties China has encountered in discussing these four issues with the United States. Therefore our demands are different from the American demands: ours are more specific, more targeted, and will take more time. In insurance, for example, we only want life insurance—in this area the European Union is more competitive than the United States. In telecom, we only want mobile telecom, not land lines, satellite phones, and international Internet. This is because our European mobile phones are very easy to use. I have one that works very well in Beijing, but it doesn't work in Washington.

The issues we are raising are different, and after seeing the content of your negotiations with the United States, we did not make the same demands. That is why I asked you to have another look at our position and to show flexibility when we have discussions with Minister Shi. Of course you said just now that you cannot make any further concessions because you want a principle of reciprocity, but what we're asking for is not a very great concession. Rather, because of some political and technical reasons, we are asking you to consider some individual European interests. I have to be responsible to the European Commission and the EU Council. If I can't help you clearly understand our position, I won't be able to answer to them. I can show flexibility, but I must be able to resolve these important issues.

ZRJ: Mr. Lamy, this is our first meeting, and I had intended to make friends with you by being earnest, frank, and very relaxed, but you've taken economic issues and elevated them into political ones, which has made me more wary. I hope you'll listen to my words more carefully and not misconstrue them. I did not say that things we had not promised to the United States could not be promised to the European Union. We promised you we would improve 125 tariff numbers—isn't that a concession? Haven't we made concessions to you that we didn't make to the United States? How can you say that we're discriminating against the European Union politically?

What I said just now about the four issues of telecoms, insurance, and so forth is our bottom line for any country. It isn't our bottom line for only the United States, nor is it for the European Union—it's for all countries. Therefore we cannot make [these] concessions to the United States, and we can't make them to the European Union. Didn't I make this very clear? There's no political content at all. Mr. Lamy, I hope you'll take note that China's current relations with the European Union are very good. They're very good in all political and economic aspects, and there are no political issues.

On these four issues, I see no difference between the European Union and the United States. You say you're more competitive than the United States in insurance and in mobile telecoms, but I don't believe it. Of course I don't believe it has an edge over you either. True, right now European mobile telecoms have the edge in the China market, but that's mainly the result of the U.S. embargoing us and of our cooperation with Nokia of Finland. In life insurance, it's mainly AIG, which was originally founded in Shanghai and later went to the United States. At the time it applied to enter the China market, no European company had applied. We approved the American company, so the American company gained an advantage in the China market, but we've never said that American companies are always better run than European companies, or that European companies are always better run than American ones—I've never felt that way. We don't delineate by countries or regions, but by companies. So if you ask me to judge which is an American strength, which is a European strength and which is a Japanese strength, and to draw up corresponding provisions to meet everyone's demands, we wouldn't be able to do it.

That's why this is all we can do for now—that is, on the most critical issues we can only establish some general principles that are applicable to all countries. At the same time, we can give some special considerations directed toward each country's unique features, but these special considerations are applicable in turn to all countries, and cannot be solely directed toward any one country.

I don't know if I've made it clear and if you've heard clearly? I hope you'll point out anything you're not clear about, and not create any misunderstandings.

PL: I listened very attentively to what you just said. I'm sorry if I spoke too frankly—that only demonstrates my lack of experience. The major issues I want to discuss are automobiles, life insurance, mobile telecoms, and state-sponsored trade. Will you be able to meet the demands of the European Union over a very long transition period in way that addresses these demands?

I agree with your saying that these are sensitive issues. That's why we would give you a very long transition period and are so pleased to have an opportunity to discuss things with Minister Shi.

In terms of insurance, the United States has a larger market share in China. AIG has been established for a longer time and has a large market share. That's why we want to maintain a balance in the numbers of insurance companies before China joins the WTO.

In terms of state-sponsored trade, the European Union is not asking for this to be abolished; rather, we hope to bring in other participants in a steady, gradual way. I think you can understand our position, and I also hope to make myself clearer; that is, we don't want to ask the Chinese government to make any commitments that would put it in a difficult position. I hope you will also show flexibility and also not put us at a disadvantage.

I'd like to ask you to agree to a general guiding principle for our next round of negotiations, namely that agreements between China and the European Union must have prominent EU features.

And this is something that we can achieve only when, without any preconditions, we discuss all the topics and analyze the positions of both sides. I hope to bring the negotiations to a conclusion, but the results reached by the negotiations must have European features. Otherwise, given the members of the European Union and given the European Parliament, my authorization would not be sufficient to complete this task.

All I ask of you is that when you give instructions to Minister Shi, there should be no preconditions and no topics that cannot be discussed, and when each topic is discussed we have to see if the European Union is getting balanced treatment.

ZRJ: If you had spoken so clearly from the very start, perhaps the atmosphere around our negotiations would have been a bit more relaxed. I too apologize. I also had some misunderstanding about what you said. But perhaps that's because we're extremely sensitive about the word "political," and we're very afraid of turning an economic issue into a political one, thereby complicating matters. As you said just now, I think we can reach a consensus on these four issues.

For example, on the matter of life insurance, I said very clearly that there can be no concessions at present on shareholding percentages, but that will certainly improve in the future. As for the number of insurance companies, we've never said that there must be more American companies than European ones. Why?

Because the United States is 1 country and you're 15 countries, so you should have more than it does. Right now there are more American companies, so we'll just continue approving European ones. Just keep increasing! Provided they meet the conditions, we'll approve them.

As for exclusive [state] distribution, during my last negotiation with the Americans on November 15, 1999, Ms. Barshefsky said that President [Bill] Clinton told her over the phone that we had to abolish exclusive distribution of chemical fertilizers; otherwise he wouldn't be able to answer to people in American business circles. I did not agree. I told Ms. Barshefsky, "Go explain to President Clinton that I cannot make this concession. Let's sign now and discuss this later." As you said just now, and I fully agree with your view, in the future we will definitely gradually give consideration to this question. We could even make a certain degree of concession to the European Union on the issue of quotas. As for what you were saying just now, that the Sino-European agreement has no European features, that you can't go back and won't be able to answer for it—but, Mr. Lamy, I think that the present outcome of our negotiations already has a considerable number of European features. We never made so many concessions to the United States on so many tariff numbers. Of course we can't make any more concessions on auto tariffs. If we made any more concessions, the American industries would destroy ours. Now this isn't just our worry; companies including your Volkswagen of Germany are very worried, and GM of the United States is also very worried![4]

SGS [Shi Guangsheng]: Europe has the most companies in China.

ZRJ: But on the other issues, we've authorized Minister Shi to negotiate with you in earnest and make concessions to the greatest extent possible, so that our agreement can have more European features. But I also ask you to understand us—we can't make such great concessions all at once, because the concessions we make are not only applicable to you; they'll also be applicable to the United States. You also have to consider for our sake whether or not we can handle them. If China's economy were to suffer negative effects from joining the WTO, I think it wouldn't be good for the world, or for any of our partners in cooperation.

PL: Mr. Premier, Europe agrees with you on one point, namely that China's economy is in the process of transitioning and China has been very successful at it.

The European Commission sees China not only as a market but also as an important future partner, but this sort of partnership needs nurturing, it needs care. That's why the final agreement must clearly display European features. You mentioned proposed customs tariffs—China has indeed improved, but

---

4. Translator's note: both Volkswagen and GM had large joint-venture operations in China.

the average weighted tariff rate that China is proposing to the United States is clearly much lower than the one it is proposing to the European Union.

ZRJ: [Asking Shi Guangsheng] Is that true? He [pointing at Shi Guangsheng] hasn't done the calculations, so let's exchange materials. You really are very sharp. I hadn't noticed Lord Brittan raising this question.

SGS: It's because he used to be a banker.

PL: Lord Brittan started off as a lawyer, whereas I'm a businessman; he is a Liberal whereas I'm a Social Democrat.

In Europe and in France, I've discovered there are two types of Social Democrats: one type knows what numbers are, and the other type doesn't. I completely agree with what you said just now about automobiles. Some Chinese auto factories, such as Volkswagen and Citroen that have investments from European companies, are not especially enthusiastic about lowering tariffs and gradually opening up to joint ventures. More concretely, I will go over all the specific issues once with Minister Shi. If necessary, we will also ask you to make a decision during the discussions as to whether or not our demands are balanced.

ZRJ: I think you can conduct comprehensive, frank, and earnest negotiations. You can talk about anything, but I still hope that you can accomplish your mission during these historic talks.

Finally, I also want to say that we have very good relations with all the countries in the European Union, and political relations in particular are very good. We definitely regard the European Union to be one of the regions friendliest to us. If I were to say our relations aren't better than Sino-American relations, then at least they're not worse than Sino-American relations. I can point out some facts. Our relations with the United States are sometimes good, sometimes bad, and they follow a tortuous path. But our relations with the European Union are different. Ever since we established ties, relations with the European countries have been good. During the so-called elections in the Chinese territory of Taiwan, only President Clinton issued a statement expressing congratulations to the leaders in the territory of Taiwan, and no European country expressed congratulations. Therefore I want to thank the European Union for supporting us on the issue of "One China." We are good friends politically, and good partners economically. We don't want to see the European Union become the last region to sign a bilateral agreement with us on China's joining the WTO. Hence we place great hope in you, Mr. Lamy, and we hope that even as you make your arguments you will show some flexibility and accomplish this mission. Thank you.

29

THREE ECONOMIC RISKS
WE MUST GUARD AGAINST[1]

April 18, 2000

At the time of this year's "Two [Annual] Meetings,"[2] we saw a great increase in the number of social disturbances all over the country, marked by protest marches, railroad and highway blockages, deaths in coal mines, and so on. General Secretary Jiang Zemin and I were both extremely anxious and didn't sleep well for several nights in a row. When I discussed this with him, I pointed out that we have to carefully guard against three risks: (1) the risk at state-owned enterprises (SOEs), which might also be called the risk in social employment; (2) the latent financial risk; and (3) the risk in the rural areas and in agriculture. I'm talking about these in economic, not political, terms.

We came to Jiangsu to investigate and research these concerns and concluded this stage of our work today. We learned a great deal here and also corroborated and enriched some of our original ideas.

Risks at SOEs

It's fair to say that we'll be able to achieve our goal of rescuing SOEs from their difficulties within three years, but this won't actually solve their problems. SOE problems can only be resolved if three basic conditions are present.

—First, SOEs must have good mechanisms, mainly multiple forms of public ownership. In the spirit of the 15th Party National Congress, we must implement shareholding systems, clarify enterprise ownership rights, separate government from enterprises, operate and manage openly and transparently, move toward the market, and accept market oversight. Otherwise it will be very hard to change the practice of "eating from the same big pot."

---

1. On April 12–19, 2000, Zhu Rongji visited Xuzhou, Huaiyang, Yangzhou, and Nanjing during an inspection trip to Jiangsu Province. This is the main part of the remarks he made after listening to work reports by the provincial Party committee and the provincial government.

2. Translator's note: the annual meetings of the National People's Congress and the Chinese People's Political Consultative Conference.

—Second, they must have a good management system. I'm referring to a modern enterprise management system.

—Third, they must have a good and well-developed management method, that is, a method of rigorously selecting and overseeing enterprise leadership teams.

Our SOEs haven't met these three conditions yet, and it will still take many years of hard work to do so. A very important step in this direction is the establishment of a social security system.

In 1997 we proposed to "standardize bankruptcies, encourage mergers and acquisitions, lay off and reassign [employees], trim staff and increase efficiency, and implement reemployment projects." In reality, however, we did not take the initiative to "lay off and reassign, trim staff, and increase efficiency," so we still have 5 people, or perhaps even 10, doing the work of 3. Why? Because we still haven't established a social security system. Enterprises can be run well only if they can trim staff at any time, in keeping with the needs of production and management. They can't be run well without such a mechanism, but in order to trim they must be backed by a social security system.

The "three-thirds"[3] system currently in use at reemployment services centers is [only] a transitional measure: enterprises can't afford it, unemployment insurance funds are insufficient to support it, and fiscal departments also have difficulty propping them up. As a result, it isn't really working, particularly in provinces with faltering economies. That's why we must establish a social security system that is independent of the enterprises and socialize the distribution of aid; otherwise we won't be able to maintain social stability. And to establish such a social security system, we must first solve the problem of funding. We're now trying to prepare the necessary groundwork for such a system before the end of the year and then expect to start establishing the system next year.

This social security system will have minimal standards and be tailored to fit Chinese conditions: it will allow laid-off workers to have enough to eat and to get by, but they still won't be able to eat very well. We had initially proposed that reemployment service centers handle laid-off workers for only three years, but I'm afraid this won't do—we'll have to keep supporting them all the way until they find new jobs. That's why we need a single national standard, a single system of collections and payments, and a single method of funding.

To begin with, provincial governments must be in charge of overall planning and should complete this basic work as soon as possible. The present "three lines of security" (a guarantee of basic living costs, a pension insurance system,

---

3. The "three-thirds system" refers to a State Council regulation regarding laid-off workers who were receiving reemployment services. Their enterprises, society at large, and government finance departments were each to be responsible for one-third of their basic living costs, including health care and old-age insurance costs.

and a guarantee of minimal living costs) must be handled well. Then we have to gradually incorporate the measures planned at the provincial levels, increase the scope of [fund] collections, and increase the collection rate. If we can improve and refine this system and achieve 100% socialized collections and payments, then national master planning and resolution of the funding problem will be fairly manageable. Provided the central authorities are determined, it won't be impossible to solve the funding problem either. After all, there are only a few ways to achieve this:

—Make adequate provision in the fiscal budget for social security funds.

—Improve and refine the current methods for collecting social security funds in order to collect enough of these funds.

—Designate a portion of taxes (for example, the tax on interest) for the social security endowment, thus establishing a national social security endowment and ensuring it has a fixed income.

—Reduce holdings in or sell off state-owned assets, either listing them abroad or domestically, and hand over 10% of the money raised to the state for establishing a social security endowment.

—Operate and manage social security funds [for higher returns]. Many countries have been successful in this regard; that's why we believe that such a social security endowment can be established and that we now have the ability to do so.

With such an endowment, we would not only be able to guarantee that SOEs will have a good opportunity to trim staff on the basis of need, but we would also be able to ensure social stability and have fewer disturbances. After the disturbances in Zhenjiang, I remarked that blocking traffic has become a fad. This won't do. We need to distinguish between the issues here. On one hand, if you cause a disturbance it must be because of shortcomings in our work, so we need to do better. If the rural cooperative funds, sales-and-marketing cooperatives, and whatnot aren't paying up, then we need to put out a notice to reassure people and guarantee payments—we'll solve your problem. On the other hand, you may not block traffic. If you do, you'll be most unceremoniously dealt with as the law requires, and we'll also get to the bottom of who is organizing things behind the scenes. If traffic was blocked from morning to night, how could we maintain order and how could the economy develop? Problems should be handled as problems, and we must be sure to resolve them for you, but if you block traffic and disrupt public order, then you should be subject to criminal penalties.

On this visit to Jiangsu, I've gained insight into this question as it relates to the State Council's decision this year—mentioned in the "Report on the Work of the Government"—that laid-off workers should have their basic livelihoods guaranteed by the reemployment service centers of their enterprises and then gradually transition to receiving unemployment insurance, with these [two systems] eventually merging. It now appears that the conditions are not yet present for us to immediately start pilot programs. Unless the funding sources are in place, how can they merge? Thus it wasn't prudent to decide to start pilot programs in some provinces and municipalities in eastern China. This might be possible in some localities that have strong economies, such as Shenzhen and Xiamen, but there aren't too many such places. That's why we've now decided not to start pilot programs immediately. Those provinces with the conditions to do so may try it on their own.

The main thing is to refine the existing social security system and put the "three lines of security" fully in place—that would be quite an achievement in itself. Then you could devote your energies to broadening the scope of coverage, raising the collection rate, strengthening management, realizing the socialization of collections and payments, figuring out the size of pension arrears, and not reporting false figures. Do this foundational work well in preparation for the State Council's implementation next year of a unified social security system. Even next year I'm afraid we'll still have to first operate pilot programs in a few provinces. It would be hard to expand [the program] nationally right away because the pace of economic growth differs across the country. Once the State Council draws up unified regulations, we can carry out the merging—only then will we be able to gradually establish a socialized security system.

Latent Financial Risks

I fear that the greatest risk we face is a financial one, owing to decades of debts and especially the mess left behind by a certain degree of economic overheating in 1993. Nationally, the banks have RMB 10 trillion in deposits and 9 trillion in loans, of which 40–50% are nonperforming loans—this is a very major risk. How can you use up all the people's savings? If they all want to withdraw money, what will you pay them with? Even if you printed money, you wouldn't be able to roll it out quickly enough. Of course the problem isn't yet so serious that it might blow up in our faces at any moment, because our economy is still capable of steady growth and people still trust our Party and our government. It hasn't gotten to the point where they have their passbooks in hand to withdraw money. However, if we don't attend to this matter and if the proportion of nonperforming loans continues to increase, the situation will become very dangerous. We will resolve this problem level by level.

1. The Problem at State-Owned Commercial Banks. Loans at these banks account for 80% of all loans. As long as a high proportion consist of nonperforming loans, it will be very hard to institute a series of modern financial management mechanisms and systems for evaluation and oversight, including [systems

Hearing from local farmers about their economic burdens in Wu'an Township, Gaoyou, Jiangsu Province, on April 15, 2000. (Photograph by Li Xueren, Xinhua News Agency)

for] transfers of leading officials and for in-term and end-of-term audits. Not only will it be impossible to run banks well, but it will be extremely dangerous. The Agricultural Bank has the highest proportion of nonperforming loans, now reaching 47%, followed closely by 45% at the Bank of China. I was totally shocked—how is it that even the Bank of China has gotten into such a mess? We must properly investigate and review our experiences.

Although bank presidents were responsible for creating these nonperforming loans, all of you gentlemen here also played a role! We can't just blame the banks—government intervention in the banks was also excessive. Furthermore, the banks are of poor caliber: they don't have a system for managing risk, nor do they understand economics or production, but think solely in terms of banking; they also don't know what redundant construction is, and they don't know what sorts of loans will turn into nonperforming ones—I feel these are their greatest flaws. Meanwhile, local leaders keep telephoning with requests for loans, and the banks have no choice but to comply. Cheng Kejie[4] went so far as to call local

---

4. Cheng Kejie was a former Chairman of the Guangxi Zhuang Autonomous Region who became Vice Chairman of the National People's Congress in March 1998. In 2000 he was sentenced to death for accepting bribes.

bank presidents and demand that their banks lend to companies he designated. Almost all these companies were privately run, and after they received the loans, the kickbacks went into Cheng Kejie's pockets.

Generally speaking, the interventions of local Party and government leaders were related to the development of their local economies, so were well meant and at the time thought to be beneficial. It wasn't until after the fact that they learned that a lot of the money went into redundant construction and couldn't be recovered. Ultimately they did bad things out of good intentions. That's why banks must establish risk-assessment systems and absolutely not accept any outside intervention—bank presidents must be responsible for this. During the major reshuffling of bank presidents now, we must conduct end-of-term audits and track down responsibilities. A loan might be for several billion or several tens of billions of renminbi—we have to find out who made the decision. Some of the responsibility lies with others, but some also with the bank president.

2. Financial Risk in Irregular Fundraising. This problem arises mainly in rural cooperative funds, in the capital stock divisions of sales-and-marketing cooperatives, and in various types of trust and investment companies and securities firms. At present we have 90 securities firms, 28 of which have been rectified, while most of the remaining 60 or more were set up by the banking system itself. Quite a few securities firms are in an utter mess, so if there's a problem, who the devil are you supposed to look to?! We're currently doing our best to eliminate some risks during the term of this administration, for if they were to linger on, the problems would only get more and more serious.

We've decided to use relending to help locals solve the problems of rural cooperative funds, with Sichuan being the first case. Recently we also began addressing the problems at the capital stock divisions of sales-and-marketing cooperatives, and you in Jiangsu are the first case in this regard. Following our investigation of these capital stock divisions, my rough guess is that their problems can't be resolved unless the central government comes up with RMB 10 billion—you'd better be mentally prepared. The price the entire nation will have to pay for this will be a hundred billion renminbi, and then the only course of action will be to print money. We must absolutely never do such stupid things again. After all, you can do a lot of good with RMB 10 billion—that's enough to build eight or nine bridges across the Yangtze River. You'll be spending RMB 3 billion to build the second bridge across the Yangtze, but you'll actually only have to fund RMB 1 billion of this, and that even includes Treasury bonds and various funds; the rest will come from loans from the China Development Bank. Therefore none of you should ever consider irregular fundraising again.

Looking over some materials yesterday, I was stunned by the size of debts at all levels of a certain province's government. The village and township governments and the county governments parceled these out to the farmers: on average each village owed RMB 500,000, and one township might owe RMB 4 million to 5 million. Yet many "county lordships"[5] still fail to understand this problem since many [debts] were incurred by their predecessors, and they won't discover them until there's a hint of trouble and the people demand payment.

The financial situation in Jiangsu and its irregular local fundraising are not one bit better than in other places. Henceforth you must pay sufficient attention to this problem. We did many stupid things for so many years, and now we're paying the price, which amounts to buying a lesson. Don't ever do this again! If you do things properly, you'll accomplish more, do it quickly, do it well, and do it economically. If you use improper and underhanded methods, you'll be spending money for nothing, and you'll have nothing to show for it.

On this trip to Jiangsu, we also gained insight into the remaking of rural credit cooperatives. This helped refine our original thinking, providing it with greater specificity and depth, and led us to conclude rural credit cooperatives are the best financial link for connecting farmers together, and we should turn them into financial institutions that will truly help farmers meet their production and living needs and help adjust the agricultural structure. The funding that famers require to adjust the agricultural structure as well as to ease their difficulties in production and living is also unresolved, [because] no bank is willing to lend to farmers. At the moment rural credit cooperatives can't play this role either. For one thing, their burden is very heavy, and they are seriously in debt—they were saddled with a large part of this burden when the Agricultural Bank of China split up.

After we go home, we must help the rural credit cooperatives shed this burden and handle things through separate accounts. Historical problems should be dealt with separately—we can't place this burden on the present rural credit cooperatives and render them incapable of operating normally. Furthermore, rural credit cooperatives should direct their lending toward villages and not toward county seats. Their rural deposits should not flow into cities; they should flow from cities back to the villages. The business departments of rural credit cooperatives and county cooperatives must change direction and lend to the villages. Deposits from county seats should also be loaned to villages and should not be used in county seats. This is because county seats already have branches of all the various banks, whereas nobody is looking after the villages. Of course this will not come about easily, but change it must.

3. Rural and County Credit Cooperatives. Each rural cooperative and its corresponding county cooperative should be combined into a single entity. Village

---

5. Translator's note: a traditional term for county magistrates. Here it refers to leading officials at the county level.

cooperatives should come under their direct administration and become their representative offices or branches. This will facilitate the unified deployment of funds within a county for use in promoting the development of agricultural production and the restructuring of the composition of agriculture. We should also consider establishing some cooperatives or associations in prefectural-level cities or even at the provincial level. This must be done slowly, however.

First we should properly rectify the county cooperatives, change the direction of their lending, and replenish their funds. To achieve this, we've been exploring the possibility of returning all current rural postal savings to rural credit cooperatives and having the People's Bank handle them. The postal savings system can only take deposits and may not make loans, for if it did, contradictions with the rural credit cooperatives would arise. For example, you in Jiangsu have RMB 1 billion in rural postal savings at the county and subcounty levels, which should all be turned over to the People's Bank. After it is turned over, the full amount will be returned to the rural credit cooperatives through relending, and the interest [on this relending] should be lowered. County and subcounty postal savings should be returned in full to rural credit cooperatives, while urban postal savings would be put to other uses.

Next, the rural credit cooperatives themselves must be rectified, and they must downsize. Jiangsu has over RMB 2 billion in cumulative rural credit cooperative losses—this won't do. If you're a financial institution, you should be converting deposits into loans and collecting a handling fee in the middle—how can you lose money? There's no reason whatsoever for this. The problem is that there are too many people; too many people have to be supported. Therefore agencies have to be streamlined, staff must be trimmed, and rural credit cooperatives must become a main force for developing rural finance under the new historical conditions: we should assign them this historic task.

After we go back and further investigations and studies are completed, we will formulate a document, submit it to the Standing Committee of the Politburo for review, and then issue it. The State Council has decided that before the Central Committee's document is released, Jiangsu will first conduct a pilot program.

I had been wondering all along how to meet the funding needs of the farmers but hadn't thought of any good ways. Now I feel that rural credit cooperatives are just right for taking on this historic task. The other banks need not continue to operate in villages and should pull out of all of them. They can operate in cities above the county level, and they don't need to operate in certain county seats. The loans of rural credit cooperatives should not go to township and village enterprises. If you loan to them, you'll definitely lose money, because you don't have the ability to assess risks at these enterprises and you won't be able to get your money back. I joked last night that I even question the need for the Agricultural Bank of China to exist—you're losing several tens of billions of renminbi a year, so what do I need you for! We might as well parcel out those tens of billions to the farmers and be done with it.

If the rural credit cooperatives are run well and the funding needs of the farmers are met, then there really wouldn't be much value in the continued existence of the Agricultural Bank of China, because your loans to industrial projects could be entirely taken over by the Industrial and Commercial Bank. But don't worry, you comrades from the Agricultural Bank of China, I have absolutely no intention of abolishing your bank. This is just a warning. If you don't start fending for yourselves, you'll be in danger of being abolished!

Rural Areas and Risks in Agriculture

One of our historic achievements has been to solve the problem of feeding our people. Dean Acheson's White Paper[6] predicted that the Chinese people would be unable to feed themselves. This is no longer a problem today. What's more, our grain supply exceeds demand. Our grain enterprises have 516 billion jin[7] of grain in storage, which is equivalent to 55% of our annual production. If you add the farmers' surplus grain to that, we have about 1 trillion jin. The Chinese people now have plenty to eat and wear! But the problem this creates is that grain isn't worth anything, [farmers] produce more without earning more, and their incomes might even decline. If this problem isn't solved, it could affect the farmers' enthusiasm for growing grain. Once farmers stop planting, we will immediately be in danger. Of course the threat doesn't seem so ominous at the moment because we have a buffer, but we mustn't take it lightly.

Our extensive investigations in northern Jiangsu have shown that the solution to this problem is still to make uncapped grain purchases, to still implement the "three policies and one reform."[8] We're unable to control grain prices now and have trouble selling it at a profitable price because we haven't properly implemented the policy of uncapped purchases. According to nationwide surveys, at

6. This refers to a White Paper entitled "United States Relations with China," edited by Secretary of State Dean Gooderham Acheson and published by the U.S. State Department on August 5, 1949. After the White Paper was completed, Acheson wrote to President Harry Truman on July 30, 1949. In the letter he said, "The population of China during the eighteenth and nineteenth centuries doubled, thereby increasing unbearable pressure upon the land. The first problem that every Chinese Government has had to face is that of feeding this population. So far none has succeeded." Cited in Mao Zedong, "The Bankruptcy of the Idealist Conception of History," in *Selected Works of Mao Tse-Tung*, vol. 4 (Bejing: Foreign Languages Press, 1975), p. 452.

7. One jin is equal to 0.5 kilogram.

8. The "three policies" are to make uncapped purchases of surplus grain from farmers at the protected prices, have grain purchase-and-storage enterprises sell grain at profitable prices, and operate grain purchase funds in a closed system. The "one reform" is to accelerate self-reform at grain enterprises.

present we've purchased only two-thirds of the farmers' surplus grain, so one-third is still in their hands. Jiangsu is a bit better, you've bought up 80%—this is what you reported. After his investigation in Yangzhou, Ni Zhenbang[9] concluded that they're doing good work with grain there, but their report contains a slight exaggeration for in fact they haven't purchased 80%. They're still a few percentage points off, nor have they managed to make uncapped purchases year round.

When I made some inquiries of farmers myself, they indicated that the grain departments forced down both [grain] grades and prices, that they in fact weren't purchasing, and that when the farmers needed cash they had no choice but to sell their surplus grain to private dealers. If this is the situation in Jiangsu, where this sort of commodity grain is relatively abundant, then we can see how it would be even harder for places like Henan and Hebei to make uncapped grain purchases. It's really not bad to have purchased two-thirds of the surplus grain nationally because this two-thirds has stabilized grain prices, but in the end that one-third remains unbought. If the state-owned grain stations won't buy, then the private dealers will, and once they buy it they will drive prices down.

During my investigations, 3 jin of corn went for RMB 1 in Hebei, while wheat was RMB 0.38–0.40 per jin in Xuzhou. I doubt whether farmers would be willing to sell at these prices—they're too low. The reason market prices are so low is that state-owned grain stations aren't buying. Given that the grain supply basically exceeds demand, this problem can't be solved by so-called uncapped purchases. If there are no caps on purchases and private dealers go to the villages, will they buy at prices higher than our protected prices? Of course they won't! They will only drive prices down. The way to prevent private dealers from driving prices down is to have state-owned grain stations put up a sign and buy grain every day at protected prices 365 days a year. This way, prices will stabilize. Of course we mustn't force down grades and prices and must offer prices commensurate with quality. If we do that, there will be no danger whatsoever in further uncapped purchases, and it won't matter who goes to buy grain.

Why is that? Because farmers aren't so stupid. If you're clearly making purchases without caps here at RMB 0.6 per jin, why would they sell to private dealers at RMB 0.33 per jin? That would be truly strange! Purchasing without caps is a result of our central authorities' grain policy, and in the end we will be able to make such purchases, but it is not a way to help farmers resolve their current difficulty in selling grain, and if we don't raise the percentage purchased, then we won't be able to make purchases without caps. Therefore we're preparing to convene a national work conference on grain before the summer harvest. Then we will clarify this problem, further implement the policy of purchasing without caps, and increase fiscal subsidies.

---

9. Ni Zhenbang was then Director of the State Administration of Grain.

Why are state-owned grain enterprises unwilling to make uncapped purchases? They can't afford to, so we give them subsidies—this is a "joyous burden" for the country! We must subsidize. Any country would subsidize, let alone China. To do so, we must replenish the grain risk fund. We've now basically set a protected price—for wheat, it's about RMB 0.57–0.59 per jin—and it's already begun to go down. Some provinces want this price to be lower still, but we think it can't be lowered too much or else it will affect the income of farmers and lead to rural instability.

At this price, farmers will earn RMB 8 billion less. We've now tentatively decided to return this RMB 8 billion by using it to replenish the grain risk fund. There is currently about RMB 25 billion in this fund and adding RMB 8 billion would be equivalent to increasing it by a third. This way we can go from purchasing two-thirds now to purchasing 90%. If we can purchase 90% or more, rural grain prices won't fall, and the interests of farmers will be protected; it will be easier for grain enterprises to sell at profitable prices, and they will no longer lose money. All of this will be very beneficial.

Where will this RMB 8 billion come from? We should continue using the current ratios, with the central government subsidizing so much and the local governments matching this with so much. If the locals are truly in difficulty, the central government will have no choice but to lend them money through relending. Of course these questions still need to be carefully studied and addressed. One very major question is whether this subsidy will reach the grass roots or whether it will be misappropriated and withheld at every level. The fiscal authorities will have to get a clear picture of the subsidy situation, issue a bill, and send the money down to the grass roots in one lump sum. We can't have each level allocating and dividing up the money, because by the time they finish, it won't have reached the grass roots. Only by ensuring that the central grain risk fund is really sent down to the grass roots will we actually be able to increase purchases.

We've learned a lot about this issue through this investigation in Jiangsu and are now even more confident about the benefits of "three policies and one reform." Some places in northern Jiangsu are doing fairly good work and should continue to do better. You still have to trim staff, however. You also have to separate government from enterprises, but Jiangsu Province has already established a grain company. County grain bureaus should be separate from the grain company. They should supervise it and should not "eat" it—it would be awful if they did that! They should supervise to make sure it is making purchases without caps and not forcing down grades and prices.

The grain bureau and the state-owned grain company must not be one and the same. If government and enterprise are not separated, there will be a monopoly, which will breed corruption. The government must be standing at the side [of the company] to supervise it. In short, I feel that villages and agriculture are the foundation of our national economy. If this issue is not handled properly, our economic growth won't last long, and great dangers will arise.

The three issues I've just discussed are ones that the State Council is most concerned about. Our investigations and studies during this visit to Jiangsu provided tremendous insights. Comrades, you 've have done a great deal of work, offered us valuable experiences and lessons, and enabled us to formulate some policies that have guidance value for the entire country. For this I want to express my thanks to you.

30

THE ELECTRIC POWER SYSTEM MUST BE REFORMED[1]

June 13, 2000

Please ask [Jiang] Zemin to read this. The Ertan power plant is not discharging large volumes of unused water because of high electricity prices. (The cost of power generation is low; electricity prices are high because the interest on investment loans is high, so recouping costs is expensive.) The regulated price of electricity is RMB 0.31 per kilowatt-hour, whereas the regulated price of power supplied to the grid is only RMB 0.18 per kilowatt-hour. It's so cheap, yet they're not allowed to generate—in 1998 they discharged enough unused water to generate 1.5 billion kilowatt-hours, in 1999 it was enough for 8.1 billion kilowatt-hours, and this year they might discharge enough for 10.2 billion kilowatt-hours.

The main cause of such great waste is that power sector reforms have been lagging. We must change the present arrangement of having the province be the entity that generates power and must establish a system of transregional companies, with power plants separated from grids, and price competition in supplying power to grids; we must also encourage hydropower, restrict thermal power, and close down small power plants. This way we can save tens of billions of renminbi a year in power-generation costs.

Zhu Rongji
June 13, 2000

---

1. The Ertan Hydropower Station is located in Panzhihua City in Sichuan Province. It was built to meet the increasing power needs of the Sichuan-Chongqing region; all construction was completed and put into production in December 1999. Because of changes in the power market and factors in its management system, from the time its first set of generators started producing in August 1998, the Ertan Hydropower Station never received the full benefits of its power production. It was forced to discharge large volumes of unused water, and its normal operations were seriously affected. These are Zhu Rongji's comments on a report entitled "Conditions at the Ertan Hydropower Station."

215

请泽民、岚清同志：二滩电站大量弃水并不是由于电价高（尽管成本偏低、好投资贷款还息高，导致成本电价高），因投产电价0.3元/度，实际上网电价只执行0.2几元，主管使值也不让发。二滩水电站有关情况1998年弃水电量15亿度，1999年弃水31亿度，今年可能弃水120亿度。造成如此大的浪费，主要是电力体制改革滞后，必须加速。有力实体的现状，实行建电厂网分开，竞价上网，多发水电，限制火电，实行小电网，降解了时的发电成本以伍计。

朱镕基 6.20

二滩水电站位于四川省攀枝花市，是雅砻江上建设的第一座水电站，总装机容量330万千瓦(6×55万千瓦)，多年平均发电量170亿千瓦时，是我国目前已建成的最大的水电站。现将二滩电站的概算、上网电价及有关情况汇报如下：

一、关于概算问题

二滩水电站于1991年9月正式开工建设，1999年12月全部建成投产，但二滩水电站从1986年最初审查初步设计以来，工程概算几经调整，投资总额增幅很大。具体情况是：

(一)1986年初步设计概算审定工程投资为37亿元，当时是按1985年价格水平计算的，且按全部内资拨款建设，未计入建设期利息。1987年决定利用世行贷款后，于1990年编制了利用世行贷款的项目概算，按1989年价格水平，其静态投资为63.5亿元(含外资6.28亿美元，按3.7314汇率折合人民币23.4亿元)，计入价差预备费后总投资为75亿元(未计入建设期内资利息)。

(二)1993年二滩水电站在土建工程国际招标并主体工程全部由外国承包商中标后编制了内外资概算，当时按1991年价格水平计算，其静态投资为105亿元(其中内资63.11亿元，外资7.77亿美元，按5.4478汇率折合人民币42.33亿元)，动态总投资为210亿元。动态投资比静态投资高出一倍的原因是93年正是物价和银行贷款利率的高峰时期(物价上涨指数为10%，贷款利率为9.9%)，仅建设期还贷利息就达66亿元，价差预备费39亿元。

Zhu Rongji's directive on a report entitled "Conditions at the Ertan Hydropower Station."

31

ON USING RELENDING TO HELP LOCAL FINANCIAL INSTITUTIONS REPAY DEBTS AND GUARANTEE PAYMENTS[1]

August 1, 2000

Xianglong:

Yesterday, we exchanged views on preventing and mitigating financial risks. The policy of using central bank relending to help local financial institutions repay loans and to guarantee payment is very important and complex. Such relending is in fact a form of fiscal relending because apart from a very few provinces, most do not have the ability to repay debts, so this is equivalent to having the central government print money to repay local debts. If we don't handle macroeconomic controls seriously and prudently, there will be a dangerous potential for financial risks and inflation. I've been considering this problem for a long time and after thinking it over repeatedly last night, I feel it is still necessary for me to make my views on it clear.

According to the materials you provided, as of this July 26, central bank relending has been or will be needed to resolve a cumulative total of approximately RMB 230 billion of financial risks. Of this amount:

---

1. This letter was written by Zhu Rongji to Dai Xianglong, Governor of the People's Bank of China. After the national conference on financial work of November 1997, rectification of the financial order was intensified across the country, and a decision was made to dissolve a number of local financial institutions whose assets were seriously outweighed by debts. In order to maintain social stability, the State Council agreed in November 1999 to allow the People's Bank of China to engage in relending for the purpose of paying the legitimate high-risk natural-person debts and foreign debts of local financial institutions. The relending was to be done by qualified local financial institutions, and local governments were to assume the responsibility for debt repayments. Zhu Rongji felt that using central bank relending to help local financial institutions repay debts and guarantee payments was a form of fiscal relending that bore financial risk and the hidden danger of inflation. He therefore wrote to Dai Xianglong asking that the central bank strictly control such relending and undertake its measure carefully. In accordance with State Council regulations and the expectations in this letter, the People's Bank of China, the Ministry of Finance, and other departments would draw up strict conditions and procedures for relending.

1. RMB 83.8 billion of relending has already been approved for resolving local financial risks, of which 37.4 billion will be for rural cooperative funds, 15.6 billion for urban credit cooperatives, 28.1 billion for trust and investment companies, 1.5 billion for the capital stock services departments of supply and marketing cooperatives, and 1.2 billion for the rectification of the "three financial irregularities."[2] Estimates based on the requests of locals indicate that we will have to increase this by an additional 101 billion. RMB 184.8 will be needed for these two together. It is said that the Ministry of Finance's estimate is even higher, that [it calculates] 220 billion will be needed.

2. A total of RMB 45 billion will be used for bailing out small and medium financial institutions and for relending, rebating interest to commercial banks, and advancing funds for debt repayment by Chinese [government-]owned enterprises in Hong Kong and Macao.

In the final analysis, this sort of central bank relending to local governments is a type of fiscal relending that basically cannot be recovered. In order to mitigate the financial risk involved, which is due mainly to historical causes, in order to maintain social stability, and in order to create a good environment for the sustained, rapid, and healthy growth of the national economy, the current policy of using central bank relending to conditionally guarantee payments is both correct and necessary—and appears to be a price that must be paid. But given the present state of macroeconomic development and the circumstances surrounding the implementation of this policy, it seems that first, the demand for central bank relending by the locals and by financial institutions is too great; second, quite a few people in economic circles feel there are already hints of inflation in our country; and third, we are beginning to see signs that some local governments and SOEs are deliberately avoiding debt payments or failing to pay, and financial moral hazard is increasing.

Therefore if we don't strictly implement this policy and don't strictly control total relending, we will not only fail to achieve our goal of preventing financial risks, but we might even turn good work into bad, covering up wrong decisions by those in charge at various levels along with the misdeeds of corrupt elements, which would be unfavorable for strengthening the awareness of preventing financial risks by local governments and state-owned enterprises as well as their ability to deal with it. At the same time, we would also be leaving behind hidden dangers for the future growth of the national economy.

Thus from now on we must be stricter than ever in controlling and in tightening fiscal relending used for resolving financial risks. However, we will not be

---

2. The "three financial irregularities" were irregular fundraising by some local governments, agencies, enterprises, public institutions, and individuals; irregular approvals for the establishment of financial institutions; and irregular conduct of financial transactions.

"closing the valve," nor will we be changing this policy. Rather, in the spirit of being highly responsible to the Party and to history, we must handle the degree [of controlling and tightening] properly. Regardless of whether a financial risk was caused by a central government enterprise or a local one, we are going to take charge. But we must assign responsibilities clearly—we cannot fail to make distinctions. At present, we are implementing a system of central and local tax streaming as well as fiscal budgeting at both the central and local levels. We have to make it clear that the locals must bear the main responsibility for the financial risks of local governments and enterprises, and they must think of every means possible to raise funds on their own and work hard to mitigate them. They cannot pass everything over to the central bank (and ultimately to the central government's finances).

Of course the central bank has also been somewhat lax in exercising its oversight responsibilities. If the locals have really made the greatest possible efforts but still have difficulty in finally resolving the payment problem, or if cases of social instability should even arise (now that the financial risks are so serious, it is impossible to expect no "troublemaking" to occur), the central government of course has a duty to lend a hand. Nonetheless, there is still the matter of degree, because even the central financial authorities are stretched very thin.

Also, "guarantees of payment" can only be conditional guarantees; they cannot be unconditional guarantees of payment in full. The people's participation in fundraising entails an element of coercion but also an element of their seeking high yields. Creditors (depositors) should also assume some of the risks and some of the losses themselves; debts cannot all be repaid by the government.

Likewise, the risks in international debts of local trust and investment companies cannot all be assumed by the government. We should publicize the successful experiences of Guangdong Holdings Ltd. and Dalian State-Owned Assets Management Co. Ltd.[3] in reducing their debts and use methods such as debt restructuring to force foreign parties to reduce debts. Don't be afraid of the so-called effect on the country's reputation. Debts of local financial institutions are

---

3. Guangdong Holdings Ltd. was established in Hong Kong in 1980 by the Guangdong provincial government. It was a "window to the world" company that was to raise money from abroad. Because of management problems and the effects of the Asian financial crisis, the company accrued more debts than assets. The provincial government decided to separate the Yuehai Group from the government; at the same time, it entered into negotiations with international creditors, who would have to assume part of the losses. In accordance with market principles, Yuehai was then reorganized into a shareholding enterprise. After restructuring, the company's debt-to-asset ratio and finances improved markedly. The Dalian International Trust and Investment Company was a fundraising enterprise of the Dalian Municipal Government. By the end of August 1999, its debts exceeded its assets. After negotiations with its international creditors, a debt reduction agreement was signed that waived a portion of the principal and interest it owed them.

not guaranteed by local governments, and even less should the central government be expected to repay them—that would make no sense! In accordance with international practice, creditors (the foreign financial institutions) must also assume operational risks!

Zhu Rongji
August 1, 2000

32

WE SHOULD USE ECONOMIC MEASURES TO ELIMINATE OVERCAPACITY[1]

August 3, 2000

For the past two years, the State Economic and Trade Commission has been actively organizing and implementing the work of industrial restructuring, with notable results. As experience has shown, enterprises that pollute the environment, destroy resources, are poor in quality, or fail to meet production safety standards must be administratively shut down in accordance with the law; otherwise, these enterprises will not withdraw from the market on their own. However, we can only use economic measures to shrink and constrain those enterprises manufacturing products that are already oversupplied and force them out through elimination by the market.

By so-called economic measures, I mean stopping banks from lending to enterprises whose costs are higher than market prices and that are operating at a loss. Moreover, local fiscal authorities must not protect these backward enterprises by using measures like subsidies. At present, the best way to prevent eliminated enterprises from coming back to life is still to use the levers of market mechanisms and prices. For example, the price of sugar has already risen from RMB 2,000 per ton to RMB 3,400. A profitable selling price has already been achieved, and in some places it has already risen to RMB 3,700 per ton. We should sell off excess inventories of sugar in a timely manner to keep sugar prices steady. Otherwise, small sugar factories and beet sugar factories that have already been eliminated will undoubtedly be encouraged to resume production.

Zhu Rongji
August 3, 2000

---

1. These are Zhu Rongji's comments on a report from the State Economic and Trade Commission entitled "Progress Report on the Closing Down of the 'Five Small Enterprises,' on Eliminating Backward Production Capacity, and Reducing Overcapacity." (On the "five small enterprises," see chapter 14, n. 4, p. 123.)

两年多来，国务院各部门积极组织实施产业结构调整工作，取得显著成绩。实践证明，对污染环境、破坏资源、质量低劣、不符合安全生产条件的企业，必须依靠采取行政关团的措施，不如此，这些企业不会自动退出市场。但是，压缩、限制长线产品生产的企业，只能采取经济办法，通过市场调味使其（供求平衡）退出。所谓经济手段，主要是指对那些成本高于市场价格、销售三块的要企业停行止贷款，地方（银行）财政更不能以补贴等手段来保护已亏损的企业。

关于关闭"五小"、淘汰落后、压缩过剩
生产能力进展情况的报告

当前，防止那些被淘汰企业死灰复燃的最好办法，仍然是利用市场机制和价格杠杆，例如，若钢价现已经每吨4000元，降到2000元乃至更低，就可以实现技术销售，部分也百企业可能降到3000元，应该及时抛售去大的储备，重存以年抑提价格，否则必将鼓励已淘汰的小钢厂和钢铁新厂重新恢复生产。

邦国副总理并报镕基总理：

长期以来，相当一部分国有企业之所以陷入困境，其中一个重要原因，就是多年来的重复建设，造成了生产能力低水平的过剩。特别是"五小"企业污染环境、浪费资源、质量低劣、技术落后、不符合安全生产条件，不关闭，不让它们退出市场，就无法实现结构调整。不淘汰落后的工艺和设备，就无法实现产业的升级，就无法应对加入 WTO 后所面临的挑战。根据市场需求实施总量控制，把过剩的产量压下来，关闭"五小"、淘汰落后的生产能力，是改善企业经营环境和市场环境的重要措施，也是推进经济结构战略性调整的重要步骤。

按照党中央、国务院的统一部署，我们用了两年的时间，基本完成了纺织压锭、减员和整体扭亏的突破口任务。到 1999 年底，全国累计压锭 906 万，分流安置职工 116 万人，国有

Zhu Rongji's directive on the "Progress Report on the Closing Down of the 'Five Small Enterprises,' and on Eliminating Backward or Reducing Excess Production Capacity."

33

SEVERAL ISSUES REGARDING XINJIANG'S DEVELOPMENT[1]

September 10, 2000

Xinjiang is very important strategically. It covers one-sixth of China's total land area and lies adjacent to most of our neighboring countries. The Central Committee pays a lot of attention to our work in Xinjiang, and Jiang Zemin in particular has spoken about the region many times at meetings of the Politburo Standing Committee.

I've been to Xinjiang four times since 1987. On this trip, we went to Ili in northern Xinjiang and then Aksu and Bayingolin in southern Xinjiang. We visited oil fields and gas fields and gained a deeper understanding of the region. At the same time, we saw how much Xinjiang has changed over the past few years. Its economy has shown striking growth, with major adjustments in its industrial structure, considerable infrastructure construction, and significant increases in its fiscal revenues; the lives of the people have also improved greatly, and there has been notable progress in ethnic unity. As a border region populated by ethnic minorities, Xinjiang has had to deal with factors from many sources that disrupt and destroy the unity of its peoples. Its success in overcoming many difficulties to achieve so much is extraordinary.

I've come to Xinjiang this time because, together with all of you here, I want to deepen our insights and understanding of the strategic concept of "the great development of western China" and explore how to further implement this concept. Because of the region's strategic importance, its development is the most important component of the "great development of western China." Through this study tour and the constant exchanges of views with you here in Xinjiang, we have arrived at the following observations about how Xinjiang should implement this strategic concept.

---

1. These are the highlights of Zhu Rongji's remarks during an inspection tour of Xinjiang. They were previously published in *Selected Writings on Work in Xinjiang (1949–2010)* (Beijing: Central Documents Publishing House, 2010).

1. Speed Up the Growth of Resource-Oriented Projects

This refers mainly to oil and natural gas, the most important project right now being the shipping of gas from western to eastern China. The prospects for exploiting oil in Xinjiang appear good at present, and our hopes for natural gas are even higher. According to current verified resources, conditions are ripe for the construction of a 4,200-kilometer gas pipeline from Xinjiang to Shanghai. Although this enormous project will require an investment of RMB 120 billion, we are still determined to do it, and the faster the better. You can't turn natural gas into wealth when it's buried underground—it must be put to use in order to turn into wealth! Is it possible to use it all up in Xinjiang? You can't use it all! You must ship the gas out. You will benefit from shipping it out not only because the areas along the pipeline in Xinjiang will develop economically, but you will also earn tax revenues.

Wang Lequan[2] told me that the present resource tax on natural gas is too low. The resource tax on oil is RMB 20 per ton, which is an average figure that varies from place to place and is determined by costs. By contrast, the resource tax on natural gas is RMB 4 per 1,000 cubic meters. This needs to be thoroughly studied, but please set your minds at ease—we won't put you at a disadvantage. We'll do everything to support Xinjiang, but it must be within reason. I think that the increase in Xinjiang's tax revenues will be considerable, and this figure must be carefully calculated. As the gas fields and oil fields are developed and as the gas pipeline is built, these will give strong impetus to the economic development of Xinjiang. I believe that the region will gradually become one of China's most important [production] bases for oil and natural gas.

2. Concentrate Your Energies on Developing Xinjiang's Water Resources

Over half of Xinjiang's 1.6 million square kilometers is composed of desert or gobi,[3] but as long as water is present, there can be oases. With ecological problems worsening by the day and if development [of water resources] is ignored, the future will be very worrisome. Development will bring great benefits. Xinjiang has an ancient civilization. Foreigners would all like to visit, but it's too far away. Yesterday in Urumqi, I met with Robert Rubin, the U.S. Treasury Secretary. I invited him to come. He said he very much wanted to, but that it was too far— the time spent on the road would be even longer than the time he could spend here, so it was not worth it. Don't we say that transportation is the key? If we develop oases, properly fix up and preserve ancient sites and relics, and improve

---

2. Wang Lequan was then Party Secretary of the Xinjiang Uyghur Autonomous Region and First Political Commissar of the Xinjiang Construction Corps.

3. Translator's note: "gobi" is an arid stretch of land covered primarily by small rocks, whereas "desert" is covered primarily by sand.

transportation and services, I am sure Xinjiang will become a fine tourist destination that everyone will want to visit.

Xinjiang's water resources amount to 5,700 cubic meters per capita, but they haven't been exploited or fully utilized. The water is just allowed to flow away or else used for flood irrigation in putting new land under cultivation, thereby salinizing the soil. The central leadership cares very much about developing water resources in Xinjiang, and you should speed up this endeavor. After exchanging views on this repeatedly, we feel that first, you should complete the already approved Ertix River development project as soon as possible. Now that the project for diverting water from the Ertix has been completed, the planning for guiding water from the Ertix to supply Urumqi and its entire basin should be stepped up.

Second, in terms of priority, it's still the planning, management, and utilization of the Tarim River that is more important. Southern Xinjiang could be a land of great abundance, but it still won't be if you just solve the transportation problem and not the water problem. The Tarim River has 30 billion cubic meters of water, but this hasn't been used well. Currently there are only flatland reservoirs and flood irrigation—the upstream water is all used up while the downstream gradually dries up. For the past 20 years, ecological degradation has been worsening steadily—the *Populus* forests are all dying and the Taklimakan and Kumkuduk deserts will soon join into one.

On this trip, we looked at the midstream and downstream portions of the Tarim River. We feel that [the use of] this river really needs to be well planned and managed: the Tarim should be restored to its original state, and its water should be sent into Lop Nur—there's enough water. This project must be undertaken. If you develop tourism once southern Xinjiang has water and transportation, it will become much wealthier and truly become an oasis in the desert.

Third, it is also extremely urgent that you develop the Ili River. Ili has a good climate and long hours of sunshine—anything planted there grows well, so you should speed up the development of the Ili River.

In developing water resources, you mustn't try to do everything at once because funding is limited. Besides, this is not just a question of funding but also of how to use the water after it is retained. For example, after a hillside reservoir is built in the upstream portion of the Tarim River to take the place of those flatland reservoirs, how will the water be used? After the Ili River Chapuqihai waterworks hub is built, what will you do with the water? You have to study this carefully. It will easily require an investment of around RMB 10 billion. After spending so much money, the water will be retained, but are you then going to use it for flood irrigation? That would not be fitting—it would even be harmful and would bring no economic benefits. Can the state spend this sort of money? No. That's why the most important question is how to use this water, and it must be fully considered during planning.

How should the water of the Ili River be utilized? You say you can open up 5.7 million mu[4] of land. What will this 5.7 million mu be used for? According to a report of Ili Prefecture, it is looking at a ratio of 6:2:2, that is, 60% will be used to develop animal husbandry, 20% for planting forests, and 20% for growing grain. I say that if you were to do that, this river won't be usable for a very long time. Once the Chapuqihai waterworks hub is built, the water will be retained, but you still won't have a way to use it. I think your best option would be to use 70% of the land for forests—this is the fastest way to use it.

What I'm saying isn't the last word on the subject because I haven't researched this scientifically, but my thinking is based on practice, specifically on the Kekeya forestation project we saw northwest of Aksu City. It is 25 kilometers long and varies in width from several to 15 kilometers. This was started in 1986 when Xie Fuping was the prefecture's Party secretary—he was the one who suggested planting this forest. At the time it was desert everywhere, crisscrossed by gullies and lacking in waterworks. [The project] was begun during his term and continued over the terms of four Party secretaries covering a span of 14 years, and now the poplars are fully grown and there's a forest of fruit trees. Anyone who sees that "long green corridor" will be stunned—this is how people can triumph over nature! It's truly extraordinary that they were able to achieve such great results through little more than a decade of hard work in such a harsh environment! I was much moved after seeing the forest and would have forever regretted it if I had not seen it this time.

Afterward I wondered, can't we just use this model for the development of the Ili River? That's why I will be bold and say that you should plant forests on 70% of the land, and plant grasses and develop animal husbandry on 20%. It won't do to develop too much animal husbandry—where would you sell the products? Mutton can't be easily shipped out; it can only be shipped by refrigerated trucks. As for wool, I'm in favor of that, but it must be the kind of fine wool you see in Australia. We import over 500,000 tons of fine wool a year. If Xinjiang can produce this, we won't have to import it and will be able to save several billion dollars. But you still can't produce it at the moment—the necessary equipment is all hi-tech and this must go through a process of development. It won't do to have too much ordinary animal husbandry—there's no outlet for it, and the herders will remain very poor.

In Ili, I saw a place with a good climate and an abundance of various resources, yet the people aren't rich and the homes they have built also look poor. Perhaps in the future there will be mountains of grain and plenty of cattle and sheep, but because these can't be shipped out, they won't find markets and cannot be turned into goods or money, so the people still won't be able to get

4. One mu is equal to 666.7 square meters.

rich. That's why you must first develop things the market needs. You must turn Xinjiang into a base for fine wool, a production base for high-quality wool—you must be resolved to do this. Learn a lesson from cotton and go for quality, not quantity. After you have the quality, then you can go for quantity, because having the quality means that all the equipment is in place. Developing quantity on such a foundation is very easy. That's why you shouldn't have too much grassland at present—20% will be enough—and you must concentrate your energies on consciously bringing in foreign investment, foreign technology, good stock, and [efficient] management in order to develop and produce high-quality wool.

In Ili they also told me that tree leaves can be fodder for cattle and sheep, so forestation can also develop animal husbandry! That is to say, by using only 20% for grasslands, the value of your animal husbandry can account for 50–60% of your total production value. By contrast, if you use 60% of the land to plant grasses, you won't be able to achieve such a good result. It's enough to use only 10% of the land to grow grain—just enough for food, [because] even if you have a surplus you won't be able to ship it out. Also, forestation can improve the eco-environment, and it will bring very good ecological and economic benefits.

When building waterworks projects and developing water resources, the critical thing is not how much money you request from the central authorities or what year you must start the work. Since the central leadership has decided to develop Xinjiang and western China, it won't be reluctant to provide the money. The problem is that if you derive no benefits from spending the money, won't your finances collapse? The key lies in the fact that you must produce results: you must let the people of Xinjiang benefit, and what's more, you must let them feel that they are benefiting every year. Only then will they feel motivated to do these projects.

Projects must be scientifically validated and go through the review and approval process; the guiding principle is that there should still be priorities and you mustn't start everything up at once. Provided you do the preparatory work well, projects will proceed very quickly once they're under way. If you try to do everything at once, projects will take a very long time as nothing will ever be completed.

Some of the things I've just discussed have already been decided on and are formulated projects—their feasibility studies and preparatory activities are complete, and work can commence once they have been reviewed and approved. For those that are not yet decided on, we will study them again when we go back, but we will approach this matter with a very positive attitude.

3. Work Hard on Industrial Restructuring

Adjusting the industrial structure is a key task for the period of the 10th Five-Year Plan. Xinjiang should therefore concentrate its energies on the following activities: exploiting oil and gas resources, and working on shipping gas from western to eastern China; developing water resources so that Xinjiang becomes an oasis; and putting equipment in place for building transportation infrastructure, which will drive the entire economic development of the region, especially the development of tourism.

You must bear in mind that Xinjiang is very far from the heartland. Right now the supply of industrial products exceeds demand all over the country. It also has so many imported goods that there would be no future in still building processing industries in Xinjiang. And what if you built up iron and steel? Or petrochemicals, or downstream petrochemical products? The distances are great and you would not be competitive. And what if you built up textiles? Nationally, the textile industry has improved only slightly after a 10-million-spindle reduction, so why would you add to their number? In the past, the Ministry of Textile Industry was in favor of moving all the spindles in the heartland to Xinjiang, but I opposed this all along. There are so many spindles in the country, what would be the point of moving all those broken-down things to Xinjiang? In short, you must be cautious about starting up new processing-industry projects.

I've been reading local newspapers in all the prefectures on this trip and get the sense that you seem to be especially keen on investment fairs and trade fairs. Comrades, I'm not saying that you shouldn't have any fairs, but can't you have fewer of them? Investment and trade both require careful thinking and ample validation—how can you sign contracts just through a fair? Is it the case that the greater the contracted amount, the greater the achievement will be? That the commissioners and Party secretaries should therefore be promoted? This kind of logic must be refuted. Does a contractual amount stand for political achievement? Does it stand for benefits to the people? I think a lot of these will become burdens. If you can say that you have your own unique features, your own strengths in resources other regions lack, if you can make products that others can't, I will agree with your developing them. It's not that you mustn't have any industries at all, or any processing industries. But if you're producing the most commonplace goods and your location is so distant, will you be able to sell them all? That's why I hope you will concentrate your energies on achieving a breakthrough in infrastructure construction and environmental improvement. Do more solid, down-to-earth projects and fewer showy ones.

4. Transform Government Functions

Recently, at a seminar sponsored by the Leading Group on National Science, Technology, and Education, I pointed out that there should be fewer staff and greater efficiency in government. Mind the business you should be minding, and don't mind the business you shouldn't be minding. At the moment the number of government employees is too high—too many people are eating "imperial rations,"[5] while the populace shoulders a very heavy burden, what with arbitrary fee collections and fundraising. Won't the people rise up in revolt if their burden becomes unbearable?

Government agencies in Xinjiang also need to be streamlined. Your government staff is currently composed of almost 5% of the entire population of the autonomous region, which is two percentage points higher than the national average. You're a region of ethnic minorities, and the proportion of cadres should be a bit high, but you should still streamline a bit. When I went to Shaanxi, to northern Shaanxi in particular, I found the proportion of cadres there too high. The farmers can't cope with this burden, which is one reason why they're poor.

The crucial issue isn't whether the population can support so many officials—but whether having a large number of officials means there will be a surfeit of ideas. If these were all good ideas, then I would thank heaven and earth, but unfortunately quite a few are bad ideas, and some are nothing but stupid ones. When there are too many people in government, they'll want to do things, and once they do things, they'll want to start projects. Then the "image-building projects" and the "vanity projects" will start appearing and if they don't have the money, they'll arbitrarily collect fees and arbitrarily raise funds. This is called playing the wrong role.

Government agencies are supposed to be very fair and just minding the business they should be minding: managing the markets, so that no one is allowed to violate the rules; managing security, so that no one is allowed to break the law. That's what the government is supposed to be minding, yet some agencies focus on nothing but "getting projects started," and they micromanage even more than a factory director. They go to fairs all day long and the minute they do, they are duped out of tens of millions of renminbi.

What goals can you achieve by minding fewer things and having fewer people? Everyone will be able to eat first, and then go to work—pay wages first. Right now you're behind in paying wages, and your staff can't even afford to eat—what can you build? There will also be social unrest. You must streamline. If you are having difficulties or specific problems and are temporarily unable to streamline, then you should first ensure that your staff can afford to eat and their wages are paid in full. Do as much construction as you can with whatever money is left over. I've always insisted on this concept. This isn't just my own idea; many leaders of the older generation would agree. If you do construction that yields immediate benefits, then you can pay more wages. The problem is that many of the projects that are started up produce no benefits.

---

5. Translator's note: that is, they are paid by the government and supported by budgetary expenditures.

Let me draw your attention to a specific project in this regard. PetroChina spent over RMB 3 billion to build a 2.5-million-ton capacity oil refinery in Korla. However, it was shut down upon completion because no crude oil was available. With the oil refineries in Urumqi and Karamay fully utilized, where would you find crude oil, so why build yet another refinery? This was a wrong decision made by the China National Petroleum Corporation, but since the State Planning Commission and the State Council agreed to the refinery's construction, we are also at fault. If we hadn't undertaken this project and donated over RMB 3 billion to Xinjiang, wouldn't that have solved your problem of paying wages? Now that over RMB 3 billion worth of equipment is just sitting there and we have to spend money every year to maintain it, as well as to pay interest on the loans—can you deal with that? It's a harsh lesson! Henceforth, don't start up projects randomly. Comrades, when you start one, you must complete it, and when you complete it, it must yield benefits—that is my hope.

5. Pay Close Attention to Fiscal Issues

Just now you said that last year Xinjiang had fiscal revenues of RMB12.2 billion, of which 4.7 billion was turned over to the central government and 7.5 billion retained by you. Anyone who sees this will think, "How can this be! How could a third of fiscal revenues be turned over to the central government? If the central government is supporting Xinjiang, how can it take away RMB 4.7 billion?" What is the problem? The problem is that you failed to mention the central government gave you almost RMB 10 billion of subsidies last year, and this doesn't even take into account the 3.9 billion of subsidies given to the Xinjiang Construction Corps. That is to say, the central government gave Xinjiang over RMB 13 billion in subsidies, which is far more than the 4.7 billion you turned over, far more than the 7.5 billion you retained, and also far more than your total fiscal revenues of 12.2 billion.

Today, I particularly want to give you a clear breakdown of last year's figures: you received RMB 2.95 billion of fixed subsidies, 2.105 billion of tax rebates, 704 million of transfer payments, 500 million of hardship subsidies, and 2.95 billion of various targeted subsidies. Last year, the increases in your wages, in the basic living costs for laid-off workers, and in pensions were all subsidized by the Ministry of Finance. Doesn't that indicate the central government's deep concern for ethnic minority areas, and isn't that great support for the Xinjiang Uygur Autonomous Region? This year's subsidies to Xinjiang will definitely exceed those of last year. Why? Because last year's subsidies for Xinjiang's wages, basic living costs for laid-off workers, and pensions were for half a year whereas this year they'll be for a full year, so this sum alone will be doubled; add to that the increases for other subsidies, which will be well over RMB 10 billion this year. Where is this money coming from? It's collected from the coastal areas, and it's paid to you out of the transfer payments collected from municipalities and provinces like Shanghai and Guangdong. This transfer would become a problem if we were to revise the taxation system.

Yesterday, on an inspection tour of Changji Prefecture, we saw a factory making a special type of transformer, with exports valued at US$30 million annually. We visited an 180,000-ton capacity tomato sauce plant that also exports quite a lot, so these two enterprises could be considered very rich. However, they said it would be best to let them keep their 75% value added tax. I replied, if we let you keep that 75% VAT, then Shanghai and Guangdong will also want to keep theirs, and each percentage point there is worth several dozen of yours. If they were to turn over one percentage point less, the central government would have no money to give you. That's why we say that the tax-streaming system mustn't be altered. It is only by maintaining this system that we can justify sending money from the east out to the west. Otherwise you wouldn't be able to cope with it!

This "great development of western China" is very different from the building of special economic zones (SEZs) that began in 1979. These SEZs are near Hong Kong and Macao. They could process orders, build "3 + 1" industries,[6] and import components and export finished goods to earn forex, with everything growing like a snowball. Now they're already moving into hi-tech industries. Xinjiang is far away, at our western borders—who would come here to place processing orders? How would you ship out the goods you produce? That's why it won't work to keep using the SEZ policies of the past. Besides, that policy already had a great setback in 1993. At that time, the whole country was involved in processing industries and real estate. This resulted in economic overheating and left us with a pile of debts that still haven't been fully paid off—right now there is still RMB 700–800 billion of real estate loans from that time that have become bad loans at the banks. We mustn't use this policy again but must tilt toward construction.

The infrastructure construction, eco-environment improvement, and development of science, technology, and education that western China needs will depend mainly on fiscal inputs—it won't work to rely only on bank loans. It would be unworkable for us to arrange projects for developing western China and then ask the local governments for matching funds. We say eat first, then build. If the locals can't even pay wages, where will they get the matching funds for construction? Therefore the most important policy that we have drawn up this time is that henceforth the central government will arrange funding for all projects arranged by the state. This will include grants from the Ministry of

6. Translator's note: these are industries that process imported materials, process according to imported samples, assemble imported parts, and engage in compensation trade.

Finance, funding through Treasury bonds, and also bank loans. But I'm not saying that the locals don't have to match anything. I've already told the Party secretary and chairman of the Uygur Autonomous Region that first, you mustn't try to extort the central government and collect lots of matching funds—don't try to do that. Second, your land usage fees mustn't be too high. This is the most commonly used method in some coastal areas, and under no circumstances should you learn from them. When the central government invests in projects in these places, the land is ridiculously expensive. In other places, RMB 4 billion is enough for a 140,000-ton ethylene project, but in Guangzhou it costs RMB 8 billion. Perhaps you can't imagine why it could be so expensive. Isn't it because of all those local fees as well as the land compensation charges? It's ridiculously expensive!

That's why you don't have to pay for projects arranged by the state and you also shouldn't charge the central government—I see this as the greatest support. Also, don't apply other policies haphazardly. If you don't handle these well, you'll encourage redundant construction and small factories will blossom everywhere. These are all going to become burdens and will have to be shut down. In the future, we will increase the level of investment from the central government and do our best to minimize the matching funds you must pay. The central government is very supportive of Xinjiang in major projects like railroads and river development. We must continue to take this path in the future, continue to increase the level of support, and increase the force of the tilt policy.

In short, the Party Central Committee with Jiang Zemin at its core attaches great importance to Xinjiang. In implementing the decisions of the Central Committee, we at the State Council will be giving the utmost support to Xinjiang. We hope that this support will be transformed into benefits, that it will truly make Xinjiang's economy prosper, enable its people to live better, and strengthen the unity between ethnic groups—that is our greatest hope.

34

PAY GREATER ATTENTION TO
ENVIRONMENTAL PROTECTION AND
BUILDING THE ECO-ENVIRONMENT[1]

January 11, 2001

Over the past few years, our country has done a great deal to protect and manage the environment, and our progress has been encouraging. However, the present trend of environmental deterioration has still not been effectively checked and is still very challenging.

The signs of desertification and grassland regression are quite serious and very worrisome. The Hunshandake Desert in the Inner Mongolia Autonomous Region is a direct cause of sandstorms, and it is vital that we do something about this. Although we have no control over the sands that blow in from the Mongolian People's Republic, we can cooperate more closely [with the Mongolians] in desert management. We do have a say in [the affairs of] the Inner Mongolia Autonomous Region and must step up environmental management and prevent desertification.

Last year, Beijing experienced quite frequent sandstorms, which I hear were caused by external factors, but irresponsible construction projects also contributed to the problem by increasing the airborne dust and sand in the urban areas. Beijing is applying to host the 29th Olympic Games, so we should make a greater effort to improve the vegetation cover. We must reinforce construction management: you can't dig up a place and then leave the ground exposed for several years without covering it. We must have responsible construction.

Judging from the yearly chart on water pollution, the Hai and Liao rivers were severely polluted when treatment began and improved somewhat afterward, but now the pollution is increasing again. I don't see much improvement following treatment at the other river basins either, or at Lake Tai—we must pay close attention to this problem and deal with it more forcefully.

---

1. These remarks were made by Zhu Rongji after listening to a work report by the State Environmental Protection Administration.

Inspecting homes almost completely covered by sand in Xiaobeizi Township, Fengning Manchu Autonomous County, Hebei Province, on May 5, 2000. (Photograph by Ma Zhancheng, Xinhua News Agency)

Xiaobeizi Township, Fengning Manchu Autonomous County, Hebei Province, in 2007 after erosion control measures.

Qian Zhenying[2] recently forwarded a letter to me from Qian Yi, the academician.[3] She also appended an essay expressing disagreement with the State Environmental Protection Administration's views, noting, "You think the problem of industrial pollution has already been solved and we should now turn our attention to resolving other major environmental issues. In fact, water pollution is still very serious and treating water pollution is even more important than solving the problem of water shortages." I've signed this letter over to you all and hope you will seriously consider these different opinions.

I hope that environmental protection specialists will pay particular attention to the question of whether cities, especially cities in the north, should plant more trees or more grasses. I think that trees are easier to plant and have a greater environmental impact than grasses, so I favor planting more trees and fewer grasses. The costs of planting grasses are also high, plus they consume a great deal of water and are very hard to protect. I don't know if you scientists agree with my view or not? I hope you will conduct some scientific studies on this—it's a very interesting research topic. I'm worried that right now people are trying to achieve quick results, so there is a craze for planting grasses, and no attention is being given to planting trees. This may lead us away from the correct path in the future.

The head office of the State Environmental Protection Administration should, in conjunction with the other departments concerned, use visuals through TV and other news media to inform the country's entire population about the research results of environmental scientists and about the continuing environmental degradation. By doing so, you can make our people more alert and cause leading cadres at all levels to pay more attention to environmental protection and eco-friendly construction. You should compile the conditions you just reported on in a form suitable for publicizing and give them broad exposure. Turn your research results into visualized TV films for broadcast and send these to all the responsible people in the various regions and departments for viewing. Let them all understand that the eco-environment is still deteriorating, that the pace at which forests and grasslands are being destroyed surpasses the rate at which they are being reforested and replanted, that arable land is still constantly being destroyed, and that water pollution is still very serious. We must make China's leaders everywhere understand that it won't do for them to pursue only economic growth of the moment and not think about sustainable development. Otherwise, we will have to pay a price that is all too high—this is

2. Qian Zhengying is a hydropower specialist, a Member of the Chinese Academy of Engineering, and a former Vice Chairman of the Chinese People's Political Consultative Conference.

3. Qian Yi was then a member of the Chinese Academy of Engineering and a Professor in the Department of Environmental Science and Engineering at Tsinghua University.

a profound lesson to be learned from [experiences] past and present, Chinese and foreign.

Regardless of whether it's farmland or grassland, once destroyed, it's very hard to restore. The head office of the State Environmental Protection Administration and the environmental bureaus at all levels have the principal responsibility for environmental protection. You should work with the publicity departments and the radio, film, and TV departments at all levels to publicize the country's environmental worsening. Don't be afraid—there isn't anything that needs to be kept secret, and there's also no need to cover up shortcomings. The point is not to negate our achievements in environmental work; rather, it is to remind everyone to pay a great deal of attention to protecting the environment. The problem is already so serious—we would be derelict in our duty if we still failed to warn the entire country! Environmental scientists should join together with artists as well as with experts in film and video to produce publicity films about environmental science research results, and these should be broadcast nationally. The *Topics in Focus* programs on CCTV should be shown repeatedly as a warning to all cadres and people. I hope all parties will work together to do a good job of publicizing and educating.

In the new century, we must seriously implement the strategy of sustainable development and pay more attention to protecting and managing the environment. We should further build up the eco-environment and halt ecological deterioration. We should make great efforts to plant trees and grasses and work more forcefully to prevent and manage sandstorms. We should strengthen the comprehensive treatment of atmospheric pollution, water pollution, trash pollution, and noise pollution in cities and control and manage industrial pollution. We must start greening our cities on a broad scale. We must build up our environmental and atmospheric monitoring systems. In implementing the great development of western China, we must be sure to build up and protect the environment and focus on reverting farmlands to forests and grasslands in a planned and phased way.

35

HUNAN MUST GIVE PRIORITY TO MANAGING ITS MOUNTAINS AND WATERS[1]

April 11, 2001

In 1998 and 1999 I came to Hunan mainly to direct its flood-control efforts. This time I've come to have a look at western Hunan. Fifty-seven years ago, I studied at senior high schools in Xinhua and Huatan. When I saw them during this trip, they had changed greatly, with some places no longer recognizable. Today people also appear to be living quite well. Jishou, for example, used to have only a single [granite-] paved street, but now it's a very large city, and Jishou University is nicely constructed. Back when I was studying at Tsinghua University, it only had 2,000 students. At that time, Tsinghua's auditorium and library were all built by Americans using "the Boxer Indemnity."[2] Every single brick was shipped over from the United States. Now Jishou University has a far bigger auditorium and library than the ones at Tsinghua when I was a student there, and it has over 10,000 students. What an earth-shattering transformation!

Although the farmers in western Hunan haven't been completely lifted out of poverty and some even still struggle with basic subsistence, on the whole their living standards have risen considerably. During yesterday's discussion, I indicated that work in Hunan is being conducted quite well and summed it up in three phrases: "The direction is correct, the efforts are diligent, and the achievements are great." You have truly realized the goal of basically getting the vast majority of large and medium core-industry state-owned enterprises out of their difficulties. Since last June or July, Hunan Province has also achieved the "Two Assurances."[3] None of this was easy. That's why I feel that overall, the Hunan Provincial Party Committee and the provincial government have

---

1. These remarks were made by Zhu Rongji after listening to work reports by the provincial Party committee and the provincial government during an inspection tour of Hunan Province.

2. Translator's note: in 1900 (the "gengzi" year in the traditional Chinese calendar), armies of 8 nations occupied Beijing in the aftermath of the Boxer Uprising. The following year, under the terms of the "Boxer Protocol," the Qing government was compelled to pay reparations of 450 million taels of silver at 4% interest a year over 39 years.

3. That is, assuring retirees that their pensions will be paid on time and in full, and assuring laid-off workers that funds to cover their basic living expenses will be paid on time and in full.

achieved a great deal in their work and should be fully recognized. The facts are there, with no room for doubt.

However, quite a few problems do remain that require us to unite as one, align our thinking, and solve each of them seriously and responsibly. Of course some problems are already being addressed, and the next step is to get a firmer grip on them. I'm going to focus my remarks on one key aspect of work in Hunan, namely improving the eco-environment. This comes down to two words: "waters" and "mountains."

By "waters," I mean Hunan's "one lake and four rivers": Lake Dongting and the Xiang, Zi, Yuan, and Li rivers, all of which have yet to be transformed from a harmful to useful state. Perhaps I should say, they're still not very useful and still harmful in many ways. If this problem isn't resolved, Hunan's economy won't be able to grow, its people's living standards won't rise, and society won't be stable. By "mountains" I mean the "Three Mountains and Five Ranges." Southern Hunan can be said to lie within China's Five Ranges—I don't mean the entire Five Ranges, only one of them. Most of Hunan is thus surrounded by mountains: the Wuling Mountains to the northwest, the Xuefeng Mountains (where Huaihua is located) to the west, and the Luoxiao Mountains to the east, so these can be called the "Three Mountains."

To do good work in Hunan, the first thing is to tame the mountains and waters. I inspected flood control work in the Lake Dongting area in 1998 and 1999 and had also visited Lake Dongting earlier. I feel that the eco-environment there has deteriorated very badly. The surface area of the lake has shrunk greatly, and its capacities for flood prevention and floodwater retention are very poor. The Party Central Committee and the State Council have therefore drawn up a program to manage Lake Dongting, and the concrete planning is being carried out step by step. We must focus further on implementation. In particular, the management of the Xiang, Zi, Yuan, and Li rivers must be coordinated, and their flood prevention measures must mesh with the management of Lake Dongting. This project can't be completed within one Five-Year Plan—perhaps it can't even be completed by a single generation of people, but we must persevere in seeing it through.

As for mountains, on this trip I saw them in three cities and prefectures in western Hunan. I found great changes there and am very satisfied with all aspects except for one: damage to the mountain forests has been far too severe: they've basically been cut bare and are completely different from what I saw 57 or 58 years ago. In the past, I had seen "big-character poster"[4] farms only in

---

4. Translator's note: "big-character posters" were written with large Chinese characters and pasted onto walls. Here the phrase alludes to the scattered places on slopes where all trees have been cut down, creating bare spots that give the entire slope the appearance of a big-character poster.

A laughter-filled conversation with villager Yang Zaibao in Aizhai Township, Jishou, Xiangxi Tujia Autonomous Prefecture, Hunan Province, on April 7, 2001.

Sichuan, where land was cultivated on slopes so steep there weren't even terraced fields—farmers simply planted right on the slopes, [creating an effect] like the "big-character posters" of the "Great Cultural Revolution."

I had originally thought there were no "big-character poster" farms on Hunan's mountains, but some can still be found in western Hunan, although most are terraced fields. Because Hunan has so many people and they don't have enough to eat, they cultivate fields all the way up the mountains and thereby destroy the eco-environment. Fortunately, Hunan has a good climate and grasses can still grow, so it still has a bit of vegetation cover. Otherwise soil erosion would become a problem, the "one lake and four rivers" would flood disastrously, and there would be no way for people to survive. That's why the work of protecting and managing the eco-environment in Hunan has gotten to the point where it cannot be put off a moment longer!

We have to make a great effort and give priority to managing the mountains and waters as a key task. Plans have already been completed for river management, and now we have to execute them more quickly. The management of mountains will require better planning and implementation: of course managing mountains also includes managing waters. Unless Hunan solves this fundamental problem, conditions won't improve.

To protect the eco-environment, the first thing is to stop destroying it. I think the Hunan provincial Party committee and provincial government must have the firmest resolve about this. It won't do to hesitate or to shrink back—you must act decisively. Forests must not be cut down at will, waters must not be polluted, and the environment must not be destroyed. We are implementing a strategy of sustainable development, and things that destroy the eco-environment must not be permitted to go on!

When I came to Hunan, I received a letter from its people stating that some miners were refining gold haphazardly near the Liaojiaping Reservoir in Anhua, that the reservoir's waters are becoming more polluted by the day, and that the local government turns a blind eye to all this. I've forwarded this letter to Yang Zhengwu[5] and Chu Bo.[6] Actions like this that destroy the eco-environment must be dealt with severely. I said this again in western Hunan: whether it's manganese or some other type of mine, no one is allowed to mine at will, and we must now shut down the "five small enterprises."[7] If you want to build modern smelting plants and mines, you must have concentrated resources. You can't have any more of those "hen's nest mines." That's the only way to reach international standards. Otherwise how can you industrialize? How can you modernize? You must take strict measures and immediately put a halt to actions that damage the eco-environment.

When I was in Huayuan, I saw a very fine piece of farmland. Unfortunately, a building was being constructed on it. I later heard that a transformer station was being built there. Transformer stations must be built, rural power lines must be upgraded, electricity must be made available to the farmers, and power prices must come down. But why did you have to use such a fine piece of land? Planting is extending all the way up the mountains because it's hard to find such a good piece of level farmland at the bottom of gullies, yet it's being used for a building—why? Besides, they didn't even go through review and approval procedures. This is wrong. The people who should be punished must be punished, and those who should be fined must be fined.

The first step in addressing this problem is to stop destroying the eco-environment. Only after that do you revert farmlands to forests. I'm in favor of reverting farmlands to forests within the three cities and prefectures of western Hunan if possible. You needn't worry about grain—we're not asking you to be

---

5. Yang Zhengwu was then the Hunan Provincial Party Secretary.

6. Chu Bo was then Governor of Hunan.

7. See chapter 14, n. 4, p. 123.

self-sufficient. The expressways to these three places will soon be completed, so grain can be shipped in. Don't overemphasize self-sufficiency in grain, because what we want is to restore the beautiful mountains. The speed at which farmland is reverted to forests should be based on the actual situation in each city and prefecture. It should be fact-based and handled in a sound way. Don't start everything up in a rush through coercive measures. Don't proceed too quickly if preparations aren't adequate, for example, if there isn't enough time to prepare the saplings. The speed should be commensurate with the state of preparations. Also, questions like which types of trees to plant should be fully studied in advance, all of which will take time.

As farmlands revert to forests, adjustments must be made in the rural energy structure; otherwise even the planted forests will still be cut down. That's why I told people in western Hunan not to use a slogan like "a year of hardship to be followed by eight years of spring." Don't create the impression that after a year of reverting farmland, the state will provide grain for eight years. Under the policy of reverting farmlands to forests, the state will provide grain without compensation for eight years after farmers stop planting, and they will be required to plant trees without compensation, so that barren mountains can be turned green. At the same time, it must be stressed that you can't ask the farmers to do things like build roads without compensation just because the government is providing grain without compensation, because the grain subsidies are for the purpose of reverting farmlands to forests. You can only ask farmers to plant trees, not to do more voluntary work. You also have to adjust the energy structure and use a variety of ways to help farmers gain access to the fuel they need for daily living—they can't keep on burning firewood.

In dealing with Hunan's waters, it is essential to speed up the restoration of Lake Dongting. Some are saying that the pace is too slow and that the farmers are not very motivated. The main reason is that the state subsidies are too low—around RMB 15,000 per household, plus another RMB 2,000 from the province. It's been suggested that if each household were to receive RMB 30,000, the pace of relocation could be stepped up and thus the surface area of the lake could be increased more quickly. Please do some research and see if it's possible to add some fiscal grants (including grants from the central government) as well as some bank loans, because after the area around the lake is developed, the farmers will still have a certain ability to repay loans. I hope the work of reverting farmlands to lakes can be carried on unceasingly to the very end. As officials in Hunan, it would be a dereliction of duty if you failed to manage Lake Dongting!

You might call it an emotional outpouring, but while in western Hunan, I wrote a poem: "Feelings on Revisiting Western Hunan and Memories of Lake Dongting." I'll recite it today to convey both my feelings and my hopes:

Sixty years of western Hunan in a single dream,
Where former sites faintly resemble another world.
There are great talents in the schools of Jishou,
While gods gather on the peaks of Zhangjiajie.
People are bustling in the beautiful new city,
But the sight of barren hills saddens me.
When will we see their grandeur again?
My dream won't come true until all is green.

Manuscript of Zhu Rongji's poem "Feelings on Revisiting Western Hunan and Memories of Lake Dongting."

The poem is about arriving in western Hunan long ago filled with great expectations upon seeing its lovely environment. I was in Xinhua in 1943 and went to Huayuan (then called Yongsui) in 1944. That was 57 years ago, but let me round it off to 60 years. Today I can't recognize any of the places that I recall living in back then—everything has changed and seems blurry. I went to what used to be Public High School No. 8 but couldn't recognize it either. The original buildings all burned down, and a primary school has been built there; the city wall is also gone, now replaced by buildings. I remember a couplet taught in the Yuelu Academy:[8] "Chu[9] has much talent/ Hence it is great." It referred to Hunan as having talented people, and I applied this allusion to Jishou. Education there has developed to the point that 10,000 students now attend Jishou University. Its founding was a wonderful thing spearheaded by Yang Zhengwu while he was Party Secretary of the Tujia-Miao Autonomous Prefecture in western Hunan.

The scenery in Zhangjiajie is like a fairyland, but unfortunately too many people live in the area now—there are swarms in every city you visit. Though very large, the plaza of the Xinhua Rail Station in particular is crammed full of people, which is why I said they were bustling. If you look at those mountains now, they're as bald as a young child's head. I felt truly awful when I saw all the trees had been cut down! "The Yueyang Tower," written by Fan Zhongyan at the time of the Northern Song Dynasty, describes Lake Dongting as "majestic as far as the eye can see." When will such a sight appear again? This is my hope, and I place my hopes on all of you here!

It is my fervent hope and dream that western Hunan will revert its farmlands to forests and grasslands, that it will improve and protect the eco-environment, and that it will restore its green hills and blue water—I hope you will all work toward this. I think that "managing Hunan" means managing its mountains and waters, its "one lake and four rivers," its "Three Mountains and Five Ranges." Once the chapters on mountains and waters are written well, there will truly be hope for Hunan.

8. Translator's note: the Yuelu Academy was one of the four famous academies of learning in traditional China. It is located in Changsha, Hunan Province, and was built in AD 976 during the Northern Song dynasty (AD 960–1127).

9. Translator's note: an ancient Chinese state (approximately the 10th–2nd century BC) that was founded in the Yangtze River Valley and eventually expanded to include parts of present-day Hubei, Hunan, Henan, Anhui, Jiangsu, Zhejiang, Jiangxi, and Sichuan Provinces.

36

TEACHERS ARE THE BASIC DRIVING
FORCE OF EDUCATION[1]

April 27, 2001

In this vibrant spring, you have all come to the verdant Tsinghua campus to join us in celebrating the 90th anniversary of the founding of Tsinghua University, as well as to offer suggestions for how to run the Tsinghua School of Economics and Management well. For this, I thank you from the bottom of my heart!

It has been half a year since the last meeting of the International Advisory Committee. With the support of all of you, we have made definite progress in establishing a first-rate school of economics and management. The training program for senior executives organized jointly by Tsinghua and Harvard universities has achieved good results: the quality of instructors has been improved, students have indicated that they have learned a lot, we have accumulated experience in management, and have also increased mutual understanding and consensus. This is an important step forward for the school and also a result of the joint efforts of everyone on the International Advisory Committee. Like all of you, I take the greatest pleasure in this. I particularly want to thank all of you here for directly promoting our work.

During the past half year, the International Advisory Committee has done a great deal of work and proposed many good suggestions and comments on how to elevate the school's teaching standards. The discussion we had just now drew up a fine blueprint for the Tsinghua School of Economics and Management and proposed measures for realizing it. This is most inspiring and fills us with great expectations. Now I'd like to share some thoughts on how to build up the school.

The core issue for making this a good school is the quality of the teaching staff. "A teacher is one who points the way, transmits expertise, and resolves perplexing questions."[2] Teachers are the basic driving force of education. They not only transmit knowledge and skills and improve the all-round caliber of students, but they are also important discoverers and inventors of new science and technology and new concepts of management. The quality of its teachers is

---

1. These remarks were made by Zhu Rongji at the second meeting of the International Advisory Committee of the Tsinghua University School of Economics and Management.

2. A quotation from *On Teaching* by Han Yu of the Tang Dynasty.

Attending and speaking at the second meeting of the International Advisory Committee of the Tsinghua University School of Economics and Management on April 7, 2001. To the right is Henry Paulson, Chairman and CEO of Goldman Sachs.

the most important measure of a university's excellence. The Tsinghua School of Economics and Management has first-rate students, and its facilities are also being improved. Now the basic task in improving its teaching standards is to focus on the quality of its instructors.

More specifically, the means to this end is, first, to recruit, and second, to cultivate. That is, we must resolutely strive for a breakthrough by attracting instructors who are considered first-rate by international standards. To the best of our ability, we must provide them with good living conditions and a good research and teaching environment. We must rely on these highly accomplished professors to rapidly elevate the standards of teaching and research at the school, and at the same time nurture a large group of young and middle-aged faculty members.

Our experience in running the school has shown that to develop a field and cultivate talent, it must have one or more professors who will take the lead and act as standard-bearers. Precisely with this in mind, the school is forcefully promoting a system of chair professors. Cultivation is an even longer-term measure, especially in the case of young faculty members and students who might become instructors in the future. We should send our top students to study in internationally renowned, first-rate schools of management, because "the best way to learn is to learn from the best." We must let our people enter the mainstream of international scholarship as soon as possible so that they will have the ability to conduct dialogues and exchanges with the great masters. This is fundamentally different from building chariots behind closed doors[3] and is the long-term approach to building up the teaching staff.

Of course we still have to make a concerted effort to attract professors who are master teachers. Although the school has done a lot in the past to bring outstanding instructors here, we still have to try harder and must concretely implement the suggestions of the International Advisory Committee. Besides offering better material benefits, we should provide a good environment for teaching and research and clearly assign responsibilities and privileges, so that the professors we engage will have an opportunity to realize new and greater achievements professionally. I believe that the Tsinghua School of Economics and Management will definitely make considerably more progress in this regard.

My great hope is for us to build a high-quality school of management that can make enormous contributions to the prosperity of our country and of the human race. I have benefited greatly from your incisive comments and now have even greater confidence that we will do a good job of building up this school. I thank all of you for coming and hope you will plant the finest seeds in this hope-filled spring.

---

3. Translator's note: an expression used to describe a person who acts willfully without regard for objective conditions.

37

THE SPIRIT OF TSINGHUA IS THE PURSUIT OF PERFECTION[1]

June 5, 2001

I'm very nervous today. I wasn't so nervous even when speaking on the South Lawn of the White House because I'm not the least bit afraid of foreigners. But in front of you students I'm very tense—perhaps because "it is the young who are formidable!"

The President of Tsinghua University and Party Secretary asked me to say a few words, and I hope my remarks will be of some benefit to you because after all, I'm speaking from experience. However, you will have to be the judge of their value. If what I say is correct, if you feel it is reasonable, you may study it and discuss it; if you feel what I say is incorrect, then please forgive me because every day there are way too many documents that I must read, meetings that I must attend, and speeches that I must make. It would be too unrealistic to expect me to never misspeak.

When the Tsinghua School of Economics and Management was established in 1984, Liu Da[2] asked me to serve as its Dean. I was then the Deputy Party Secretary and Executive Vice Chairman of the State Economic Commission. At the time I hardly knew anything—and in fact I had never studied economics and management—but I was very interested in the subject and therefore agreed to serve in this position. I became increasingly aware of how inadequate and unqualified I was; at the same time, I was very busy with my work and really never did much for the school, for which I feel very embarrassed. Several times I said that I could no longer serve, but they kept saying, "It's still very helpful [if you stay]."

Recently, I again talked to Wang Dazhong[3] and He Meiying[4] about this and said I could no longer continue as Dean no matter what. After thinking it over, they finally agreed to my resignation but asked me to serve as Honorary Dean. I felt that this was a post I shouldn't accept. Many foreign universities

---

1. On June 5, 2001, Zhu Rongji was invited to give a presentation at Tsinghua University. This is part of that presentation.

2. Liu Da was the Party Secretary and President of Tsinghua University in 1984.

3. Wang Dazhong was then President of Tsinghua University.

4. He Meiying was then Party Secretary of Tsinghua University.

have offered me a doctorate or asked me to accept a prize of some sort, but I've always declined. If I'm going to receive a doctorate, it must be one that I earned through my own efforts and my own abilities; if I didn't acquire it through study, then I don't want it as a gift from them. That's why I cannot accept the position of Honorary Dean. Later they asked, "Can you be the Honorary Chairman of the School's Advisory Committee?" That I could agree to, because the Honorary Chairman has a great deal of freedom and will not affect the work and the operations of the Advisory Committee in the least.

So, admittedly I don't have to come back, since my position is "Honorary." But please don't worry. My heart will always be with Tsinghua University; it will stay with the school. Today I've come to resign my deanship, but I ask you all to bear witness: I have not left Tsinghua, for my heart is still here. Every achievement of Tsinghua University and of its School of Economics and Management will be something I take pride in; each and every problem of yours will be a concern of mine; if you have any shortcomings, I will most unceremoniously point them out, because I am a Tsinghua man.

During the Tsinghua anniversary 10 years ago, I wrote these four lines:

Like the warm spring breezes and the timely rain,
The waters and woods of Tsinghua
Have taught and nurtured me
And will be remembered all my life.

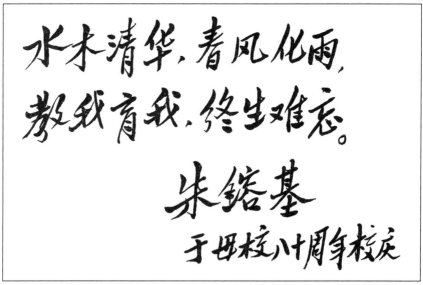

An inscription written by Zhu Rongji in 1991 on the occasion of the 80th anniversary of Tsinghua University.

Tsinghua has given me too much and I have done too little for Tsinghua. I sincerely hope that Tsinghua gets better and better and becomes a world-class university. Let every student here deserve to be called a student of a world-class university—that is my hope. I believe that all of you here have already made up your minds to make Tsinghua a world-class university and to make the School of Economics and Management a world-class school of management so that they may serve our homeland and turn China into a world-class power. Now I'd like to discuss some of my other hopes for you.

I didn't sleep well last night because I kept wondering what to talk about. Nine years ago, at the request of the students then, I wrote an essay titled "On Being a Scholar and Being a Person"[5] to celebrate the 60th anniversary of the founding of the Department of Electrical Engineering at Tsinghua. The essay was about Zhang Mingtao, who was Dean of the Department of Electrical Engineering while I was studying at Tsinghua. During an assembly in 1950, he spoke on the subject of being a scholar and being a person. I therefore used this as the title of my commemorative essay.

It has been many years since Zhang Mingtao passed away. He said that between being a [good] scholar and being a [good] person, it is more important to be a [good] person. If you're not a good person, no matter how good a scholar you may be, you might become a bad apple; to be a [good] person, you must be a Chinese with backbone. I have always remembered the phrase, "be a Chinese with backbone." Tsinghua is not a place that just pays attention to how to be scholars; it truly teaches us how to be people.

I recall my own maturation at Tsinghua. Tsinghua taught me not only how to be a scholar, but also how to be a person. Tsinghua has fine traditions: traditions of democracy, science, and revolution. I remember encountering so many new things when I came to Tsinghua from Hunan. At that time, the people I most worshiped were Wen Yiduo and Zhu Ziqing.[6] Although I was studying electrical engineering, Zhu Ziqing's lectures were my favorite. To this day I still have vivid memories of him speaking at an assembly in Tongfang Hall. He was a good essayist but not as adept at speaking, yet his words were so earnest and moving—I admired him as a person. I also admired Wu Han and Zhang Xiruo.[7] Before the liberation of Beijing (1949), we loved to go to Zhang Xiruo's home. Many students would sit on the floor and listen to him discuss the world situation and heap scorn on the KMT [Kuomintang, or Chinese Nationalist Party] reactionaries—it was so satisfying!

---

5. See *Zhu Rongji on the Record, 1991–1997* (Brookings Institution Press, 2013), chap. 9.

6. Wen Yiduo (1899–1946) was a poet and scholar; Zhu Ziqing (1899–1946) was an essayist and poet.

7. Wu Han (1909–69) was a historian; Zhang Xiruo (1889–1973) was a political scientist and educator.

Under the influence of some progressive students, I joined in some student movements and did some [political] work. Particularly after the liberation of Beijing, I served as class president and president of the student association at Tsinghua. What left the most lasting impression on me was how I learned all my basic knowledge of Marxism at that time, how I read many books and laid the foundations of [Marxist] theory. That's why I say that Tsinghua is not a place that just specializes in scholarship; it is also a place that teaches you how to be a person.

I must say frankly that as far as scholarship goes, I wasn't a very good student. Of course those extracurricular activities affected me, but on the other hand, I am by nature not very fond of engineering. My English is quite decent, and I like both foreign and Chinese literature. At one point I wanted to switch to the Department of Foreign Languages but didn't succeed. At the time, I only read books about literature. When I went to the library, it should have been to read books on electrical engineering, but I kept wanting to read plays by Cao Yu.[8] It was after arriving at Tsinghua and reading his plays that I discovered that Cao Yu's real name was Wan Jiabao, and that he, too, was a Tsinghua graduate.

Tsinghua imparts to people a sort of tradition that makes you always want to reach higher. I greatly admired those who excelled in their studies. I once said to my schoolmate Zhang Fengxiang (who later became Vice Minister of Water Resources), "I was always first in my class from elementary school all the way through high school. Why is it that since coming to Tsinghua I have more difficulties with my studies than those schoolmates who are doing well?" It's been almost half a century now, but I still remember his reply very clearly: "Is there anyone in our class who wasn't first in high school?" That shows how intense the competition at Tsinghua was—there were indeed a great many outstanding talents. Our electrical engineering class alone produced three academicians.

I wasn't very good at my studies, but then I don't have President George W. Bush's sense of humor about it. Didn't he graduate from Yale? During a speech at Yale, he congratulated those who had done well but said those who had not done well need not be anxious, as they could still become president. He noted that Vice President [Dick] Cheney had also gone to Yale but did not finish; hence he could only be Vice President. Today, I absolutely did not come here to say that I didn't do well in my studies but can still be premier—I have a different sense of humor. What I mean to say is that it's more important to be a person than to be a scholar.

Let us also think about what the Tsinghua spirit is. Many interpretations are possible: the tradition of democracy, the tradition of science, the traditions of

8. Cao Yu (1910–96) was a playwright.

Attending the tenth anniversary celebration of the Tsinghua University School of Economics and Management on March 30, 1994.

"Mr. D," "Mr. S,"[9] and of revolution. You can look at it many ways, and each person will have a different interpretation. I have an interpretation, and this is my understanding: it is the pursuit of perfection. An environment like that of Tsinghua makes you feel surrounded by talent. Everyone's task is to build our homeland—this is our historic mission. When we study here, we feel that we must pursue perfection, that we must be the very best.

To be a person, one must be a Chinese with backbone, a Chinese who can stand tall. To run a school, one must be down-to-earth and rigorous, and must give absolutely no thought to seeking fame, let alone to appropriating the achievements of others—one must view this sort of behavior with utter disdain. When we act, it must be with substance and must truly be for the people. It is impossible for someone to be flawless, but we must do our best to be incorruptible and impartial, and not develop a reputation for notoriety.

It is this kind of Tsinghua spirit that has encouraged me. Even though I was wrongly designated a "rightist" and lost my Party membership for 20 years, I never lost my Communist beliefs, and I never slackened one bit in my work or my studies. I still constantly demand of myself that I live up to the education given to me by my Tsinghua teachers, by Tsinghua University, and by the Party. I always want to have no regrets on my conscience—this is my greatest hope.

9. Translator's note: these terms refer to "Mr. Democracy" and "Mr. Science," which were popularized in the early 20th century.

I make the same demands of my daughter. She was born in 1954 and my son in 1958. They came under great pressure during the "Cultural Revolution." I feel terrible whenever I think about this, but I've always made strict demands of them. I remember very clearly how my son, when he was a little over 10 years old, wanted to grow vegetables on our balcony. One day he found a tattered piece of linoleum that he put on the balcony, preparing to put soil on it in order to grow vegetables. As soon as I saw this, I told him that no matter how poor we were, we could not take things from others. Then I casually slapped him on the ear. It was the first time I had ever struck him, and it was also the last.

He told me he had taken nothing from anyone, that he had retrieved this broken piece of linoleum from the trash. At the time I very much regretted hitting him, but perhaps because as a father I couldn't get off my high horse, I said, "All right then, I shouldn't have hit you. But we must bring this piece of linoleum back regardless of whether it belongs to someone or if it came from the trash." Then I accompanied him in throwing this piece of linoleum back into the trash heap. I feel very bad whenever I think of this. However, I'm very pleased that although he didn't come to study at Tsinghua, he has carried on the Tsinghua spirit.

My daughter and son both studied abroad. While they were in school, I had already become Mayor of Shanghai and then Vice Premier, but not a single foreigner knew that their father was a Chinese mayor or vice premier. They went through school through their own efforts, by doing dishes and by working in school. Now they've finished their studies and returned to China.

Today I'm speaking to you from the heart, and my remarks might seem a bit rambling. But I truly hope that while at Tsinghua, all of you will not only learn to be scholars but also to be people, to learn to do things, and to pursue perfection—you must be the best. You must set this goal. We must build a first-rate university. For China to become a world-class power, it must basically depend on science and education, and education is the foundation of science. You are entirely capable of doing this. One day, who knows how many members of the Academy will emerge from among you. I hope you will all do your best.

My hope for the Tsinghua School of Economics and Management is that it can compare with the best schools of management in the world, whether it be Harvard, the Massachusetts Institute of Technology, or a school of management in whatever country—that it can stand comparison with them. To compare with them, one condition must be met: namely, we must pay attention to building up our instructional ranks. We must have first-rate teachers and must be willing to offer high wages to hire them from abroad, to invite them here if only to lecture. Former President Mei Yiqi of Tsinghua once said, "A university[10] does not mean

10. Translator's note: "daxue," the Chinese term for "university," also means "great learning."

a place with great buildings; it means a place with great teachers." That is to say, a university is not called a place of great learning because it has great buildings; it is because it has great masters—masters of Chinese studies, of science, of management—only then can it be called a place of great learning and only then can it be called a first-rate university. I hope that henceforth the school will devote a lot of effort to building up its instructional ranks.

I also want to raise one other issue: I hope that all future instruction in the school will be conducted in English. I absolutely do not worship foreign things. I urge this because the economy is now globalizing—if you can't have exchanges with foreigners, how can you integrate into the global economy? Our economic growth depends on reform and opening up. It absolutely won't do to not know English, particularly in management.

I never studied abroad, but I benefited greatly from the Tsinghua textbooks of my university days, which were mostly in English. Only one book, *Basic Physics* by Sa Bendong, was a Chinese text—all the others were in English. Some professors taught half in English and half in Chinese. Zhuang Qianding, a native of Wuxi who taught thermodynamics, once said, "You're not going to understand me anyway if I speak in Wuxi dialect, so I'll speak in English. I'm sorry." That's why it's very important to teach in English. If the level of English of instructors isn't good enough, they can study it further. We can give you a year or two of training, and you can go abroad to practice—it isn't too hard.

At the two meetings of the International Advisory Committee that I convened, for example, there were foreign participants. That's why I insisted we all use English. If you're in economics and management and can't speak with foreigners in English, it will be very hard for you to integrate into the world's economic currents. Is this also the case for the university's other departments? Not necessarily, because for many in engineering it's enough to be able to read English, and it isn't essential for them to speak it, but those in economics and management must be able to do so.

As I bid farewell to the Tsinghua School of Economics and Management—it's not yet a total farewell, as I'm still keeping the title of Honorary Chairman of the Advisory Committee—I offer my best wishes to the university and to the school and hope that all you young people here will do better than I did.

38

On Economic Development Issues in Three Autonomous Ethnic Minority Prefectures in Sichuan[1]

June 11, 2001

My first goal in coming to Sichuan this time is to fulfill a promise to visit three autonomous minority prefectures. In 1996 I went to Liangshan, in 1999 to Ngaba, and this time to Ganzi. Another consideration is the fact that the Party Central Committee is about to convene a conference on our work in Tibet, and after the conference is over, we will announce the commencement of work on the Qinghai-Tibet railroad. This railroad will play a very important part in the development of Tibet. We must make the construction of this railroad a "first in the world," because it will be built on a frozen plateau, and there is no precedent anywhere for anything like it. It is to be used mainly for passenger traffic and will allow people from countries all over the world to visit Tibet and see the actual conditions there. The Qinghai-Tibet railroad has great significance [for China], both politically and economically, and also for the people of Tibet. I wanted to take this opportunity to visit the Tibetan areas in Sichuan and hope I can help resolve some of their problems.

My second goal [in coming] is to see the results of reverting farmlands to forests in Sichuan. It's fair to say that the insight I gained in Sichuan helped shape the policy of reverting farmlands to forests. After the exceptionally heavy flooding along the Yangtze, Nen, and Songhua river basins in 1998, I submitted a report to the Politburo in Beidaihe focusing mainly on reverting farmlands to lakes and proposing a 32-character approach to this work.[2] Subsequently, Xie Shijie[3] and Zhang Zhongwei[4] told me that we now have quite a lot of grain and asked if it would be possible to have the farmers grow less grain and plant more forests by offering them grain in lieu of relief aid. That's why I can say

---

1. On June 8–12, 2001, Zhu Rongji visited Ya'an, Ganzi, and Chengdu during an inspection tour of Sichuan Province. These are remarks he made after listening to work reports by the provincial Party Committee and provincial government.

2. See chapter 7 in this volume.

3. Xie Shijie was Party Secretary of Sichuan Province from March 1993 until December 1999.

4. Zhang Zhongwei was then Governor of Sichuan Province.

that after gaining this insight, I conducted studies nationwide, particularly in several western provinces, and it was only when I was in Yan'an in 1999 that I formulated the 16-character approach and formally proposed reverting farmlands to forests.

In 1999 Xie Shijie suggested to me that Sichuan revert 3 million mu[5] of farmland to forests, and I expressed my approval. All our work is similarly enriched [by ideas from] the leadership and the entire population, enabling us to propose an approach to the central authorities, who then make the decision. We can now see the significance of this [reforestation] even more clearly and recognize that it is more vital than ever. Although last year's drought was so severe that grain production fell by over 90 billion jin[6] and another drought is under way this year, this apparently did not affect the grain supply, which still exceeds demand, nor did grain prices rise. That's why I say that this is a historic opportunity, a heaven-sent chance, or a chance that comes but once in a thousand years: it allows us to catch our breath and make up somewhat for the damage we did to nature in the past.

We used to pay no attention to a strategy of sustainable development and destroyed nature, destroyed its ability to heal itself, causing today's deterioration of the eco-environment. A ditty going around Beijing sums it up: "The poor people of Beijing get one dose of sand a day; they don't get enough by day and must get some more by night." That is how nature punishes us. Now we can make up for it—but this restitution will require the efforts of several generations, and we must start right now.

You could say that I have also come here to inspect work that has been done. I did visit some areas and saw their great achievements. The feedback from the local population was also very good, but we mustn't become self-satisfied. I also saw goats running around the hills where farmlands had been reverted to forests—they hadn't been penned up. We paid such a high price to revert farmlands to forests: we provided grain, we provided saplings, and we provided subsidies. Yet houses are still being built on hilltops or halfway up the hills—this shows that the hills still haven't been closed off. A lot of work still hasn't been done thoroughly, so don't be complacent.

The Party Secretary of Tianquan County, a very capable woman, had all the goats penned up, but the pens are next to the river. She said this is "making money off goats," enabling people to increase incomes by raising goats. I replied, "How can you place the goat pens right next to the river? You might be 'making money off goats,' but the people downstream will have to drink goat piss!" The goat excrement was all discharged into the river and polluting it.

---

5. One mu is equal to 666.7 square meters.
6. One jin is equal to 0.5 kilogram.

To reiterate, there's still a lot of work to do in reverting farmlands to forests. For example, the document granting a subsidy of 300 jin of grain for each mu of land explicitly stated that the farmers would still have to pay the agricultural tax. But in order to lighten their burden, you're not collecting the agricultural tax. If you don't think of ways to offer some fiscal subsidies, the difficulties will become even greater. At the same time, we must understand that while a subsidy of 300 jin of grain per mu of land isn't a lot, this grain is free. In the past, farmers might harvest 300 or even 400 jin of grain per mu, but they had to pay a very high price—they would need seeds, chemical fertilizers, and labor. Now sacks and sacks of rice for reverted farmlands are delivered straight to the farmers' doors, whereas many of these places basically couldn't even afford to eat rice in the past. In Kangding, we saw sacks printed with "Farmland Reversion Rice" in large characters—this is a very good idea from Sichuan. The local people also said that highway tolls are not charged for rice transported in such sacks, which shows that everyone supports this policy.

Now everyone is asking that the scale of farmland reversion be increased and that the quotas be set higher. Increasing the quota means increasing the grain [provided], which would moreover be free. I hope that to the greatest extent possible, the increased quota can be used to take care of the three autonomous minority prefectures, because they are the sources of the Yellow River and the Yangtze! Improving the eco-environments in these places will have a great effect on the entire nation. The 300 jin per mu of grain subsidy from the state is not only for one year. We've promised to give it for eight years, and when the time comes, we can consider extending that period. If by then the farmers' incomes are very high and grain is cheap, it won't matter whether or not we provide grain subsidies. That's why we have to attentively nurture the forests to maturity—I feel this is not too great a demand. Policy in this regard still needs to be developed and perfected; we must be strict in our demands and pay attention to quality. There's still a lot to do in this area.

I came here with these two goals, and after my visit, I feel I've learned a lot and gained many insights. Just now the provincial Party Committee and provincial government made some requests of us. We should also help resolve some problems.

Problems of the Three Autonomous Minority Prefectures

We can resolve the problems of these prefectures with three approaches:
    —First, increase the scale of reverting farmlands to forests.
    —Second, reinforce infrastructure construction.
    —Third, increase revenues.

Visiting a Tibetan family in Ganzi Tibetan Autonomous Prefecture, Sichuan Province, on June 8, 2001, and examining state-subsidized rice given to promote reversion of farmlands to forests. (Photograph by Qi Tieyan, Xinhua News Agency)

Wang Chunzheng[7] has already responded to the call for more extensive refor-estation by increasing the quota by 1 million mu, and I entirely agree. Therefore I next turn to infrastructure projects.

Infrastructure Construction. The first question to tackle is transportation, with other infrastructure construction projects close behind. Our most important policy for the great development of western China is to use state funds as much as possible: that is, arrange [financing] through Treasury bonds and bank loans, so that local authorities pay little or nothing in matching funds. Now some peo-ple keep saying they don't see any preferential policies for the great development of western China—but this is the most preferential policy of all. We have taken into consideration the western region's fiscal difficulties and the relatively heavy burdens of its people, and this is the policy [we are implementing] when we use Treasury bonds for projects.

Three projects—the Sichuan-Tibet highway,[8] the Nanchong-Guang'an expressway, and the Ya'an-Panzhihua expressway—were all based on the

77. Wang Chunzheng was then Vice Chairman of the State Development Planning Commission.

8. The Sichuan-Tibet highway runs from Chengdu in Sichuan to Lhasa in Tibet. Its northern route is 2,412 kilometers long and was formally opened to traffic in 1954; its southern route is 2,149 kilometers long and was formally opened to traffic in 1958.

principle I just described and were financed through Treasury bonds and bank loans. This is special treatment for minority and old [revolutionary] areas, and it is also the most important preferential policy for the great development of the west.

A word about roads. From now on, roads going from the administrative centers of these three minority prefectures to counties within their jurisdictions—for example, the roads from Kangding in Ganzi Prefecture to its 19 counties—these roads will be incorporated into the national plan and will be built with state funding. When Jiang Zemin came to Sichuan in 1991, he remarked that "for Tibet to be stable, Kang must first be peaceful." "Kang" refers to Xikang, which is where those three ethnic minority prefectures are located. I would add a word or two to that: "For Kang to be peaceful, it must first be accessible." If transportation is inconvenient, it won't be possible to develop the economy and improve the lives of the people. Of course these roads will be different from the national highways I discussed earlier.

In our discussions with Kangding and with the prefectural government, we said that the state will provide as much funding as possible, but the following conditions will apply:

—First, you mustn't charge for expropriated land.

—Second, the local governments mustn't exploit [us].

—Third, you mustn't charge fees for the necessary labor; it will be up to the governments of the autonomous prefectures to think about how to compensate for the labor.

In short, the central government's fiscal departments will arrange the funding needed to build these roads, but you must really work with us. These three autonomous prefectures have 48 counties in all, some of which may already have roads. Road construction can be planned in phases and batches. Draw up a plan indicating which counties are to be reached first and which later; this should be based on their populations, the importance of their economic growth, and their strategic importance. Don't try to finish everything within a year. Road surfaces may differ, but you should at least start on asphalt-paved roads because only those can be permanent structures. Roads from the administrative centers of these prefectures to their counties should be included in their plans and implemented in phases.

After we go back, Zhang Chunxian[9] will organize people to come on a study trip, and they will then propose a plan to the State Planning Commission. We will put the funding for the roads in these three prefectures into our Treasury bond program, draw up a plan for them, and carry it out in phases and batches. I'm sure the autonomous prefectures from other provinces and regions will

9. Zhang Chunxian was then Vice Minister of Transportation.

want similar treatment. They can come [to us] if they wish; we'll treat them all equally. However, there must be priorities, and we'll start with these three prefectures, arranging for their roads in phases and batches.

How should we develop the economies of minority areas? We've previously gone down many wrong paths in allowing the "five small enterprises;"[10] in the end we wound up with an assful of debt and hardly any benefits. If the roads are built and are accessible from all directions, the first thing to develop can be tourism. Our trip to Ganzi this time was very productive and well worth the time, as we were able to see our country's magnificent scenery. There were also many places we didn't visit, but some of the young people who came with us used their afternoon breaks to go exploring and viewing the scenery at an elevation of 4,300 meters above sea level. I have yet to visit Seashell Gorge, but I'll return when you complete these roads and the Kangding Airport. I think this is the best way to support the minority areas. First help them complete their infrastructure, then complement that with a couple of decent hotels—the foreigners will start coming. Heaven has given us such fine resources, and these areas should be able to earn a lot, but without transportation, it will amount to nothing.

I'd like to do a pilot program here. Originally, the state need not get involved in such matters as the division of labor; it only needs to be in charge of the "five verticals and seven horizontals."[11] It can't be in charge of roads beneath the prefectural level, but I'm willing to use these three autonomous prefectures for a pilot program. I believe this will be very helpful for their economic development.

At the same time, I hope you will properly protect your resources. Don't start developing haphazardly if your plans aren't complete and if you haven't received approvals from the province or the State Council. Otherwise you will destroy your resources.

A word about tourism. On two recent evenings, I watched a program in which Phoenix TV from Hong Kong broadcast a local group's travels in western China. As soon as they got off the plane in Xi'an, its members were dragged off to discuss [investment] projects, which left them with a poor impression. When they arrived in Xinjiang, however, they enjoyed ethnic music and dancing as soon as they got off the plane, with no discussion of projects, yet in the end they successfully negotiated the most projects in Xinjiang. Most of these successful projects were tourism-related.

It's very obvious that there's no place for processing industries and whatnot in western China—supply basically exceeds demand for all consumer goods, yet you still think you can compete in the heartland? You're so far away! There's a

10. See chapter 14, n. 4, p. 123.

11. The "five verticals and seven horizontals" are the five north-south and the seven east-west national trunk roads.

very famous marketplace in Urumqi called "Erdaoqiao." When you talk about Urumqi with people from Hong Kong they may know little about the place, but when you mention "Erdaoqiao" they've all heard of it because it's a booming marketplace. Now Urumqi wants to rebuild that marketplace—to move it and then put up large buildings there. Wong Man Kong from Hong Kong is a big capitalist. After visiting, he said you shouldn't move and you absolutely mustn't demolish the market. You can remodel it, preserving its original appearance and adding a cultural plaza in front of it—he's willing to invest in this. I feel his line of thinking is more astute than ours. If you casually destroy something that is famous inside and outside China and replace it with a large building, it would have no appeal.

Then there's Nina Kung Wang of the Chinachem Group, who signed deals for RMB 800 million to 900 million worth of projects. I noticed that the majority of the contracts she signed were commercial. There was one gold mining project but no other industrial ones—they were basically all commercial projects that attach great importance to tourism. Ganzi wants to promote tourism, but it has no hotels that are up to international standards, so foreigners won't come. If you only pay attention to "what goes in" and not to "what comes out,"[12] people will feel that you're not civilized enough. The "software" of tourism is extremely important. Of course Liangshan has industries, but I feel tourism is the most important direction for the other two minority prefectures to follow. Jiuzhaigou is in Ngaba [Prefecture]. If the tourism resources there are properly protected and properly developed, it will become rich and can make up for past losses caused by halting logging in its natural forests.

What we are doing now is helping you create conditions, helping you to complete roads. Once the roads are built and your own efforts are added in, your economy will definitely pick up, which is why I've added this project. You really must understand my intent, as it wasn't easy for me to make this decision. There is no precedent for [the state] being in charge of roads at the county level below the prefectures. This exemplifies the concern of the central authorities for our minorities and our hopes that your economy can grow a bit faster.

A word about waterworks. The key step for waterworks, including hydropower, is to do sound feasibility studies and good early-stage work. These can all be conducted in phases and batches and should be reported to the Ministry of Water Resources and the State Planning Commission. In principle, I agree with all of them and hope their construction can be accelerated. However, I think the most important thing to establish is where Sichuan's electricity will be sent. If it is to be delivered to Guangdong through national allocation, then you must step up planning and construction. Sending it to Guangdong via Guangxi,

---

12. Translator's note: this refers to the importance of good sanitary facilities.

Guizhou, and Yunnan poses no problem at all. Their plans are already complete and they are speeding up construction. However, power can't yet be sent out from Ertan.[13] The first generator at the Three Gorges[14] will start operating in 2003 and its power is to be sent to Guangdong. You must hurry up with your planning, decisionmaking, and construction. In accordance with the principles I described just now, most of the funding for all these projects will be arranged by central fiscal authorities.

The Question of Finances. Your plan is too ambitious, and I'm afraid we can't manage it. In view of actual current needs, we are making one request of the three minority prefectures: namely, that you yourselves explore how to increase revenues and decrease outlays, how to reduce unnecessary expenses.

First of all, you must guarantee wages and must absolutely not be in arrears on wages. To ensure that you can pay the wages of civil servants, including teachers, you must streamline agencies. Some local government agencies are as large as can be, yet few people are actually doing anything. There are also many among the ranks of teachers who can't teach. You must think of ways to address these problems, to streamline agencies, increase efficiency, to promote clean, diligent, and effective government.

Second, you must guarantee that public security agencies have funds to investigate suspected crimes. Without the rule of law, how can there be construction?

Third, you must guarantee funding for departments that manage markets. How can a disorderly market economy develop? If you don't strike at the fake, you will be striking at the real, and if you don't strike at the shoddy, you will be striking at quality. You must strengthen the bureaus of industry and commerce and of technical supervision. Guarantee funding for them, but be thrifty. In a word, you must also rely on yourselves to increase revenues and reduce outlays in order to make up for the shortfalls you described just now.

Xiang Huaicheng[15] just said—and as he has reported to me—that beginning this year the central fiscal authorities will give the three minority prefectures RMB 400 million in subsidies annually. I will add another RMB 100 million, making it RMB 500 million a year. I can't let Xiang Huaicheng alone be the nice guy. I also want to be a nice guy. Of course this isn't settled just because we said

13. The Ertan Hydropower Plant is the largest hydropower plant built in China during the 20th century. It is situated at the downstream section of the Yalong River in Sichuan Province. Construction on it began in 1991 and was completed in 1999. Its reservoir has a capacity of 5.8 billion cubic meters, and the plant has an installed capacity of 3.3 million kilowatt-hours. It generated an average of 17 billion kilowatt-hours annually for many years.

14. The Three Gorges Hydropower Plant, with an installed capacity of 18 million kilowatt-hours and average annual generation of 84.68 billion kilowatt-hours.

15. Xiang Huaicheng was then Minister of Finance.

so. We still have to discuss it with the departments concerned after we go back; then we have to report to the State Council. It will be decided after discussions by the State Council leadership.

There is also a basis for setting this figure at RMB 500 million. It was quite clear from listening to the reports in Ganzi that they have fiscal revenues of RMB 500 million and expenses of over 700 million. The shortfall of over RMB 200 million is covered by misappropriating specially designated funds. I suggest that you focus on finances. Your top two people must know finances like the back of your hand: you must know where the money comes from and where it goes. This was the most important thing I learned from the time I was Mayor of Shanghai and then also Party Secretary. Now that I'm Premier, I keep all the fiscal accounts in my head. I estimate that Ngaba is about the same as Ganzi in both population and territory and that its shortfall is also upward of RMB 200 million. At least the Liangshan Autonomous Prefecture has industry! Xichang has industries. Its industrial population is a bit larger than those of Ganzi and Ngaba; it also has slightly higher revenues and can basically guarantee the wages of its people. The RMB 500 million is mainly for Ganzi and Ngaba, though of course we'll also give something to Liangshan. Its support will come from an increase in the quota for cigarettes produced by its tobacco factories. As for how much will be given to Ganzi and Ngaba each, that is for the provincial government to determine. You must tell everyone that we have done our utmost for them.

39

FURTHER SPEED UP TIBET'S ECONOMIC DEVELOPMENT[1]

June 25, 2001

With its vast territory stretching along our country's southwest, Tibet is of great strategic importance. The Party Central Committee and the State Council have always considered it a pressing task to accelerate the region's economic development. As far back as the 1980s, Deng Xiaoping pointed out that we must "stimulate rapid development in the region and bring it into the forefront of the drive for modernization."[2] In 1994 Jiang Zemin stressed that "the most fundamental means of accelerating Tibet's development is to speed up economic development. If its economy improves, other matters will be easier to deal with."[3] Further speeding up Tibet's economic development is not just a regional issue; it has great political as well as economic significance for the entire country.

Focus on Speeding Up Tibet's Economic Development

In the 50 years since the peaceful liberation of Tibet, the region has undergone democratic reforms and socialist construction, has greatly liberated and

---

1. On June 25–27, 2001, the Party Central Committee and the State Council convened the fourth symposium on Tibet-related work in Beijing. Participants included leading members of the Party and government of the Tibet Autonomous Region; the principal leading members of the various areas and cities in Tibet and the agencies directly administered by the Autonomous Region; leading members of various provinces, autonomous regions, centrally administered municipalities, and the relevant cities separately listed in national plans; and leading members of the Party Central Committee, departments concerned of the State Council, the four general departments of the People's Liberation Army, and the headquarters of the People's Armed Police. The speech Zhu Rongji made at this symposium was published under the title "On Speeding Up the Economic Development of Tibet" in *Selected Writings on Tibet-Related Work, 1949–2005* (Beijing: Central Documents Publishing House, 2005). Portions have been omitted in this edition.
2. Deng Xiaoping, "China's Policy, Based on the Equality of Nationalities, Is to Accelerate Development in Tibet (July 29, 1987)," *Selected Works of Deng Xiaoping*, vol. 3: *1982–1992* (Beijing: Foreign Languages Press, 1994), pp. 242–43.
3. Jiang Zemin, "Our Tibet Work Must Effectively Ensure the Region's Stability and Development (July 20, 1994)," *Selected Works of Jiang Zemin*, vol. 1 (Beijing: Foreign Languages Press, 2010), p. 378.

developed its forces of production, and made ample progress in building up its economy. Particularly after the third symposium on our work in Tibet,[4] the Party Committee and government of the Tibet Autonomous Region have led the people of all ethnic groups in a united effort and obtained notable results in economic and social development. From 1994 to 2000, Tibet's GDP rose by 12.4% a year. The central government made key investments in a batch of core infrastructure projects in transportation, energy, communications, agriculture and animal husbandry, and social enterprises. There was also considerable progress in science and technology, education, culture, and public health. The incomes of farmers, herders, and urban residents rose continuously, as did their standard of living.

However, because of historical, natural, and social reasons, the level of Tibet's economic development remains very low. Its total economy is small, and its ability to build up assets and develop on its own is poor. Its agriculture, animal husbandry, and eco-environment are fragile; constraints due to infrastructure bottlenecks are serious; and science, technology, and education are backward. Only by further speeding up its economic development can we fundamentally change Tibet's backwardness in these areas.

The acceleration of Tibet's economic development is also an important guarantee of its ethnic unity and our homeland's unity and security. Hence the two major tasks facing Tibet are speeding up development and maintaining stability: stability is the precondition of development and development is the foundation of stability. Only by stepping up economic development, building up economic power, and constantly improving the lives of the people can we reinforce cohesiveness, and only then can we strengthen and develop the great unity of all our peoples. We must lay a solid material and social foundation for the sake of Tibet's social stability and long-term governance. With almost 4,000 kilometers of borders [with other nations], Tibet is an important frontier area for the defense of our nation's territory and security. Only by speedier development can we build a "Great Wall of Steel" along our southwestern border to defend our nation's unity and security.

The present time, with its favorable conditions, is one of the best periods in history for Tibet's economic growth, social progress, overall stability, ethnic unity, and border strengthening. All the peoples of Tibet have a strong desire to achieve these ends as soon as possible, and this is a powerful impetus for accelerating development. Our country's implementation of the strategy for the great development of western China also offers a rare historic opportunity for Tibet to speed up its growth.

---

4. After two symposiums on Tibet-related work in 1980 and 1984, the Party Central Committee and State Council convened the third symposium in Beijing on July 20–23, 1994.

Have Clear Goals and Focus on Key Priorities

In an outline of its 10th Five-Year Plan for economic and social development, drawn up with the assistance of the central government departments concerned, Tibet laid out the following goals for the period of the plan:

—An annual growth rate of over 12%.

—Per capita production that would be among the highest in western China by 2005.

—Per capita production that would reach the national midrange by 2010, thereby laying a good foundation for Tibet to modernize along with the entire country.

These development goals are aggressive and necessary. The Tibet Autonomous Region must join its efforts with all sectors of the entire nation and work hard to realize these goals.

Economically, Tibet's growth should be sustainable and rapid so that it can close the gap between it and other provinces and municipalities as quickly as possible, but it must also be sustainable. Therefore it must be centered on improved economic performance as well as speed. You must be driven by reform and opening up and by scientific and technological progress, and your industrial structure must be forcefully optimized and upgraded. You must utilize resources and protect the eco-environment in a reasonable way and take the path of sustainable development. You must constantly increase the incomes of urban residents and make marked improvements in the lives of the people. Only then will Tibet's economy enter a virtuous cycle and achieve sustainable, rapid, and healthy development.

You must clearly recognize that the fundamental transformation of Tibet's backwardness is a long-term and arduous task that will require unremitting efforts. You must actively take the initiative and strive for faster development; at the same time, you must proceed from realities, act in accordance with objective rules, and pay attention to actual effectiveness. The following are the most important steps on the path to Tibet's development: speed up infrastructure construction, nurture and strengthen unique economic features, reinforce the protection and conservation of the eco-environment, and develop science, technology, and education.

Infrastructure Construction. Poor infrastructure is the main constraint to Tibet's economic growth. You must speed up infrastructure construction in railways, roads, airports, power, communications, and waterworks. After ample validation and preparations, work is about to start on the Qinghai-Tibet railroad. The building of this great rail artery across the Qinghai-Tibet plateau will not only have a great impact on Tibet's development but will also play a major role in the strategy of the great development of western China. It must be meticulously designed, meticulously organized, and meticulously constructed. You should do your best to have the entire line open to traffic within six years. At the same time, you must focus hard on a batch of infrastructure projects that affect Tibet's long-term development and lay a solid foundation for Tibet's all-round resurgence.

Unique Features. You should take full advantage of your strength in resources and create an economy with unique features as well as pillar industries in its markets. In reinforcing and strengthening the foundational status of agriculture and animal husbandry, you should focus on adjusting their economic structure, developing them comprehensively, and using every means possible to increase the incomes of farmers and herders. Work hard to develop distinctive industries like traditional Tibetan pharmaceuticals, high-elevation biologicals, green food-stuffs, and ethnic handicrafts, and make every effort to turn your advantage in resources into a real economic strength.

I especially want to emphasize that you must pay great attention to tourism and you must soundly develop it. Tibet is at the roof of the world. It has unique snowscapes, high-elevation scenery, and cultural sights that will attract both domestic and international tourists. Tourism has tremendous potential and great scope for development. You must make it one of Tibet's pillar industries. That way, you will not only drive the growth of related industries and enable most farmers and herders to leave poverty behind sooner, but you will also increase Tibet's contacts at home and abroad and be better able to show the people of the entire world the great achievements in Tibet's development.

The State Council has already asked the departments concerned to assist the government of the Autonomous Region in drawing up mid- to long-range development plans for tourism. They should include the following measures: speeding up the construction of tourism-related transportation and other facilities, gradually opening up more areas to tourism, simplifying approval processes, making a concerted effort to train people in tourism management and services, developing all sorts of tourism products, and raising the standards of tourism management and services as quickly as possible.

The Eco-Environment. Tibet's eco-environment is very fragile, and large-scale construction will place a great deal of stress on it. Thus in speeding up the region's economic development, you must pay great attention to protecting the eco-environment in all project validations, designs, construction, and operations. Some of the projects you initiate should be dedicated to protecting natural forests and strengthening the construction of nature preserves, and to carefully developing and protecting natural grasslands and keeping in check their desertification and regression. You must also do more and better

Attending a ceremony on June 29, 2001, in Golmud, Qinghai Province, to mark the start of construction of the Qinghai-Tibet Railroad and to announce the start of construction along the entire line. (Photograph by Fan Rujun, Xinhua News Agency)

surveying, monitoring, and scientific research on your [natural] resources and the eco-environment.

Science and Education. To speed up Tibet's economic development, you must truly implement the strategy of "revitalizing Tibet through science and education." Therefore you must constantly raise the cultural and educational level of the population by making great efforts to train all sorts of talent, use local talent well, and actively recruit urgently needed talent from outside. Your primary objective should be to improve basic education and eliminate illiteracy among the young, as well as to vigorously promote all levels of education. That means you must continue to run Tibet's high schools, Tibetan classes in the heartland, and Tibet University well. You must also focus on forcefully promoting scientific and technical progress and innovation, and on applying appropriate advanced technologies so that modern science and technology can play a greater role in your economic development. Part of this "revitalization" should entail developing a stronger set of socialist ethical and moral values, and actively promoting endeavors in the social sphere such as culture and art, radio and TV, news publications, public health, and sports. In particular, be sure to strengthen work on protecting cultural relics.

Increase the Level of Support for More Rapid Development

In order to help Tibet speed up its economic and social development, the central authorities have for many years implemented special preferential policies for Tibet, directly arranging construction projects and funding. The central government departments concerned and 15 provinces and municipalities have also given assistance to designated counterparts. These entities have played a major role in promoting Tibet's development. Current circumstances call for a further increase in construction funds for Tibet, more forceful preferential policies, and further assistance to counterparts, so as to better speed up Tibet's development.

After fully consulting all parties, we have now determined that the state will directly invest a total of RMB 31.2 billion in 117 construction projects (including the RMB 12 billion investment in the Tibetan section of the Qinghai-Tibet railroad). This is an increase of 87 projects over the 30 centrally supported projects decided upon at the third symposium on work in Tibet; it is also an increase of RMB 27.4 billion over the 3.8 billion invested in completed projects. These are all major projects urgently needed in Tibet for which the [necessary] conditions are present and on which work can begin within this year or the next. Some other key projects must also be undertaken but are not counted here because work on them cannot commence in the near future. In principle, there will be no cap on the projects needed in Tibet in the future—as each one matures, it can be approved.

During the period of the 10th Five-Year Plan, we should try to start up more projects that will affect long-term development. In light of the special circumstances in Tibet, funds for its key construction projects will be provided by the state. State investments and support from the central fiscal authorities should be used mainly for developing agriculture and animal husbandry, infrastructure, science, technology and education, facilities for grassroots [level] government agencies, and the protection and development of the eco-environment. The emphasis should be on eliminating bottlenecks that constrain Tibet's development and resolving prominent problems.

Even as it increases direct investment, the central government will implement special support policies. Current preferential policies that can continue to be carried out should be carried out; those that need refining should be carried out after refinement. This time, we have also added some new preferential policies. There will be stronger policy support for fiscal work, taxation, financing, investment, pricing, helping wages and industries grow, opening to the outside, the development of human resources, construction of cities and townships, industrial reforms, and science, technology, and education. After these preferential policies are put in place, central support and fiscal subsidies for Tibet will reach RMB 37.9 billion during the period of the 10th Five-Year Plan, which is double the level of the period of the 9th Five-Year Plan.

We also have to strengthen assistance to designated counterparts. After careful preparations and coordination, we have decided on 70 aid projects by the provinces and municipalities concerned, for a total investment of about RMB 1.06 billion. In terms of the number of projects and the sums involved, these are considerably higher levels than those decided on during the third symposium on our work in Tibet.

The adoption of measures such as increased investment, preferential policies, and assistance to designated counterparts exemplifies the great attention the central authorities are paying to the development of Tibet and the deep feelings of the nation's entire population. We must use these inputs and policies well so that they yield the intended benefits in full. All these projects must be incorporated into Tibet's development plans. You should act strictly according to the systems and procedures for basic construction, strengthen project oversight, rigorously control quality, use first-rate project teams and first-rate oversight to ensure first-rate quality, and you absolutely must not engage in any "tofu dreg"[5] projects.

All aid projects should be oriented toward Tibet's long-term development, but they must also endeavor to improve the people's production and livelihoods in the short term and raise their standard of living. Direct investments by the state, fiscal subsidies from the central authorities, assistance to counterparts, and local investments and fiscal outlays in Tibet should all be directed as much as possible toward projects that directly benefit the majority of farmers and herders. At the same time, you must work harder at poverty alleviation and resolve as quickly as possible the difficulties in the livelihoods of those who still reside below the poverty line.

Take the Big Picture into Account

All departments of the central government and all regions must take the big picture into account and work hard to help Tibet develop more rapidly. This policy of having the whole country help speed up Tibet's development is an important

---

5. See chapter 11 in this volume.

On June 29, 2001, ceremonies were held simultaneously in Golmud, Qinghai Province, and Lhasa, capital of the Tibetan Autonomous Region, to mark the start of construction of the Qinghai-Tibet Railroad. Zhu Rongji and others laid the foundation for the project in Golmud. (Photograph by Fan Rujun, Xinhua News Agency)

strategic decision made by the central authorities. It is the common duty of all ethnic groups across the country and a duty that no department or region can shirk. In improving their support and assistance for the development of Tibet, all departments and regions must approach this work from the loftier perspectives of politics and the big picture.

First, all departments and regions must make sure that the projects to assist counterparts already agreed to are implemented. The central government departments, provinces, and municipalities providing aid to counterparts and the Tibetan Autonomous Region must all soundly implement the various tasks decided upon at this conference, make sure that the work of meshing and coordinating is done properly, and ensure that aid projects are completed on schedule. During the course of project construction, we must focus on training Tibet's local management talent. The keys to a project cannot be handed over unless a qualified management team and other necessary conditions are in place to carry it forward.

Second, we must continue to establish aid relationships that are relatively stable over the long term. Depending on their own capabilities and the actual needs of Tibet, all departments and regions should use a variety of financial, technical, and material means to support and assist in accelerating development. Talent is an important ingredient of support. We should continue to select outstanding officials and other types of talent to work in Tibet.

Third, we should adapt to the new situation of development in a socialist market economy and actively search for new forms and mechanisms of assistance. We should encourage and support investment in Tibet by enterprises under all types of ownership and by individuals. We should use a variety of ways to promote the establishment of businesses and commercial and trading activities that can offer mutual benefits and be developed jointly.

Fourth, we must ensure local ethnic unity as well as the nation's unity and security. In adopting special forms and policies for supporting Tibet, the central authorities are not only considering the unique difficulties of Tibet. They are also mindful of maintaining unity among the various ethnic groups and the security of our homeland. Both the current situation and the big picture make this a necessary consideration. Speeding up Tibet's development and maintaining Tibet's stability are both in the direct interests of the Tibetan people as well as ethnic groups throughout the country. The central authorities also care deeply about the difficulties and development problems of other minority areas and have adopted many types of measures to address them. Of course in setting policies, they must proceed from the big picture, considering all sides in their planning. They must also take into account different situations [where necessary].

Emphasize Tibet's Role

Tibet must continue to rely on its own efforts, be united in its endeavors, and work hard to open up new vistas in economic development. The central authorities and all parties are now taking measures of unprecedented force to support Tibet. These are creating favorable conditions and a rare opportunity to accelerate its development. Ultimately, however, the revitalization and development of Tibet will depend on the self-reliance, arduous work, and drive of its own officials and people. You must turn the caring of the central authorities and the support of the entire country into a powerful force and make great efforts to forge ahead with your development.

Officials are the key to making Tibet develop more quickly. For a long time, its officials have worked hard and selflessly, making great contributions to the region's development and stability. Current circumstances demand that they continually improve their political and professional caliber while keeping the spirit of "Tibet old-timers" in mind. All levels of government should be clean, diligent, pragmatic, and efficient; they should care about the lives of the people, be attentive to their methods of work, and serve all the ethnic groups in Tibet wholeheartedly. Education in patriotism, socialism, and collectivism should be thorough and continuous; it should include information on policies pertaining to minorities, religion, and law. We must take a clear stand against ethnic separatism, crack down hard on destructive separatist activities in accordance with the law, and uphold ethnic unity as well as our nation's unity.

40

In Attracting Foreign Investment, We Must Achieve the "Three Integrations"[1]

July 4, 2001

Four years have passed since the 1997 national conference on foreign investment. The present conference is particularly significant because great changes have occurred in the interim, both domestically and internationally. To help us move forward better, we need to do timely studies of the new circumstances relating to foreign investment, must resolve new problems, and be clear about our new tasks.

Study the New Circumstances in Depth

To begin with, we should fully acknowledge the achievements of our work on foreign investment. Amid the international complexities during the Ninth Five-Year Plan, we persevered in "utilizing foreign investment actively, reasonably, and effectively" and sustained good momentum in this endeavor. Despite the impact of the Asian financial crisis, we still absorbed US$45.4 billion in direct foreign investment (FDI) during 1998. The figures were slightly lower in the past two years—$40.3 billion in 1999 and $40.7 billion in 2000—but the scale was still very large. This doesn't even include the roughly $30 billion raised by our companies that listed abroad. If we include that amount, then our country still ranks second in the world in attracting FDI, behind only the United States. This is clearly a great achievement in foreign investment work and has played an important role in increasing investment demand and export trade, in promoting reforms and expanding opening to the outside, and in stimulating development.

---

1. This is the main part of Zhu Rongji's speech at a national working conference on foreign investment held in Beijing on July 3–4, 2001. Participants included leading officials in charge of foreign investment from the various provinces, autonomous regions, and centrally administered municipalities, leading members of the Xinjiang Construction Corps, and leading members of the relevant departments of the Party Central Committee and the State Council. The speech was previously published under the title "Adapt to the New Situation and Work Hard to Elevate Our Work with Foreign Investment to a New Level," in *A Selection of Major Articles since the 15th National Party Congress*, vol. 2 (Beijing: People's Publishing House, 2000). Some parts have been omitted in this edition.

Of course we should also recognize that some shortcomings and inadequacies remain, primarily in the quality and performance of investments attracted. We should carefully take stock of our experiences and work hard to improve.

In the past, our country lacked capital, commodities were in short supply, and we were inexperienced. The main reason for attracting foreign capital was to attract more capital, start up more projects and increase production capacity. This was necessary under those historic circumstances. However, our economy has now changed profoundly, and we are facing many new conditions that have bearing on foreign investment.

First, Changes in Domestic Supply and Demand. There has been an important shift in domestic supply and demand, with a seller's market turning into a buyer's market. Current supply exceeds demand in the vast majority of materials of production and consumer goods; about one-third of capacity of ordinary processing industries is not fully utilized. The supply of capital is also relatively ample, and capital is no longer a prominent problem in economic operations. Hence we should no longer focus on simply seeking scale when attracting investments. Rather, we should work at raising quality and standards when utilizing foreign investment.

Second, Changes in the Systemic Environment. The systemic environment of our economic growth has changed drastically. As our reforms continue to deepen, a socialist market economy has begun to be established, and market mechanisms are playing an increasingly large and fundamental role in resource allocation. If we continue to abide by certain concepts and methods carried over from the traditional planned economy, this will interfere with economic growth and prevent us from getting good results by using foreign investment.

Third, Changes in Our Opening Up. Major changes have occurred in our opening up to the outside. With our accession to the World Trade Organization (WTO), our opening up will enter a new phase. This can create better opportunities for attracting foreign investment but at the same time will expose domestic industries to more intense competition. After joining the WTO, we'll have fewer sectors and rules that restrict FDI and see foreign investment coming in on an upward trend.

Fourth, Changes in Global Economic Growth. This year global economic growth has slowed down. As a result, international capital is seeking new investment opportunities and outside investors are viewing the China market favorably. For instance, according to a recent survey by J. P. Morgan Chase, American multinationals are still increasing direct investments in China despite reducing other investments abroad because of the global slowdown. Therefore we have no

Attending and speaking at the National Conference on Foreign Investment on July 4, 2001. To the right is Politburo Standing Committee member and Vice Premier Li Lanqing. (Photograph by Lan Hongguang, Xinhua News Agency)

reason to worry that foreign investors won't come—what we need to do is think about how to better channel foreign investment into the areas where it is needed for our modernization.

New Conditions Call for New Approaches. These new circumstances call for new strategic thinking and measures in our foreign investment work. Concepts must be changed, sectors must be broadened, structures must be optimized, and formats must be improved. If we disregard the new situation before us and stick to old ways, if we continue to care more about quantity than quality, if we focus on capital rather than technology, if we attach little importance to the rules of the market and great importance to policy preferences—all these practices will make it more difficult for the entire national economy to rise to a higher level, and we will also increasingly lose the initiative in the face of intense global competition. Therefore we have no choice but to work to raise the quality and standards of our foreign investment work.

Adjust and Optimize the Structure of Foreign Investments

As we enter the new century, we face arduous tasks in our reforms, opening up, and modernization. But the current moment is favorable, with its global economic restructuring and ample international capital, so we must seize its opportunities and strive to use more foreign investment to serve our modernization. In doing so, we must persevere in following the guidelines laid out by the central authorities, which emphasize "utilizing foreign investment actively, reasonably, and effectively." In the new circumstances, we'll also have to adjust and optimize the structure of foreign investments on the basis of the new tasks in our economic development. In a nutshell, this means that henceforth in attracting foreign investment, we must achieve "three integrations."

1. Integration with Economic Restructuring. Foreign investment must be integrated with economic restructuring, industrial upgrading, and improvement of enterprise performance. The central authorities have already made it clear that the main theme of the 10th Five-Year Plan is strategic economic restructuring. This is the first year of the plan. Our work in foreign investment should adhere closely to this theme, should optimize [investment] structures, improve quality, and promote economic restructuring.

Since the domestic market for ordinary industrial goods is saturated at present and there is a relative excess of production capacity, our use of foreign investment should be redirected from ordinary processing industries toward more hi-tech industries. At the same time, we must bring in new and advanced technologies to transform and upgrade traditional industries, mainly in order to increase the variety of products, especially the types that we do not make or that we make too little of, and we should improve the quality, technology content, and market competitiveness of our products. If we continue to ignore technology and management quality and keep attracting investment just for low-quality redundant construction, we will intensify structural contradictions and create greater difficulties and burdens. The idea that we can increase revenues merely by attracting foreign investment and increasing production capacity has already fallen far behind the times.

We must also approach the upgrading of industries from a loftier and more far-sighted perspective. This applies not only to the restructuring of the primary, secondary, and tertiary sectors, but also to the restructuring of our export trade. The primary emphasis in our use of foreign investment must shift from industry to the development of tertiary industries, including transportation, communications, urban public works, tourism, and environmental protection. We should also channel more foreign investment into market intermediary services such as finance, trade, consulting, accounting, law, information, advertising, and asset evaluation. At the same time, we should expand joint ventures and cooperative projects in areas such as education, science and technology, and public health, all of which are very much in the public interest and will have decisive influence on social and economic development over the long term.

2. Integration with Improving the Socialist Market Economy and Increasing the International Competitiveness of Enterprises. Our socialist market economy has begun to take overall shape, but a great deal remains to be done to improve it. In particular, enterprise operating mechanisms and management standards are far from what is required to engage more broadly and more deeply in international competition. After joining the WTO, our country will open up more in banking, insurance, and securities, and we will allow more foreign investment in these sectors. The objective here is not only to expand the areas open to foreign investment and optimize its structure, but even more to bring in advanced management practices, advanced technologies, and talent that is familiar with international norms and capital operations, so that we may raise our management standards and increase international competitiveness.

Intermediaries are instrumental in the development of a market economy. At present, quite a few state-owned enterprises (SOEs) are not constrained by any rules during the course of mergers and acquisitions, nor do they act in accordance with international norms, the result being massive losses of state-owned assets. One important reason for this is the lack of reputable and authoritative intermediaries in their mergers and acquisitions. Such intermediaries can make fair and reasonable evaluations and analyses of enterprise finances, asset values, and trading conditions; they can also assume responsibility for the legal consequences of their services. Therefore we should be bold in attracting internationally well-known asset management companies and investment firms to engage in joint ventures with us. At the same time, we should speed up the development of joint-venture intermediaries such as accounting firms, law firms, and investment consulting firms so that foreign financial companies, multinationals, accounting firms, asset assessment firms, and investment consultancies can participate in the remaking and restructuring of SOEs.

Talent is the decisive element in international competition now. Without talent, nothing can be done well. We must recognize and use talent and recruit many talented people, but we need a mechanism and methods to do so. As Jiang Zemin has pointed out, "It is necessary to accelerate the establishment of an income distribution mechanism conducive to retaining the talented and bringing out the best in them and to implement a system that guarantees that their rewards are commensurate with their work and contributions."[2] In this regard, we must also act according to international norms to some extent; otherwise we won't be able to attract any talent. However, we mustn't simply compete to offer the highest wages, because the structure of our domestic prices and consumer spending differs from that in developed countries or territories. Professionals can receive high salaries, but they must truly be capable and be able to create more benefits for enterprises.

---

2. Jiang Zemin, "Speech at a Meeting Celebrating the 80th Anniversary of the Founding of the Communist Party of China (July 1, 2001)," *Selected Works of Jiang Zemin,* vol. 3 (Beijing: Foreign Languages Press, 2013), p. 284.

As for how to attract various types of urgently needed talent, the State Administration of Foreign Experts will have to do more work and play a greater role in light of the new situation. Talented people from Hong Kong, Macao, and Taiwan, as well as talented overseas Chinese, can all be brought in. Banks, insurance companies, securities and listed companies, large and medium SOEs—these should all boldly hire managerial and technical talent from outside.

3. Integration with the Expansion of Enterprise Exports and the Development of an Externally Oriented Economy. Under the influence of the continuing slowdown in the global economy, our exports have been declining since the beginning of this year. We should be on our guard about this. A reduction in exports will affect not just our international balance of payments, but more significantly, many enterprises will have to close down and some workers will also be laid off. Therefore we must use every means possible to increase exports. This also places greater demands on our foreign investment work.

One place to use foreign investment is the processing trade, which played an important role during the course of reform and opening up. Its contribution is unarguable, and it will continue to play a role in the future. But with international economic competition becoming increasingly intense, our market prospects are going to be very limited, and we'll have ever more competitors if we rely on processing-trade exports based on low labor costs and low technology content. If we do not adjust the composition of our exports now, we will be increasingly at the mercy of others. The substantial decline in Guangdong's exports this year is a warning bell.

In short, our work in foreign investment must be appropriate to the demands of the new conditions and new tasks of our economic development. Its prime concerns must be to raise the overall caliber of our economy, increase our international competitiveness and ability to withstand risk, make timely adjustments to our major work objectives and methods, and truly achieve the "three integrations." Now that the magnitude of foreign investment is quite large and domestic capital (including forex) is relatively abundant, we should shift the emphasis in our foreign investment work from simply attracting foreign capital to attracting advanced technologies, advanced modern management, and professional talent, so that we may better utilize foreign investment to promote the sustained, rapid, and healthy development of our economy.

3. Use Domestic Capital Nimbly and Well

We currently have forex reserves in excess of US$180 billion, and banks are holding $134 billion of forex deposits from enterprises and individuals outside China, for a total of over $310 billion. The vast majority of this forex is held abroad through purchases of foreign bonds and interbank loans, so in fact foreigners are using our capital. At the same time, the renminbi deposit imbalance [between loans and deposits] at commercial banks is increasing each year and has now reached more than RMB 2 trillion. We must adopt forceful measures to combine the utilization of foreign investments with the effective use of domestic capital.

1. *We Must [Actively] Make Good Use of the Forex Capital in China.* At present, some $63 billion of forex deposits in domestic banks is used for interbank lending abroad. Current international money market rates are very low: the six-month Libor rate is only 3.7%, while the domestic interest rate on one-year dollar loans is 5.8–5.9%, so commercial banks are better off lending forex deposits at home than making interbank loans abroad.

Banks must draw up some rules to make it more convenient for domestic enterprises to use forex loans. They should give priority to forex loans for domestic purposes such as large domestic infrastructure projects and projects involving technological upgrading. They should also encourage commercial banks to make more forex loans to domestic enterprises and individuals for service-related expenditures. We can allow foreign-invested enterprises that have insufficient working capital but meet lending conditions to borrow forex from banks within China.

2. *We Must Make Full Use of Domestic Renminbi Deposits.* All commercial banks should carefully analyze the reasons for their growing deposit imbalances. They should speed up innovations in their systems, mechanisms, and management and make a major effort to improve service quality and efficiency. By increasing lending and improving operational management, they can better prevent financial risk while providing support for economic growth.

They should actively offer loan support to all enterprises and construction projects with markets and good performance. Although they must not give out loans arbitrarily, neither should they withhold loans from those who deserve them.

3. *We Should Reduce Our Use of International Commercial Loans.* Such loans have relatively high interest rates and are very risky. Since our forex is quite abundant at present, there is no need to keep using these loans. US$80 billion of our forex balance consists of mid- to long-term international commercial loans. For some time to come, besides continuing to try to obtain concessionary loans from foreign governments and international financial agencies, domestic enterprises should, in principle, minimize their use of international commercial loans. For loans that have already been made, they can use the opportunity presented by

the current low international money market rates to try to repay some loans ahead of time or use new loans to repay old ones.

4. We Must Prevent the Exodus of Forex. Analyses have shown that in the last few years there has been considerable illegal outflow of forex. We must employ effective measures to strengthen our oversight of forex. Customs and the State Administration of Foreign Exchange must strengthen their management over illegal forex outflows and watch out for domestic capital being used for speculation in H shares[3] in Hong Kong. We absolutely must not be trying to attract foreign investment with every means possible on the one hand, and then allow it to illegally leave the country on the other.

Further Transform Government Functions and Improve Methods in Using Foreign Investment

To strengthen and improve foreign investment work in the new environment, all levels of government must transform their functions and improve their work methods as follows.

Truly Separate Government from Enterprises. We must make it clear that attracting business and foreign investment is not the main task of government—these are enterprise activities. Local government leaders at all levels and those in charge of government agencies must have a clear understanding of their own responsibilities. For some time now, the leaders of some provinces and municipalities, even of some counties, have led large numbers of agencies and enterprises abroad to engage in large-scale activities to attract business and investment. This trend is now gaining momentum but is a prime example of misplaced government functions. The principle of separation of government and enterprise must be observed in attracting foreign investment, and we must insist on having enterprises play the leading role in this area.

If in attracting foreign investment we are to truly achieve the "three integrations" I described earlier, we must get ready for a great deal of arduous work. The rules of a market economy must be obeyed, commercial factors such as markets and technologies must be fully considered, and ultimately enterprises must be accountable for the results of their investments. Therefore administrative leaders may absolutely not act in their place. If they try to directly attract business and investment, they will not only distort administrative behavior, but

---

3. Translator's note: H shares are shares of Chinese companies listed on the Hong Kong Stock Exchange.

they will also waste our people's efforts and money and foster a great deal of corruption. The State Council feels that we must firmly put a halt to this trend.

Resolutely Correct the Practice of Competing to Offer Preferential Policies. In order to attract business and investment, some locals are violating central policies, national laws, and regulations. They are following unauthorized preferential policies on tax reductions and exemptions, land use, disposition of state-owned assets, access to industries, and approval procedures. Some have even set quotas for each [local] level, demanding that Party and government agencies, social organizations, and individuals all try to attract business and investment, and they have instituted responsibility systems and rewards/penalties systems in this regard. Some locales have gone so far as to create an atmosphere of competition through news publications, advertisements, radio, and TV, causing quite a few places to see who can offer foreign investors the most preferences. This approach is wrong: it must be firmly halted and corrected. Our country already has clear laws, regulations, and policy measures on the utilization of foreign investments. Not long ago, we also promulgated some policies on using foreign investment for the great development of western China. All locales should conscientiously implement these. Let me emphasize again that local governments at all levels must administer according to the law and absolutely not destroy the uniformity of national administrative orders. No locale has the authority to go beyond central policies or national laws, regulations, and policy measures. Local people's congresses and governments have the power to set local laws and regulations, but these must not contravene the laws passed by the National People's Congress or the regulations of the State Council. We will absolutely not permit the phenomenon of "each acting in its own way." All locales must comprehensively clear up their own policies and methods for attracting foreign investment; any policies and methods that do not accord with the requirements of central policies or national laws and regulations must be corrected.

Work Hard to Improve the "Soft Environment" for Investment. In order to utilize foreign investment and consolidate its results to our best advantage, it is essential to give priority to improving the investment environment, particularly the "soft environment." This is the government's principal function in the utilization of foreign investment.

After many years of effort, the "hard environment" such as infrastructure facilities has indeed been greatly improved in many places. The most prominent problem now is the lag in construction of the "soft environment." Areas in urgent need of attention include the protection of intellectual property, protection of legitimate interests of foreign businessmen, refinement of the legal system and credit system, and improvement of policy transparency, policy approvals, and work efficiency.

Quite a few foreign businessmen are complaining that their brands are being counterfeited, fees are being collected arbitrarily, and it is difficult to get anything done. One of their particular concerns is the nature of the "soft environment." Some say that the good faith and reputation of a place are priceless, a bottomless source of earnings, whereas bad faith and a poor reputation will cut off the road to riches and create shackles that can never be shaken off. These words are worth reflecting on. A place that really wants to do good work with foreign investment must look inward and try very hard to improve its investment environment—this is something that can be achieved through its own efforts. If the investment environment is poor, no matter how you try to attract them, foreign businessmen won't come.

As locales further rectify and regularize the economic order of their markets in accordance with central plans and requirements, they must seriously investigate all cases of complaints by foreign businessmen. At the same time, they must strengthen the rule of law, reform their project approval systems, protect intellectual property, and improve efficiency so as to create a good environment for attracting foreign investment and all types of talent.

Look into the Question of National Treatment for Foreign Businesses without Delay. This is part of the broad trend since we joined the WTO and is one aspect of improving the investment environment. It is also a condition for optimizing the composition of foreign investment and improving the quality of its usage. So-called national treatment should mean treating domestic and foreign enterprises equally and allowing them to compete fairly. If you allow foreign enterprises to sell their products domestically and also give them tax benefits, how will domestic enterprises be able to compete against them? Of course this is a rather complex issue. It will require careful consideration, and we should take appropriate measures to address it.

41

A CONVERSATION WITH GEORGE SOROS[1]

September 17, 2001

ZRJ: I welcome your participation in the international forum organized by the Chinese People's Institute of Foreign Affairs. Your new book has been published in China, and I congratulate you on that. I received the copy of *The Crisis of Global Capitalism* that you sent me. It's my pleasure to meet you. Did you fly from the United States to Japan and then to Beijing?

GS: I flew over from Mongolia.

ZRJ: Were you in the United States when the attacks took place?

GS: I had already left.

ZRJ: I was shocked by the losses suffered by the American people on September 11 and want to express my condolences and sorrow. To the best of my knowledge, at least 51 Chinese have died.

GS: I feel very sad.

ZRJ: Two of them were on a hijacked plane, and the others were working at the World Trade Center. I was just watching TV. There was a wife and child from a Chinese family who were in tears, and I was also in tears. How great an impact do you think this attack will have on the United States?

GS: From an economic perspective, the existing trends in the American economy such as the economy entering a downturn, consumer mind-sets turning cautious, the Federal Reserve lowering interest rates, and the stock market falling— these will all develop more quickly because of this incident, the timeline will be advanced, and the speeds will be greater. Of course the length of the downturn

---

1. This conversation between Zhu Rongji and George Soros, the American financier, took place in the Hall of Purple Light at Zhongnanhai. Soros established Soros Fund Management in 1969 and served as its Chairman and CEO.

283

will also shorten as a result, so this is the good news amid the bad news. At the same time, Americans will travel less, which is the same as postponing demand into the future, which is conducive to fiscal and monetary stability. In short, the economic decline will speed up greatly, but its duration will shorten.

As for how great an impact this incident will have on America, to a large extent that will depend on how America reacts. At present Americans are all angry, but if the American government were to take any actions that harm civilians in Afghanistan or other countries, that would lead to a vicious cycle. I hope that can be avoided.

ZRJ: We're also worried that an excessive reaction from the United States will lead to opposition from the Arab world, which would worsen the contradictions. We understand the grief of the American people but hope that efforts to find [Osama] Bin Laden won't create a tragic situation wherein civilians are harmed or killed.

GS: Personally, I think that Bin Laden is an evil genius. The planning of this terrorist attack demonstrates his vision. Many armed groups in Afghanistan oppose him. Almost at the same time as the attacks (or the day before), there was a suicide attack on [Ahmad Shah] Massoud,[2] who was an opponent of Bin Laden. That's why Bin Laden is psychologically prepared for a military response from America.

ZRJ: So you're quite sure that Bin Laden is the chief plotter?

GS: I don't have any definite proof; it's only a guess.

ZRJ: Most people had originally expected the American economy to revive next year. Will that expectation change because of the attacks?

GS: Before the attacks, the American economy was already in the second phase of a decline. The first stage was concentrated mainly in the technology industries; consumers and consumer spending, which play a critical role, were basically unaffected. Now there are already signs that consumers are beginning to be affected. The economic decline is entering its second phase. And precisely because this incident is accelerating the decline of the American economy, I now feel all the more that the economy will revive next year. But because investment

2. Ahmad Shah Massoud, former commander of the Northern Alliance in Afghanistan, who was murdered on September 9, 2001.

in technology industries was overheated, their recovery will need more time, perhaps several years. The situation in 1973 was the most similar to the present. At that time, the stock markets were thriving, the structure was unreasonable, and it took 10 years to overcome that situation.

ZRJ: Congress has already authorized President [George W.] Bush to use US$40 billion to deal with the attacks. If a war starts, that sum won't be nearly enough. This implies that there'll be a budget deficit in the United States this year. What kind of effect will that have on its economic production?

GS: It can stimulate the American economy, but it will have an adverse impact on interest rates, especially long-term rates. I had originally expected the American economy to decline and therefore purchased large quantities of Treasury bonds. But today I've begun to sell off 10- and 30-year long-term Treasury bonds, though I won't sell my 6-month short-term bonds.

ZRJ: That means the federal government will lower interest rates even more?

GS: Short-term rates will go down, and the difference between long- and short-term rates will increase further.

ZRJ: I've asked all the questions I wanted to ask. Now I want to hear what you'd like to say.

GS: I'm very pleased to revisit China after 12 years. I haven't been able to come since 1989. China's changes and progress have impressed me deeply. Before 1989, I had some understanding of China, but now I know very little about it. What I'd like to ask is: what are the principal tasks China is facing and what is its greatest problem?

ZRJ: You've immediately singled out the hardest question to answer. What is the greatest problem we're facing? Professor Wang Mengkui[3] is an economist. You say something about this.

WMK: China's greatest problems are those of agriculture and increasing the income of farmers, employment for the urban populations, and the reform of the financial system.

---

3. Wang Mengkui was then Director of the State Council's Development Research Center.

ZRJ: I'd like to elaborate further on Professor Wang's reply. The greatest problem that we face is our unreasonable industrial structure, which will require major adjustments. Traditional industries have already developed to very high levels, and in many sectors such as iron, steel, and coal, we're the world's top producer. But these traditional industries now depend mainly on government efforts and infrastructure investment to sustain their current production capabilities. Without a push from the government, these industries would not be able to operate at full capacity.

The producers of consumer goods depend mainly on selling cheap goods to Europe and the United States, but they are imposing increasingly stringent restrictions on such goods, and it's becoming harder and harder to export. If we don't make timely adjustments, if we don't use information technologies to stimulate a scientific and technological revolution and industrial restructuring, the problem will get worse. In particular, farmers account for 80% of China's population. Because they produce surplus grain that can't be exported, and because prices are higher than in the international markets, farmers' incomes either can't grow or can only grow slowly, and the urban-rural gap will become greater. If we don't adjust the industrial structure, and especially if we fail to raise the standard of agriculture, the entire national economy will encounter difficulties. Of course these are all long-term problems. We still have a few years in which to do something. No sharp contradictions will emerge for now.

The current problem is that as the American economy weakens and the Japanese economy stagnates, it will be harder and harder for China to export, yet exports are becoming more and more important to China. Last year's total exports amounted to $255 billion. At present exports have decreased sharply, and I'm worried that there might even be negative growth this year, which would become a negative factor for our national economy. Therefore we already started making preparations in the second half of last year to resolve the problem by stoking domestic demand. Right now people have confidence in the government. They're willing to consume, and consumption is growing, so a decrease in exports won't affect our realizing the plans we had originally drawn up.

The second problem lies with the state-owned enterprises (SOEs). We can see that our present SOEs are increasingly unable to meet the needs of economic development. In the past few years, we've achieved a great deal in transforming SOEs into shareholding companies, especially those SOEs that listed abroad and have already raised tens of billions of dollars in funding. Companies that list domestically can also raise RMB 100 billion to 200 billion a year. We've made very great progress in promoting the shareholding system, that is, in reforming the ownership system. Over the past three years, foreign direct investment in China has stayed at over US$40 billion annually, and will approach $50 billion this year. But after the attacks, it's hard to predict.

The problems now are that the stock markets are developing quickly but irregularly, there is too much speculative activity and not enough government oversight, and there is lack of confidence in the renminbi. How to strengthen oversight and make things more standardized is giving us headaches, and I'd like to hear your thoughts on this.

The third problem has to do with reform of the banking system. In the past, we had a state-owned commercial banking system, its biggest problem being an excessively high ratio of nonperforming assets. At its peak, this was as high as 40%. Later we drew on the experience of the U.S. Resolution Trust Corporation, established asset management companies, and hived off the nonperforming assets so that these commercial banks could become more standardized and operate autonomously, but there are still a lot of problems. Through reforms and strengthened oversight, the ratio of nonperforming assets at the four large state-owned commercial banks has been lowered to 3–5% this year. We hope to turn them into shareholding banks. Although a considerable portion of their nonperforming assets has already been hived off, a lot of problems remain, and it will be very difficult for them to be listed.

I've been talking a lot about things that give us headaches, but we've also accomplished a good deal. The results over the past two years in establishing and improving a social security system have been rather good. The social security system has basically achieved a balance of income and expenditures, though of course there are still debts from the past. We've established a system to guarantee a minimum livelihood for urban residents. If a family's per capita income is lower than the local minimum livelihood standard, the state will provide subsidies.

GS: Have you considered establishing trust funds to manage social insurance funds such as pensions?

ZRJ: Yes. The central government has a Ministry of Labor and Social Security, and all levels of government have departments of labor and social security. An independent system is responsible for fund management. After workers pay into its pension fund, it pays pensions to workers at enterprises all over the country.

GS: Have you considered dividing these into several pieces in order to strengthen the financial markets, permitting enterprises to establish independent pension accounts and allowing individuals to choose from among several management agencies?

ZRJ: Because we lack experienced and capable people, the fund is used mainly to buy government bonds or for interest-bearing bank deposits. Only 10% of the fund is allowed to be invested in the stock market. We're thinking about how to use the fund better. I'm talking here mainly about social insurance, not commercial insurance.

GS: I'd like to share a few thoughts. China's external situation is very good. In terms of competitive strength, trade surplus, fast-growing domestic markets, and attractiveness to foreign direct investment, you could say it's the strongest economy in the world. After joining the World Trade Organization (WTO), China will have no choice but to open up its financial markets—this will be a real challenge. I think that China should first develop its domestic financial markets as a cushion for opening up its financial markets to the outside. The sequence of opening up is very important. You should proceed step by step, first pushing hard to open up the domestic financial markets, then working on opening them to the outside. Other countries such as Japan have had similar experiences. Japan was at one point the strongest economy in the world, and its economy was growing rapidly. At present, although Japanese industry is still strong, its financial system is a mess. However much Japan's industry produces, that's how much the financial system loses. China should avoid repeating Japan's mistakes.

The main reason why China avoided the impact of the Asian financial crisis was that its financial system was closed. If it had been open to the outside, you would have faced greater risks. Therefore first strengthen [your markets], then open up. You already talked about the problem of bad debts. I feel that the first thing is to develop an internal banking system. China has a high savings rate, and you should provide savers with other financial tools besides banks for them to choose from. As for talented overseers, China does not lack any. I recently met two superb talents in this area. But there are basically only retail investors in the Chinese stock markets and no institutional ones, yet the stability of stock and bond markets depends to a large extent on the participation of institutional investors. Pensions and the like can be operated by having institutional investors and nongovernment organizations entering the market according to business principles. Japan's problem is that its financial institutions only listen to the Ministry of Finance, and they haven't learned to respond to market signals. After they entered the international market, they had to deal with the international banking sector and as a result, they lost their shirts.

ZRJ: You're putting it very politely: you didn't say they lost everything but their pants.

GS: You should establish institutional investors, and they shouldn't be controlled by the government. I feel that China has talent in this area. If those who have studied abroad return, and if Chinese from Hong Kong and Taiwan have abilities in this area, you can nurture China's financial market before opening it up.

One last point: to open up, China will also have to permit the free flow of information, freedom of discussion, freedom of thought—if I might put it that way. I spent quite a long time in the Soviet Union and the Eastern European countries. I've established foundations in these countries and know something about them. I compared China and the Soviet Union: China is politically successful, its people support the government and are optimistic and enthusiastic. Perhaps because I've only been to eastern China, I might not understand China sufficiently, and my view may be biased, but I feel that the present environment is favorable to China's political opening and to the building of an open society. The mind-set of the people is constructive. You have to understand that the course of change is nonlinear. Sooner or later the situation won't be so favorable. If [by then] you still haven't established an open system that allows free expression, a serious collapse will occur.

Indonesia in Southeast Asia was developing very quickly at one point. Jakarta was like Shanghai in China, but parts of its system were ossified, such as its political system and the linking of its currency to the U.S. dollar. Because it lacked a mechanism for adjustment, once problems occurred they led to collapse and crisis. That's why you should make some flexible arrangements at a time of economic prosperity.

ZRJ: Your observations are very keen, and your perspective is also very penetrating. China's greatest problem at present is the financial market. China has already enabled full convertibility of the renminbi for current accounts, but we're still a long way off from full convertibility for capital accounts. Many problems have yet to be tackled. In terms of talent, there are many talented Chinese, but many have already been hired by foreign enterprises to become their representatives in China.

GS: You might consider establishing a joint venture to put these people's talents to use.

ZRJ: The US$40 billion of foreign direct investment we get every year is all used for establishing joint ventures. China needs a system of incentives for talent. Wages in China are low. When people see someone with a high salary, they get jealous. It will be hard to attract domestic talent if this mind-set doesn't change.

GS: As I understand it, China has yet to allow foreign mutual funds to establish joint ventures in China. Through this visit, I've become interested in setting up a joint-venture enterprise in China to attract young people to come manage it.

ZRJ: China has yet to allow foreign mutual funds to invest here because even some of our own funds lack credibility. Owing to inadequate oversight capabilities, these funds of ours are behaving deceptively in the stock markets. Perhaps we can consider your idea and collaborate with foreign mutual funds. This might be a bit better than our own funds.

GS: This way you could also attract retail investors in the market. Right now they're like gamblers in the stock markets, whereas they could get better returns through the professional management of mutual funds. The development of financial markets is not just a question of oversight. It's mainly also a question of culture, such as investment mind-set, behavior, standards, and so on. You should move toward institutionalization. China has talent in this area that can be attracted over.

ZRJ: When China joins the WTO, there will also be a timetable for the opening up of the financial markets, including mutual funds.

GS: The schedule should still be advanced. Before opening financial markets to the outside, you should use foreign technology and experience to nurture domestic institutions. Japan made a mistake in this regard. It waited until the last minute to allow Morgan Stanley and Goldman Sachs into Japan. Up to then, they had not remade Japanese enterprises through internationalization and modernization. Therefore, China should compete with foreign enterprises for talent through joint ventures.

ZRJ: I've learned a great deal from your comments, and hope we have an opportunity to talk again. If you have any ideas, you can tell me directly. You can write to me, or you can look them up [pointing to Wang Mengkui and Xin Futan].[4]

GS: I should still go to them. My company is different from an investment bank. If I can find a Chinese partner to cooperate with, I'd be willing to establish a joint venture in China and also to be a minority shareholder.

ZRJ: You'd be welcome.

GS: Major banks or other institutions can also benefit from joint ventures.

ZRJ: I value your experience more.

---

4. Xin Futan was then Vice President of the Chinese People's Institute of Foreign Affairs.

42

Toward a More Open and Prosperous Chinese Economy[1]

September 19, 2001

As we enter into the new century, it is particularly meaningful that the Sixth Convention of the World Chinese Entrepreneurs Association is being held in China. On behalf of the Chinese government and the Chinese people, I would like to express a warm welcome to our honored guests who have come from all corners of the world!

Since the founding of New China over 50 years ago, especially since our reforms and opening up, China's economy has continued to thrive and has achieved tremendous growth, attracting the notice of the entire world. From this new historic starting point, our economy is taking mighty strides forward and is becoming more open and more prosperous.

During the past few years, the global economic environment has been complex and ever changing, and China's economy has been tested. We have successfully fended off the impact of the Asian financial crisis and realized sustained, rapid, and healthy economic growth. This year, at a time when the global economy has noticeably slowed down, our economy has maintained good growth momentum. In the first half of this year, GDP was 7.9% higher than in the same period last year. From January through August, compared with the same period last year, industrial value added grew 10.4%, fiscal revenues 24.7%, fixed asset investments 18.9%, retail sales of social consumables 10.1%, and the consumer price index 1.2%. Total imports and exports amounted to US$330.521 billion, a 9.6% increase, and of this, exports accounted for $170.994 billion, a 7.3% increase; actually utilized foreign direct investment (FDI) amounted to $27.44 billion, an increase of 20.4%, and by September 15 of this year, our forex reserves reached $193.5 billion. Even though some unfavorable factors may appear in the global economic environment, we believe that China's economy

---

1. The Sixth Convention of the World Chinese Entrepreneurs Association was held in Nanjing on September 17–19, 2001. Participants included almost 5,000 Chinese businessmen and businesswomen from around the world, as well as from the Hong Kong and Macao special administrative regions, the Taiwan region, and the Chinese mainland. Zhu Rongji delivered this speech at the forum on the Chinese economy at the convention.

Giving a speech at the forum on the Chinese economy at the Sixth Convention of the World Chinese Entrepreneurs Association on September 19, 2001. (Photograph by Lan Hongguang, Xinhua News Agency)

will continue to move ahead in a virtuous cycle of rapid growth, high performance, and low inflation.

These results did not come easily. They were achieved because the Party Central Committee with Jiang Zemin at its core was in overall command, assessed the situation, and adopted a series of forceful policies in a timely manner. Our starting point was to increase domestic demand. We implemented a proactive fiscal policy and a steady monetary policy, always ensuring policy continuity and the necessary degree of forcefulness. We focused on strengthening infrastructure construction; increasing investment in science, technology, education, and the environment; and raising urban and rural incomes, particularly the incomes of low and medium earners. At the same time, we stepped up industrial restructuring and reforms and restructuring of state-owned enterprises (SOEs) and took many measures to encourage exports. Experience has shown that our policies have been entirely correct; they have played and will continue to play an important role in the healthy development of the national economy.

With the arrival of the new century, China's reforms, opening up, and socialist modernization are entering a new stage of development. Despite being faced with new challenges—notably accelerating economic globalization and the rapid onslaught of revolutionary technical advances—we will go with the

flow of world development and forcefully implement the strategies of economic restructuring, the great development of western China, revitalization of
the nation through science and education, and sustainable development. These
measures can markedly improve our capacity for economic innovation and our
ability to compete and fend off risk, so that China's economy can move ahead
on an even larger scale and to an even higher level.

1. Strategic Economic Restructuring

Strategic economic restructuring is a major and pressing task. The list of figures I just read out shows that China's total economy is not small, though of
course it is very small on a per capita basis. Some traditional industries constitute a major part of our total economy. For example, last year we produced
140 million tons of steel, 1 billion tons of coal, and 1.2 trillion kilowatt-hours of
electricity. With such high levels, we rank first in the world in these traditional
industries. However, our hi-tech industries and modern financial services are
still very backward.

Of course we're not lagging in some sectors such as information technology (IT). For instance, we now have 150 million telephone lines with program-
controlled switching nationwide, and the total switching capacity for mobile
phone lines has already reached 120 million lines. These volumes rank first in the
world, surpassing those of the United States. The production of such IT equipment is also based in our domestic market and has reached advanced world technical levels, but the core technologies such as integrated circuit production technologies and research and development still fall short of advanced world levels.
We therefore still have to work harder, so if we don't restructure our economy, it
will be very difficult to maintain sustained, rapid, and healthy economic growth.

Thus even as we continue to promote industrialization, we must seize the
moment to speed up the application of IT to achieve its widespread use for economic and social purposes, and to drive industrialization and overall economic
modernization. We will make a major effort to develop hi-tech industries; to accelerate the development of modern service industries such as banking, securities, and
insurance; and to use advanced technologies extensively to remake and upgrade
our traditional industries. At the same time, we must speed up agricultural restructuring and transform traditional practices in this sector into modern ones.

One issue I'd like to discuss here is how to feed the Chinese population,
which now numbers more than 1.2 billion. This has always been a major concern. Some have predicted that China won't be able to feed its populace. It's true
that we met with great difficulties in 1993–94, when some of our grain harvests failed and we had to sell off half of the national grain reserves in order to
stabilize the grain markets. But through a series of correct agricultural policies

beginning in 1995, particularly the decision to raise grain purchase prices three times, we became self-sufficient in grain by the fall of 1995. Moreover in the following years, grain supply exceeded demand, and every year several tens of billion jin[2] [of surplus grain] are stored away in granaries.

Now, including national grain reserves and circulating grain inventories, we have 500 billion jin of grain reserves. Our headache at the moment is that there is too much grain—although we exported 30 million tons, that's still not enough. Despite serious droughts this year and last, grain prices did not change in the least because we still have a huge amount of grain in storage. Although the state adopted a policy of making open-ended purchases of surplus grain from farmers at protected prices, grain prices continued to fall each year because supply exceeded demand. As a result, it's been very hard for farmers to increase their incomes. Although their incomes have increased each year across the country, in the major grain-growing regions such as the northeastern and central provinces, the trend has been one of decreasing farm incomes.

If we don't take immediate measures to adjust the composition of crops planted, the gap between urban and rural incomes will grow wider. Therefore we are speeding up adjustments to crop compositions and gradually opening up markets for commoditized grain. The coastal provinces and municipalities should grow whatever makes the most money and don't need to grow more grain. We should let the main grain-growing regions play up their particular advantages. Of course the most important measure of all, which I'll discuss later, is that of reverting farmlands to forests. There's plenty of grain, so stop planting along mountainsides and let forests grow there. Stop enclosing parts of Lake Dongting to create farmland—revert the farmland, enlarge the lake area, increase its flood prevention and floodwater storage capacities, and improve the eco-environment. Return Lakes Dongting, Poyang, Hongze, and Tai to their former appearances, restore those "infinite vistas of majesty" described by Fan Zhongyan[3] in *On the Yueyang Tower*—I think this can be done quite rapidly and will facilitate all-round adjustments to and optimization of the economic structure; it will help promote beneficial interaction and joint prosperity of agriculture, industry, and service industries, of traditional and hi-tech industries, and of rural and urban economies. This is our most important strategy for industrial restructuring.

2. Speeding up the Great Development of Western China

This is an important strategic measure that will help balance regional development and open up broad new areas for national economic growth. For a while

---

2. One jin is equal to 0.5 kilogram.
3. Fan Zhongyan (989–1052) was a writer and an official of the Northern Song Dynasty.

to come, our great development of western China will focus on strengthening infrastructure and building the eco-environment. We will do our best to make breakthrough advances over the next 5 to 10 years. A series of core projects that are significant for the overall development of central and western China have already been started up and are proceeding smoothly. These include the transportation of gas and power from west to east, the Qinghai-Tibet Railroad, protection of natural forests, and reversion of farmlands to forests. Let me discuss each of these briefly.

Transportation of Gas and Power from West to East. This refers in part to a pipeline 4,200 kilometers long that will bring large quantities of natural gas from the Tarim Oilfield in Xinjiang to Shanghai. With the resulting adjustments to the industrial economies of the nine provinces and municipalities along its route and to their urban heating supplies, the benefits of such a project will be very great. International bidding for this project has already taken place, work will commence this year, and it will be completed rapidly.

During a visit to Russia not long ago I signed an agreement with Russia to build a 1,400-kilometer oil pipeline to bring oil from Irkutsk to Manzhouli, from Manzhouli to Daqing, and then from Daqing to the entire country. It's cheaper to import oil [overland] from Russia than to transport it by sea—the sources are more reliable and stable.

"Sending power from west to east" refers to the vast hydropower resources of Sichuan, Yunnan, Guizhou, and Guangxi in southwestern China. Their generation costs are very low, and power prices are much cheaper, whereas much of Guangdong's 30 million kilowatt-hours of power come from burning oil, and burning heavy oil and diesel is very expensive. Moreover, Guangdong may need to increase its power consumption by 15 million kilowatt-hours during the period of the 10th Five-Year Plan. Therefore the best approach is to use 500,000-kilovolt power transmission lines to bring hydroelectricity from the southwestern provinces to Guangdong, where it will be much cheaper than the power they have been using. This will both meet the power needs of coastal areas, especially of Guangdong, and help the poor residents in the southwest lift themselves out of poverty. Because of this, we have not only started basic work on all the hydropower plants we have thought of building for decades but did not build, but we are also rushing to concurrently install several 500,000-kilovolt transmission lines to Guangdong.

The Qinghai-Tibet Railroad. This railroad will run from Qinghai to Lhasa, a distance of more than 1,000 kilometers. Construction will be very difficult because of the terrain: a plateau of frozen earth at altitudes of more than 4,000 meters. This undertaking is unprecedented in the world and requires enormous investment, but we are determined to build it. I personally went to Golmud in Qinghai to proclaim the start of work on the Qinghai-Tibet railroad. The line could have been completed in four to five years, but in order to protect the vegetation cover and eco-environment of the Qinghai-Tibet plateau, we are keeping the area under construction as small as possible and extending the construction time to six years, which means it will be completed in 2006. I have already asked foreigners, aren't there some among you who keep saying that there's no religious freedom in Tibet? Now we're building a comfortable and luxurious passenger rail line, so I invite those of you who are interested to go to Tibet and see if they have human rights, see if they have freedom of religious belief—go see for yourselves!

Reverting Farmlands to Forests. Last year and this year I made separate study trips to the Ngaba Tibetan-Qiang Autonomous Prefecture and the Ganzi Tibetan Autonomous Prefecture in Sichuan Province. In the past, to ensure people had enough to eat, these areas planted crops all the way up the high mountains and ridges. Today we have grain that's growing moldy in storage, so why do we need to plant crops on mountainsides? Because there's basically no longer any need to do so, we are returning farmlands to forests and converting all the land in the mountains planted with grain into land for planting forests. In Ganzi, I saw how, after only a year and a half, all the cropland has turned into green forests—it looks very hopeful. I believe that within 5 to 10 years, the appearance [of these places] will be entirely different.

Dear friends and guests, you can see how green Nanjing has become. It must be acknowledged that the greening of Nanjing, particularly of the Sun Yat-sen Mausoleum, was the result of many years of work. I said to the leaders of Nanjing Municipality and of Jiangsu Province, "You can't just plant trees outside the city. You also need to move large trees into the city, and then the farmers will get rich. Otherwise, how are they going to increase their incomes?" That's why the Nanjing you see today is lush and green—it took a lot of work. [For tree-planting alone] more than 40,000 large trees were brought in from inside and outside the province. I can't describe all the urban infrastructure development that has taken place over the past few years, because China is so large and I haven't been everywhere, but it has truly taken on a new appearance, and this is the result of our implementing a correct development strategy.

Encouraging Investment in the Great Development of Western China. Now that the state has decided on a key policy of tilting toward the west, we will increase the forcefulness of our support in funding construction, arranging projects, and making fiscal transfer payments. We have also drawn up policy measures to encourage domestic and foreign investors to participate in the great development of western China. The vast expanses of the west are awaiting this great

Meeting on September 19, 2001, in Nanjing, Jiangsu Province, with some of the guests attending the Sixth Convention of the World Chinese Entrepreneurs Association. (Photograph by Lan Hongguang, Xinhua News Agency)

development. People throughout the country are eager for it to happen, as are foreigners. Almost every major oil company in the world has joined in the bidding for the project to transport gas from west to east. I met with President [Vladimir] Putin in Russia and made a point of discussing the great development of western China. The Russians indicated a desire to participate in it, so we have just formed a small team to coordinate Sino-Russian work. This development will be the work of several generations, but we want to have a breakthrough advance during the next 5 to 10 years—this is an important development strategy of ours.

3. Revitalizing the Nation through Science and Education

We will attach great importance to developing science, technology, and education, giving strategic priority to scientific and technical innovation and the cultivation of talent. We will continue to develop new systems of innovation for our country, encourage enterprises to become the main pacesetters for technical progress and innovation, and strengthen our ability to initiate innovation. We will concentrate on making major breakthroughs in hi-tech efforts and work very hard to industrialize scientific and technical results. We will revitalize education and comprehensively improve the caliber of our people. We will implement a strategy to attract talent from all over the world, to cultivate and train large numbers of new talents who can meet the needs of the times.

In the past, many of our outstanding people went to the United States, but very few returned. Now this situation has begun to change: many Chinese who have studied abroad, including some with a considerable amount of experience, are willing to return to their homeland because they feel there is a future and there is hope in China. We welcome their return and hope they will return. We've adopted many preferential policies to welcome them back. If they're making a certain amount abroad, we can also offer them the same amount. In fact, many talented people who are studying or working abroad aren't seeking very high salaries. Rather, we must give them a chance to develop. That's why I believe that more and more of these people will be returning to their homeland, and hopes for the revitalization of the Chinese people will continue to rise.

Maintaining a Strategy of Sustainable Development

Our awareness of the importance of sustainable development evolved through a long and tortuous process. Our per capita natural resources are very few by world standards. In the past, we had so many people who needed food and who wanted development, so we took the path of sacrificing the environment for rapid growth. Perhaps I shouldn't say this was the wrong path, because very possibly it could not have been avoided. If we hadn't taken this path and planted crops all the way up the mountainsides, how could we have fed our billion-plus people? But this has led to serious consequences. Isn't planting on mountainsides going to lead to soil erosion? The Yangtze and Yellow rivers silted up and then problems followed.

We can now say that we have learned this lesson profoundly and are therefore determined to implement a fundamental national policy of protecting the environment. We will comprehensively strengthen the coordinated management of our land and of our environmental construction, and we will work hard to create a consumption pattern and a production structure that are conducive to conserving resources and protecting the environment. Build a lovely land with a thriving economy and a beautiful landscape—that is our goal.

In order to implement the development strategies I just described, we will unwaveringly deepen reforms, further open up, and create a powerful force for greater economic growth.

First, We Will Continue with Deeper Reforms of the Economic Structure. We will further adjust and refine the structure of ownership systems and strengthen and develop an economic pattern in which public ownership is dominant but develops jointly with multiple forms of ownership. The current pattern has already undergone great changes. My friends, when I went to the central government from Shanghai in 1991, the output value of SOEs accounted for 55% of the entire national economy, while that of collectively owned enterprises, including township and village enterprises, accounted for about 35%. Foreign-invested enterprises and individually or privately owned businesses accounted for only 10%. What is the situation now? The kingdom is divided into thirds. [The share of] SOEs is now only one-third and is continuing to shrink; collective enterprises make up one-third, and private or nongovernment businesses plus foreign-invested enterprises already account for over a third. Thus the composition of ownership has undergone a major adjustment, and the forms of public ownership have themselves changed considerably.

In accordance with the direction of the 15th National Party Congress, we are actively exploring many forms public ownership might take, the most important of which is the shareholding system. The market value of the domestic stock market has already reached RMB 5.5 trillion; many enterprises have listed and increased their transparency and are also exploring forms of public ownership. Growing numbers of companies are listing abroad. In particular, our large enterprises—including PetroChina, Sinochem, China Mobile, and China Unicom—have listed on exchanges in Hong Kong and abroad (for example, in London and New York). They have raised about US$30 billion of capital. We are at present continuing to establish a standardized modern enterprise system and to comprehensively deepen reforms at SOEs. We are also studying and adopting measures to promote systemic reforms of monopoly industries such as power, railroads, civil aviation, and communications. By refining the market system and rectifying and standardizing market behaviors, we will build up a new order in our socialist market economy. We will speed up the construction of a social insurance system and establish a social "safety net" in order to create a stable social environment for our reforms and development.

Next, Even More Proactively, We Will Open Up across the Board. This will take place at many levels and in broad areas. It is a certainty that China will soon join the World Trade Organization (WTO). The resolution was passed at the 18th meeting in Geneva of the WTO Working Party on the Accession of China and only awaits the November meeting of all members of the WTO Ministerial Conference for formal passage.

I'm not entirely sure myself how intense the competition will be after we join the WTO. There will surely be quite a few headaches, but I still believe that China's enterprises have enough competitiveness to deal with the challenges of fully opening up after we join the WTO. We still do have this ability.

We will live up to our promises and step by step further open up domestic markets along with more sectors and regions, including service sectors such as finance, insurance, telecommunications and trade and tourism. We'll also proactively explore new forms and paths for utilizing foreign investment. We want to tightly integrate efforts to attract foreign investment with the restructuring of domestic enterprises, the promotion of the great development of western China, and the deepening of SOE reforms. The emphasis throughout will be on bringing in advanced technologies, modern management, and professional talent.

Friends, please take note of what I'm saying: henceforth in opening up and bringing things in, our emphasis will not be on capital—we are not very short of capital now. I just mentioned that China now has $193.5 billion of forex reserves, and this will reach $200 billion by year's end; we [also] have $130 billion of domestic forex deposits. We utilized over $40 billion in foreign investments last year, which might reach $48 billion this year. At the same time, we have $300 billion of domestic forex assets held abroad through bond purchases and interbank lending. China is using foreign capital, and other countries are also using Chinese capital. That's why China is not very short of capital right now, including forex.

What we lack now is advanced technology and modern management, particularly talent. Economic competition today is focused on talent. We hope in particular that our overseas compatriots, students studying abroad, and people living abroad can return to their country. There is a lot of room for growth if you come back to grow your businesses. Of course we must continue to improve the investment and operating environments here, including the social environment. That's why it is so important that this year we started to rectify the social order, crack down on organized crime and the forces of evil, and standardize and rectify order in the market economy—we've put a lot of effort into this. People can come only if we improve the investment and operating environments and protect the rights of investors in accordance with the law. I think this will take time, but we are very determined, and I believe this goal can be realized relatively quickly.

At the same time, we are encouraging domestic enterprises that can do so to invest and operate abroad, to increase their exchanges and collaborations with the economies of countries all over the world. For example, we feel the prospects for the Russian market are great. I just returned from Russia—they are progressing very rapidly and the growth rate is very high. They have [natural] resources, an area where we have no advantages. Therefore as soon as I returned from Russia, I called upon the large and reputable Chinese enterprises to enter the Russian market and not be risk adverse—Russia's future growth will be immeasurable.

Although China's economy is running into quite a few difficulties right now, and challenges of one sort or another are bound to arise in the future, many factors work in our favor. The most important ones are our huge domestic market, abundance of human resources, social and political stability, and development path, which is suited to China's conditions. We have friends all over the world, and we especially have the caring and support of the many Overseas Chinese[4] and ethnic Chinese in other countries. We will continue to go down our own path without wavering, totally confident and capable of overcoming all obstacles in our way, so that our economy can better develop and scale new heights.

The further opening up of China's economy and increasing prosperity will not only greatly enhance the well-being of China's billion-plus people, but it will also offer vast markets and boundless opportunities to businessmen from all over the world, including ethnic Chinese businessmen. As we move forward along this path, we'll also undoubtedly make increasing contributions to world prosperity and development.

We estimate that there are 60 million Chinese outside China. I had originally thought that we had the most emigrants in the world, but after my recent visit to Ireland I have changed my views. Ireland has 80 million emigrants, 45 million in the United States alone. Their situation is very similar to ours. People left their homes and families to seek their livelihoods abroad because of war and famine, and now they're all thriving. They have played a significant role in Ireland's development by supporting it financially, bringing in talent, and transforming its technology. That's why Ireland was able to leap from an agricultural nation to an industrial and hi-tech nation in a very short time. My visit there was very brief, only two or three days. I went to the Shannon Development Zone and saw its latest technology. I was particularly interested in the contributions overseas compatriots have made to the country's development.

Let me digress a little. As a country, Ireland has its unique characteristics. It is fiercely independent, and its people fought long for independence. My visit left me with the impression that the senior leaders of Ireland as well as the ordinary people are very friendly toward us. When we walked around on the streets, people nearby all waved at us. The press, however, was really unfriendly. During my stay, whenever I looked at local newspapers, the largest photos would feature protestors marching for "Tibetan independence" and "Falun Gong," whereas there would be only one picture of me with their president, placed on the very back page. Nowadays I can't say I still have the "aggressiveness of youth," but I do have a bit of it despite my age, so I mentioned this in a speech at a public breakfast meeting with business leaders. I said, "We Chinese understand and care very much about you in Ireland; we know you're a people who fought long for independence and have struggled to build up your country through your own efforts. You have developed very quickly, and we are full of admiration. But do you understand China? You know only three things about China: first, human rights; second, Tibet; third, 'Falun Gong.'" I said, "Apart from these, what do you know about China? Not much else."

---

4. Translator's note: Overseas Chinese are Chinese citizens residing in other countries.

It wasn't very courteous of me to say this, but I had no choice: I had to say it. I also said, "You may be developing very quickly in Ireland, but did you know that China's development is even faster than yours? In Ireland, you have 70,000 square kilometers of land, a population of 3.8 million, a GDP of US$78 billion, and a per capita GDP of over $20,000—that's no mean feat! But do you know that Shanghai alone covers 6,300 square kilometers and has a regional GDP as large as yours? I want to let you know that 'beyond the skies, there are heavens.'"

Toward the end, I had a one-hour meeting with their president, Mary McAleese. Fifty minutes of that meeting was spent debating the issue of "Tibetan independence." This lady was born in Northern Ireland and had previous contact with the Dalai Lama, so she was particularly interested in Tibetan "independence." I therefore debated her on this and asked, "Tibet used to be a society of serfs—what kind of lives did they lead then? Now in one leap they've entered an era of modern civilization. Living standards and per capita incomes there are substantially higher than the national averages, all because of fiscal subsidies from the central government." She replied that people not only need material lives, they also need spiritual lives. I said that regarding spiritual life, freedom of religion is stipulated in China's constitution. We haven't violated this, but I can't speak to individual incidents.

But say what I might, she wasn't convinced. She said that she had met the Dalai Lama, who had visited Ireland. Many Buddhists there had kissed his hand, thereby expressing their love. She said, "Mr. Premier, I hope you can demonstrate this sort of love so that the people of Tibet will also love you," to which I replied, "Madam President, much as one might wish, it would be impossible to be loved and liked by everyone. I know that in China, quite a lot of ordinary people like me very much, but there are also some people who thoroughly hate me. How can anyone make everyone love him? Among my delegation, all the ministers who have accompanied me on this trip are present here. I believe that most of them like me, but I also believe that a few of them are very dissatisfied with my criticisms of them and might be waiting for me to leave office to take their 'revenge.'"

The President then said, "My goodness, you have a very good sense of humor." She said she had heard that the Chinese people are humorless, and she liked my sense of humor very much. At that point, it was very hard for me to reply. How could I reply? I could only say that our country is an open one, that our people have always been all-embracing and learned the best from all sides. There are 56 ethnic groups in China that have blended together well for long periods throughout history.

One thing that I didn't say, which would have been hard to translate, was this: "You say that the Chinese are humorless, but the *Records of the Grand Historian*, written over 2,000 years ago by Sima Qian during the Western Han Dynasty, contained a section called 'Biographies of Jesters.' In China, a jester is a humorous person. How could the Chinese people be humorless? They were humorous over 2,000 years ago."

Let me return now to the subject of us Chinese. Deng Xiaoping, the chief architect of China's reforms and opening up, once pointed out that the tens of thousands of Overseas Chinese and ethnic Chinese abroad are a remarkable force providing a unique opportunity for China's great development. For a long time now, a great many of them have enthusiastically supported and participated in China's economic construction in a variety of ways. So far, among the foreign enterprises that have invested in China, the vast majority of projects and funds have come from Chinese businessmen. Overseas Chinese and ethnic Chinese abroad have made indelible contributions to the glittering achievements of the Chinese economy. You have never forgotten your special feelings for and ties with your homeland. You have overcome one obstacle after another and made many contributions. Your innovative spirit has already been recorded in the glorious annals of China's economic growth. Our Chinese businessmen friends from all over the world include talented professionals in all fields. You have a thorough understanding of the workings of the international market economy and are also familiar with traditional Chinese culture, so you have unique advantages with which to assist in China's development. Whether you have already invested in China or are seeking projects, you will all be able to find many opportunities for growth and realize your great dreams in that piece of home that is China. We warmly welcome all of you to continue your eager participation in China's modernization through a variety of forms.

With its tremendous vitality and great prospects, China's economy is climbing to new heights from a position of strength. Let us join hands and work together to realize China's modernization and the great revitalization of the Chinese people in the new century!

43

The Impact of 9/11 on Our Economy, and Our Countermeasures[1]

September 27, 2001

Uncertainties in the international situation have increased in the aftermath of the 9/11 attacks in the United States. It's still too early to predict how great an impact they will have on the American and global economies. It seems that the United States is sure to resort to arms, but fighting won't be so easy, and we won't know what will result once the fighting starts. Therefore we should be prepared early, plan strategies in depth, and study what measures to take once war breaks out.

The events of 9/11 and their aftermath will affect our own economy in a number of ways, which we must clearly recognize and fully assess. It would now appear that the most direct impacts will be in the following three areas: forex reserves, exports, and Chinese stock markets.

Forex Reserves

The most sensitive [area] to be affected will be our forex reserves. I was visiting Moscow the day 9/11 occurred. The next day, I told the Russian leaders that on the previous day alone, our forex reserves (mainly dollar-denominated assets) suffered a book loss of US$4 billion because of devaluation of the dollar: the dollar-euro exchange rate went from $0.89: €1 to $0.91: €1; the Japanese yen also rose against the dollar. In light of this, we can continue to look into altering the exchange rate mechanism, but we should not change it now.

Because the renminbi closely follows the dollar; once the dollar devalues, the renminbi exchange rate against the yen and euro will fall correspondingly. This will increase the competitiveness of our exports to Japan and the European Union and achieve part of our original goals. This is not the time to alter the exchange rate mechanism. If we were to link the renminbi to a basket of currencies now—including the dollar, yen, and euro—the renminbi might even become stronger. That's why this issue must be considered on a long-term basis.

1. This is part of a speech by Zhu Rongji at the 16th meeting of the leading Party Group of the State Council.

For now, it's still better to closely follow the dollar and keep the exchange rate steady. I believe that subjectively, the United States still wishes to keep its policy of a strong dollar, but a slight devaluation of the dollar would be quite helpful for our exports to Japan and the European Union.

As for the size of our current US$200 billion in forex reserves, first, I don't think that's very large. Japan, with a GDP of $4 trillion, has $390 billion of forex reserves; the Republic of Korea has a GDP of $470 billion and its forex reserves reached $96 billion at the end of last year; the Hong Kong and Taiwan regions only had GDPs of $160 billion and $300 billion, equal to a fraction of the mainland's GDP, yet their forex reserves exceeded $100 billion and $110 billion, respectively; even a country as small as Singapore has $72.7 billion in forex reserves. Compared with the reserves of these countries and regions, $200 billion of forex reserves in a large country like ours with a GDP of $1.1 trillion cannot be considered very large.

Second, according to the new method of calculation, our foreign debt already exceeds $180 billion. Of course this includes foreign debt incurred by enterprises, but these establishments still need to buy forex from the state to repay their debts. Relative to the size of these foreign debts, our forex reserves are even less large.

Third, having large forex reserves is a good thing. They indicate our country is strong, which helps keep the value of the renminbi stable. People will be willing to do business with us only if we have ample ability to pay in forex at any time. The monthly increase in our forex reserves is a result of our foreign trade surplus and our attracting foreign investment, so this is an even better thing. We can't just blindly increase imports to reduce the surplus—if we did so, our domestic enterprises wouldn't be able to cope.

Fourth, the current world situation is very volatile. In light of the complex international environment, we need to have sizable forex reserves in order to push ahead with reforms and opening up and ensure our economic security. Particularly because we are about to join the World Trade Organization, holding abundant forex reserves will allow us to deal with any unforeseen contingencies.

Fifth, national forex reserves are capital and can generate interest. The crux of the question is how to manage these reserves well. I should say that over the past few years, our management of them has been quite good. We've been able to guarantee annual returns of over 5%, which is several hundred million dollars a year. Even taking into account the cost of forex locking up renminbi funds, the net returns are still quite substantial. If those renminbi were invested in China, they would never yield so much money.

Exports

There will also be a major impact on our exports. Following a rapid rise over the past few years, exports reached US$249.2 billion last year, which is in excess of RMB

2 trillion and is equivalent to 22.4% of our GDP of RMB 8.94 trillion. If exports were to fall 10% in a year, our economic growth in that period would decline by two percentage points, and even more people would become unemployed—what a huge impact that would be! We absolutely must not underestimate it.

The major effect will be felt next year, not this year. It's possible that next year's exports will indeed be 10% less than this year's because ordinary Americans have adopted a wait-and-see attitude, their confidence in consuming and investing has been weakened, they are in general spending less on consumption and investment, they don't dare fly on airplanes or go on tours, and quite a few of the industries affected are laying people off. This has a very great effect on America's purchasing power. Given these circumstances, we must do our best to maintain the volume of our exports to the United States. After all, its market is still seeking consumer necessities that are high in quality but low in price.

Of course, the marked slowdown in the American economy won't make it easy for us to increase exports to the United States. The most optimistic projection for the U.S. economy right now comes from the International Monetary Fund (IMF), which is forecasting sustained growth of 2.5% this year and next—these are flattering words. At the end of this July, the U.S. Department of Commerce announced that the American economy grew by 0.7% in the second quarter; the most recent amended figure announced was 0.3%. It's very clear that there will be negative growth in the U.S. economy during the third and fourth quarters of this year, and this negative growth will continue during the first half of next year. This is the estimate of most people. [Alan] Greenspan[2] thinks that the U.S. government will have to spend $100 billion to make up for the losses caused by the events of 9/11, and this may not even be nearly enough to make up those losses. Therefore it's certain that the U.S. economy will enter a recession, and it's also certain that the Japanese economy will remain in the doldrums. We have to take this fully into consideration.

The Chinese Stock Markets

The direct impact on our stock markets won't be very great. This is mainly because our stock markets are closed [to the outside]. Even though our stock indices have oscillated since 9/11—with a few more downs than ups—this is related to many events in the previous period, notably the listing of the Guangxia Company of Yinchuan, which deceived stock buyers, and our investigation of how banks' credit funds went into the market, how they reduced their holdings of Treasury bonds, and how they issued additional shares. All these things had a definite impact on the psychology of share buyers.

---

2. Alan Greenspan was then Chairman of the U.S. Federal Reserve Board.

Our stock markets have been behaving in a most unusual way for many years now. They fall when other markets [abroad] rise and rise when others fall. Externalities don't have a very great impact on our stock markets—domestic factors are the key. There is some benefit to the current drop in stock prices. We can shrink things a bit, trim some fat, and use this opportunity to squeeze out some bubbles. How can we have price-to-earnings ratios in the dozens? The moral hazards are too great. If enterprises are all busy speculating in stocks, who will engage in production? But there is one thing [to remember]: namely, we mustn't allow any great shock or even a collapse to happen to the stock markets. We must work hard to avoid creating any social unrest. Overall, the current stock markets still haven't been greatly affected.

Countermeasures

I've just spoken mainly about the impacts in the preceding three areas, but some other effects require close study as well. To put it simply, we have to consider both short-term and long-term consequences. We must look at various possibilities, prepare many contingency plans, and be fully prepared for anything that might happen.

We must soberly observe the new international economic situation and new developments and deal with them calmly. At the same time, we should focus on studying effective countermeasures. I'd like to discuss three such courses of action.

1. The Most Fundamental Countermeasure Is to Expand Domestic Demand. Over the long term and especially the short term, we must adhere to a strategic plan that is anchored in domestic demand. Where will domestic demand come from? Right now, an important measure for increasing domestic demand is production, which means issuing Treasury bonds and matching that with additional bank credit in order to drive economic growth. And where will the money for Treasury bonds come from? Although the bonds are issued mainly to banks, the money still comes from the savings of ordinary people. In the sphere of consumption, the way to directly increase demand is to raise incomes for urban and rural populations, including officials and staff, and to reduce the burden on farmers.

I feel we now have to make one requirement explicit: that is, we must nurture and protect domestic demand emanating from ordinary people. Expanding domestic demand can't be infinite, and we can't get as much as we want. Someone told me that [during the first two years] when the Ministry of Finance issued certificates for purchasing Treasury bonds, people started lining up for these the night before. By shortly after 9 a.m. the next day, they were sold out. This time the Ministry of Finance issued RMB 20 billion of these certificates and started selling them 20 days ago. They're still selling them, and nobody is scrambling to buy them. This is because the purchasing power of our residents is beginning to be diverted. Those of us in charge of macroeconomics, especially those at the State Planning Commission, the State Economic and Trade Commission, the Ministry of Finance, and the banks, need to study this issue well and determine exactly how much social purchasing power is still there and how much potential remains for increasing domestic demand. We can't say that we can drive the economy just by issuing Treasury bonds—it isn't that simple. There are also limits to issuing Treasury bonds, so we must pay attention to nurturing domestic demand.

What does it mean to nurture domestic demand? This is a multifaceted task. Ultimately, it means we must continue to increase urban and rural incomes, particularly for low-income people. A very important part of this move is to continue giving raises to civil servants and resolutely guarantee the "Two Assurances."[3] Salary increases help civil servants feel secure in their work and also help reduce corruption. The actions of civil servants have a direct effect on the economic performance of enterprises. If government work can become more efficient, if rent-seeking behavior can be halted, if administrative interference and arbitrary fee collections can be reduced, enterprises will be profitable. Only when they are profitable will enterprises be able to give their staff raises, and only then will they be able to motivate staff and retain talent. These measures will set people's minds at ease, strengthen their confidence to consume, and drive an increase in consumption. The Ministry of Finance should think of issues in terms of nurturing domestic demand.

An important aspect of nurturing domestic demand consists of working hard to increase farmers' incomes and raise rural purchasing levels. These past few years, because of a current phase in which supply exceeds demand in grain production, grain prices have gone back down, structural contradictions in the rural economy have become very pronounced, the growth of farmers' incomes has slowed, and farmers' incomes in the major grain-producing regions have even dropped. This is a prime reason why domestic demand doesn't rise. Our greatest potential domestic demand lies in the vast rural areas. We must take more effective measures to make farmers' incomes increase more quickly.

The key is to push hard on reforming the structure of agriculture and the rural economy, on transforming traditional agriculture into modern agriculture, and on broadening the channels for farmers to increase their incomes; at the same time, we must truly reduce the burden on farmers and lighten their taxes. I would like the central leading group on agriculture to be responsible for

---

3. That is, assuring retirees that their pensions will be paid on time and in full, and assuring laid-off workers that money to cover their basic living expenses will be paid on time and in full.

studying and suggesting policies to increase farmers' incomes; the Ministry of Agriculture to study in depth measures for speeding up agricultural restructuring; and the State Council's working group on reforms of rural taxes and fees to quickly sum up the experiences of the pilot programs in Anhui and other provinces, and to propose ideas for introducing reforms of rural taxes and fees next year.

2. We Must Prevent Ineffective Construction. The past few years, the central government has used almost no Treasury bond funds for projects in the processing industry. Yet quite a few locales are still starting up many redundant projects of this nature using bank credit. In the past two years, for instance, over 30 new float glass production lines alone were started up. We should also bear in mind that even infrastructure construction should not be redundant or excessively cutting-edge. We can't say that it's always good to build expressways. If there are many roads but few cars using them, that is in fact also a form of waste. Similarly, it's not the case that the more ring roads a city builds, the better. All construction projects must consider actual performance, while infrastructure construction must also consider returns. Otherwise funds will be locked up there and be unable to yield returns. Then in the future we will exceed our capacity [to repay] and we won't be able to sell our Treasury bonds because we won't be able to recover the capital invested, which would weaken our ability to increase fiscal revenues.

3. We Must Strictly Practice Frugality and Oppose Extravagance. At a time when the international economic environment is steadily worsening, we must use all resources reasonably and thriftily in order to overcome difficulties and achieve sustained and stable economic growth. At present, whether it is in production, construction, circulation, or consumption, there are many signs of burdens on the people and of wastefulness. Some places are eager to start up "vanity projects" and "political achievement projects" that are showy but lack substance and are detached from reality. Some places aren't even paying wages on time, yet they run wild with construction projects and spend as if there were no tomorrow. Some erect fancy halls and buildings in violation of the rules, and their offices are becoming ever bigger and ever more lavish. Some organize a profusion of celebratory activities, vying to be the grandest and most extravagant; it is fairly common to find banqueting at public expense, using public funds for foreign travel, and wining and dining without regard for cost. All these phenomena squander huge sums of money, and no matter how much we have, we can't afford this kind of wastefulness. We must firmly put a halt to this tendency to be wasteful and decadent. This will not only help us use our limited funds and materials where they are most needed for our economic reforms and development, but it will also help us correct the work styles of our Party and our government.

On this matter, I want to stress several points:

First, we must implement the spirit of this meeting. We must use the opportunity of implementing the spirit of the 6th Plenary Session of the 15th National Party Congress to urge with much fanfare that the entire Party and the whole of society work arduously, build our country through diligence and thrift, and be frugal in all our endeavors. We must also firmly halt all incorrect behaviors that are unrealistic or disregard effectiveness.

Second, we must work to cut spending. We should make a big effort to lower costs and expenses in production, construction, and circulation. Enterprises, public institutions, government agencies, and schools should all count their pennies and cut out all types of unnecessary expenditures. Next year, we should lay out clear and specific cost-cutting goals and expectations for all regions, sectors, and work units.

Third, we must strengthen fiscal oversight and exercise more rigorous fiscal discipline. We should strengthen budget management and oversight audits and implement specialized fiscal account management. We must strictly investigate all sorts of irregular spending in violation of the rules and prohibit feasting, tourism, and costly entertainment at public expense. We must also prohibit leisure travel abroad under various pretexts.

Fourth, we must proactively adjust the composition of our fiscal outlays. We should assign priorities and ensure funding for those that ought to be guaranteed, such as increased inputs for agriculture, science and technology, education, environmental protection, national defense, and legal-political work; implementation of the "Two Assurances"; and raises for staff at government agencies and publicly supported institutions. Those outlays that should be cut back must be cut back. Adjustments in the composition of fiscal outlays should be integrated with economic restructuring and a major campaign for an arduous work style.

The 9/11 attacks will surely trigger enormous changes in the international political situation and the global economic picture, and we absolutely must not underestimate the effects on our economy. This might present us with yet another major challenge, one that may be even greater than the 1997 Asian financial crisis because its impact was confined to Asia, while the American and European economies were still doing well. But even before 9/11, the American economy had started slowing down, the Japanese economy had entered a recession, the overall European economy was not doing well, Latin American countries like Argentina were experiencing serious financial crises, and the southeast Asian nations were also having great difficulties. For some time to come, the world economy may be in a downturn. The external economic environment will undoubtedly have a rather negative effect on our economic growth, and that impact will be even greater next year. However, this can also turn into a great opportunity, provided that our thinking is aligned, we are united, and we handle it properly. We must seriously implement all the policy measures of the Party Central Committee and the State Council, improve our Party's work style, transform government functions, rectify and standardize the order in the market economy, and improve the investment environment. That way, China will not only become one of the largest markets in the world, but it can also become an investment paradise, a factory for the world, a very safe place for tourism, and a great, prosperous, and stable socialist country.

44

CHINA CAN BECOME THE WORLD'S INVESTMENT PARADISE[1]

October 22, 2001

Compatriots and friends, we have shared roots, so I should call you overseas compatriots. I know you have tremendous professional expertise in many areas and that your achievements are outstanding. I admire you very much. Why? Because I studied engineering, and to this day I continue to have a strong interest in engineering. Unlike you, however, I have no practical engineering experience—at most, I laid some low-voltage power lines and built a couple of transformer stations. As soon as I left the university, I worked basically in macroeconomics, where the biggest headache is finance. I still don't know how far the stock market will fall this year. I've asked the departments concerned to report to me as soon as possible, but there's nothing I can do—the government can't control whether stocks go up or down. It would have been wonderful if I had studied economics at Tsinghua University. Now I have to take make-up classes, and it's really difficult.

I have an American friend named [Joseph] Stiglitz, a Stanford professor working at the World Bank and former economic adviser to President [Bill] Clinton. I hear he won the Nobel Prize in Economics for his work on asymmetric information. He's a very forthright person, and his criticisms of the International Monetary Fund have been very sharp. He also criticizes the World Bank, but because he is a senior vice president and chief economist there, he is gentler in criticizing the World Bank and harsher on the IMF—that is also

---

1. This speech was delivered by Zhu Rongji when he met with Chinese experts from many countries attending the Fifth Sino-American Technology and Engineering Conference. The symposium was jointly sponsored by the State Commission on Economics and Trade, the State Administration of Foreign Experts, the China Association for International Personnel Exchange, and the Chinese Institute of Engineers–U.S.A. Sixty-seven experts from North America and over 210 experts from over 60 Chinese enterprises participated. After visiting 25 Chinese enterprises, the North American attendees engaged in discussions with their Chinese counterparts on 8 areas of interest: computer networks and software, photoelectricity and communications, environmental digital appliances, machinery, petrochemicals and chemical industries, medicines and bioengineering, new materials, and energy and environmental engineering. They also offered many relevant recommendations.

"asymmetrical." If any of you are from Stanford, please congratulate him on my behalf.

Yesterday I looked at the résumés of all 67 of you and found your specialties very interesting. In the aftermath of the terrorist attacks on 9/11, you still took the trouble to come to China to attend the Sino-American Technology and Engineering Conference. We should learn from your spirit. I greatly admire you and welcome you most warmly!

The first Sino-American Technology and Engineering Conference took place in 1993, and this is its fifth meeting. It has played a great role in raising the levels of science and technology in China, particularly the level of technological reform at enterprises. Tsai Hwan-tang[2] showed us the technology for repairing convertor steelmaking furnaces. This can greatly increase the lifespan of convertor furnaces and has great practical value; of course it also has great scientific and technological value. I'm only giving this one example, but I believe many others have played equally fine and important roles in raising the level of China's economic construction and the living standards of our people.

I know you've already visited many factories in the heartland, including Haier, the Wuhan Iron and Steel Works, the Baogang Iron and Steel Works, the North China Pharmaceutical Group, and Sinochem. These are some of the better enterprises—you still haven't seen the poorer ones. I'm sure that you'll be able to offer many good ideas to help us improve our technical progress and raise the standard of our technological reforms. We will definitely take your ideas very seriously.

We have gained a much deeper understanding of the significance of this conference and hope it will continue to take place, because I believe that such a meeting will definitely be of inestimable value to China, to the United States, and to friendship and cooperation between China and the United States. The recent Asia-Pacific Economic Cooperation (APEC) meetings[3] held successfully in Shanghai were not only conducive to promoting cooperation and friendship between the Asia-Pacific member nations, but also helped Sino-American friendship develop better by taking advantage of this opportunity. I wish you all in advance a pleasant trip in China and hope you will make even greater contributions to friendship and cooperation between China and the United States.

Not long ago, I said a few words in Nanjing at the Sixth Convention of the World Chinese Entrepreneurs Association, but I had not realized that it was being broadcast live on Hong Kong's Phoenix TV. If I had known, I wouldn't

2. Tsai Hwan-tang was born in Taiwan in 1950. He chaired the metallurgy group at the Second and Third Sino-American Technology and Engineering Conferences.

3. This refers to the 9th APEC Economic Leaders' Meeting and the 13th APEC Ministerial Meeting held in Shanghai on October 15–21, 2001.

Meeting on October 22, 2001, at the Great Hall of the People in Beijing with Chinese experts from abroad attending the Fifth Sino-American Technology and Engineering Conference. (Photograph by Qi Tieyan, Xinhua News Agency)

have been so "uninhibited" and emotional in calling upon Overseas Chinese, ethnic Chinese in other countries, and Chinese studying abroad to return home and take part in our economic construction.

Some say that China's economy is "the only beautiful blossom." I don't see it that way. There would be a problem if only one blossom was beautiful. In that case, it wouldn't be beautiful for long. Everyone must do well if you are to do well. I'm afraid there's no such thing as everyone else doing poorly and you alone doing well. No matter how you look at it, China's economy must rely on its own domestic market. We're adopting many policy measures to increase domestic demand.

What is domestic demand? It is the people's purchasing power. If the people don't get rich, where will the banks get so much money from? If the banks don't have money, to whom will the government sell Treasury bonds? If the people don't have money, how can they buy consumer goods? We're taking many measures to nurture, support, and protect the people's purchasing power. To civil servants alone, we've given two raises this year. To tell you the truth, my salary is much lower than yours, but then again, things in China are much cheaper than where you come from. If it costs ten yuan to buy something where you are, one yuan will be enough here.

Our salaries may be low, but our people are living quite happily. That's why they're quite highly motivated and quite confident about consuming. As a result, our domestic demand has been growing steadily. We're also not disregarding foreign markets. For the past few years, exports have been very important to us. Last year, our exports approached US$250 billion, which is almost one-quarter of our GDP—this is a very large figure.

At present, the U.S. economy is slowing down, the European economy is in the doldrums, and the Japanese economy has in fact already entered into recession, so our exports will undoubtedly be greatly affected. However, we're still taking various measures to increase exports. After all, I believe the American people still need consumer goods that are high in quality but low in price. You can't say that people won't consume because the terrorists knocked down the World Trade Center. Consumption is still necessary, and there is hope yet for our markets.

At the same time, we have to open up new markets. This year, we've had great growth especially in attracting foreign investment. From January through September, we attracted US$32 billion in foreign direct investment (FDI) (actually received, not contracted). This represents an increase of 22% over the same period last year, an increase that exceeded my expectations. This is proof that our investment environment has improved.

With respect to China's investment environment, we have a handle on the hardware, namely the infrastructure, but the soft environment is indeed less than ideal—I'm referring to those laws and regulations that still haven't completely merged with international norms and that have a lot of room for improvement. However, our social order is still very good, and I guarantee you'll be absolutely safe here. We're attracting about US$40 billion a year of foreign investments. If we do well this year, we can exceed US$40 billion. So you can see that we can be very hopeful about attracting foreign investment. After all, we're safe and stable.

People in the West keep criticizing our human rights, but to tell the truth, our human rights situation isn't that bad. You say we're corrupt, but we're going after the corrupt elements one by one—what more do you want? You say you have democracy, freedom, a multiparty system, and universal suffrage—true, you're handling these very well. And aren't we also absorbing good things from you? But we don't have to take things that aren't good or that aren't suited to our circumstances. There isn't necessarily a single model for everything. It's not that you're free of corruption; you just have a bit less than we do. And we, too, have legal institutions—this is not a lawless place.

Regarding the world situation, I admit that we absolutely must not underestimate the impact of 9/11, as it might alter world political and economic conditions. But I'm still optimistic, and I still believe that as long as China handles things appropriately, as long as our measures are suited to the actual circumstances, our economy will still be able to maintain rapid growth for the next few years—that is, it can be kept at about 7%. It won't do for it to be higher than that. This is the kind of speed that can be maintained.

We won't rely just on domestic demand; we also must rely on foreign investments and exports. Most important, we will rely on you, who represent the descendants of the Yellow Emperor. Chinese living abroad are a very powerful force in support of our country. At the Sixth Convention of the World Chinese Entrepreneurs Association, I loudly urged, "Please come back!" After saying that, I felt very insecure because our investment environment is subpar. What will I do if you all come back and then complain to me? But as I also said, it isn't as if you will all return once I make the call. If our investment environment isn't improved, if we can't enable you to live very happily here, if there isn't room for you to use your skills, if you're not free to start your own endeavors, you won't come back anyway.

I believe that although we have quite a few shortcomings, overall we are still getting better, and overall we are still moving forward. Now even foreigners admit that China is still the safest place in the world. President [George W.] Bush is so busy directing a war, the Pacific Ocean is so vast, and Air Force One needs an escort of fighter jets—if China weren't safe, how could he come? So you can see, this is still a paradise.

I believe that China will become a paradise in this world and it will become a huge global factory. Everyone will move here because costs here are low and products made here are competitive. China will also definitely become a global tourist attraction. With 5,000 years of civilization, we have countless relics and heritage sites! We're building the Qinghai-Tibet railroad and preparing to have deluxe passenger traffic on it so that people all over the world can conveniently visit Tibet, see the Tibetan Buddhist culture there, and see whether or not there is freedom of religion in China. Those who say we interfere with freedom of religion don't understand the realities.

Dear compatriots, I hope you'll come often and that afterward you'll tell the American people about the realities in China. I'm hoping you'll talk not only about good things but also about bad things. Moreover, you should let us know about the bad things, or else write about them in newspapers. This is an information world, and we can all see [what you publish]. Only by doing this can we improve our work, and only by doing this can the American people have a genuine understanding of China. I believe that the friendship and cooperation between China and the United States will definitely grow on such a foundation, and all of you here can play a very great role in this.

45

STRENGTHEN OVERSIGHT THROUGH THE MEDIA[1]

December 6, 2001

It's very important that we strengthen oversight through the media. Our current administrative and legal capabilities alone are inadequate for resolving many serious immediate problems. Why do I take so much time to read letters from the people, to read "Internal References," and to watch *Topics in Focus?* Nowadays it isn't only CCTV Channel 1 that features *Topics in Focus.* Several CCTV channels and many local TV stations all have similar programs that expose certain problems and criticize some signs of corruption. I think this is a fine thing.

I read "Internal References," including the *People's Daily's* "Information Bulletin," more than anything else. Recently 70 to 80 people died at the Nandan tin mine in Guangxi. If it hadn't been for the report in the *People's Daily's* "Information Bulletin," I really wouldn't have known about it, and nearly a hundred people would have died without redress. The owner of that mine had bought off the leading cadres, including the Nandan County Party secretary and magistrate. He operated this mine on his own without any safety measures. The workers he hired were all poor people from Hunan and Guizhou, with no one to care about them when they died. Once the waters rushed in, those 70 to 80 people were inundated, yet the county covered it up and said there had not been a single fatality.

After this was revealed by the *People's Daily* reporter, I forwarded instructions to the Party secretary of the Guangxi Zhuang Autonomous Region, noting that the *People's Daily* reporter's description was accurate. No matter what, you must pump all the water out, I said. If they're alive, find the people; if they're dead, find their corpses—you can't treat people's lives casually. Once the water was pumped out, all the bodies were found. That mine owner paid the county magistrate and the Party secretary hush money and kept the leadership of the autonomous region in the dark. This sort of problem has been addressed who knows how many times in the Shanxi coal mines, and I don't know how many notices and documents have been sent out or how many people punished, yet things go on as before.

---

1. This is part of Zhu Rongji's remarks at a meeting with leading members from the various departments of the Xinhua News Agency.

317

Recently, there were five explosions in a mere nine days, killing more than a hundred people. These were all cases in which small mine owners had bought off the responsible officials in the departments concerned. They showed no regard for people's lives, nor did they pay taxes or assume any responsibility, while huge sums of money went into their pockets. Now coal prices have shot up 30% and they're making fortunes, yet they don't care about people's lives at all. How can we go on if such things aren't seriously exposed and strictly handled? How can the Party's policies be implemented?

I'm the most loyal reader of the Xinhua News Agency's "Domestic Affairs Press-Proof." I read every issue, and after I read it, I write instructions. As far as I know, nobody has indicated that [the reports] I wrote instructions about were incorrect, although of course parts may not have been entirely accurate. That's why "Internal References" and "Domestic Affairs Press-Proof" play a very important role. They can help keep leaders sober and let us know what problems exist and how far these problems have developed.

Last year, I wrote instructions on about 200 items; this year, I reached 200 by November. But now the instructions don't seem to be as effective as before. When I first started writing them, the locals were very tense, and their leaders would personally go on-site to investigate. Now they don't deal with [the problems] as seriously as they used to, so my instructions are having less and less effect. When Caoji Township in Xiayi County of Henan Province illegally raised funds to build an office building, the township leader only received an internal warning within the Party. It broke my heart to read about this. This sort of thing is a criminal offense—how can it be addressed by an internal Party warning?

I say all this not because I am discouraged, and even less because I want to dampen your enthusiasm, causing you to think that I no longer take the Xinhua News Agency's "Domestic Affairs Press-Proof" as seriously—that isn't the case. I continue to read your "Domestic Affairs Press-Proof." As for what sort of instructions to write, I still have to give that some serious consideration. I care about effectiveness. You work very hard and report many things to us. These are taken seriously not just by me—the Party Central Committee and the Standing Committee of the Politburo all take them very seriously. I will keep reading what you write for that way I will understand what is going on around China.

Of course it's entirely appropriate for coverage to be primarily positive. You've followed this guideline very well—we mustn't cause the people to lose confidence. But I wonder, regardless of whether the ratio [of bad news to good news] is 3:7, 2:8, or 1:9, surely it won't do to not expose problems, right? Surely we can't fail to have oversight through public opinion, right? We Communist Party members pay attention to science, and we pay attention to contradictions. If contradictions are not revealed, it would be contrary to the facts.

As Communist Party members and servants of the people, we should of course serve the people with all our heart and soul, reveal their hardships, and expose bad things in our speeches and through our writings. Only then can we win the support of the people, and only then can they feel confident. We can't say that talking only about how wonderful things are will inspire confidence. If we cover up contradictions and don't solve problems, people will still lack confidence. They'll have confidence only after they see that problems are being solved. That's why we stress that reporting should be primarily positive, but that oversight through public opinion is also needed.

Of course we also know that oversight through public opinion can only do so much—that rule of law is essential. Not just rule of law—the building of a whole set of ethical and cultural values is very important. This central working meeting on the economy also discussed the issue of trust. If society as a whole does not establish a culture of trust, if it does not build spiritual strength and moral strength, we won't be able to operate sound banks and securities markets. If you don't pay a price after committing fraud and don't have to repay after borrowing money, social trust will vanish.

However, I'm not attaching excessive weight to the power of oversight through public opinion. It can't do the job in all areas, such as oversight of state-owned enterprises (SOEs). Systemic problems are especially important. We've been implementing enterprise reforms for many years now, but the vast majority of large and medium SOEs still haven't established a modern enterprise system and corresponding mechanisms. By now it's very clear that a simple system of SOEs has gone as far as it can go because it has no constraints—whatever the first-in-command says is the final word. The Party Central Committee has explicitly said we should have shareholding systems, but if a shareholding system only allows SOEs to own and cross-own shares, and if the shareholders' meeting and board of directors have no powers to constrain management, then a modern enterprise system still can't be established.

We are in favor of revealing information to the public when stocks are listed so that stockholders and the public can exercise oversight, but it now appears that even this isn't quite enough. There's also talk about having independent directors who can represent the interests of small shareholders. Right now those independent directors are all economists who don't dare offend anyone—would they dare to speak up on behalf of small shareholders? That's why if we don't establish a system of constraints through oversight and if we continue to let the factory director or manager alone have the final say, we still won't be able to run SOEs well. If enterprises don't have internal mechanisms by which to constrain their leaders, the problems at SOEs still won't be resolved. Therefore we must continue to explore various forms of public ownership and truly establish

Visiting an exhibit on the history of the Xinhua News Agency during an inspection tour of the agency on December 6, 2001.

systems to constrain and oversee management. Above all, we must put a stop to the falsification of accounts. In a recent audit of 1,290 enterprises, the National Audit Office found serious cases of falsification in 68% of this group. This piece of information was picked up by the media all over the world as soon as it was released. Newspapers in Hong Kong played it up and said we were corrupt.

I don't know if you at the Xinhua News Agency released this news or not—I suspect you might have had reservations. Actually, you needn't have reservations. You don't have to wait for foreigners to report this news first because they will post it on the Internet soon enough, and Hong Kong newspapers will also spread the news far and wide into China. These won't matter because after it's reported, it will attract everyone's attention.

The first person who should be criticized is me. I've been in charge of economic work for 10 years, and so far 68% of SOEs are still falsifying their books. I should be the first to atone by resigning—this does not concern others who do only routine work. I have become deeply aware of the seriousness of the problem. I recognized it in 1995, when I wanted to set up national institutes of accounting to train some real accountants. If accountants [abroad] falsify books, the partners of their accounting firms will fine them down to their last pennies, destroy their reputations, and revoke their professional qualifications.

They will be held responsible for "unlimited liability" and pay all their savings in compensation. To this day, we still haven't established such a system.

In the 1,290 cases of falsified bookkeeping at SOEs that I mentioned just now, losses to the state amounted to RMB150 billion—that's how serious it is! Therefore, I proposed to create three national institutes of accounting, one each in Guangzhou, Beijing, and Shanghai. They still weren't set up after several years of discussions—the Ministry of Finance wouldn't provide the funds and only procrastinated. It was only after I became premier that these institutes were established. The one in Shanghai was the first to be completed; I've also seen the one in Beijing, which has now been completed. Guangzhou wasn't enthusiastic enough so [that one] has been shifted to Xiamen, which is very enthusiastic and set aside a most beautiful piece of green space, 500 mu^2 in all, for the institute. When I visited the state accounting institute in Shanghai this year, I inscribed a school motto for them: "Do not falsify accounts." Just those four words. I was the one who proposed to set up these three state institutes, and they were finally built after untold troubles.

If you were to falsify accounts, you would break my heart! If you were trained at these state institutes of accounting that we have taken so much trouble to create and still rigged the books, would there be any hope for China? Of course we must maintain the rule of law. As I said just now, if they can be fined down to the last penny and their reputations can be totally ruined, we'll see if they still dare to manipulate the books. We must work diligently in this regard, so as to establish a culture of trustworthiness and rule of law where good faith matters. Otherwise, banking, securities, and insurance will be in an utter mess, as will SOEs. If the basic problems aren't solved, even a strong economy and good finances will only be temporary phenomena.

When I inspected the state accounting institute in Beijing this October, they also asked me to inscribe a school motto for them. The institute leaders suggested that I write, "None of our graduates falsify accounts!" Does that mean people who aren't their graduates may rig the books? I therefore changed it to "Honesty is basic and integrity is key; adhere to principles and don't falsify the books." That is somewhat more comprehensive. If I can achieve only one thing while I'm in office, it is to have no more falsified books in China—that would allow me to die happy. I would not be able to die happy if in the future graduates trained at the state accounting institutes still tampered with the books. If we don't solve this problem, how can we industrialize and how can we modernize?

What I mean to say in all this is that I do hope you are aware of how great a responsibility you bear. Your work can play a seminal role, and you represent the

---

2. One mu is equal to 666.7 square meters.

An inscription written during an inspection tour of the State Accounting Institute in Beijing on October 29, 2001.

ordinary people. I hope you continue to do better in publicizing the Party's policies and in reporting on the hardships of the people. I will absolutely support you. If the lower levels don't take seriously any of the instructions I send out, including those pertaining to letters from the people, "Internal References," and "Domestic Affairs Press-Proof," I will have the Bureau of Letters and Petitions and the General Office of the State Council prod them into action. If they make excuses in the details of reports sent back to me, I will rebut them. I've already rebutted many such responses. In short, please believe that I will always be your loyal reader and supporter.

46

STRENGTHEN OVERSIGHT
THROUGH PUBLICATIONS[1]

December 13, 2001

Today, Li Lanqing, Ding Guan'gen, and responsible members of the departments concerned have come with me to the General Administration of Press and Publication (GAPP) with three goals in mind:

—First, to express our congratulations, to congratulate GAPP on its restructuring and upgrading. This shows that the Party Central Committee and State Council have entrusted you with an even more difficult mission and expect that you will play an even greater role.

—Second, to express our affirmation: under the leadership of the Party Central Committee and the State Council, you've done a great amount of work, and your achievements should be affirmed. Just now we saw the exhibit on "Cracking Down on Pornographic and Illegal Content," which is an achievement in strengthening oversight, and an exhibit on the flourishing publications market. It is clear that you've done a great deal.

—Third, to encourage you, to support you, and to express our hope that you will achieve even greater results.

But we should also see that there are still a great many problems in the publications market, and there is no end to cracking down on pornography and illegal content. We must keep on cracking down, every year and every day. This is not the sort of work where we can rest on our laurels—it might recur in waves, and the problems will reappear if there is the slightest letup. Therefore we must make great efforts, and we should also expect a good deal of resistance. There's a bit of protectionism in every region. If you praise them, they welcome it, but if you criticize them, they get very tense and think of all sorts of ways to prevent

---

1. This is part of a speech by Zhu Rongji at a meeting of deputy department directors and above at the General Administration of Press and Publication. On April 30, 2001, the State Council had reorganized the Press and Publications Administration (State Copyright Bureau) into the General Administration of Press and Publication (State Copyright Bureau), which in 2013 was merged with the General Administration of Radio, Film, and Television to form the State Administration of Press, Publication, Radio, Film, and Television.

you from criticizing them. But without criticism there would be no oversight, and there would be no [effective] rule of law.

Today we have all come to express how much the Party Central Committee, the State Council, and the various departments all support you as you fulfill your oversight responsibilities and promote the prosperity of the publications market. We will support you no matter how much resistance you encounter— what is there to be afraid of! I believe that when it comes to strict law enforcement and strict oversight, the Party committees and governments at all levels will also support you. Now I'd like to discuss three hopes.

1. Hopes for GAPP

I hope GAPP will transform its functions, strengthen market oversight, and set up legal institutions for the management of news and publications. At the same time you should gradually overcome and correct bad work styles.

Work in the realm of news and publications is in fact work on the ideological superstructure. This is extremely important work, and without legal institutions, it will be very hard to oversee its issues. Yesterday, the State Council passed the newly revised "Regulations on Management of Publications" and "Regulations on Management of Audio-Video Products." In order to adapt to further marketization and particularly in light of the new conditions that will confront us after we join the World Trade Organization, we will have to add some supplementary articles.

On the one hand, we want to open up to the outside; on the other hand, we still have to resist the ideological infiltration and corrosion of hostile forces. It is worth our while to make unstinting efforts and put up a relentless fight in this regard. The problem of bad conduct in this sector is quite serious. Several major problems have arisen at news and publication units, and political errors have been made—all because book publication licenses can be bought and sold and review procedures ignored. Although the current methods of review are not very effective, they cannot be entirely abolished. That's why we must adopt methods that are legally institutionalized to put an end to bad work styles and to stop behaviors that merely seek profit and disregard political consequences.

2. Hopes for Market Order

You should be more forceful in rectifying and standardizing market order. Just now I said that cracking down on pornographic and illegal content is not a short-term task and must be sustained over the long term. Similarly, the job of rectifying and standardizing order in a market economy must be performed continually. The publications market is an extremely important one. As much as fake, imitation, counterfeit, and shoddy foods and medicines can harm people's lives, illegal publications can harm an entire generation of young people, with immeasurable consequences. That's why you must have the utmost determination to address this problem; you absolutely must not ease up, nor should you be satisfied with your present results.

There are profits to be made in illegal publications. What's more, these are windfall profits. Unless a great deal of energy is expended to crack down on them, it will be very hard to suppress them. We will need cooperation from all sides, and everyone should join in this fight. You must understand that the rectification and standardization of the cultural market are an extremely important aspect of the rectification and standardization of order in a socialist market economy—we could also say that it's an extremely difficult part, one that requires joint efforts.

3. Hopes for Intellectual Property

You must better protect intellectual property. The principle that intellectual property should be protected is an international norm. In joining the World Trade Organization (WTO), we signed three agreements, one of which pertains to protecting trade-related intellectual property. We must live up to this commitment. If intellectual property is not protected, the publications market won't be able to flourish; if fake, imitation, counterfeit, and shoddy goods can be found all over China, it will never be able to modernize. Because fake, imitation, counterfeit, and shoddy goods, with their low prices, have taken over the market in profusion, high-quality goods can't be produced.

I attach a great deal of importance to teaching materials for primary and secondary schools because these are part of our policy on rural areas. What we're most worried about right now is the large-scale dumping of American farm products after we join the WTO. Although we have some systems for protection such as customs duties, quotas, and licensing and they can remain in place for a transitional period of five years, they may not be able to fully protect us even during this period. Once imported agricultural goods are being dumped, market prices will go down, and farmers' incomes will immediately fall.

Because American grain is produced on a large scale, it is 30–40% cheaper than ours. Therefore we will be under tremendous pricing pressure. Now, besides restructuring agriculture, we also have to significantly reduce the burden on farmers and increase their incomes. This is a very demanding task. The cost of books for primary and secondary schools alone is a heavy burden for farmers, as they can't really afford to pay several hundred renminbi a year for textbooks. Moreover, the quality of these books is very poor: some are pirated and some are even photocopied. This problem is definitely worthy of our attention.

On an inspection tour of the General Administration of Press and Publication on December 13, 2001.

We are now going to conduct some pilot reforms that will put the publishing of primary and secondary school teaching materials up for bidding. The provincial governments where the pilot programs are located will ask for bids, and qualified publishers can submit bids. Only after winning a bid can a publisher publish and print [the materials]—this is the only way to do it. They will receive authorization to print after the bidding and competition. This authorization must be protected, and if any further piracy is detected, it must be subjected to a fierce crackdown.

Today, I've come especially to ask you to pay attention to teaching materials for rural primary and secondary schools, and to exercise strict oversight of printing and publication. Treat this as an important policy of our Party for lightening the burden on farmers and increasing their incomes. First of all, ensure the quality of teaching materials and protect intellectual property; then reduce the burden of textbook costs in rural primary and secondary schools. You now still operate one agency under two titles—the State Copyright Bureau is also located here. During bidding, the most important thing is to look at the costs of the various bidding publishers—try to lower the costs as much as possible. Teaching materials, especially those for rural primary and secondary schools, need not be printed so beautifully. It's not that we don't want teaching materials to be beautifully printed; the problem is that farmers can't afford it, and we have to keep realities in mind. There's no need for a lot of color printing—just bring the costs down. I'm entrusting you with this and hope you will pay attention to it.

47

Halt the Tendency to Blindly Seek Increases in Urban Size[1]

January 9, 2002

The overall economy performed really well last year despite many hidden problems that may gradually come to light this year. At present, many sectors—especially urban construction—show a tendency for overkill, extravagance, and disregard of realities. The "Happy Homes" project hasn't been resolved, and ordinary people still find a great deal of housing unaffordable at over RMB 10,000 per square meter. For whom is this being built?

This very dangerous tendency is now worsening. One hundred and eighty-two cities across the country all want to build international metropolises—how can this be? They've forgotten that there are still several tens of millions of people in China living below the poverty line! Some places can't even guarantee the "minimum living standard," can't even guarantee the payment of wages, yet they're guaranteeing that they'll build so-called international metropolises. If they can't build a real one, they'll build a fake one so they can complete a 15-year-plan in 15 months: if they can't put up the buildings, they'll put up a wall along the street—they're deceiving themselves and deceiving others!

This work style is truly awful, and it's all for the sake of promotions, of higher office. Ordinary people see this very clearly, but some of our local leaders haven't recognized the seriousness of this problem. I feel that the document we are preparing now on strengthening oversight and management of urban and rural planning is not solely for the sake of strengthening this management but also for the sake of very forcefully halting this improper trend. Employees aren't getting their wages and farmers are as poor as can be; yet officials want to build large cities everywhere, to create international metropolises filled with tall buildings, all to serve the rich. I think that the emphasis in this document should be on this matter, and that strengthening the management of urban and rural planning can be discussed in a later section along with the [specific] measures.

---

1. On January 9, 2002, Zhu Rongji chaired a Premier's working meeting on how to strengthen urban and rural construction planning and management. These are the key points he raised after listening to a report on these issues by leading members of the Ministry of Construction.

We have to raise this issue clearly at the beginning and point out that this tendency currently exists. Some places need to be criticized by name, examples should be given, and then we lay out some rules. I wonder if we should now consider whether we should first stop expanding cities. As for when city expansion should be allowed, you should first draw up a plan, and then we can discuss it after you've completed a five-year plan. For now, don't take any more of the farmers' land—don't go any further. Whatever the size of the urban population now, that should be its size. After all, the population will increase naturally!

The focus of work should be on the construction of urban infrastructure such as water pipes and sewers and on dealing with urban transportation and the like. The emphasis should be on solving the people's housing problems, not building those skyscrapers. If a master plan already exists, go slow in construction; if there is no master plan, continue to draw one up, but don't do anything for the time being, and focus your efforts on doing a good job with urban infrastructure.

The title of this document needs to be changed somewhat: it is both a notice and [a list of] rules, followed by several measures. The Ministry of Construction should work together with the relevant departments—the Environmental Protection Bureau, the State Planning Commission, the Ministry of Tourism, the Ministry of Culture, and the State Administration of Cultural Heritage—and should focus on research. The State Council will discuss this once more, then report to the Standing Committee of the Politburo. We have to put a halt to this tendency in urban construction of disregarding realities and trying to be grandiose. This includes tourism—don't destroy our scenic resources, human environment, and natural resources.

Also, I suggest that the Ministry of Construction work with CCTV to film a TV program that exposes the ugly side of urban construction: a three-story building in which one story has only one sidewall that is a facade; a tiny city constructing a grand square of more than a hundred thousand square meters; or tourism facilities arbitrarily built in violation of laws and regulations. Let's make them all "famous"!

48

INNER MONGOLIA SHOULD PLAY TO ITS OWN STRENGTHS IN ITS DEVELOPMENT[1]

March 7, 2002

I'm delighted to be with the delegation from Inner Mongolia to hear your thoughts on the "Report on the Work of the Government." Inner Mongolia is the largest minority autonomous region in northern China and has always received a great deal of attention from the Party Central Committee and the State Council. In 1966 I was sent to work for a year in the Abag Banner of Xilingol League. I have a great deal of affection for Inner Mongolia. These past few years, it has developed very quickly and very well. Provided the peoples of all ethnic groups are united and work on economic development with one mind, Inner Mongolia will continue to prosper.

In summing up your opinions, I'd like to make two points.

1. You Must Make Full Use of Inner Mongolia's Strengths

You have all sorts of resources but relatively speaking, your grassland resources are the most abundant and should be used to play up your advantages in animal husbandry. At present, our country produces about 1 trillion jin[2] of grain a year, or about 800 jin per capita, which approximates the global average. Most of our people's spending on food is for grain. Current levels of grain consumption indicate we already have a surplus of grain. If most people's diets were to consist of meat, eggs, and milk, however, we would have too little grain because it takes several jin of grain to produce one jin of meat. Our standard of living will have to go up, the total quantities of meat, eggs, and milk consumed will gradually increase, and products made from these commodities will be in ever greater demand.

Inner Mongolia should become a great base for our country's animal husbandry. Developing animal husbandry is the most realistic path to riches for farmers and herders. Its products can also be exported. Right now many of the

---

1. These remarks were made by Zhu Rongji at a plenary session of the Inner Mongolian delegation during the fifth session of the Ninth National People's Congress.
2. One jin is equal to 0.5 kilogram.

Addressing the delegation from the Inner Mongolia Autonomous Region on March 7, 2002, during the fifth session of the Ninth National People's Congress. (Photograph by Rao Aimin, Xinhua News Agency)

dairy products in Beijing's markets are imported. Why can't we claim this market for ourselves?

Just now the mayor of Tongliao said that breeding should be given priority over planting—I think that's absolutely correct. At the same time, he said industry should be given priority over agriculture—I don't entirely agree with that. Inner Mongolia doesn't necessarily have to take the same developmental path as the heartland, thinking that industrialization is the only way you can modernize and get rich—that isn't the case. Inner Mongolia's industrial strengths, its geographic strengths, and its environmental strengths all favor the development of animal husbandry. This market has a lot of room for growth in China, and it is the road to riches for Inner Mongolia. I feel that Inner Mongolia's thinking on development should be clearer on this point.

However, this absolutely does not mean that Inner Mongolia shouldn't develop industries. Places like Baotou have [ample] mineral resources [of their own]. They have a foundation for developing industries and have already developed these to a significant scale. But this, too, does not mean that industries should not be developed in agricultural or herding regions. When I visited New Zealand, I saw their ranches as well as their factories for meat and dairy products. These were completely modernized and complemented their strengths in animal husbandry. In particular, New Zealand has quarantine and inspection facilities that ensure its animal and dairy products are of high quality. Not only are these establishments extremely modern, but processing is very meticulous, and hygienic conditions are excellent. This is modern industry, the kind of industry that must be developed in conjunction with animal husbandry. Without such modern processing industries and without advanced quarantine and inspection facilities, people will be concerned about the foods produced, and our markets will be taken over by animal and dairy products from countries like Australia and New Zealand. That's why, for these industries and matching facilities, we should build to the world's most advanced and most modern standards.

On no account should we go back down that [old] path to industrialization, what with the "five small enterprises"[3] sprouting up all over, smoke billowing from every village, and every household lighting fires to refine iron and steel—that path must not be taken. After we did those things, we had no competitiveness whatsoever, and now we are wracking our brains on how to shut those enterprises down. We mustn't build any more small coal mines, small chemical plants, and small paper mills. If we build industry, it should be modern industry with economies of scale; otherwise we won't be able to compete in these markets. Especially in the remote areas, transportation is inconvenient and shipping costs are high. Never mind exports—we wouldn't be able to compete even in the domestic market. We must learn the lessons of history.

Don't think that you're sure to make money by building a factory—often it won't even last a couple years before it has to shut down. Quite a few of those township and village enterprises that were all the rage have now shut down. Their production costs were high, and their quality was poor—how could they be competitive? In developing industries, Inner Mongolia must develop modern industries, ones able to compete internationally—otherwise don't develop them. You should be entirely focused on playing to your strengths in animal husbandry and develop the grasslands; at the same time, develop some complementary modern industries for processing animal and dairy goods.

You also have to play to your strengths in grain production. Grain is already abundant across the country, so it doesn't need to be grown on the grasslands. There is also a surplus of corn. The corn that isn't exported is just rotting in the granaries, yet its price isn't competitive—foreign corn is cheaper. So places that have no advantages in grain production should not produce grain. I hope Inner Mongolia's line of thinking on its development will be very clear. Some of the old concepts from the past are no longer suited to current conditions.

Infrastructure must be built, roads must be accessible, and telecommunications must reach the villages. Inner Mongolia's land area is so vast, if disaster were to befall any one place and there isn't even telephone communication with

---

3. See chapter 14, n. 4, p. 123.

it, how can rescues be organized? This is the kind of money that must be spent. Urban construction should move toward small but high-quality projects. Inner Mongolia doesn't have that many people, so don't build on too large a scale. That is why Manzhouli has suffered losses—its scale was too large. Urban construction should be suitably concentrated. That way, infrastructure—including water pipes, sewers, gas, electricity, and centralized heating—can be readily built.

2. You Should Substantially Strengthen Protection and Conservation of the Eco-Environment

There is not a minute to lose in improving the eco-environment—this is an extremely urgent task in the face of continuing desertification, increasingly serious soil erosion, and environmental degradation that is worsening by the day—we can't ignore these facts. As an important ecological screen for northern China, Inner Mongolia must, no matter what, give very high priority to its eco-environment. This work will have a direct effect not only on the survival and development of the peoples of all ethnic groups in Inner Mongolia, but also on our strategy of sustainable development for the entire country.

The year before last, several ministers and I went to inspect the management of desertification. We drove all the way from Beijing to the edge of the Onqin Daga Sandland. En route our hearts grew heavy as we saw the large areas of soil that had turned to sand. Some parts of Fengning County, Hebei Province, that have turned to sand are less than 100 kilometers from Tiananmen as the crow flies. That's why all along the way I kept telling the provincial and municipal leaders in Hebei that everyone must mobilize to protect the ecological security of the place where the Party Central Committee is located! This desert will soon be invading Tiananmen. Inner Mongolia must give top priority to managing and building its eco-environment and must stop the deterioration there as quickly as possible.

Both the Party Central Committee and the State Council attach great importance to this issue. The state has drawn up a plan and also set aside a lot of funding in order to prevent desertification. But the work needs to be done by people, and everyone needs to be mobilized for it; it can't be done just with money. You already have many methods—the key is to work more forcefully.

Animal husbandry must absolutely not be developed at the expense of the eco-environment. You must really solve the problem of overgrazing in the grasslands. The grasslands cannot be subjected to any more overgrazing, and their capacity to sustain livestock cannot be increased. You should divide up usage rights in the grasslands and implement a system that would make families contractually responsible for usage. On this basis, you can promote dry-lot feeding and captive feeding; at the same time, you can step up grassland development,

In conversation on May 13, 2000, with Bilig, a herder who had contracted for 2,300 mu of pastureland, during a visit to the Xilingol League of the Inner Mongolia Autonomous Region to inspect a pilot program to contract out grasslands. (Photograph by Ma Zhancheng, Xinhua News Agency)

work hard to improve pastures, develop high-quality breeds of livestock, and create a virtuous cycle in which the eco-environment of the grasslands improves even as animal husbandry develops and herders' incomes increase. You must strengthen the construction of various types of complementary facilities, particularly those for quarantines and inspections. You must create a disease-free zone. This will truly require a great deal of effort, and I am very much in favor of strengthening construction in this area.

You should talk to the departments concerned about how to resolve specific problems. If you need only RMB 20 million of support from the central fiscal authorities, that will be no problem. The problem is that if we permit you to develop a disease-free zone, you must really achieve that; otherwise you will lose your international reputation. Just now you asked if the animal husbandry tax could be waived and if you could get some support from the central authorities through fiscal transfers. I'm inclined to approve, but we have to study the actual way to do this. Please discuss it with the departments concerned—I think this is something that can be considered. After all, we should give the herders some support, both fiscal and material, so that they can implement the policy of halting herding and reverting the grasslands. Otherwise, without [concrete] measures, this would all be empty talk. The central fiscal authorities should give as much support as possible, and the local fiscal authorities must also make some effort in this regard.

I very much support improving the eco-environment and playing to the strengths of the grasslands—I place great hope in these endeavors. We must have comprehensive plans and reasonable arrangements that highlight key issues, focus on actual results, and are carried out with perseverance. We must be resolved to see these vast grasslands once again turn lush and green and to see verdant landscapes on our northern borders.

49

A Conversation with Former U.S. Secretary of State Henry A. Kissinger[1]

April 14, 2002

ZRJ: I'm delighted to be able to meet with Dr. Kissinger, Mrs. Nancy Kissinger, and Ambassador [Stapleton] Roy today. I just returned from Hainan yesterday. This year is the 30th anniversary of President [Richard] Nixon's visit to China and the Sino-American "Shanghai Communiqué." I think this day is not only an important one for relations between China and the United States; it's also an important one for Dr. Kissinger. Dr. Kissinger, you've had a very good relationship with three generations of New China's leadership. There are no longer many leaders like you in the world today, so I wanted to be sure to get back from Hainan to share a meal with you.

HAK: I'm very sorry I wasn't able to go to Hainan. I know you've played a very important role over the past 10 years, and I believe the relationship between our two countries is the key to peace and stability in the Asia-Pacific region.

ZRJ: You've made outstanding contributions to Sino-American relations, and no way of welcoming you would be too much. Of course we can't welcome you with a military review, but we can welcome you with genuine friendship.

HAK: If you were to have a military review, you would ruin me in Washington.

ZRJ: You've dealt with three generations of our leaders. I'm of a later generation, but I've also had dealings with you for a long time now and can be considered an old friend. In my dealings with you, I've always gotten very well-meant and friendly help, for which I'm very grateful. In particular, I received a lot of help from you during my visit to the United States in 1999, and I thank you for that. At a time when Sino-American relations suddenly turn hot and cold, we especially need your help.

---

1. This conversation took place at the Great Hall of the People in Beijing, where Zhu Rongji met with Henry Kissinger and hosted a lunch in his honor. Kissinger had come to China to participate in activities commemorating the 30th anniversary of the Shanghai Communiqué.

Meeting with former U.S. Secretary of State Henry Kissinger at the Great
Hall of the People, Beijing, on April 14, 2002. (Photograph by
Hu Haixin, Xinhua News Agency)

HAK: I appreciate the hospitality you've shown me during my many visits to China and the importance you attach to discussions with me. All the people who mentioned you during talks with me expressed admiration for your talent, courtesy, and dedication to your work. In the current situation, relations between our countries have entered one cycle after another. Part of the problem is that each new administration must formulate a new foreign policy, and there may also sometimes be differences between how different departments implement foreign policy. However, the fundamental direction of U.S.-China relations is a positive one. All the Americans I've met hope that China will not do anything confrontational.

ZRJ: We're still not quite used to some of President [George W.] Bush's ways.

HAK: He comes from Texas in the central United States and thinks differently from New Yorkers. He relied on support from the conservative wing of the Republican Party to get elected. He is now transitioning from previous China policy and needs to reconcile the Chinese style with the Texan style. The Chinese style is more indirect while the Texan style is very direct.

ZRJ: So we should watch more Westerns.

HAK: That would help. The important thing is to find an appropriate style. After I return, I will convey my impressions of this China visit to Ms. [Condoleezza] Rice,[2] but the United States needs to understand the Chinese style.

ZRJ: At first, we also had some differences with Presidents [George H. W.] Bush and [Bill] Clinton, and we didn't get along so well, but later we had more contacts and began to understand each other. Relations became quite good, and friendship developed.

HAK: I believe this will also be the case with President Bush, but the Middle East question will interfere with everything.

ZRJ: How do you see the Middle East question? I read our embassy's report on your speech about the Middle East question.

HAK: My view is that we should make progress diplomatically, but we cannot let terrorists think that we are supporting them. Concessions are necessary for reaching any agreement, but they cannot be perceived as concessions to terrorism. Therefore we have to move carefully. As I see it, the withdrawal of Israeli troops from Lebanon two years ago made matters even worse. That withdrawal was done very abruptly; we can't let people think that Israel might now also abruptly withdraw its troops from Palestine. That is my view. As for the view of the U.S. government, it changes every few months. Sometimes it is similar to mine, and sometimes it's different.

ZRJ: Is that also the Texas style?

HAK: That is a sign of lack of experience. Palestine and Israel think about issues in different ways. Israel thinks in terms of law; the Arabic world is more romantic—they believe some methods are reliable, but in fact these are not reliable.

ZRJ: But there must be guarantees for [Yasser] Arafat's[3] safety; otherwise the entire Arab world will oppose the United States.

HAK: Personally, I feel it was unwise of the Israeli soldiers to rush into Arafat's official residence. The result was that it turned Arafat into a respected martyr even while he was alive. There must be absolute guarantees for his safety.

2. Condoleezza Rice, then National Security Adviser to the President of the United States.
3. Yasser Arafat, then President of Palestine and Chairman of the Palestinian National Authority.

Secretary of State [Colin] Powell will be meeting with Arafat today, and this will ensure Arafat's safety.

ZRJ: Our embassy says that you feel Secretary of Defense [Donald] Rumsfeld is very easy to get along with, but I feel that those people at the U.S. Department of Defense all side with Taiwan.

HAK: Many people do, but Rumsfeld sees farther, and everyone thinks very highly of him. My views aren't always the same as his. He still doesn't understand Chinese thinking. In the United States, critics of China all feel that the Chinese mainland is determined to have a showdown with Taiwan—they look at the Taiwan issue from a military viewpoint. The vast majority of people don't understand that China wishes to resolve the Taiwan issue through peaceful means unless Taiwan declares independence.

ZRJ: I feel that those in power in the United States don't understand China and hope more of them can come visit China.

HAK: I think it would be very good if Vice President [Dick] Cheney and Secretary Rumsfeld could visit China. If they were to visit China, the topics discussed should not be technical ones—they should be like the ones today.

ZRJ: I hope their visits can change their views to some extent. [Condoleezza] Rice came once, and I hope her view has changed.

HAK: Secretary Rice doesn't have any particular views about China, but it's always helpful for her to understand certain things.

50

ON VISITING THE FORMER
RESIDENCE OF HU XUEYAN[1]

May 5, 2002

At the former residence of Hu Xueyan,[2] I saw carved beams and embossed tiles, and clusters upon clusters of buildings. These were supreme examples of southern Chinese garden landscaping and the embodiment of Wu and Yue[3] cultures. Hu was as rich as any prince or noble and owned half the wealth in the land. There's an old saying, "Wealth does not last more than 3 generations." For all his guile, the wealth of this red-tasseled merchant did not even last 10 years. Pride and extravagance caused him to forget himself—should this not be a warning to us all?

Zhu Rongji

1. On May 5, 2002, Zhu Rongji, his wife, Lao An, and his daughter, Zhu Yanlai, visited the former residence of Hu Xueyan in Hangzhou, Zhejiang Province. (Translator's note: this piece was written in classical Chinese.)

2. Hu Xueyan (1823–85) was a native of Anhui Province who founded a money-changing shop in Hangzhou and handled finances for the local government. He then became responsible for logistics for the Hunan-based army of General Zuo Zongtang, and through this association, he amassed a fortune by engaging in money-changing, pawnbroking, and trading in herbal medicines, tea, and silk in many provinces. After General Zuo became Governor-General of Shaanxi and Gansu provinces, Hu Xueyan set up a procurement office for him in Shanghai to handle military pay and provisions, purchase arms, and raise funds. He was rewarded by the Qing court by being permitted to wear a red-tasseled hat, the mark of a high-ranking official during the Qing Dynasty, and became known as "the red-tasseled merchant." He went bankrupt in 1884 because of competition from foreign merchants and died the next year.

3. Translator's note: Wu and Yue were ancient kingdoms located in parts of present-day Jiangsu, Shanghai, Zhejiang, Anhui, and Jiangxi provinces.

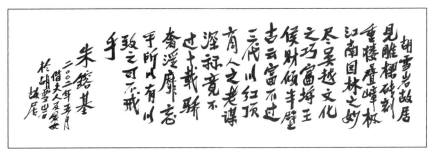

Manuscript of Zhu Rongji's note written after a visit to the former residence of Hu Xueyan.

51

A Conversation with an American Congressional Delegation[1]

May 30, 2002

ZRJ: I'm delighted to meet with both of you and your wives today, as well as with Vice President [Arnold] Wellman.[2] I hear that you went to Zunhua in Hebei Province, that you went to a village, donated to educational work there, and personally participated in manual labor. I'm very moved by that. Our Foreign Minister tells me that two department heads from the Foreign Ministry also went with you. If I had gone, I would certainly have done as well as you, because I worked on a farm for five or six years. I want to thank you on behalf of the farmers of Hebei—you've done a very good thing for them. On this visit you've gained some understanding of China's villages, as well as a better understanding of China. This is beneficial for fostering good relations between our two countries

I understand you visited the Great Wall there. That section of the Great Wall has never been visited by foreigners before. The roads are poor. I'm sorry—in some places, roads still haven't been built in villages. Over the past four to five years, roads have been built at all the city and county levels, but the task of building roads below the county level is still an enormously difficult one. I welcome you on your visit to China, and would like to first hear your thoughts.

Representative Jim Turner: On behalf of myself as well as Mr. and Mrs. [Spencer] Bachus and Mr. Wellman, I want to thank you for the warm hospitality and friendship that we have received in China. This trip to China was made possible by United Parcel Service (UPS). UPS donated US$100,000 to build a new primary school in Zunhua. It also donated a computer lab equipped with computers. In two days' time, we and 50 UPS employees built this computer lab together. This time we visited Beijing, and we also visited villages. The warmth and friendship of the Chinese people is unforgettable. The 50 UPS employees, the three Representatives, and their wives don't know much about architecture,

---

1. This is the main part of a conversation between Zhu Rongji and an American congressional delegation. It took place at the Hall of Purple Light at Zhongnanhai.
2. Arnold F. Wellman was then Vice President of UPS.

341

but completed the job in two days and got very good results. Chinese children are very smart. They're all studying English, and they also want to learn about computers and the Internet. They left a very deep impression on us.

Speaking of rural roads, I'm from a Texas farm myself, and there are dirt roads in my electoral district. There are gaps between cities and farms in America as well as in China. This time we were very glad to see both sides of China, the urban and the rural. I agree with you that we should work together to strengthen U.S.-China friendship. Mr. Wellman of UPS is a good-hearted person who wants to give back to China what he has gotten from China. Representative Bachus also said that from now on, if any Chinese go to Washington, he will give them a similarly warm reception.

Representative Spencer Bachus: Mr. Premier, I've been learning about China ever since I was very young. China has a history of several thousand years, while America has a history of only several hundred years. What both countries have in common is that they love peace and don't like war. The area around the section of the Great Wall that we visited was invaded by the Japanese during World War II. In American history, there were also foreigners who wanted to take our land and who attacked us. Like China, America has no designs on other people's territory, and it's most appropriate that our two countries become partners. I hope that the peace-loving people of both countries can work together for world peace. I saw Chinese students in the Zunhua school. I myself have five children. Whether or not all children can have a beautiful future will depend on how our countries get along, whether we are friends or enemies. We always talk about the future of children and young people, but in fact their futures depend on us. I assure you that as a member of Congress and as a friend of President [George W.] Bush, I would like to build better relations with my peace-loving Chinese brothers and sisters and make a contribution to world peace. You're a person who is very considerate to others, as could be seen in the way you posed with us individually for pictures. Chinese children are very friendly, and the mayor of Zunhua is a very fine person. After meeting you today, I've increasingly realized that I've always liked Chinese people and would like to become friends with Chinese people, and even more so I hope America can become a good friend of China.

AFW: Mr. Premier, I'm very pleased to have this opportunity to say a few words. Our company doesn't do any business in Hebei, but we're aware of the needs there. I went to Hebei after the Asia-Pacific Economic Cooperation (APEC) meeting in Shanghai last October. I visited several places and went to a Manchu village and a Han village. Finally we decided to donate to both villages. Giving money isn't hard—what's hard is to visit personally. This period is a critical time for members of Congress because their colleagues at home are participating in Memorial Day activities, and they also have to prepare for elections. They've brought their wives with them. Chairman Mao said, "Women hold up half the sky." The women in our delegation took care of half the project.

We also experienced a special moment this time. The Zunhua school organized an essay-writing contest. Each child wrote an essay on the topic of "What the New School Means to Them." A 6-year-old girl in the Han village who had never seen a computer read her essay out loud in front of everyone. She read it really well, and it was filled with feeling. This made a very deep impression on us. I think my 12-year-old can't do what she did.

China has many needs and so does the United States. We hope to help China meet some of its needs. This time, we only took a small step forward. There's a Chinese expression, "A journey of a thousand miles begins with a single step." We've already taken the first step, and what we've learned from China is much more than what we've given.

ZRJ: This small step of yours is something I had not heard about, and you've told a very touching story. You say you've done something small, but I feel it's a very meaningful thing. May I ask the two ladies to also share their thoughts?

Linda Bachus: Thank you so much for giving me this opportunity—I'm very touched. I don't know where to begin in describing the past few days. In America, I work as a teacher. I'm very honored to be able to visit your country—the children here are so beautiful, charming, and adorable. As these gentlemen said just now, we've gotten something very precious on this trip—we now know what kind of people we are. Now I'm even more determined to work to promote friendly relations with the Chinese people.

Virginia Turner: Premier Zhu, thank you for receiving us this morning. This trip to China has been one of the most memorable experiences in my life. As these gentlemen just said, we lived in the school for two days with the Chinese children, and this is something we will always treasure. We helped them build a computer lab, and I look forward to getting e-mails from our friends in Zunhua after I return to America.

My husband and I are from Texas, and we've always felt that Texas is the biggest and the best in the world. Now that I've come to China, I've discovered that it's China that is the biggest and the best. Chinese and Americans speak different languages and have different appearances, but our hearts are the same.

ZRJ: As Mr. Turner said, I'm very pleased to meet with American members of Congress. Not long ago, I met with 20 Senators and Representatives. We were originally scheduled to talk for an hour, but wound up talking for two hours and kept a leader from Turkey waiting for an hour. If I added up all the Senators and Representatives I've met, it would be half of Congress.

JT: Wonderful. It's very important that they come have a look at China.

ZRJ: Why do I always meet with American members of Congress whenever possible? Because I feel that the vast majority of bills directed toward China in both Houses are unfriendly, including the recently passed "National Defense Authorization Act for 2003," which is also unfriendly. I've always had very good talks when meeting with American members of Congress, and we're all friends. There are no fundamental conflicts of interest between our two countries, and we can become friends. Contradictions arise mainly because of a lack of mutual understanding. In other words, some American members of Congress don't understand China. In order to promote mutual understanding, I hope they will come to China and have a look. Each time you come, most of the misunderstandings between China and the United States can be dispelled. I think UPS has done a fine thing in inviting Representatives Bachus and Turner to come here. I hope you'll continue to work at it and invite all members of Congress here. There are no differences between us that cannot be resolved.

It's been 30 years since Sino-American relations were normalized. During these 30 years, bilateral relations have sometimes been very good, and sometimes not so good. On the whole, these relations have stayed friendly. The basic issue is Taiwan—there is no issue more sensitive than this one. Actually, I've told all the members of Congress I've met with that the reunification of Taiwan with the mainland would be good for both Taiwan and the United States, and there is no downside.

First, after Taiwan and the mainland are reunified, existing institutions [in Taiwan] will not change and cannot change. Taiwan can have its own armed forces, and we would not change Taiwan's present institutions, nor do we have the means to do so. Second, Taiwan has neither resources nor markets. To further develop, it must rely on the mainland's resources and markets. Let me tell you something that you may not know. In its trade with Taiwan, the mainland runs a deficit. Last year the mainland's deficit was US$25 billion. Without the mainland's support, Taiwan could not have developed like this. Frankly speaking, [what we want from] reunification is the wording "One China"—nothing else changes. But we must have this wording; otherwise our people won't agree to it. We are determined not to allow "Taiwan independence."

In coming to China, you and your wives have seen how the Chinese people are working to develop their economy and change their poverty-stricken condition, how they yearn for peaceful lives. Cooperation between China and the United

Meeting with an American congressional delegation at the Hall of Purple Light in Zhongnanhai, Beijing, on May 30, 2002: Vice Foreign Minister Li Zhaoxing (second from left), UPS Vice President Arnold Wellman (third from left), Mrs. Linda Bachus (fourth from left), Rep. Spencer Bachus (fifth from left), Rep. Jim Turner (seventh from left); Mrs. Virginia Turner (eighth from left), Chen Haosu, President of the Chinese People's Association for Friendship with Foreign Countries (ninth from left); Li Xiaolin, Vice President of the Chinese People's Association for Friendship with Foreign Countries (tenth from left).

States, and between China and the world, is good for both sides as well as for world peace. We hope for reunification and will not use force against the people of Taiwan. Taiwan's existing institutions will not change after reunification. I hope that the members of Congress will understand this and not give Taiwan misinformation that causes it to go further down the path of "Taiwan independence."

You're still young—perhaps you were born around 1946 or 1947? I was born in 1928. World War II had ended by the time you were born. I spent my childhood and my youth drifting, always on the move. We've had different experiences. You don't want war, and I want war even less. We don't want to use force; we want to use peaceful means to reunify with Taiwan. We're very sure that peaceful reunification is possible provided that the United States doesn't give Taiwan misinformation. Why not do that? They could get markets and dollars, and they wouldn't need to change anything. I don't want to impose my views on you—I just hope you can understand our position.

I know the gentleman from UPS has a question regarding express mail services. After the 9/11 attacks, we found many instances in China of anthrax spores being sent through the mail. In order to strengthen antiterrorism controls, we promulgated new management rules for express mail services that require foreign enterprises to get approvals from the responsible Chinese departments before starting up mail services. I know that after these rules were announced,

UPS and Fedex had objections about the content, methods, and transparency of the law, and they were strongly dissatisfied. I want to ask you to be understanding of China's situation. We're forced to do so by circumstances and have no choice. Of course we will give full consideration to your views. You can talk with the Ministry of Foreign Trade and Economic Cooperation and the Ministry of Information Industries, and ask them to make some additions. We will protect fair competition for foreign enterprises in China. Personally, I'm very willing to help you, because you've helped us. You've done a fine thing in inviting members of Congress to come to China. Just for that alone, I myself would like to give you a license.

JT: I'd like to say a few words. America has always insisted on One China, and I believe that both the American government and Congress support the peaceful reunification of China. But the Taiwanese are very skillful in lobbying the U.S. Congress.

ZRJ: We're far less skillful than they are.

AFW: The best lobbyist is Chinese Vice Foreign Minister Li Zhaoxing.

JT: Sometimes Taiwanese discuss their views with us—those are just views. We will also offer some responses—those are also just responses. We hope that the Chinese mainland and the other side of the Strait will maintain good relations. We have indeed given very confusing signals to Taiwan, but the position of the American government is that there is One China.

I've been in Congress for many years, and the thing I remember most clearly is casting a vote to support giving China permanent normal trading status, opening the door to China's accession to the World Trade Organization. As a member of the House Armed Services Committee, I cast that vote because I believe that the world's peace, stability, and prosperity depend on the cooperation and development of friendly relations between America and China. You understand that under our government framework, each member of Congress can freely express his or her own views. Sometimes the views of Congress aren't the same as those of the President, and the media sometimes takes things out of context. You may have heard conflicting statements. America will abide by its commitment to One China. Mainlanders and Taiwanese are all Chinese, and their economic ties are growing very quickly. We should stand on the right side and understand the meaning of One China. What the Chinese government is doing in Hong Kong is a very good example. We're willing to make a contribution to the peaceful reunification of China.

ZRJ: Have you been to Hong Kong?

JT: No, but I'd very much like to go.

SB: There's only one way to solve the Taiwan problem, and that is peaceful reunification and One China—that's the correct way, and it's the basis for resolving the problem. As Representative Turner just said, in America, members of Congress aren't responsible for making foreign policy; the President is responsible for making foreign policy. The President represents the country while we only speak for ourselves. For the past 50 years, there have been misunderstandings, fears, and prejudices between us. Once these things occur, they're very hard to dispel. [Nikita] Khrushchev once said he would bury America, and America was afraid of the Soviet Union's military power. Because we felt that China was an ally of the Soviet Union, we were also afraid of China. Now that Khrushchev has passed away, and Russia doesn't want to bury America, there's been a 180-degree turn in America's policy toward Russia. We should do likewise with China.

Today you spoke about China's good hopes for peaceful reunification. I think that was very appropriate and hope that China will be peacefully reunited as soon as possible. The American people want to develop friendly relations with the Chinese people and want to work with the Chinese toward peaceful reunification. Sometimes our government's words are at odds with its actions. Our policy is to have One China, but sometimes our actions deviate from this. I have publicly questioned in Congress whether the Taiwan question should be decided by us. Taiwan is part of China, and that should be decided by the Chinese people themselves. Right now we lack capable, open-minded, sincere, and efficient people like you to deliver messages to America. You have the ability to influence our policy. You have very strong communication skills and would certainly win respect in America.

ZRJ: I wish you a successful visit in China, and welcome you to come again. I hope next time there won't be just three members of Congress. More should come, and 30 would be best. Hong Kong, which Representative Turner mentioned just now, is a very good example. After Hong Kong's return, the central government has not interfered. Every day, some newspapers in Hong Kong are lambasting China's leaders even more harshly than the American media lambasts your leaders. That shows that we're not putting any pressure on Hong Kong.

52

PUT "ACCURACY" FOREMOST
IN STATISTICAL WORK[1]

October 28, 2002

The National Bureau of Statistics recently celebrated its 50th anniversary. It so happens that in 1952 I was transferred from northeastern China to the State Planning Commission. At the time, the State Planning Commission and the National Bureau of Statistics were both located in Beiheyan. Xue Muqiao was then the Director of the National Bureau of Statistics as well as Vice Chairman of the State Planning Commission; the Deputy Director of the Bureau was Wang Sihua, who later became Director. I was working in the General Affairs Bureau of the State Planning Commission, and many of the people there are no longer with us today. Our study of Soviet statistical methods then went much deeper than our studies of statistical methods today. As soon as we started working, we practiced using forms, studying them one at a time.

I once said that when you do economic work in China, you should not put too much trust in figures. I said this not to deny [the importance of] statistics, but to emphasize how hard it really is to guarantee the accuracy of statistical figures. Inaccuracies in level upon level of figures are not the fault of a single person. That's why, under certain circumstances, we have no choice but to combine statistics with estimations—if we were to base decisions solely on statistics, we would likely make mistakes. For someone doing economic work, it's extremely important to assess the accuracy of statistics through information gathered from all sides: from social and economic research and your own understanding of circumstances. You also have to understand how the numbers were derived and computed.

At present, it is indeed the case that quite a few people haven't followed these steps. I'm quite familiar with statistical methods used in the past but haven't really studied the methods currently in use; however, I feel this is really worth looking into. It's impossible to be perfect in any kind of work, or for [figures] to completely reflect reality. If we understand how statistics are created, how many

---

1. During an inspection tour of the National Bureau of Statistics, Zhu Rongji made these remarks at a discussion with officials from the Bureau's subdepartmental level and above, and with principal leading members of publicly supported institutions directly under the Bureau.

Inspecting work at the National Bureau of Statistics and inscribing the words "Do not falsify figures" on October 28, 2002.

processes they undergo, and what methods of calculation are used, then we can analyze them using our experience and various types of information, and we can judge their reliability relatively accurately, which would help us formulate correct policies.

Statistical work is an important basis for our economic decisionmaking, or rather, it is the primary basis, although we cannot limit ourselves to it alone and must also conduct many studies, especially of a practical nature. It's impossible to formulate correct economic policies if we don't understand the situation, but some things are truly hard to grasp. That's why we say that statistics are very important both for judging economic trends and for making economic decisions.

You said just now that in 1998 I had proposed the terms "quick, precise, and accurate" to describe the requirements for statistical work, but now it would seem that this way of putting it isn't quite right—perhaps I hadn't given it enough thought on the spur of the moment. "Accurate" should be foremost. Although it's very hard for statistics to be absolutely accurate or even relatively accurate, you must still try your best to ensure their accuracy. What use are they if they're not accurate? The most important thing is to try your best to aim for accuracy, which after all is the whole purpose of statistics; otherwise they would be deceiving others. Today I wrote a four-character inscription for the National Bureau of Statistics: "Do not falsify figures." When we suffered the huge setback during the "Great Leap Forward" of 1958, wasn't it because we believed those inexplicable figures?

Trying to be a bit "quicker" should only be in second place. Putting "quick" first will not work. It's useless to be quick but inaccurate—in fact, that would harm others. There's a system of annual and monthly statistical reports that stipulate when various types of statistical figures must be produced, but in order to meet the needs of macroeconomic decisionmaking, they should come out as soon as possible. Only this way can we be sure decisions will be timely and firm and can we use them effectively; otherwise they will come too late.

Looking back at the economic overheating of 1993, [we can see] it took shape very rapidly. It started in 1992 and was already out of control by January 1993. I remember very clearly that on January 1, 1993, Jiang Zemin asked the Party secretaries and governors from 18 provinces to come to Beijing in groups for discussions. What did they discuss? He told them that the printing of money couldn't keep up and asked them to issue no more money before the Spring Festival under any circumstances. If large quantities of money were to be issued at the start of 1993, inflation would become increasingly serious after the Spring Festival. Economic overheating takes shape very quickly, and its first jolts strike the banking system. If we had gotten an accurate indication of this problem early on, we would have been able to make timely decisions, and things might not have gotten out of hand. Likewise, I recently pointed out that there's some overheating in the property sector. If we don't pay attention to halting it, it will develop very quickly. Everyone who lived through the "Great Leap Forward" of 1958 and the three difficult years had this experience and understands this. The statistics of that time were also reported by the National Bureau of Statistics.

During this National Day, I saw a statistic of yours in Guangzhou indicating that 60% of the increase in fixed asset investments in Guangdong Province for the first nine months of this year comes from real estate. Isn't that heated enough? If these houses were sold for people to live in, the risk would still be relatively small: even if real estate prices were to collapse in the future, only the individual [buyer] would lose, but he would still be living in the housing. In fact, 20–30% of bank loans go to real estate developers who only put up high-end buildings—this practice fuels great risk. Many developers have no capital of their own, so if real estate prices were to collapse, they might not repay this money or have the ability to do so. We already learned this lesson in 1993. To this day, Hainan has yet to clear up all its "rotten tail" buildings[2]—I call it "a body covered with scars."

At present basic construction is growing very quickly and is again being driven mainly by real estate so there's a bit of overheating there, which will quickly rise higher if we don't pay attention it. Steel production this year has

2. Translator's note: a building that is started but not completed.

reached 180 million tons, more than the total of Japan and the United States, the world's two largest steel producers. This has correspondingly fueled rapid inflation in industries that manufacture construction material and equipment. You only have to watch the news on TV to realize this. Some previously unheard-of steel factories are increasing their scale of production one after the other. Colleagues! Did you live through the "Great Steel Refining" of 1958? At that time, we "took steel to be the key link," and this pulled all the equipment-making industries along with it. Now, over 60% of our 180 million tons of steel is used for construction, and what's more, much of it is substandard. What good can come of going on like this?

As I told the leaders of Guangdong Province and Shenzhen Municipality, the whole of Shenzhen except for its mountains is entirely built up, and now it's asking Huizhou to carve out several hundred more square kilometers for it. What for? To put up more buildings. What good will that do for the national economy? It doesn't need any more "impetus." Guangdong can't keep going on like this. Internally, you should talk about "putting on the brakes," not allocating any more land and not allocating away all farmland; externally, you should talk about strictly tightening controls. They entirely agreed with my view.

The task now is to adjust industrial structure, to develop hi-tech industries and the tertiary sector. We can't be like rats that only know how to bore holes— surely the Chinese people don't only know how to put up buildings? Building from morning to night with construction sites everywhere—how can this be? In the past, I couldn't believe that we really produced over 100 million tons of steel—to whom could they sell it? Now I'm a believer, especially after the China International Engineering Consulting Cooperation completed a study showing that steel production had actually reached 180 million tons. We also had to import 25 million tons, for a total consumption of over 200 million tons. Is our national strength so great?

If we go on like this, we will definitely be unable to restructure our industries. If we again "take steel to be the key link" as we did in 1958 and drive up the growth of all the equipment-making industries, the scale will become very large, and once it collapses, tens of millions of people will become unemployed or be laid off. I'm not bluffing. CCTV's *Topics in Focus* program has demonstrated but a small part of the problem, which in fact is much greater. Some real estate developers care about nothing but profits: they cut corners in materials and workmanship, misrepresent [construction] areas, fail to meet promised conditions, and don't pay workers' wages on time. The situation is very serious, and there's already no way to oversee it. In some places government agencies are colluding with developers, and this is outright corruption.

We must think about such consequences, which is why I hope the National Bureau of Statistics can use the information I've talked about, follow up on it promptly, conduct in-depth studies, and provide some basis for decisionmaking by the central authorities. In matters like these, I think you should work more quickly. As for annual and monthly reports, you should publish these on time; but there's no way to speed them up. For matters beyond institutional requirements, matters that can provide information and a basis for central decision-making, you should try to provide these as soon as possible.

The third [requirement of statistical work] is to be "precise," which simply means doing more detailed and more precise statistical work. No matter how you put it, statistical work is very important. You deal with information all day long and must report information accurately and quickly. If you are good at capturing information and analyzing it in depth, if you are good at grasping and discovering the significance of information and relaying this in a timely way to the central authorities, then that is your great skill, and you will be making a major contribution to the development of the national economy.

Statistical work has a lot of room for talent; you should recruit and retain talented people. Of course we can't afford salaries as high as those offered by foreign-invested enterprises. Although salaries at these enterprises are very high, perhaps several times to several dozen times your salary levels, you must also see that first, that sort of work is very demanding, and not every person can get used to it; second, the risk is also higher, and staff might be laid off at any time; and third, foreign-invested enterprises can't compare with government agencies when it comes to the sense of achievement and pride you can get from working there. That's why, provided we create an environment that can attract and retain talent and allow people to show what they can do, I think we will still be able to attract more talent with relatively lower wages.

The key is still the environment. Our leaders should create an environment in which people can feel happy in their work, can be of one mind and one heart, can have shared ideals, can work together smoothly, and thus can feel they are being treated fairly, rather than having to rely on relationships and handing out favors to get promotions.

I hope that under the leadership of the Party Central Committee and the State Council, the National Bureau of Statistics will continue to work hard, build on its past achievements in further developing its work, attract more talent, raise the levels of its own technical methods and equipment, and at the same time undertake some systemic reforms in order to move the work of national statistics up to a new level. That way I, too, will feel very honored, because I grew up together with the National Bureau of Statistics.

53

Hong Kong Has a Bright Future[1]

November 19, 2002

I want to thank Chief Executive Tung [Chee-hua],[2] the government of the Hong Kong Special Administrative Region (SAR), and our friends here from all circles for your great friendship and for hosting such a grand dinner to welcome me and the members of my delegation. Allow me to take this opportunity to offer our genuine regards and best wishes to our Hong Kong compatriots! I also want to express our deep admiration and heartfelt thanks to all the friends and colleagues here for the great efforts you have made and for your outstanding contributions to the work of reenergizing Hong Kong.

The Chinese Communist Party just held its 16th National Congress and elected its new collective central leadership with Hu Jintao as General Secretary. I believe that the new Central Committee and its leadership team will uphold Marxism, Mao Zedong Thought, and Deng Xiaoping Theory and, in accordance with the demands of the important thought of the "Three Represents,"[3] will comprehensively build a modestly prosperous society, refine the socialist market economic system, and achieve even more notable results! I also believe that the Party Central Committee and the State Council will continue to maintain the policies of "one country, two systems," letting Hong Kong exercise a high degree of autonomy under [the principle of] "Hong Kong run by Hong Kong people." We will also continue to do our utmost and to use all resources and methods at our disposal to promote Hong Kong's prosperity and stability.

Hong Kong is currently encountering some difficulties, but we have always believed that they are mainly the result of historical factors. For the past several decades, our Hong Kong compatriots have created a prosperous and magnificent

1. On November 18–20, 2002, Zhu Rongji traveled to Hong Kong to attend the 16th annual meeting of the International Federation of Accountants. He made these remarks at a welcoming dinner hosted by the government of the Hong Kong Special Administrative Region.

2. Tung Chee-hua, then Chief Executive of the Hong Kong SAR.

3. The "Three Represents" is an important concept propounded by Jiang Zemin in 2000. It means that the Chinese Communist Party must always represent the developmental needs of China's advanced productive forces, the orientation of advanced Chinese culture, and the fundamental interests of the vast majority of China's people.

Speaking on November 19, 2002, at a welcoming dinner hosted by the government of the Hong Kong Special Administrative Region.

society through their spirit of hard-working entrepreneurship. However, bubbles have built up amid the prosperity, and some concerns lay hidden within the joys of success. Once the Asian financial crisis was added to these, structural contradictions came to light. These difficulties absolutely did not form over the course of a day or two, or even a year or two. However, I believe that under the leadership of Tung Chee-hua and the SAR government, you will certainly be able to overcome them.

You might want to ask, "As Premier of the State Council, what good policies for governing Hong Kong can you propose?" Let me be very frank: I am not familiar with Hong Kong, but I can tell you this story. In 1998, when American Vice President [Albert] Gore met with me, he said, "I hear you really worship Mr. [Alan] Greenspan."[4] Not very pleased when I heard that, I replied, "I greatly

4. Alan Greenspan was then Chairman of the U.S. Federal Reserve Board.

respect Mr. Greenspan and want to learn from him. He's doing a very good job in the United States, but if he came to China, he might not necessarily do better than me." I've been doing economic work for over 50 years and can detect every pulse and twitch in the economy of China's heartland, but my knowledge of Hong Kong is merely limited to the two, sometimes three Hong Kong newspapers I read every day—these are far from enough. I've never lived in Hong Kong—could I propose a good policy for governing Hong Kong on the basis of what I have read in these two or three papers every day? That would be quackery.

But I am entirely sure of one thing, namely that the strength and methods needed for Hong Kong to overcome its current difficulties exist within Hong Kong's systems. This is because Hong Kong has a very open economic system, a fairly complete legal system, a rather efficient civil service, and most especially a large number of talented enterprise managers; it has extensive ties around the world and is a financial, trade, and service center serving both the world and Asia. Hong Kong has not lost its advantages. Its competitiveness and its abilities remain intact, and it is entirely able to overcome its current difficulties relying on its own strength.

This perception of mine is rooted in analysis. Looking around the world, we "have yet to see many celebrating, but have seen quite a few worrying." Japan has already been economically stagnant for many years. Its structural contradictions won't be easily resolved, and so far we've seen no signs of recovery. This November, I attended the "10 + 3" meeting[5] in Cambodia. After the meeting between the leaders of China, Japan, and [the Republic of] Korea, I said to Japanese Prime Minister Koizumi Junichiro, "I fully support your reforms. The methods you're using are ones we also used in the aftermath of the 1998 Asian financial crisis, and they were also used by your two predecessors. However, in implementing this proactive fiscal policy and stable monetary policy, you have not been as consistent, as resolute, and as effective as we have been. If I were in your position today, I would do what you're doing, and I wish you success." That's why these difficulties are not exclusive to any one party.

Now look at Europe. Its economy is relatively dynamic, but its growth rate is also very low, and its unemployment rate is very high. Didn't we say that Hong Kong's unemployment rate is high? But the average unemployment rate in the EU countries is 11%—it's between 8.7% and 8.9% in Germany and France. According to the latest figures, it's already gone down to 7.2% in Hong Kong, so compared with the European Union, you're "left in their dust!"

These past two days I've been having discussions with Chief Executive Tung. He is terribly worried about Hong Kong's fiscal deficit and has thought

5. The meeting of leaders of the 10 countries of the Association of Southeast Asian Nations, China, Japan, and the Republic of Korea.

exhaustively about how to resolve it. I said, "Didn't you have a deficit of HKD 60 billion to 70 billion last year? The number for this year will probably be about the same. But don't you have fiscal reserves of more than HKD 270 billion?" I then said, "For a 'Deficit Chief Executive,' there's still a great gap between you and me, the 'Deficit Premier.' Our deficit last year was RMB 259.8 billion and it will be 309.8 billion this year. We have cumulatively issued RMB 2.58 trillion of Treasury bonds so you're far behind us." On the other hand, compared with the United States, I'm still "left in their dust!" I think the U.S. deficit will continue to grow because right now America is concentrating entirely on "antiterrorism." I think its economy won't be able to recover right away, and its deficit will still grow.

As I told Chief Executive Tung, "With the deficit at HKD 70 billion, you can still hang in there for at least three years without incurring a net deficit because you have fiscal reserves. Economic recovery will depend on adjusting the industrial structure, which won't be easy and will require a cushion of time. Even if you use up all your fiscal reserves after three years, you can go to China's interior to issue 50-year long-term Hong Kong bonds, and I'll be the first to buy! I believe the people in the interior will join me in buying because they have confidence in Hong Kong! Hong Kong is one of China's most lustrous pearls—it has hope, and it has a future. What is there to be afraid of?"

However, I think that Chief Executive Tung is entirely correct to be worried and is behaving very responsibly. We must not make light of a fiscal deficit. I also don't think Hong Kong's difficulties have bottomed out. Compatriots and colleagues, they haven't bottomed out! You must be mentally prepared. Nor do I think we can easily draw up a timetable for solving Hong Kong's economic problems. If I were to do that, it would not just be quackery, it would be fraud. It's impossible! What is needed now is ample mental preparation, preparation for even more difficult times to come—you will have to transform yourselves yet once more!

But there is one thing I am fully confident about: Hong Kong can overcome these difficulties and can reclaim its former glory. I place my hopes in the 6 million people of our Hong Kong, particularly in our younger generation—our Hong Kong university students and those lovable primary and secondary school students who welcomed me at the airport yesterday. Hope rests with them. I hope that all the people of Hong Kong will be fully prepared mentally, prepared to show the same spirit as their forebears, and to transform themselves once more.

Hong Kong's future is bright, and we have always been proud of Hong Kong. I cannot believe that it can't be well run. If Hong Kong is not run well, the responsibility will not only be yours—we, too, will bear responsibility. If it were to return to our homeland and then be ruined at our hands, wouldn't that be a "crime against our people?" It won't happen.

I read a report saying that not long ago, Anthony Leung[6] either sang or recited the lyrics to "Under Lion Rock"[7]—I forget which. I've never watched this TV drama, and I certainly don't know how to sing this song. But I looked up the lyrics—the melody was by Koo Ka-fai, the lyrics by Wong Jim, and it was sung by Roman Tam, who was still alive when Anthony Leung recited those lyrics. He [Roman Tam] recently passed away, but I believe that the contributions he made to Hong Kong will be forever etched in the hearts of its people.

I was very touched after reading the lyrics to this song, and I am sure that those veterans here who helped build up Hong Kong feel this even more strongly, because every word of this song is filled with true feeling, and such true feelings will forever shine brightly. Let me now recite these lyrics so that we may urge each other forward for the sake of Hong Kong's future.

Since we are on the same boat,
Then, under Lion Rock, we must help each other,
Set aside our differences and seek each other's company,
Put away our disagreements
And pursue the same ideals.
When those in the same boat are sworn to each other,
There is nothing they will fear.
They can go together to the ends of the earth,
Holding hands as they flatten obstacles.
Together, all of us
Through our strenuous efforts
Will write those
Immortal lines about Hong Kong.

I love Hong Kong! Thank you!

6. Anthony Leung Kam-chung was then Financial Secretary of the Hong Kong SAR.
7. Translator's note: Lion Rock is an iconic site in Hong Kong that to local residents is a symbol of the spirit of Hong Kong's people.

54

SPEECH AT THE 2002 CENTRAL CONFERENCE ON ECONOMIC WORK[1]

December 9, 2002

This meeting has great significance for implementing the spirit of the 16th National Party Congress and for properly handling next year's economic work. I entirely agree with the speech by Hu Jintao just now in which he analyzed the domestic and international situations and laid out the overall expectations and main tasks for next year's economic work. We hope that all locales and all departments will implement these in earnest. Now, proceeding from the spirit of the Central Committee's discussions, I'd like to make a few points about the state of the economy this year and the overall arrangements for next year's economic work.

1. How to View This Year's Overall Economic Performance

The economy this year was in very good shape. With the growth rate above 8% almost everywhere except in a few areas where the economy is lagging, we can exceed the projected rate of about 7% and may even move past 8%. It's fair to say that this is one of the higher rates of the past few years. Performance was also quite good, particularly with the increase in profits at state-owned enterprises. We expect fiscal revenues to grow by about RMB 160 billion over last year. Import-export trade will increase by 18%, while exports alone will rise by more than 20%. Forex reserves already reached US$274.6 billion by the end of November and are expected to exceed US$280 billion by the end of the year, an increase of US$62.4 billion over the beginning of the year. We estimate that

---

1. Zhu Rongji delivered this speech at the conference on economic work convened by the Party Central Committee and State Council in Beijing on December 9–10, 2002. Participants included the principal Party and government leaders from the various provinces, autonomous regions, centrally administered municipalities, cities separately listed in national plans, and the Xinjiang Construction Corps; the principal members of the relevant departments of the Party Central Committee, State Council, and related units; and leading members of the four general departments of the People's Liberation Army and the headquarters of the People's Armed Police.

actual foreign investment this year will top US$50 billion, which is 20% higher than last year. The situation is indeed heartening.

Some have asked whether the central conference on economic work last year was too pessimistic in its assessment of world economic trends at that time. Now we feel that wasn't the case. I'd like to explain a little about this issue.

Last year's assessments of the global and Chinese economic trends were actually correct and in line with the facts. At the global level, the present economic situation is even worse than the central conference had projected, which was global growth of 2.5% from October to November of last year, dropping to 2.4% by January of this year. In fact, it didn't even reach 2.4% and is now between 1.5% and 2.4%. Although the American, Japanese, and European economies were still performing decently even during the Asian financial crisis, they are now in a swoon, and the global economy has entered a downturn. The Japanese growth rate may drop to just above zero or even suffer negative growth.

All in all, events have shown that the central authorities' estimates were not overblown, and that this year's world economic situation is indeed more serious than it was even during the Asian financial crisis. Moreover, we still see no signs of a turnaround and expect further challenges next year—you must all be aware of this.

From this one can see that it truly wasn't easy for us to achieve the results that we did. We took over other people's markets during a global downturn. Why were we able to do so? It was mainly because the Party Central Committee was farsighted, fully anticipated the difficulties surrounding global economic trends, and took decisive countermeasures in a timely way. Let me be specific.

First, the Drive from Investments Was Brought into Play at an Early Point. We started paying attention to investments as soon as the year began, and the State Planning Commission focused on it very intently. Thus in the first quarter, the bulk of projects funded by Treasury bonds were already assigned. This was earlier than in any previous year and gave a timely push to the entire national economy. It is a very important factor, as can be seen in the case of expressways, for example. In 1989 there were only 200 kilometers of expressways nationwide. By 1997 the figure was 4,700 kilometers, and by the end of this year it will have reached 24,000 kilometers because the total investment of the past four years is greater than the cumulative total of the several decades since the founding of New China.

A Second Drive Came out of Consumption Demand. Another timely assumption was that an investment drive alone would not suffice, so last year we twice increased salaries in government agencies and publicly supported institutions

Hu Jintao, Zhu Rongji, Li Lanqing, Wu Bangguo, Wen Jiabao, Jia Qinglin, Zeng Qinghong, Huang Ju, Wu Guanzheng, Li Changchun, and Luo Gan from the central leadership attending the Central Conference on Economic Work on December 9, 2002. (Photograph by Ma Zhancheng, Xinhua News Agency)

as well as the pensions of their retirees. And this year we paid extra attention to increasing the incomes of low-income groups; we also raised the pension standards for enterprise retirees, raised the levels of the "Two Assurances"[2] and doubled the levels of urban "minimal assurances" from the year before. The state made substantial investments in all the above areas, thereby greatly increasing the volume of social consumption. Therefore the drive from consumption demand also played an extremely important role.

A Third Drive Arose from Exports. The increase in exports truly exceeded my expectations. At this time last year, I said that if we didn't handle things well, we would have zero or negative growth because market demand had fallen. But in fact exports rose by 20% this year, even though this did not come about easily. We export mainly to the United States, Europe, and Japan, where the competition is very intense.

Policy factors lay behind this sizable increase in exports: that is, we rebated export taxes more vigorously—we refunded over RMB 110 billion in export taxes this year—and instituted various reforms of our foreign trade system that were also conducive to increasing exports. Another favorable factor was the 10% or more devaluation of the dollar against the yen and the euro. Since our renminbi closely follows the dollar, a dollar devaluation meant the renminbi also went down against the yen and the euro, which helped with exports.

Yet another factor was that after China's accession to the World Trade Organization (WTO), many countries removed trade and non-trade barriers and relaxed quotas. This allowed us to expand exports, which in turn helped boost

---

2. That is, assuring retirees that their pensions will be paid on time and in full, and assuring laid-off workers that funds to cover their basic living expenses will be paid on time and in full.

the production of many consumer goods and drove up our economic growth. Joining the WTO also had a downside, however: import duties were lowered by three percentage points, causing us to lose RMB 30 billion in fiscal revenues.

A Fourth Impetus to Growth Was a Corresponding Increase in Imports. Although this was two percentage points less than [the increase for] exports, it was still very rapid. With such large forex reserves as well as a trade surplus, we could of course import more. While we collected no taxes from exports and even had to provide rebates on them, we could collect taxes on imports, which formed an important pillar of our fiscal revenues. Although we lowered import duties by three percentage points, we were able to make up for the loss in tax revenues by relying on increased imports. That's why we deliberately imported extra goods in the first half of the year. These goods didn't affect production by domestic enterprises and weren't redundant imports.

For example, we could import large quantities of crude oil. We still don't have strategic reserves of crude oil and can now increase some strategic reserves. Unfortunately, we don't have any oil storage tanks and can only use PetroChina and Sinochem's existing tanks to import a little more. The State Planning Commission has already made arrangements for building oil storage tanks and increasing strategic oil reserves, but it seems that our long-term strategy should still be to cooperate with Russia and ship its oil and natural gas from Central Asia. This is very important for our energy strategy.

Because we increased imports this year, the reduction in fiscal revenues was less than the RMB 60 billion we had projected last year. In light of the commitment we made on joining the WTO, import duties will have to be lowered by an additional percentage point next year. Import duties are closely linked to fiscal revenues, so next year we should still pay attention to this issue. The boom in both imports and exports this year is related to some special measures we took, but they might not be effective every year.

One Aspect of the Global Economic Downturn Also Worked in Our Favor. After the 9/11 attacks, many people didn't dare go to the United States because of security concerns, and investments in the United States from Europe and the Middle East shrank greatly. Everyone was on edge and the atmosphere grew very tense. In a further blow to America's reputation, several of its large accounting firms were found to be falsifying their records. As a result, foreign investments in China increased. At least the investment environment in China is stable.

In addition, there have been great improvements in infrastructure, particularly in the coastal areas; things are cheap, and labor and management are high in quality but low in cost, so foreigners are willing to invest. That's why we set a record this year for attracting direct foreign investment: at US$50 billion or more,

Inspecting the Xiamen International Conference Center in Fujian Province in May 2001. Xi Jinping, Governor of Fujian Province, is first from left in the front row.

it's the highest in the world. In short, the Central Committee was not mistaken in its assessment of the world economic situation. Rather, through our efforts, we overcame difficulties and achieved unexpected growth. This is the result of our common efforts, the result of correct decisions by the Central Committee.

Don't Have Too Rosy a View, However. We should indeed recognize that many fundamental problems have yet to be solved. Otherwise it will be hard to carry on. What are the problems? Surplus labor has always been one of China's biggest problems. The structural adjustments in agriculture are progressing at a snail's pace, farmers' incomes are slow to rise, and the employment problem in rural areas is in urgent need of attention. The reemployment of laid-off workers in cities is also a major issue. We did a great deal this year to solve some problems, but the labor surplus is a perpetual concern.

A new problem has also emerged since we began increasing [university] enrollments in 1998 as those students will graduate next year. What will we do if they can't find jobs? Employment pressure is growing by the year. Provided we work with them, laid-off workers won't make trouble, but it's hard to say the same for college students. Nowadays college students also have excessive expectations. They want high salaries as soon as they finish school—how is that possible? Nor are they willing to go to rural areas—how can that be? This problem merits our attention. It's a major mismatch that will be hard to deal with for a long time to come. That's why even as good as the situation is this year, we should still fully anticipate our difficulties and absolutely not take them lightly.

2. How to Manage Next Year's Economic Work

A very important point is that we must continue to work hard to solve the problem of inadequate effective domestic demand. How can we develop without demand? How can a 7–8% growth rate be sustained? That's why it is essential to address this issue. First, however, we must break down effective demand into its components.

Demand includes investment and consumption demand. Right now the boost from investment is already substantial and can't be increased. Total fixed asset investments have reached RMB 4 trillion, which is almost double [the level of] 1997—this increase has been too rapid. Apart from 660 billion in Treasury bonds, this amount is all bank loans, and that is where the risk lies. By contrast, infrastructure construction carries no risk, provided there is no redundancy and provided it isn't completed long before it is needed. But processing industries and construction industries are all prone to risk.

These past few years, the scale of investment has been huge and has shot up all at once, surpassing total investment over the past few decades and driving up production by the infrastructure and equipment industries—what a frightening push! In 1997 we produced just under 100 million tons of steel, but this year [we'll produce] 180 million tons of steel and 190 million tons of steel products. Why would there be more steel products than steel? Semi-finished steel is imported. Because the 200 million or more tons of imported steel include semi-finished steel that is then rolled into [steel] products, we have more steel products than steel. This production volume equals the total of U.S. and Japanese output.

For many years now, Japanese steel production has been around 100 million tons and American production around 90 million tons. Our total economy isn't as large as theirs, only US$1.2 trillion compared with Japan's more than US$4 trillion and America's US$10 trillion—we're far smaller. If by any chance the drive can't be increased—right now we rely on Treasury bonds and bank loans—if by any chance mishandling creates risk, and there is a contraction, a large number of workers will immediately have to be laid off. Moreover, the composition of our steel production is also very irrational. Of the 180 million tons produced, only upward of 40 million tons, or about 20%, is produced by large mills with a capacity of 5 million tons or more, while the rest is produced by small mills. Although South Korea produced only 40 million tons last year, its Pohang Iron and Steel Company alone turns out 27 million tons annually. This is large-scale production with high efficiency, low costs, and few workers.

Meanwhile our steel industry expands by using "human wave tactics." It grows quickly but can't solve the problem of product variety. Why did we have to import 25 million tons of steel products? Because we couldn't produce auto plates and we couldn't produce many types of stainless steel products, so we still had to import them.

Like steel production, the manufacture of construction materials, cement, and glass has become as bloated as can be. What's more, much of this is from factories in the "five small enterprises" and of poor quality. That's why an excessive investment drive in fact leads to some redundant production, redundant construction, and substandard production and construction, which is very dangerous. It won't do just to churn out large volumes. We also have to improve quality, [product] diversity, and performance.

So what have the large quantities of steel been used for? Buildings. Foreigners come to Shanghai and Beijing and say this is such amazing progress. Actually, they haven't been to the villages and haven't been to the county seats—they're also putting up buildings everywhere. Almost half the steel products are used by construction industries, and the scale of construction has gotten so large. The kinds of buildings being erected have also become an issue. There won't be enough housing to meet the needs of China's 1.3 billion people, no matter how much you build. But now they've built so much high-end housing—can ordinary people afford that? Yet if they don't build high-end housing there won't be any returns. The vacancy rate for housing is now increasing, and many high-end residences can't be sold. Foreigners have yet to come, but the housing is already built and the capital is all locked up there.

Moreover, 70% of the capital consists of bank loans. Bank loans go mainly to developers and not to ordinary people who buy housing—the risk here is very great. The corrupt practices within the real estate sector are as bad as can be, with its many tricks of the trade. In Shenzhen I said that there's currently a bit of heat in real estate, that I don't dare call it overheating, [but] we can't go on like this. The way I would describe it now is that there is still some real estate heating in parts of some areas and in some individual spots. Colleagues, a bit of heat can turn into overheating very quickly. Half a year is enough—I have had several decades of experience with this. What does this tell us? That we have to think about sustainable growth.

If we go all out to increase the strength and intensity of investment, the consequences of such a drive would be unthinkable, and we would be saddled with many problems. In the end, when there is no longer such a strong push, the economic growth rate will suddenly plunge, and there'll be immediate chaos. Of course we're not reducing this intensity right away. In the case of investment with Treasury bonds, for instance, we arranged for RMB 150 billion this year, and next year we'll issue RMB 140 billion, but this year we can carry over

RMB 10 billion, so it will be about the same as this year, and the scale of investment won't be reduced. The ratio of Treasury bonds to total investment will be smaller, but [the intensity] still won't be weakened by much.

What I want to point out, too, is that while we must pay attention to the economic boost from investment, we must pay even greater attention to the boost from consumption. Only the drive from consumption is dependable. This is the purchasing power of the people; it is real purchasing power. Over the past few years, the Party Central Committee and the State Council have encouraged consumption by ordinary people, but not through the use of public funds. We cannot manage to move ahead without the drive from consumption.

In order to solve the problems left over from the past five years—such as those at rural cooperative funds, urban-rural credit cooperatives, trust and investment companies, equity departments of sales-and-marketing cooperatives, and various financial services firms—we loaned out RMB 200 billion to the various provinces and municipalities. These entities had lost the people's trust because they had borrowed from farmers and failed to pay them back, so our loans not only helped solve this problem but also increased farmers' incomes, stimulated consumption, and played a very useful role. Once this RMB 200 billion or more was put into the economy, it became purchasing power. When we reverted farmlands to forests and gave the farmers grain and money, that immediately turned into consumption. For the past two years, in the reform that converted fees into taxes, the central fiscal authorities spent over RMB 40 billion to subsidize the central and western regions, which directly drove up farmers' consumption. The "Two Assurances"—the "guaranteed minimum living standard" and the higher level of retirement pay for retirees at enterprises and publicly supported institutions—have increased consumption as well. Without these engines of growth, would we have been able to push our economy forward just by relying on Treasury bonds?

At present, our consumption rate is still low compared with average world levels. What is the consumption rate? It is the proportion of GDP that final consumption accounts for, which is why it's also called the final consumption rate. Our rate has now reached 60%, while the world average is 78–79%, so we still have a gap. The boost from consumption is very important for us. I hope that all levels of government and all departments will continue to pay attention to this driver next year. In short, we have to care about the lives of the people—that is truly the real driver.

We haven't increased wages this year but have already put next year's pay raises into the budget. We must raise wages and raise the standard of living of low-income people. We have to expand the pilot programs for converting rural fees into taxes and expand the scale of reverting farmlands to forests—these all stimulate and induce mass consumption. Right now product quality is unacceptable: many brands are fakes, and ultimately the people will lose faith in the markets and have no desire to consume. A while back, we focused on the problem of "unconscionable cotton," and now the problem of "unconscionable mattresses" has appeared, which the State Economic and Trade Commission is currently investigating. Recently, I saw a news item online indicating that the number of wineries in Tonghua, Jilin Province, has grown to over 200. That means they are making fake goods. This, too, must be investigated—we mustn't destroy our own brands.

Nowadays it's easier to register an enterprise than to have a child. Some have basically no production equipment or quality inspection measures, yet their products are marketed in large quantities. One of the functions of government is to maintain order in a market economy—there must be "rules of the game." If the government doesn't take charge, who will? A perpetual issue in a market economy is the need to rectify order, which is also a very important responsibility of our government.

Therefore I want to remind everyone to have a firm grasp of the principles for next year's economic work:

—We want to step up the drive from investment and increase even further the drive from consumption.

—We must increase the volumes of production and focus even more on improving quality.

—We must pay attention to the rate of growth and pay even greater attention to structural adjustments.

I hope that leaders at all levels of government will keep these firmly in mind. There isn't much sense in simply pursuing a [high] economic growth rate. I'm not that interested in this year's growth rate of 8%. If we could have the same fiscal revenues with a 7% growth rate, I would be very pleased. Why would we want an 8% rate that contains bubbles and is bloated?

3. Some Remarks on Our Government's Work Style

A great many new people have been elevated to leadership positions before and after the 16th National Party Congress. This is a valuable mechanism for strengthening our Party so that it can flourish and so that our nation can develop better. In this way, "the back waves of the Yangtze push the front waves"—we are constantly renewing [ourselves] and constantly raising our standards. This is the rule, and it's a very good rule. However, I feel we must also ask the leaders at all levels of government and in all departments, especially those newly promoted individuals, to be sure to take note: your most important task is to care about the people's comfort and about the people's hardships, as the important thought of the "Three Represents" expects of us. If we don't care about people's lives and hardships, how can the "Three Represents" be put into practice? If we as leaders don't care, who will care?

I'm now a bit worried because we're spending far too much! Look at how the Jingxi Hotel glitters. The Diaoyutai State Guesthouse does too, and the Great Hall of the People glitters even more. Every place glitters, and the same is probably also true in the provinces. Even the guesthouses of yours that I stayed in when I traveled had all started to glitter. It's not that we shouldn't build these facilities, but might we not "hold back" a little? Our level of economic development still hasn't reached such a stage. China can have only one Beijing, only one Shanghai. Each province can have only one provincial capital. We can't have "flowers blossoming" everywhere! Now even county-level cities are filled with new construction, with industrial parks everywhere. It makes me think back to 1993—things can heat up very quickly.

We should never forget that we still have 30 million people living in poverty in rural areas [despite] the very low poverty threshold. These people are very poor. There are also 20 million urban residents living at the "guaranteed minimum standard" as well as more than 10 million laid-off workers, many retirees, and people struggling to make ends meet. Can we set such high standards? After new officials arrive on the job, they need to change cars and housing, their offices need to be decorated, and new offices might even need to be built. The number of new officials is also sizable. In terms of creating [suitable] working conditions for them, all these things should be done. But can't we "hold back" a little?

I'm not afraid of solving problems for a few people. What I am afraid of is that the whole country will get caught up in the same rush, that everyone will want to industrialize, that every place will want to urbanize, that industrial parks will be built everywhere—that would be unthinkable. What we should constantly bear in mind is how to care about our people's lives and hardships, how to share their burdens, how to think what they are thinking, and how to worry about what they worry about. Yesterday I looked up an old adage from the *Zhenguan Zhengyao* [Essentials of Governing during the Zhenguan Reign]. Emperor Taizong of the Tang Dynasty paid a lot of attention to how to govern his country. He said,

—"If you understand danger, you will be safe." If you know that danger is imminent and know why danger exists, you will be secure in your position.

—"If you understand turmoil you will have order." If you can see where turmoil will appear and know why it would occur, you can make society peaceful.

—"If you understand extinction, you will survive."

I don't think it was pointless to say such things at a time when the country was doing well.

I will soon step down from the premiership and will not have fulfilled my duty if I did not recite these sayings before leaving office. While present conditions are excellent, we should all still think of risks during tranquil times such as this. A great many problems have yet to be solved and may occur at any time.

These are the three points I wanted to discuss. They're unscripted, and I offer them for your consideration. For the main issues, you should refer to my prepared remarks—that's the official version. Today I speak from the heart, and please be critical if you feel I was wrong.

55

Comprehensively Understand and Implement the Party's Policies on Religion[1]

January 10, 2003

Today, I've come to join with you in discussing guidelines and policies on religious affairs. To tell you the truth, you know more about this than I do. So what should I talk about? I suppose I should say something about my own understanding of the subject. Perhaps this can serve as a point of reference for your discussion of guidelines on work regarding religious affairs.

We Should Firmly Believe That Our Party's Guidelines on Religion Are Correct

Our guidelines are based on the teachings of Marxism, are the most comprehensive and correct policies on religion, and accord with historical materialism. This has been tested through practice—through our country's 50 years and more of practice, which have shown that this policy is entirely correct.

At the global level, [we can see that] religion is at the center of a great deal of tension. The Palestinian-Israeli conflict is one hot spot on the international scene—it involves both ethnic and religious differences, with all sorts of conflicts concentrated in one place. Similarly, the India-Pakistan discord stems from an intertwining of ethnic and religious differences, manifested in saber rattling on both sides. In Russia, the Chechen issue has long been a major problem, recently culminating in a hostage crisis[2] and explosion at the Chechen government building.[3] Both incidents reflect conflicts of religious and ethnic views. Even developed countries such as England and Northern Ireland are experiencing religious struggles and also seem unable to come up with any good solutions, despite their high level of economic development.

---

1. Zhu Rongji made these remarks at a national conference of directors of bureaus of religious affairs and at a retreat to discuss work regarding religious matters.

2. This refers to the hostage crisis at the Dubrovka Theater in Moscow on October 23, 2002.

3. This refers to the truck bombing of the government headquarters at Grozny in the Chechen Republic on December 27, 2002.

Meeting with Erdini Qoigyijabu, the 11th Panchen Lama, at Zhongnanhai, Beijing, on July 31, 2002. (Photograph by Li Xueren, Xinhua News Agency)

Our country has 56 ethnic groups as well as many religions and believers. We can say that for the past few decades, we have handled ethnic and religious issues quite well. You can't find another place in the world doing as well because so far we haven't had any major conflicts. There will always be minor problems, but nothing major has happened yet. Of course we are also constantly summing up, generalizing, improving on, and developing [what we have learned from] our work experiences. In short, practice has demonstrated that our Party's policies on religion are correct. We should believe in them unwaveringly and continue to carefully implement and practice them.

Basic Guidelines for Work Related to Religious Issues

Here are four statements that provide basic guidelines for religious work.

1. "Comprehensively Implement the Party's Policy on Freedom of Religious Belief." After all, when implementing guidelines and policies on religion, we ought to have a main concept. I feel this statement conveys the most important one, and we should always firmly bear it in mind in our work.

Some departments of our Party and government, particularly at the grassroots levels, tend to intervene excessively in religious beliefs in certain places and in certain respects. Religion is a product of history. Every religion and every ethnic group has created its own culture. Excessive intervention will intensify not only religious and ethnic conflicts, but also other differences among people. Some people working on religious issues tend to be overanxious, often using their powers to interfere with freedom of religious beliefs and confusing two conflicts of different natures. This is incorrect. Although terrorist ideas and organizations of the "East Turkestan Islamic Movement" (ETIM) do exist in Xinjiang, not all ethnic minorities in Xinjiang are like this, and they mustn't be considered the same thing. The very few people who believe in ETIM terrorism are even hired and trained abroad, then sent to our country to engage in sabotage and separatist activities. But these people constitute a tiny minority and should not affect the freedom of religious belief in Xinjiang. I have always felt that this is the most important thing.

2. *"Handle Religious Affairs in Accordance with the Law."* At the same time that we stress upholding Party policy on religion, we must not neglect to handle religious issues according to the law. Though religious beliefs are part of the spiritual realm and we cannot interfere with them, the actions of believers must not violate the law—this is an extremely important point and is precisely where our handling must be measured. There is no way to intervene in matters of the spiritual realm, but if its activities violate the law, they should meet with intervention as prescribed by law.

Managing according to the law requires that laws be genuinely obeyed. The State Council's "Regulations on Management of Religious Affairs" have not yet been formally issued, which shows that our laws and regulations regarding religion are still incomplete. I feel that we need to refine the State Council's regulations, as they are also part of the nation's legal system. Without laws and regulations, management will be arbitrary, and this has more cons than pros. While on the surface [a lack of laws and regulations] may seem very flexible and very convenient, it is not conducive to the establishment of a socialist country ruled by law. These laws and regulations must still be gradually refined.

3. *"Actively Guide Religion to Make It Compatible with a Socialist Society."* This statement specifies "guide"; what's more, it says "actively guide," which means administrative measures should not be used. Administrative and legal measures are only appropriate for "handling religious affairs in accordance with the law." If believers violate the country's laws, affect social stability and national security, or create discord among the people, then such behavior should be managed according to laws and regulations. "Guide" means guiding through education, culture, and publicity; administrative orders must not be used. To achieve this, you must act in a measured way and must not overdo things: if you do, it will be inappropriate.

A socialist society follows a course of gradual development. If you're not clear on this yourself, where will you "guide" people to? How will you guide them? You must be a bit looser in this regard, a bit looser than in "managing according to the law." If someone hasn't engaged in sabotage, hasn't been spying, and hasn't caused divisions between ethnic groups, in society or in the country, you mustn't be quick to pin a big label on him.

4. *"Resolutely Uphold the Principles of Independence, Autonomy, and Self-Management."* This is a special characteristic of ours. For matters involving Christianity, we have a set of three "self" guidelines,[4] which were shaped by the course of history. It's essential to be firm about these three "selfs." Particularly as we expand our opening up to the outside, things will seep in through every available channel, with foreign religions constantly trying to intervene. We have to work hard in this area.

Work on Religious Issues Merits Serious Attention

My final point is this: I hope that Party organizations and government agencies at all levels will pay greater attention to religious affairs and give this work greater support. This work is important not just in China, but also in the whole world; [religious] struggles are taking place not only domestically but also internationally, where they are even greater, and these are closely linked to the domestic ones.

The central authorities take work on religious matters very seriously. That is, we take it very seriously ideologically but haven't done enough, and we must do better. That's why I also hope that the principal leaders at all levels of Party and government as well as those in charge of work in this area will attach greater importance to it, endeavor to work with ethnic minorities, and do a good job in these areas. This is essential for maintaining ethnic and social unity, social and political stability, and economic growth.

---

4. These are the principles of self-sustenance, self-governance, and self-propagation that Christian churches in China should abide by.

56

A Memorable Five Years[1]

January 27, 2003

Today's meeting is the last plenary meeting of this administration and offers an opportunity to review the rather unique stage in the history of New China's development that emerged in the past five years. During this period, we were faced with an external environment clouded by the catastrophic impact of the downturn in the global economy and the Asian financial crisis. At the same time, we had many domestic problems on our hands, including the exceptionally large floods of 1998 and the somewhat large floods of 1999, as well as some other natural disasters. We also happened to be at a critical juncture of industrial restructuring, stagnating domestic markets, and shrinking production, leaving us with 10 million laid-off and unemployed workers in 1997. Looking back over these five years, [we can say that] it truly wasn't easy to get through all this! I never expected that we would not only overcome these difficulties but would even use this opportunity to surge ahead in our development.

While we can't say these were years of our fastest growth in history—we've had instances of the growth rate exceeding 10%—they did indeed bring us the best economic productivity thus far and sustainable and healthy growth. We can illustrate this with a few figures. For example, investment in infrastructure construction over these past five years was two to three times that of the past several decades. What a huge scale of construction this was! It changed not only the face of the landscape and society but also the living conditions of our people. I attribute this to the third generation of the Central Committee's leadership with Jiang Zemin at its core: its farsighted perspective, its constant attention to the overall situation, and its strategic decisions, which ensured success across the country. At the same time, credit must go to the State Council, which resolutely carried out the directives of the Central Committee, concretely implemented policies, overcame one obstacle after another, saw things through to the end,

1. On January 27, 2003, Zhu Rongji convened and chaired the Ninth Plenary Session of the State Council. All members of the State Council's plenary group attended the meeting, and leading members of related departments and work units were also present. This is part of Zhu's speech at the meeting.

373

Presiding over the ninth plenary meeting of the State Council on January 27, 2003: Politburo Standing Committee member and Vice Premier Wu Bangguo (first from right), Vice Premier Li Lanqing (second from right), Politburo Standing Committee member and Vice Premier Wen Jiabao (first from left), and Vice Premier Qian Qizhen (second from left). (Photograph by Liu Weibing, Xinhua News Agency)

and put in place policies, projects, funds, and various forms of oversight that ensured the smooth progress of construction.

The Importance of Perseverance in Our Various Tasks

This progress has been due in large part to perseverance in all aspects of our development: economic, agricultural, our reforms and opening up, science and education, and social security.

1. Economic Development. If we had not persevered from beginning to end in taking economic development as the central task and had not correctly implemented and strengthened macroeconomic controls, we could not have gotten the results we have today. After the Central Committee decided on a proactive fiscal policy, we focused on infrastructure construction, which changed the entire landscape. We didn't just work on transportation and shipping, but we also put a lot of effort into waterworks and other areas—these are long-term investments. They all had wide-reaching effects, not only giving a push to production and a lift to the soft domestic market, but also supporting the growth of the entire national economy.

At the same time, we carried out a stable monetary policy and strictly controlled credit lending, mainly to ensure enterprise liquidity and matching funds for Treasury bond projects, while avoiding all-round overheating. This is what allowed us to issue RMB 660 billion of Treasury bonds and make RMB 2 trillion to 3 trillion of bank loans over the past five years. It is what allowed fiscal revenues to increase every year and reach a historic high. In the past year, fiscal revenue grew by several tens of billions of renminbi, and by RMB 100 billion to 200 billion in each of the preceding few years. The central government transferred the bulk of these greatly increased revenues to the central and western regions, and it is only because of this that free mandatory education and infrastructure construction are at their current levels in the rural parts of these regions.

In these past five years, we also increased wages three times for the staff of government agencies and public institutions. The pay raises in the central and western regions were all funded by the central government. This helped gradually narrow the gap between the east and west, or at least it prevented the gap from widening rapidly.

2. Agriculture. If we had not persisted from beginning to end in treating agriculture as our foundation, and if we had not unwaveringly and solidly resolved the problems of agriculture, rural villages, and farmers, we would not have achieved the present growth. Over these five years, we put a great deal of work into the problems of rural villages, agriculture, and the agricultural population, with special emphasis on increasing the income of farmers. In order to promote free mandatory education in the villages, the central fiscal authorities helped the locals pay teacher salaries, build classrooms, and rebuild dangerous structures. In order to solve the problems of cooperative funds in villages and of credit associations in cities and townships, we made RMB 200 billion of refinancing loans, primarily to farmers.

To lighten the burden of farmers, we changed rural fees into taxes. For this, the central government had to pay out several tens of billions of renminbi. Last year we spent RMB 25 billion, this year we spent RMB 30 billion, and in the future we'll have to spend even more. By helping over 100 million farmers go to cities to find jobs, we enabled them to greatly increase their income. We must always firmly remember this: agriculture is our foundation, and we must solidly increase the income of farmers. We absolutely must not slacken up on this point in the future. We must care about the farmers every moment. We mustn't look down on farmers and think that now that the situation is so good, we can build automobiles, build real estate, build some theme park or other, and cast the farmers aside. Without the leg of agriculture to stand on, the national economy absolutely cannot move forward. Society's purchasing power lies mainly with the farmers. If the farmers' purchasing power doesn't increase, how can the national economy grow sustainably?

3. Reforms and Opening Up. If we hadn't persisted from beginning to end with reforms and opening up and dared to make bold leaps, exports would not have grown substantially. Without that growth and a correspondingly large increase in foreign reserves, without major improvements in the investment environment and large increases in foreign direct investment, we would not be where we are today.

We had originally expected that exports might incur negative growth for two or three years in the aftermath of the Asian financial crisis. On the contrary, because we implemented a series of policy measures and saw them through to the end, exports ultimately experienced a large increase—even last year, when exports stagnated all over the world and even shrank in some countries. Also, because we resolutely cracked down on smuggling and tax cheating in exports, customs revenues increased significantly. We cannot let up on those who smuggle, cheat on taxes or on foreign exchange, and must continue to focus hard on this. Without the antismuggling measures of the past few years, how could we have accomplished so much in foreign trade? It would be impossible!

Also, we truly had not expected foreign direct investment (FDI) to grow so quickly. Last year we had US$52.8 billion of foreign investment in place, the highest in the world—we're talking about foreign direct investment. FDI promotes reforms at state-owned enterprises and helps improve their operating mechanisms. These are all things we could not even have imagined before.

4. Science and Education. If we had not persisted from beginning to end with the policy of revitalizing the nation through science and education and invested large sums of money in the educational sector, education and science and technology would not be where they are today. This transformation began with a fundamental change in free compulsory education in the villages and attention to teachers' wages, which in the past were in arrears by several months or even by two to three years. Now that wages are paid on time, everyone in the villages wants to be a teacher. We centralized the payment of wages at the county level, which means they were guaranteed by the central fiscal authorities.

This measure has had a profound effect, because a people that cannot raise its educational level has no future. I think that over the past five years, the development of free compulsory education, including the expansion of secondary school admissions and development of vocational education, has been unprecedented and has greatly enhanced the strength of our people. This is not only an economic strength, but also a sustainable strategic resource.

5. Social Security. One other thing—if we had not persisted from beginning to end in treating social stability as a prerequisite and established and refined a social security system, we would also not be where we are today. Since 1997 we have done a vast amount of in-depth and meticulous work on establishing and refining a social security system and implementing reemployment projects.

We drew up quite a few policies, and the central fiscal authorities spent a lot of money on this, all of it from the central government budget. The central and western regions all need subsidies from the central government. Particularly in the establishment of reemployment centers, the central government paid for 60% while the locals paid for 10–20%. Basically they were all paid for with fiscal revenues, but a portion also came from the unemployment insurance money within the social security fund. Without this support, how could society be stable? How could people feel as reassured as they do now?

This is another point we cannot slacken up on, especially with the new reemployment policy we announced last year—it must be seen through to the very end. We absolutely must not neglect this. If we do, there will be trouble everywhere, so how would we be able to work on economic development? Liaoning Province has had a pilot program in social security that stands as an example for the entire country and has basically achieved success with it. The other provinces, regions, and municipalities can draw on its experience and make their social security systems better and better. This is a hundred-year plan to keep society calm, to keep people reassured.

The Importance of Farsightedness and Mutual Trust

All of our achievements are the result of the Central Committee's farsightedness and leadership, and they're also inseparable from the efforts of the departments of the State Council, including those of us at this plenary meeting and our entire staff. For myself, these were the most memorable five years of my life, because I was able to do something substantive for the people. I believe that for all of you here, these were the most memorable years of your lives as well. Colleagues from the Ministry of Water Resources, think back on how much you've accomplished in this period—when in the past were you ever able to achieve so much! All the dikes and embankments along the major rivers have been repaired up to [the required] standards and have safely withstood floods.

Last year, despite my deteriorating eyesight and the doctors wanting me to have an operation, I didn't have one done because I felt I had to check along the Yangtze River, the Yellow River, the Songhua River, and the Nen River. Under a blazing sun, I visited all the places I went to in 1998 and 1999. My mind could not rest until I could have a look—what if these were also "tofu dreg projects"?[2] If, on the eve of my leaving office, a major flood were to wash away a large dike, how would I answer to the people?

After I had a look, I was able to relax. Of course I could only check on a few key places, but from this I could see that the money has not been spent in vain.

2. See chapter 11.

It's not that there are absolutely no problems whatsoever with these dikes, or that some money from Treasury bond projects hasn't been misused, but on the whole it was money well spent, and the results are there for all to see. So many people live along the banks of the Yangtze, Yellow, Songhua, and Nen rivers, and they rely on these waterways for their livelihoods. If we cannot guarantee their safety through flood controls, they would have to spend several months out of every year repairing the dikes, so how would they be able to develop production? Now we can say that the entire landscape has changed.

Therefore we should never forget what has transpired in the past five years, when we all worked together and fought together. I especially feel that in working together during this period, all of us at the State Council have been in the same boat, rowing together against wind and rain. Our relationship was based on mutual trust—it was a type of tacit understanding. I truly feel that every person at the State Council worked wholeheartedly, and even though not every person's work was so outstanding, I know that you all gave it your best and have proved yourselves worthy in these five years.

I give heartfelt thanks to all of you here, thanks to everyone at the State Council for supporting our work and for supporting me personally. Without this kind of mutual trust and understanding, we could not have achieved so much. I had only to say a word or make a phone call, and everyone would know what I meant. I didn't need to say too much—everyone would just work on things together. I should say that these have been the happiest five years of my life, and also years in which I realized I was still of some value. That value lies in my being able, together with all of you, to do something substantive for the ordinary people.

Of course I've often criticized people during these years, and some felt somewhat uneasy around me. Whether or not my criticisms were valid, I ask you all for your understanding, and I ask you to believe that whatever I did was for the public good. I think you must all know me, must know that I don't engage in conspiracies and don't hold personal grudges. At this, our last plenary meeting, on the one hand I want to thank you all for your efforts and contributions and to thank you for supporting me personally; on the other hand I also ask you all for your understanding for my shortcomings, mistakes, and other problems over the past five years.

Concerns for the Future

As for future work, the 16th National Party Congress has already affirmed its direction, and plans have been laid out at the Central Committee's succession of meetings. We must resolutely carry these out. Because this administration is nearing the end of its term, I must also mention some things that worry me.

Economic Overheating. I particularly want to remind those who will be staying and carrying on to take note: the thing I'm most concerned about now is economic overheating, and I've already been worrying about it for a year. I won't publicly discuss this issue, I only discuss it at the leadership level, but I am worried about it.

There are already many signs of economic overheating, and if we don't pay attention to it, once the economy is unleashed we won't be able to keep it in check. I've been doing economic work for 50 years and am deeply aware of this "syndrome" in our country: as soon as things start getting a little better, the tendency to exaggerate appears, along with blind self-satisfaction, inexplicable self-inflicted woes, and ignorant policies. I've talked about real estate overheating before, but I've discovered that the vast majority of our people still don't understand the seriousness of this problem. They're always quick to say that "overall, things are very good," or that there may be a little problem. That is absolutely not the case!

This kind of overheating is the worst thing—in 1993 there was real estate overheating, as a result of which Hainan Island is even now "covered with scars." I read foreign newspapers, and they're all saying that a bubble economy has formed in China, that real estate is overheated and the risks are too high. Our people in banking in particular must take note of this, because the money [pouring into this sector] all comes from the banks. I again warn our people in banking: perhaps you'll be promoted in the next couple of years, perhaps you'll no longer be working in banking, so you may think that if a problem appears, you can let your successors clean it up. Although the financial reforms of this administration still haven't been completed, and we still haven't established a robust mechanism, we Communists have been working on the economy for several decades now, so we should still assume some responsibility, shouldn't we? Don't leave this burden for those who come after you and develop blindly.

Urbanization. I'm also very worried about "urbanization." Nowadays "urbanization" is already closely linked to building houses. Farmers' land is expropriated at cheap prices, and foreigners or real estate developers are then allowed to move in. Yet they don't do a good job of resettling the farmers—this kind of behavior is very dangerous. It fundamentally goes against the spirit of our central policies. We've discussed this trend many times, and it is what we're afraid of. I suggest that you all have a look at a circular from the Central Committee's Policy Research Office, entitled "The Movement to Build Townships Harms the People and Wastes Money." This report is about [real estate development in] the rural areas of Luoyang, in Henan Province.

Since 2001, developers had been building "townships" which blossomed everywhere like flowers. They did this for two years even though they had neither

A Memorable Five Years

a unified master plan nor any source of funding, but still they kept massively building real estate and enclosing land. How did they do this without money? They built walls facing the street next to what were single-story buildings, making them look like two- or three-story buildings. This is a method already in use—it wasn't something they invented—but it's all fakery! I don't know where they got the money from. Since when did township or county governments have this kind of money? It either came from the banks or was misappropriated from educational funds.

This circular of the Central Policy Research Office exposes problems even more sharply than the State Council's reports. The practice of building townships started in 1993 in large cities and places like Hainan and Beihai. If this were to spread everywhere, if everyone were to build townships, if this were to become a movement—it would be unthinkable! Our people in banking must be on the alert. You keep saying that the overall situation is excellent and that nonperforming loans are fewer in number, but I don't believe it.

New and Dangerous Fads. Also, there's a fad right now for building theme parks. They don't do this even in foreign countries—there are two Disneylands in the United States, one in France, and one in Japan. Yet theme parks are popping up in many places in China. Foreigners are not putting up any of the money themselves, while you're selling your land to them very cheaply, wrecking our country's land resources and even letting them use your money. Why do this? We still have many places where the farmers don't even have enough to eat, so why build a theme park? Who would visit it? Shanghai didn't succeed in getting a Disneyland, so they want to build a [different] theme park. Tianjin wants to build a theme park, and now Beijing wants to build a theme park. That means there'll be two theme parks right next to each other! The two Disneylands in the United States are far apart—one is in Los Angeles, the other in Florida. Why are we putting them so close to each other? We have to resolutely cut back.

The State Council did recently issue a notice in this regard. It didn't say that theme parks are not allowed beyond a certain limit; rather, none are allowed without the approval of the State Council. I'm afraid very few people have heard of the Dinosaur Park in Sichuan—it was built by the forestry authorities and takes up 9 square kilometers. They collaborated with an Australian bank, and it was all so they could build a five-star hotel.

Now there's also a fad for automobiles. Last year the price of cars fell—because of large-scale auto imports and the availability of bank loans. I feel that cars are not the direction we should be going in. We mustn't create a fever that makes young people feel it's glorious to own their own cars. We said long ago that China isn't that sort of country, and we haven't changed our view to this very day—we should mainly develop public transportation. Beijing traffic jams are already a mess—how can we host the Olympics in 2008?! The various types of infrastructure, traffic facilities, management facilities, and management standards are all unsuited [to automobiles]. At the moment, Shanghai has only half as many cars as Beijing, yet there are traffic jams everywhere. How will it host the 2010 World Expo? And parking—that's also a big problem. We mustn't waver even slightly on the policy of developing public transportation. There isn't so much oil!

Colleagues, last year we imported 70 million tons of crude oil, and that doesn't include smuggled oil products. Smuggling is still fairly rampant in some provinces, so we don't know how much oil has been imported. We produced only 160 million tons ourselves but consumed as much as 260 million tons—can this keep up? Fortunately, we now have the forex for imports, but what will we do in the future? Without oil, how can we go on developing automobiles? Public transportation has always been our weak spot, and it's never been developed properly.

Every day, I also worry about two other things: one is the constant explosions and deaths in coal mines; the other is the number of traffic accidents and deaths. This morning I read a report about an overloaded truck in the Baise region of the Guangxi Zhuang Autonomous Region. It was carrying 30 people, 17 of whom were killed when it overturned. Agricultural vehicles are substandard cars, yet they're proliferating everywhere, which is very frightening. People dying everywhere, people dying every day—as premier, I read about these things daily, yet I can't come up with any way to deal with them. You can imagine how worrisome this is to me!

We have to do so much more to develop public transportation! We have to properly develop the production of buses and long-distance vehicles and eliminate those agricultural vehicles and substandard cars. Agricultural vehicles must not be allowed on the roads, and the traffic control police must be strict about this—don't casually use "harming agriculture" as an excuse. People's lives are of the greatest importance—if a fad were to develop that focuses our energy less on this and more on building cars or whatnot, it would be unthinkable! I don't mean that we shouldn't develop automobiles, just that we needn't set our targets so high, and we mustn't have everyone rushing to build autos. Once you start building autos, you'll have to build up entire supply systems for raw materials, and if a crash occurs, they will all be brought down as well. No matter what you build, it won't do for everyone to rush into it all at once.

In short, I hope that those of you who are staying on in your jobs will make sure you don't let the "good times" go to your heads. Although the past five years have indeed been good—better than we could even have thought—you absolutely must not become blindly optimistic. That attitude will only lead to exaggerations and self-inflicted problems.

Parting Words

History teaches that there are cycles in development. But we mustn't go down the old roads of history—these are my parting words to you. Provided nothing goes wrong in this regard, other problems can be easily managed and won't turn into nationwide or irreparable problems. Economic overheating must be strictly controlled, and the State Council has to be tougher about this.

Finally, the leaders in charge of the various departments of the State Council have done quite well in being clean, diligent, practical, and efficient. I feel proud that I was able to have a team like this. I'm not saying there were no problems, only that they were relatively few. Everyone worked conscientiously and must continue to do so. Hu Jintao spoke of the "Two Musts,"[3] and we should try harder to maintain close ties with the people, to listen to their voices, to accept their complaints, to stand up for them, to speak for them, and to solve their problems. These past 5 years—or I should say these past 10 years when I was in charge of economic work—I always wanted to do these things, and I gave it my best.

If we only listen to those below who report only good news and not bad, it will go to our heads—we won't be able to hear the voices of the people, we absolutely won't be able to do our work well, and even our judgments will be wrong. After all, the *Topics in Focus* program and the letters from all the provinces, regions, and municipalities will still be there to remind us of the problems. For the past few years, I've made sure to watch *Topics in Focus* every night. I feel that as premier, if I don't care about the people's sufferings, what kind of premier would I be!

After watching each program, I would always make phone calls, either to governors or to [provincial] Party secretaries. Although I knew that a phone call could only address the problems of a few farmers or a few ordinary people, I felt a bit better in that I could right a wrong for these few farmers or ordinary people, that I could resolve their problems. If I can't do great things, then at least I can do a few small things. Sometimes I felt like not making the phone calls because there are far too many incidents of this sort, but on second thought, I still wanted to make the calls. I hope that in the future, you will do as I did while I was in office and take the people's direct complaints and their direct voices seriously and help them resolve their problems, even if it's a complaint or a letter from only one person. I don't know how many such letters I've signed off

3. In December 2002, Hu Jintao, Secretary General of the Central Committee of the Chinese Communist Party, went on a study tour to Xibaipo in Hebei Province. There he called upon the entire Party to renew its study of an important speech made by Mao Zedong in March 1949 at the Second Plenary Session of the Seventh National Party Congress, and to remember well the "Two Musts" advocated by Mao: namely that Party members must maintain a humble and prudent style that avoids arrogance and impatience and must also maintain an arduous style of work.

on—this at least counts as living up to our State Council's motto of being clean, diligent, practical, and efficient, and of doing substantive things for the people.

I hope you can carry on in this spirit and absolutely disregard those who report good news but not bad, who flatter, exaggerate, or lie. Believe in what you see with your own eyes—even though it's now very hard to see the actual circumstances, you can still find out if you just persist. This is the last hope I want to mention. I can't say that "we" must do a good job on our last watch—for me, it is the last watch, and there's only a month and a half until we change administrations. But for most of you, this won't be your last watch, and you still have to stay at your jobs. After all, this administration is coming to a close, and we still have to make sure its work ends as well as it began, to put a nice period at the end of the sentence. Provided it's something we can do, we must try our best to do it and to finish it within our term.

The "Two Meetings"[4] are about to take place. I hope you'll all participate attentively, listen humbly to suggestions, do a better job of revising our "Report on the Work of the Government" and improve on our own inadequacies. This is my hope for all of you.

4. Translator's note: the annual meetings of the National People's Congress and the Chinese People's Political Consultative Conference.

57

MAKE A CONCERTED EFFORT TO DEVELOP PUBLIC TRANSPORT[1]

February 1, 2003

Today is the first day of the lunar New Year, and on behalf of the Party Central Committee and the State Council, I bring you greetings for the New Year and wish you all a happy Spring Festival. Through you, I also want to express our best wishes for the New Year to everyone working in the Beijing public transport system and in the public bus and taxi industries. You've been working hard! While we've been home celebrating the festival, you've been here at your posts, on duty. Your hard work has, in return, allowed all the residents of the city to enjoy their New Year safely and peacefully, with good fortune, joy, and family reunions. Your work is truly very meaningful, and on behalf of my own family, I also want to thank all of you!

Comrades, I was once a mayor. I attach the greatest importance to public transport, and when I arrived in Shanghai, the first problem I solved was the traffic problem. At that time, Shanghai's traffic jams were as bad as could be. I therefore proposed a goal: in the future, it should not take more than an hour to travel from one location to any other in the city. Now this goal may soon be realized, but Shanghai's traffic jams are still awful, even worse than the ones in Beijing. That's why we have to make even greater efforts to solve the traffic problem.

To tell you the truth, I'm not in favor of each person buying a car—this does not suit China's circumstances. China has a lot of people, and there's no other country like China, with its numerous cities of a million or more people. How can every family have a car? No city would be able to cope with that—we mustn't do this. And where would we get so much oil? Most oil has to be imported! Then there are auto emissions, which will make pollution even worse and seriously affect people's health.

I feel that there's also a bit of overheating in auto production. I'm not against developing the auto industry, but it should be developed appropriately. Those with high standards of living can buy cars, but the government shouldn't spend

---

1. On February 1, 2003, Zhu Rongji visited the public security police and public transport workers who were on the job in Beijing that day. He made these remarks during a visit with staff of the Beijing Public Transport Company at the Beiguanting bus stop on Route 44.

Visiting public transit workers who were on the job through the Spring Festival holidays at the Beiguanting stop of the Beijing route 44 bus. (Photograph by Hu Haixin, Xinhua News Agency)

so much money to subsidize or promote [auto purchases]—this does not accord with the direction of China's development. For now, we should still make an all-out effort to develop public transport, to develop public buses and urban light rail, and we can also develop high-speed maglev [magnetic levitation] rail.

We should all fully understand the importance of developing public transport. We must work hard to develop it, and we also must strengthen its management. At present, there are 1.9 million cars in Beijing, and traffic is already very bad. Shanghai has only a million cars, and its transportation facilities are more advanced than those of Beijing, yet it still has traffic jams. Why? Because of poor management.

When I pointed out this problem on a recent visit to Shanghai, people were already aware of it and were studying how to strengthen management. They are planning to build the most modern citywide traffic information system, one that can be controlled electronically. They want to make it possible for people to board public transport wherever they go, and to find [men and women driving] taxis everywhere. This way, it will be very convenient to go out and individuals will feel no need to buy a car of their own, which they would have to tend to all day long.

Yesterday, CTTV's annual Spring Festival TV Gala featured several items that praised "Brother Cabbie" and "Sister Cabbie" and expressed empathy for their hard work. When I first arrived in Shanghai, there were close to a thousand taxi companies. Management was an utter mess, and arbitrary fee-charging was rampant. At that time, I asked them to create the Dazhong Taxi Company. We bought a thousand [Volkswagen] Santanas for them and laid out strict requirements for the company's services and management. With one stroke, we changed the look of the taxi industry. I know that the city of Beijing has also done a lot in the past in this area.

Nowadays there are quite a few incidents all over the country involving cab drivers. This is because they are poorly managed and heavily exploited by middlemen. That's why we still have to work hard on managing this industry. In short, we must devote more energy and attention to developing public transport rather than automobiles!

Index

Accountants, training system for, 320–21

Acheson, Dean, 211

Agency reform, 10–13, 28–36; commitment to, 32–34; defining agency role, 11; in ethnic-minority regions, 261; fairness in staff reassignment, 35; market regulation, 29; overlapping jurisdictions, 11–12; pace of, 34–35; plan for, 103; reduction in staff size, 11, 12; separation from enterprises, 28–32; stability throughout, 35–36; in Xinjiang, 228–30

Agricultural Bank of China, 74, 81, 189, 207, 209, 211

Agricultural Development Bank, 38–39, 41, 43–44

Agriculture and agricultural issues: agricultural policy, 106–08, 162, 308–09, 362, 375; animal husbandry, 329–32; corn pricing, 331; crops adjustment, 294; in ethnic minority regions, 165–66; fees as burden on farmers, 103–04; food safety, 135, 331; food supply, 211, 293, 329; grain pricing, 41–43, 325; grain risk fund, 213; grain surplus, 173, 211, 255, 293–94, 331; in Hainan, 112–14; income of farmers, 20–21; reform of the grain circulation system, 14, 37–46, 103, 294; subsidies for, 212–13, 241, 256; sugar pricing, 221; wheat production, 135. See also Forestry; Rural areas

AIG, 199

All-China Federation of the Disabled, 32

All-China Federation of Trade Unions, 20

American congressional delegation: 1999 meeting, 132–38; 2002 meeting, 341–47

Anhui Province, 37

Anti-China sentiment in U.S., 130, 132, 138

Arafat, Yasser, 337–38

Arts. See Culture

Asian financial crisis (1997), xiv, 6, 50, 89, 131, 288, 354, 373

Asia-Pacific Economic Cooperation (APEC), 313, 343

Audits of Customs, 190

Automobile industry, 197, 201, 202, 380–81, 384

Aviation agreement negotiations, 133

Bachus, Linda, 343

Bachus, Spencer, 342, 347

Bank of Agriculture. See Agricultural Bank of China

Bank of China, 207

Bankruptcy: of enterprises losing money, 175; of paper mills, 163; of SOEs, 26

Banks and banking: commercial banks, 130, 206–08, 287; and economic growth, 126, 129–30, 287; interest rates charged by, 13–14; relending policy, 217–20; and technology-based small and medium enterprises, 151. See also specific banks by name

Baogang Iron and Steel Works, 313

Barshefsky, Charlene, 131, 135, 137, 197, 201

Beijing TV, 83

Bereuter, Doug, 134, 137

Berman, Howard, 137–38

Bin Laden, Osama, 284

Bribery. See Corruption

Brittan, Leon, 194, 202

Bureau of Letters and Petitions, 322

Bush, George H. W., 337

Bush, George W., 250, 285, 316, 336

Cao Yu, 250

CCTV, 82–88, 317–22, 328, 384

Central Commission for Discipline Inspection, 187

Central Committee of Political and Legislative Affairs, 187

Central Economic Work Conference: 1998 speech, 100–11; 2002 speech, 358–68

Chen Zhili, 12
Cheney, Dick, 250, 338
Cheng Kejie, 207–08
China Development Bank, 208
China International Engineering Consulting Cooperation, 351
China Mobile, 299
China National Petroleum Corporation, 230
China Nonferrous Metals Industries Corporation, 8
China Rural Development Investment Trust Company, 8
China Unicom, 299
China Water Resources and Hydropower Corporation, 152
Chinese Academy of Engineering, 146
Chinese Academy of Sciences, 146
Chinese Communist Party, 68, 188, 353
Christianity, 372
Chu Bo, 240
Clinton, Bill, 131, 134, 139–45, 201, 202, 337
Coal mining, 101–02
Committee on Financial Work, 109
Conferences, meetings, and symposiums: antismuggling conference (1998), 55–66; central economic work conference (1998), 100–11; central economic work conference (2002), 358–68; Conference for Commending Ethnic Unity and Progress (1999), 164–69; Customs directors national meeting (2000), 183–93; foreign investment conference (2001), 273–82; grain purchases, teleconference on (1998), 37–46; International Advisory Committee meeting of Tsinghua University School of Economics and Management (2001), 244–46; International Federation of Accountants 16th annual meeting (2002), 353–57; laid-off workers conference (1998), 16–27; National People's Congress, 5th Session, plenary session of Inner Mongolian delegation (2002), 329–34; National Science Fund for Distinguished Young Scholars seminar (1999), 146–49; Party Group of the State Council 16th meeting (2001), 304–11; provincial-level officials seminars (1998), 28–36; religious affairs conference (2003), 369–72; Sino-American Technology and Engineering Conference (2001), 312–16; State Council First Plenary Session (1998), 1–15; State Council Ninth Plenary Session

(2003), 373–83; Tibet symposium (2001), 263–72; Tsinghua University presentation (2001), 247–53; urban and rural construction planning and management working meeting (2002), 327–28; World Chinese Entrepreneurs Association (2001), 291–303. *See also* Meetings with political officials and corporate leaders
Copyright protection, 323–26
Corruption, 2, 5, 315, 317, 318, 320–21, 349–50. *See also* Smuggling
"Cracking Down on Pornographic and Illegal Content" (exhibit), 323
Criminal activities. *See* Smuggling
Cultural Revolution, 252
Culture: cultural resources in ethnic minority regions, 169, 266; museums, musical performances, and arts academies, 178–82
Customs administration, 183–93; crack-down measures, 185–93; and ideology, 187–89; and law and institutional devices, 189–91; and smuggling, 62–63, 65, 183–85. *See also* General Administration of Customs

Dai Xianglong, 108–09, 125, 217
Dalian International Trust and Investment Company, 219n3
Dalian State-owned Assets Management Co., 219
Dazhong Taxi Company, 386
Deforestation, 69
Deng Xiaoping: on economic crime, 58; governmental reforms of, 2; on high-energy physics, 111; on Overseas Chinese, 303; and Schmidt, xiii; as second generation leader, 3; "Southern Tour" talks, xii; on Tibet, 263
Deserts, 224–25, 233, 332
Devaluation, xiv, 47–52, 104, 304–05, 360
Ding Guan'gen, 323
Dinosaur Park (Sichuan), 380
Disney Company, conversation with Michael D. Eisner, 92–97
Dongting Lake, 79
Duan Yingbi, 173

East Turkestan Islamic Movement (ETIM), 371
Economic development, 291–303, 358–68; 1998 growth goals, 13, 100–01; 1999 growth goals, 104–05; 2002 performance, 358–63; 2003, five-year review as of, 374–75; and Asian financial crisis, 50; and banks, 126,

construction of, 70–72, 107, 152–53; losses incurred from (1998), 101; relocation of people due to, 71, 74, 81; riverbed dredging, 71–72; in southern China, 166. *See also specific rivers*

Foreign direct investment (FDI), 111, 273–82, 286; 2001 amount of, 291; 2003, five-year review as of, 376; adjustment and optimization in structure of, 275–76; and changes in domestic supply and demand, 274, 314–15, 363–66; and changes in global economic growth, 274–75; and changes in opening up to the outside, 274; and changes in systemic environment, 274; and domestic capital, 278–80; improving methods in using, 280–82, 289–90; integration with economic restructuring, 276; investment climate, 312–16; September 11, 2001, terrorist attacks on U.S., impact on, 361; in western China, 296–97

Forestry: conversion of farmland to forests, 69–70, 156–57, 174–75, 240–41, 254–56, 294, 296; in desert areas, 226–27; and flood prevention, 80; in Hunan, 238–39; protection of natural forests, 158–63, 166–68

Forex reserves: 1998 status of, 13, 89; 2001 status of, 278, 291, 300; after September 11, 2001, terrorist attacks on U.S., 304–05; and Customs corruption, 185; Guangdong using, 184; Hong Kong using, 128; making good use of, 279; stopping exodus of, 280

The Fork in the Road (opera), 180n2

G-20 meeting, 128n3
Gansu Province, 170–75
Gas pipeline. *See* Oil and gas
General Administration of Customs, 62, 183, 187. *See also* Customs administration
General Administration of Press and Publication (GAPP), 323–26
Gezhouba Engineering Bureau, 152, 153
Global financial crisis (2008), xiv
Gore, Al, 354
Governance, 1–11; corruption, punishment of, 5; fairness, importance of, 3–4; faithful discharge of duties, 4–5; and frivolous activities of officials, 10; ground rules for, 9–10; implementation of, 6, 7–8, 366–67; and inspection entourages, 9; lessons to be learned, 6–10; and meetings of government officials, 9–10; reduction in size of

government staffs, 11; reform, 1–10; rigorous leadership, 5; serving the people, 4, 6. *See also* Agency reform

Grain circulation system, reform of, 14, 37–46, 103, 294; grain pricing, 41–43, 106; purchase funds in closed system, 43–44; and SOEs reform, 44–46

Great Leap Forward (1958), 350
Great Steel Refining of 1958, 351
Greenspan, Alan, 125–31, 306, 354–55
Guangdong Holdings Ltd., 219
Guangdong International Trust and Investment Company (GITIC), 90–91, 109
Guangdong Province: and foreign exchange smuggling, 184; and nonperforming loans, 109; and power consumption, 295; real estate market in, 350, 351; and smuggling, 59, 61
Guangxi: and mining accidents, 317; and nonperforming loans, 109; and smuggling, 59
Guangxia Company, 306

Haier, 313
Hainan, 109, 380; agricultural issues in, 112–14; real estate market in, 350
Hai River, 233
A Half Hour on the Economy (CCTV show), 83
Happy Homes project, 327
He Meiying, 247
Health care reform, 14, 103
Hebei Province: American congressional delegates visit to, 341–43; desert expansion in, 332; grain surplus in, 212
Heilongjiang Province, flooding in (1998), 67–73
Henan Province: flood relief (1999) in, 152–57; grain surplus in, 212
Highways. *See* Transportation
Hong Kong, 353–57; autonomy of, 347, 353; Customs, 192; exchange rate, 52; and hedge funds, 128
Hong Kong Stock Exchange, 190, 299
Housing reform, 14, 103, 327, 364
Howard, John, 128
Hu Jintao, 353, 382
Hu Xueyan, former residence of, 339–40
Huang Zhendong, 170
Hubei Province: flooding (1998), 73–75; Yangtze River management in, 152
Human rights, 130, 134, 138, 296, 301, 315, 316
Humor, 302–03